Vanessa Agnew, Kader Konuk, Jane O. Newman (eds.)
Refugee Routes

The Academy in Exile Book Series | Volume 1

Editorial

The Academy in Exile Book Series is edited by Vanessa Agnew, Kader Konuk and Egemen Özbek.

Vanessa Agnew is a professor in Anglophone studies at the Universität Duisburg-Essen and a senior researcher at the Australian National University. She was educated at the University of Queensland (BMus), New York University (MA), University of Wales (PhD), and Open University (BSc). Her *Enlightenment Orpheus: The Power of Music in Other Worlds* (Oxford UP, 2008) won the Oscar Kenshur Prize for 18th-century studies and the American Musicological Society's Lewis Lockwood Award. She co-organizes the Critical Thinking Program of the Academy in Exile.

Kader Konuk is a professor of Turkish studies at the Universität Duisburg-Essen. In 2017, she founded the Academy in Exile, which offers over 37 scholars at risk fellowships to continue their research in Berlin and Essen. Trained as a comparatist in German, Turkish, and English literature, Konuk focuses on the disciplinary nexus between literary criticism, cultural studies, and intellectual history. Her research is situated at the intersections between religious and ethnic communities, beginning with the Ottoman modernization reforms and continuing on to Turkish-German relations in the twenty-first century. Her work examines cultural practices that evolve in the context of East-West relations (travel, migration, and exile).

Jane O. Newman is a professor of Comparative Literature at UC Irvine. She has published on 16th- and 17th-century English, German, and neo-Latin political theory, literature, and culture and the disciplinary history of Renaissance and Baroque studies. Newman has held Fulbright, Guggenheim, and Humboldt fellowships, was the M.H. Abrams Fellow at the National Humanities Center (Research Triangle, North Carolina) (2015-16), and held a Berlin Prize at the American Academy in Berlin (2017). She is the Chair of the University of California Systemwide Coordinating Committee for Scholars at Risk.

Vanessa Agnew, Kader Konuk, Jane O. Newman (eds.)
Refugee Routes
Telling, Looking, Protesting, Redressing

[transcript]

The publication of this volume has been underwritten by generous support from the University of California Irvine, the Volkswagen Foundation, and the Andrew W. Mellon Foundation. This book is freely available in an open access edition thanks to funding from the Universität Duisburg-Essen.

Bibliographic information published by the Deutsche Nationalbibliothek
The Deutsche Nationalbibliothek lists this publication in the Deutsche Nationalbibliografie; detailed bibliographic data are available in the Internet at http://dnb.d-nb.de

This work is licensed under the Creative Commons Attribution-NonCommercial-NoDerivatives 4.0 (BY-NC-ND) which means that the text may be used for non-commercial purposes, provided credit is given to the author. For details go to http://creativecommons.org/licenses/by-nc-nd/4.0/
To create an adaptation, translation, or derivative of the original work and for commercial use, further permission is required and can be obtained by contacting rights@transcript-publishing.com

Creative Commons license terms for re-use do not apply to any content (such as graphs, figures, photos, excerpts, etc.) not original to the Open Access publication and further permission may be required from the rights holder. The obligation to research and clear permission lies solely with the party re-using the material.

© 2020 transcript Verlag, Bielefeld

All rights reserved. No part of this book may be reprinted or reproduced or utilized in any form or by any electronic, mechanical, or other means, now known or hereafter invented, including photocopying and recording, or in any information storage or retrieval system, without permission in writing from the publisher.

Cover layout: Maria Arndt, Bielefeld
Cover illustration: Vanessa Agnew, photographed by Jobst von Kunowski
Printed by Majuskel Medienproduktion GmbH, Wetzlar
Print-ISBN 978-3-8376-5013-6
PDF-ISBN 978-3-8394-5013-0
https://doi.org/10.14361/9783839450130

Printed on permanent acid-free text paper.

Contents

Dedication 9

Acknowledgements 11

List of Figures 13

Introduction

Refugee Routes
Connecting the Displaced and the Emplaced
Vanessa Agnew 17

Flight

Refugees Once Again?
Rethinking the History of Ezidi Forced Migration
and Displacement
Zeynep Türkyılmaz 33

Right to Arrive
Topographies of Genocide, Flight, and Hospitality – Then and Now
Vanessa Agnew and Egemen Özbek 51

Telling

Hunted Scholarship
How Fugitive Ideas Change the World
Ngũgĩ wa Thiong'o 89

Antaram's Journey
Nazan Maksudyan 99

Walk past the vines, past the orchards
Meltem Gürle 109

Re-Rooting

German Literary Responses to the 'Migrant Crisis'
Space and the Colonial Past in Jenny Erpenbeck's *Gehen, ging, gegangen* (2015) and Bodo Kirchhoff's *Widerfahrnis* (2016)
Christiane Steckenbiller 117

Teaching with Grief
An Exploration of Politics, Pain, and Power in *Monsieur Lazhar*
Hande Gürses 139

Looking

Calais's 'Jungle'
Refugees, Biopolitics, and the Arts of Resistance
Debarati Sanyal 159

Refugee Trajectories
Post-1945 Refugee Management and the Implications of Demography as a Field
Aslı Iğsız 193

Suffering and its Depiction through Visual Culture
How Refugees are Turned into Enemies and Figures of Hatred: The Australian Case
Claudia Tazreiter 211

Protesting

In Another's Shoes?
Walking, Talking, and the Ethics of Storytelling in *Refugee Tales* and *Refugee Tales II*
Harriet Hulme 227

The Civil March for Aleppo
Zero-Level Protest or Networking in Action?
Clara Zimmermann 247

Redressing

Academy in Exile
Knowledge at Risk
Kader Konuk 269

Scholar Rescue
The Past of the Future
Jane O. Newman 285

List of Contributors 299

Index 305

Dedication

This book is dedicated to those who have had to leave their homes and to those who set a place at the table.

And in memory of our homes, abandoned and makeshift, in Kondosu Köyü, Istanbul, Cologne, Stones Hill, and Wacol Migrant Hostel.

Acknowledgements

The editors gratefully acknowledge Egemen Özbek's and Christopher Geissler's assistance in preparing the manuscript for publication. Additional thanks are due to Amanda Swain and Julia Reinhard Lupton of the University of California, Irvine's Humanities Commons (Irvine, CA, USA) for supporting publication of the volume and Steve Hindle of the Huntington Library (San Marino, CA, USA) for facilitating editorial work on the volume. Publication has also been made possible through the financial support of the University of Duisburg-Essen and Academy in Exile.

List of Figures

Figure 3.1. Vanessa Agnew, Kindertransport, 2018, linoleum, mulberry paper. 54
Figure 3.2. Vanessa Agnew, Refugee Plaque, 2016, granite, brass flashing. 55
Figure 3.3. Vanessa Agnew, Fleeing, 1945, 2015, glass teapot, model figures. 56
Figure 3.4. Vanessa Agnew, Refugee Ludo, 2017, game set, modelling clay. 56
Figure 3.5. Vanessa Agnew, Then and Now, 2017, acrylic box, backgammon set, brass plaque, prayer beads, coin, paper, mobile phone. 57
Figure 3.6. Vanessa Agnew, Wanderlust Life Jacket, 2017, life jacket, souvenir travel patches. . 58
Figure 3.7. Map of Turkey, ca. 1915 ; source: Wallstein Verlag, Göttingen. 69
Figure 3.8. Armenian Women; source: Wallstein Verlag, Göttingen. 70
Figure 3.9. Armenian Family Portrait; source: Wallstein Verlag, Göttingen. 71
Figure 3.10. Burning Street; source: Armin T. Wegner, Wallstein Verlag, Göttingen. 72
Figure 3.11. Abandoned Child, 1915–1916; source: Armin T. Wegner, Wallstein Verlag, Göttingen. . 73
Figure 3.12. After a Massacre, 1915–1916; source: Armin T. Wegner, Wallstein Verlag, Göttingen. . 74
Figure 3.13. Corpses in the Desert, 1915–1916; source: Armin T. Wegner, Wallstein Verlag, Göttingen. 75
Figure 3.14. Refugees on the Coast, 1915–1916; source: Armin T. Wegner, Wallstein Verlag, Göttingen. 76
Figure 3.15. Armenian Mother Fleeing, 1915–1916; source: Armin T. Wegner, Wallstein Verlag, Göttingen. 77
Figure 3.16. Camp at the Anatolian Railway; source: Wallstein Verlag, Göttingen. 78
Figure 3.17. Delousing, 1915–1916; source: Armin T. Wegner, Wallstein Verlag, Göttingen. 79
Figure 5.1. Antaram at her home in İcadiye, with her beloved cigarette in hand, 1970s. 100
Figure 5.2 Armenian genocide orphans, place and date unknown. 104
Figure 5.3. The young couple, Antaram and Hmayak, managed to build a new life for themselves in the 1920s in Istanbul. 106
Figure 5.4. Antaram with her daughters Sona and Maryam at their house door, 1940s. 107
Figure 5.5. Antaram holding the hand of the author's father, Vartan, on his first school day, 1958. 108
Figure 5.6. Antaram and the author, 1980 108
Figure 8.1. Bashir taking attendance. 143
Figure 8.2. Photograph of Martine Lachance with hand-drawn wings and rope above her head. 145

Figure 8.3. Bashir looking at the framed photograph of his wife and children. 146
Figure 8.4. Bashir holding the photograph, this time without the frame. 147
Figure 8.5. Headshot of Simon. 148
Figure 8.6. Class photo with Bashir. 149
Figure 8.7. Bashir looking at the signs inside the room where his asylum case is heard. ... 152
Figure 9.1. (Top) Calais – the fence. (Bottom) Calais – the container camp. 160
Figure 9.2. Song of Ethiopia. 167
Figure 9.3. Feather on sea foam. 168
Figure 9.4. Shoe half buried in the sand. 170
Figure 9.5. Clothing on barbed wire fence. 171
Figure 9.6. Fingerprint mutilation by razor. 174
Figure 9.7. Temesghen, 'They are making us slaves'. 174
Figure 9.8. Fingerprint mutilation by burning. 179
Figure 9.9. Scarred hands. 179
Figure 9.10. 'We, the united people of the Jungle, Calais'. 186
Figure 9.11. 'Dans le calme, le face-à-face entre migrants et CRS'. 187
Figure 11.1. Portrait of Behrouz Boochani, Manus Island, 2018. 220
Figure 13.1. The Civil March for Aleppo on the route from Rataje nad Sázavou to Zruč nad Sázavou (23km), Czech Republic, in January 2017. 248
Figure 13.2. 'Tea break' in Croatia in March 2017. 250
Figure 13.3. The Civil March for Aleppo in Tyre, Lebanon, in August 2017. 251
Figure 13.4. The official end of the Civil March for Aleppo at the Lebanon-Syria border in August 2017. 252
Figure 13.5. The Civil March for Aleppo at the 'Cemetery of Refugees' near the village of Kato Tritos on Lesbos, Greece, in June 2017. 255
Figure 13.6. Morning 'news flash' before the start of the walk from Knežica to Kozarac, Bosnia, in March 2017. 261
Figure 13.7. The marching group in Glashütte, in Teupitz, Germany, in December 2016. 263

Introduction

Refugee Routes
Connecting the Displaced and the Emplaced

Vanessa Agnew

Driven from home by war, persecution, climate change, and poverty, unprecedented numbers of people are now on the move (UNHCR, 2017). This is generating social, cultural, and political challenges and raising questions about the responses of liberal democracies. Although globally insignificant as a refugee host country, Australia is key to debates over migration because of its 'Pacific Solution', a model of border externalization, incarceration, 'offshore processing', and third country resettlement (Neumann, 2004). The model has been strongly criticized on legal and humanitarian grounds, and the returning of asylum seekers deemed a violation of internationally ratified human rights (Klepp, 2010; Neilson, 2010; European Parliament Briefing, 2016). Nonetheless, border externalization, incarceration, and offshore processing are approaches increasingly adopted by European and other countries confronted by arrivees whose existence is untenable at home (Ayre, 2016; Sigona, 2018). In future, ever more people fleeing conflict, poverty, and environmental degradation will look to high-income countries for refuge (Frelick et al., 2016). The predicted tenfold increase in climate migrants alone has powerful implications for transforming social and political processes for coming generations (Brown, 2008). Better understanding refugeeism and forced migration and developing informed and sustainable responses are thus matters of profound global urgency (Betts and Collier, 2017).

State responses are often justified by invoking historical examples of migration, even though – or perhaps because – refugeeism is neither well historicized nor globally conceptualized. European historiography, for example, has only recently begun to acknowledge Europe's migration past and scholars still tend to emphasize regional rather than pan-European perspectives (Sturm-Martin, 2012; van Mol and de Valk, 2016). Refugees and asylum seekers have not just been ignored, silenced, or forgotten by mainstream historians (Marfleet, 2007), but, as Jérôme Elie (2014) argues, they have been systematically excluded from the historical record (p. 30). This contrasts with a public discourse that explicitly links the current experiences of refugees from the Middle East and North Africa to those of Europeans displaced in large numbers by the Second World War and other conflicts. In Germany specifically, responses to refugees during the 'long summer of migration' were interpreted as acts of historical reconciliation and as an exemplification of the country's 'welcome culture' (Mayer, 2016; Hamann and Karakayali, 2016; Yurdakul and zur Nieden, 2018). Yet growing populism and pressure within the European Union to apply the 'Pacific Solution' to the Mediterranean suggest that this historical lens is being eroded. A notion of Fortress Europe is increasingly shaping public attitudes and state policy.

The question arises, then, as to how refugees, exiles, and 'irregular migrants' might be inserted in collective historical consciousness. Central to this is the idea of place and its associated possibilities for remembering. The *lieu de mémoire* – something Pierre Nora (1989) calls a site 'where memory crystalizes and secretes itself' – enables a society in flux to remember and preserve what is important to it (p. 7). Since asylum seekers and refugees lack collective sites for remembering, they are often concealed from wider public view (Evershed et al., 2016; Rodriguez et al., 2017). Their expulsion from home can thus be considered simultaneously an expulsion from the 'land of memory' (Creet and Kitzmann, 2014). Prevented from crossing borders, would-be asylum seekers are subject to a temporality that cleaves them from both the past and the future (Neilson, 2010). Refugees have neither time nor place. This has implications not only for the displaced but also for potential hosts. Being 'out of time' affects common understandings of history as teleological; being 'out of place' precludes the possibility of regarding history as 'double-sided', an exchange between those who are already there and those who arrive (Dening, 2002). We can conclude then that there is a pressing need for incorporating refugee and asylum-seeker memories into existing historical narratives. Not only must such a retelling include the experiences of those considered 'worthy' refugees and 'regular' permanent migrants, but it must also provide an account of those deemed 'unworthy' and 'irregular', those who are unwelcomed, detained, or turned away. Documenting past and present refugee flight, and identifying and interpreting sites of refugee remembrance, will create a richer picture of the ways in which endogenous histories are, and always have been, imbricated with those of others.

If transnational historicization is one means of addressing the growing crisis of human mobility, another involves scrutinizing the mechanisms of state control that increasingly regulate who may belong and who may not. The concentration of asylum seekers and refugees on islands and in camps and liminal housing, along with the tightening of borders, means that refugeeism is subject to selective invisibility, on the one hand, and hyper-surveillance in border zones, on the other (Tazzioli, 2016, p. 11). This invisibility/surveillance nexus emerges as one of the dominant structures of state control. In response, scholars and activists call for what Charles Heller and Lorenzo Pezzani refer to as a 'disobedient gaze' that directs attention away from the 'illegality' of border crossings to focus instead on state violations of refugee rights (2013, p. 289). This shift will allow the border – like the refugee route

– to be thought of as a potential site of encounter (Parker and Vaughan-Williams, 2016) as well as one of investigation, redistributive justice, and memorialization.

Notions of invisibility, containment, and disobedience find expression in Debarati Sanyal's contribution to *Refugee Routes*. In the Calais 'Jungle', Sanyal says, the irregular migrant is configured as 'bare life', someone whose existence in the French camp 'is rendered invisible and inaudible'. In an unfortunate coincidence of humanitarianism and securitarianism, the irregular migrant is seen as 'a body to be saved, contained, policed, moved around, encamped, kept out, or expelled; in short, as a body to be managed'. Claudia Tazreiter, likewise, focuses on the problem of invisibility, highlighting the fact that Australia's repressive refugee policies are upheld and enforced through statutes that, on the one hand, uphold humanitarian efforts to prevent deaths at sea, and, on the other, criminalize reporting about inhuman conditions in detention centres. This 'veil of secrecy', she argues, is countered by the clandestine efforts of journalists, medical practitioners, human rights advocates, artists, and detainees themselves. The Iranian writer Behrouz Boochani, whose 2018 memoir was composed in secret via text message, for example, describes mental ill health, self-harm, and suicide as common responses to the systemic human rights violations perpetrated against asylum seekers and refugees at the offshore processing centre on Manus Island, Papua New Guinea. Voicing refugee concerns and bringing human rights violations to public attention will, Tazreiter argues, help counter state-directed efforts to 'disappear' refugees and asylum seekers.

In this vein, *Refugee Routes* argues that it is possible to counter invisibility with disobedient looking, silence with telling, extirpation with surviving, inequity with redressing, displacement with re-rooting. While the stakes are different for host communities and those displaced by need, fear, hope, or decree, commonalities may be forged through storytelling, researching, archiving, reenacting, and memorializing. Social scientists David Benček and Julia Strasheim, in their work on xenophobia in Germany, suggest that anti-refugee violence is correlated to public opinion on refugees (2016, p. 10; see also Koopmans and Olzak, 2004). To shift public opinion, then, is to take a step towards creating a society that is more accommodating to newcomers and the needy. Since participation in a society's memory culture confers the legitimacy of belonging, the possibilities for social participation and a sense of belonging are correspondingly curtailed when access to memory culture is restricted (Glynn and Kleist, 2012). From this we can conclude that developing a commemorative culture around refugeehood has implications for changing cultural attitudes and for countering what has been described as the pervasive 'moral panic' about refugees (Baumann, 2016, p. 1).

Culture is made in motion, as anthropologist James Clifford insists (1997, p. 3). This puts the refugee route and its unruly exchanges at the centre of cultural production. Rather than being seen as the agent of crisis and threat, the refugee can come to be acknowledged in his or her creative potential (Nail, 2015, p. 12). The history of hosting, moreover, emerges as a palimpsest of displacement and route-finding. Fostering an awareness of historical continuities and developing a commemorative culture around refugees and their routes of escape and survival will help to promote more humane and sustainable responses to the plight of the forcibly displaced.

Refugee Routes follows Laurajane Smith's insight that heritage is neither a site nor an object but a 'cultural process of meaning and memory making' (2011, p. 68). The performative dimension of reenactment, focused here on migration heritage, has socially transformative potential (Agnew, 2007). In examining examples of refugee reenactments, this volume investigates the historic movement of people through space. The 2016–17 Civil March for Aleppo, for example, traced in reverse the refugee trek, starting from Berlin to proceed through the Balkan Peninsula and Greece to the Lebanon-Syria border. As Clara Zimmermann shows in her essay on the Civil March, by fostering collaborations among march participants, refugees, aid workers, and hosts, the March collected stories, songs, and images and disseminated information via social media, film, and print. Rather than being a futile undertaking of the kind identified by Slovenian philosopher Slavoj Žižek as a 'zero-level' protest, Zimmermann sees in the long-distance walk the potential for future activism and social change. Through its loose retracing of the route used by hundreds of thousands of predominantly Syrian and Afghan refugees through Greece and the Balkans to Austria, Germany, and countries to the North, it might also be argued that the Civil March established historical parallels with earlier refugees traversing the same landscapes. Even now these landscapes bear the marks of successive waves of refugees in the twentieth century and earlier, with memories of flight and exile still shared by those displaced from the former Yugoslavia, the German Democratic Republic, and other communist countries, and by the Second World War. This illustrates the commemorative potential of refugee reenactment (Agnew, 2019).

The Walk in Solidarity with Refugees, Asylum Seekers, and Detainees – also an attenuated form of refugee reenactment – invokes earlier wayfaring and, with a gesture to Chaucer's *Canterbury Tales*, follows the ancient pilgrim path along the North Downs Way in southern England. Conceived as an annual protest against the United Kingdom's policy of indefinitely detaining migrants, the latter-day pilgrimage foregrounds the value of traversing historical walking routes and engaging in dialogue. As Harriet Hulme argues here, the resulting two collections of walkers' reflections, *Refugee Tales* and *Refugee Tales II*, tread a difficult line between voicing refugee experiences and ventriloquizing them. Bringing into dialogue Emmanuel Levinas, who cautions against substituting one's own voice for that of the other, and Hannah Arendt, who stresses the political value of invoking the other through storytelling, Hulme enquires into the value and ethical legitimacy of walking in another's shoes and telling her stories. Hulme concludes, with Arendt, that the telling of individuals' tales restores human dignity to them, and so constitutes an effective protest against the detention of refugees.

Inscribing displaced people into the historical and social imagination serves as a reminder that the histories of Europe and the former Ottoman Empire, like those of the Middle East, the United States, the United Kingdom, Australia, and elsewhere, are themselves a palimpsest of displacement and unruly cultural exchange. Further, incorporating recent flight into a larger complex of memory and cultivating sensibilities about multi-layered routes of displacement offer the possibility of broadening historical studies to include landscape and place-based interpretation (Niukko, 2009; McGrath, 2015). This argument is picked up in the essay dealing with Armin Wegner's 1915–16 photographic documentation of the Armenian genocide. By juxtaposing the flight of Armenians from Anatolia to the Syrian desert with the recent flight of refugees from war-torn Syria to Turkey and western Europe, Vanessa Agnew's and Egemen Özbek's essay proposes a topographic frame for reflecting on refugee issues. The selfsame landscape, crisscrossed by waves of refugee flight over the span of a century, points to the shifting identity of hosts and strangers – an insight that is often lost in populist lamentations over the burden of refugee hosting.

Topography is likewise central to Zeynep Türkyılmaz's essay on the fate of Ezidi communities during the past two hundred years. Investigating forms of Ezidi resistance against repeated *fermans* (pogroms), she argues that the refugee route was never exclusively a path of flight for minority communities in Iraqi Kurdistan: the refugee route constituted a means of survival and, as such, was a central feature of Ezidi culture. Ezidis moved horizontally through the land, retreating to new areas to escape persecution, but also up into the Shengal (Sinjar) highlands, in what may be thought of as a form of strategic transhumance. This practice allowed Ezidis to escape cyclical incursions by local marauders, official tax collectors, military conscription agents, and census-takers. Türkyılmaz traces this deeply rooted pattern of mobility to the present day and the genocide perpetrated on Ezidis by so-called Islamic State. However, the ensuing diaspora may have fundamentally transformed the refugee route, Türkyılmaz suggests. No longer predominantly a mode of survival, the refugee route may now augur the eradication of religious and cultural pluralism in the Middle East today.

In its treatment of literary and filmic responses to forced mobility, *Refugee Routes* observes that refugee experiences are often narrated according to distinct tropes. Recurring themes include persecution and suffering at home, packing and departure, the dangers of the journey, exploitation by people smugglers, the confiscation of possessions, route-finding, interpreting rumours, searching for sleeping and hiding places, practices of sharing and hospitality, and scenes of arrival. Nazan Maksudyan, in her biographical essay on the experiences of her great-grandmother during the Armenian genocide, documents the fractured family's flight prompted by forced deportation orders (*tehcir*). It was while travelling from their home in the Anatolian village of Çengiler, near Bursa, to Der Zor in Syria, that her great-great-uncle, concealed as a girl, was revealed to be a boy and killed. Maksudyan observes that, for those deportees who survived, exploitation, hard labour, forced conversion to Islam, and physical and sexual abuse were common experiences. Yet, she suggests, the tenacity of people like her great-grandmother contributed to their survival. In contrast, Meltem Gürle's literary contribution 'Walk past the vines, past the orchards' adopts a more elegiac tone. Through its allusion to a poem by the Turkish poet Cemal Süreya, the essay captures the sentiments of a couple parting at a railway station – she to remain in German exile, he to return to Istanbul. Understated is the suffering implied by the impending separation. Yet, there are powerful intimations of what exile entails – the vagaries of memory, loneliness, anxieties about self-erasure, unwitting infelicities while adjusting to a new culture and language, and the longing for an alternative future, however unlikely. For all the certitudes that exile implies, Gürle's essay demurs about its meaning. Because their fate remains uncertain, the couple will disagree about the implications of the past for the present and future. Exile will remain a cipher.

Refugee Routes suggests that through collecting and comparing refugee accounts from a range of subjects and places, it may be possible to determine the extent to which these narratives exhibit common narrative features and so encapsulate universal aspects of refugee flight and exile. It might be asked, for instance, whether the resourcefulness identified in accounts of Armenian refugees finds a corollary in the Yiddish *macher*, the Polish *kombinator*, or the French *débrouillard*. A corresponding and less well-researched set of tropes can be traced in the collective memory of host communities. A potential set of themes centres, for example, on first encounters with refugees, levels of gratitude, women's status and treatment, child-rearing practices, indolence and the squandering of material resources, comparisons with autochthonous experiences of exile and migration, and self-positioning of the host as empathic and generous. Such tropes are explored in Christiane Steckenbiller's essay on Jenny Erpenbeck's 2015 *Gehen, ging, gegangen* and Bodo Kirchhoff's 2016 *Widerfahrnis*, novels that treat German attitudes towards the influx of refugees. Steckenbiller highlights the necessity for an historical reckoning with Germany's own colonial and fascist pasts. Current attitudes towards refugees are, she suggests, a measure of that unfinished project.

Analysing the representation of refugee experiences may shed light on their commonalities, but it can also contribute to a better understanding of cultural and historical specificities. Such findings are relevant to the ways in which asylum seekers' claims are processed. Narrowly prescribed by the Geneva Convention, the asylum applicant's account must adhere to a narrative pattern that foregrounds a 'well-founded fear' of persecution. The asylum interview protocol is thus likely to be a critical determinant in how asylum seekers narrate their stories. Hande Gürses raises this point in relation to Philippe Falardeau's 2011 film *Monsieur Lazhar*, which reveals the difficulties faced by an Algerian asylum seeker in making his experiences of persecution and loss intelligible to listeners who have the power to determine his fate. The question thus arises as to whether the conditions of enquiry imposed by the asylum process help to shape the ways in which asylum seekers themselves come to view their own experiences. Further, it might be asked whether the asylum interview forms part of a larger regulatory apparatus that contributes to the state structuring of memory.

Refugee Routes recognizes a need to investigate refugeeism within a comparative transnational framework. The construction of a 'welcome culture' makes Germany, for example, the heritor of a hospitality discourse with antecedents in the Enlightenment and in earlier periods. Immanuel Kant, for example, argued that states were bound to admit newcomers and this 'right to arrive' would promote lasting world peace, a theme investigated in the exhibition treated in Vanessa Agnew's and Egemen Özbek's contribution (Kant, 1977, p. 214). The volume seeks a better understanding of how adjudications are made and how the tension between hospitality and self-preservation – welcoming and turning away – is played out in the historical as well as contemporary contexts. By investigating this nexus, *Refugee Routes* seeks to determine whether other forgotten discourses about the treatment of strangers are available for reanimation. It enquires into the paradigms available for commemorating refugee experiences and the need to identify potential sites to be marked for official remembrance. These might include boat landing places, camping spots, reception centres, camps and prisons, churches and private homes – sites of personal and collective significance that have hitherto been overlooked. It also investigates the ways in which memories are represented. Scenes of refugees crowding trains, taking leave, abandoning belongings, and being selected are redolent of the Holocaust, which is often, if problematically, drawn upon as a visual corpus for commemorating acts of unrelated mass violence, displacement, and suffering.

The numbers of refugees are predicted to grow exponentially in the coming decades as a result of deteriorating environmental conditions, conflict, hunger, repression, and state collapse. Internal displacement is also likely to increase due to climate change, making refugeeism and forced displacement an increasingly domestic problem. To date and across the globe, state policy has focused on tightening immigration regulations and revising the legal underpinnings of the state's international humanitarian commitments. In the long run, however, such measures are unlikely to assuage public anxieties about the impact of refugees on host societies or allay concerns about the erosion of civil liberties and the incarceration and deaths of asylum seekers (Tazreiter, 2015; Weber and Pickering, 2011). By addressing these issues, *Refugee Routes* intervenes in public debate, drawing attention to the refugee, asylum seeker, exile, and forced migrant as individual subjects with respective sets of memories, hopes, needs and prospects, and a place in the national narrative.

Responses to the perceived refugee crisis have put migration discourse at the centre of international debate. *Refugee Routes* contributes to the transnational study of refugeeism and forced migration by investigating attitudes, responses, practices, and experiences of asylum seekers, refugees, and 'irregular' migrants. Historicizing refugeeism and forced migration can change perceptions about what it means to be displaced. This has benefits for the displaced. But historicizing refugeeism and forced migration also pays dividends to those we might think of as the 'emplaced' – those prior-comers, rooted in place, whose autochthony is so often taken as given. By establishing refugeeism as the object of reenactment and commemoration, the volume contributes to a more expansive memory culture – one that reminds today's emplaced that they or their ancestors, too, were once on the move. Once they also sought safe places to sleep and eat and settle. Once these prospective hosts were themselves the recipients of hospitality.

It is in this spirit that Kader Konuk reports on the work of the Academy in Exile, an initiative founded in Germany in 2017 to support intellectuals persecuted as a result of their work on human rights, democracy, and freedom of enquiry, or as a result of what she refers to as their commitment to 'critical thinking' more generally. Drawing inspiration from efforts during the Second World War to rescue Jewish, communist, and other scholars endangered by fascism, Konuk stresses the necessity of supporting at-risk individuals in the current conjuncture. Offering a place of refuge and intellectual exchange redounds to the individual and to host institutions. But, she argues, in fostering cohorts of exiles what is also preserved are communal ties, memories, cultural practices, and bodies of knowledge. Traditions of critical and secular thinking, once alive in Turkey and elsewhere but now under threat, may be cultivated abroad – held in readiness for a time when they might be returned to their native soil. Similarly, Jane O. Newman traces the history of mid-twentieth-century scholar rescue initiatives, describing efforts in the United States to support at-risk scholars in resisting the challenge of ever more repressive migration policies and the criminalization of aid provision to refugees. Albeit predicated on a human rights 'regime' that fell, and still falls, short, there is a case to be made for continuing this work even when the path to asylum is barred. Structures and support networks can be held in abeyance until governmental policies change and public attitudes soften. Testifying to this from personal experience, Ngũgĩ wa Thiong'o's contribution, 'Hunted Scholarship: How Fugitive Ideas Change the World', catalogues a long personal history of challenging authority and promoting academic freedom in Kenya. The price paid by him and others has ranged from self-imposed and enforced exile, imprisonment, physical assault, surveillance, and professional and publishing bans to homelessness and statelessness. Ngũgĩ stresses that by 'shelter[ing] a fugitive idea', it is not only the outspoken critic, knowledge producer, or creative thinker who is spared; it is his or her vital contribution to human flourishing. Offering sanctuary preserves the right of scholars and independent-minded people everywhere to ask uncomfortable questions in pursuit of truth.

If this puts the burden on individuals to offer aid and elevates the displaced person to the object of individualized humanitarian concern, Aslı Iğsız issues a caution. In keeping with the point made by Debarati Sanyal, Iğsız argues in her contribution on refugee management, eugenics, and demography that there are disturbing historical continuities in the configuration of refugees as either undesirable or saveable. *Refugee Routes* concludes that global mass mobility, already at historically unprecedented levels, will only increase as the effects of climate change spill into worsening social and political discord. It remains to be seen whether the emplaced respond, as is currently the case, with ever-intensified security and surveillance measures, border externalization, and populist vitriol directed at the displaced. The refugee route – that hard slog of hope – offers a possibility of disambiguating governmental securitarianism from humanitarian aid. In the refugee route, we seek more productive forms of exchange and political subjectivity and a path to the systemic redress of global resource inequality.

Bibliography

Agnew, V. (2020) 'Songs of Flight: War and Genocide Reenactment on the Refugee Route', in A. Fauser and M. Figueroa (eds) *Performing Commemoration: Musical Reenactment and the Politics of Trauma*, Ann Arbor, University of Michigan Press.

———. (2007) 'History's Affective Turn: Historical Reenactment and Its Work in the Present', *Rethinking History*, vol. 11, no. 3, pp. 299-312.

Ayre, K.-L. (2016) 'Europe, Don't Copy Australia', *Forced Migration Review*, 51 [Online]. Available at www.fmreview.org/destination-europe/ayre.html (Accessed 29 May 2019).

Bauman, Z. (2016) *Strangers at Our Door*, Cambridge, Polity.

Benček, D. and Strasheim, J. (2016) 'Refugees welcome? A dataset on anti-refugee violence in Germany', *Research and Politics*, pp. 1-11 [Online]. Available at http://journals.sagepub.com/doi/pdf/10.1177/2053168016679590 (Accessed 29 May 2019).

Betts, A. and Collier, P. (2017) *Refuge: Rethinking Refugee Policy in a Changing World*, Oxford, Oxford University Press.

Boochani, B. (2018) *No Friend but the Mountains* (trans. O. Tofighian), Sydney, Pan Macmillan.

Boudou, B. (2018) 'The Solidarity Offense in France: Egalité, Fraternité, Solidarité!', *Verfassungsblog* [Online]. Available at https://verfassungsblog.de/the-solidarity-offense-in-france-egalite-fraternite-solidarite/ (Accessed 29 May 2019).

Brown, O. (2008) *Migration and Climate Change*. Geneva, International Organization for Migration.

Clifford, J. (1997) *Routes: Travel and Translation in the Late Twentieth Century*, Cambridge, MA, Harvard University Press.

Cole, D. (2019) 'The Path of Greatest Resistance', *The New York Review of Books*, vol. LXVI, no. 2, pp. 21-22.

Creet, J. and Kitzmann, A. (eds) (2014) *Memory and Migration: Multidisciplinary Approaches to Memory Studies*, Toronto, Toronto University Press.

Crutchfield, L. J. (2018) *How Change Happens: Why Some Social Movements Succeed While Others Don't*, Hoboken, NJ, Wiley.

Dening, G. (2002) 'Performing on the Beaches of the Mind: An Essay', *History and Theory*, vol. 41, no. 1, pp. 1-24.

Elie, J. (2014) 'Histories of Refugee and Forced Migration Studies', in Fiddian-Qasmiyeh, E., Loescher, G., Long, K. and Sigona, N. (eds) *The Oxford Handbook of Refugee and Forced Migration Studies*, Oxford, Oxford University Press, pp. 23-35.

European Parliament Briefing (2016) 'Refugee and Asylum Policy in Australia. Between Resettlement and Deterrence' [Online]. Available at http://www.europarl.europa.eu/RegData/etudes/BRIE/2016/593517/EPRS-BRI(2016)593517-EN (Accessed 29 May 2019).

Evershed, N., Liu, R., Farrell, P. and Davidson H. (2016) 'The Nauru Files', *The Guardian*, 10 August [Online]. https://www.theguardian.com/australia-news/2016/aug/10/the-nauru-files-2000-leaked-reports-reveal-scale-of-abuse-of-children-in-australian-offshore-detention (Accessed 11 June 2019).

Forced Migration Online (n.d.). 'What is forced migration?' [Online]. Available at: https://www.usf4freedom.org/about-forced-migration (Accessed 29 May 2019).

Frelick, B., Kysel, I. M. and Podul, J. (2016) 'The Impact of Externalization of Migration Controls on the Rights of Asylum Seekers and Other Migrants', *Journal on Migration and Human Security*, vol. 4, no. 4, pp. 190-220.

Glynn, I. and Kleist, J. O. (eds) (2012) *History, Memory and Migration: Perceptions of the Past and the Politics of Incorporation*, Basingstoke, Palgrave Macmillan.

Hamann, U. and Karakayali, S. (2016) 'Practicing Willkommenskultur: Migration and Solidarity in Germany', *Intersections. East European Journal of Society and Politics*, vol. 2, no. 4, pp. 69-86 [Online]. Available at https://intersections.tk.mta.hu/index.php/intersections/article/view/296 (Accessed 29 May 2019).

Heller, C., Pezzani, L. and Stierl, M. (2017) 'Disobedient Sensing and Border Struggles at the Maritime Frontier of Europe', *Spheres Journal for Digital Cultures*, 4 [Online]. Available at http://spheres-journal.org/disobedient-sensing-and-border-struggles-at-the-maritime-frontier-of-europe/ (Accessed 29 May 2019).

Kant, I. (1977 [1795]) 'Zum ewigen Frieden. Ein philosophischer Entwurf', in Weischedel, W. (ed) *Werke in zwölf Bänden*, vol. 11, Frankfurt a.M., Suhrkamp.

Klepp, S. (2010) 'A Contested Asylum System: The European Union between Refugee Protection and Border Control in the Mediterranean Sea', *European Journal of Migration and Law*, vol. 12, pp. 1-21.

Koopmans, R. and Olzak, S. (2004) 'Discursive opportunities and the evolution of right-wing violence in Germany', *American Journal of Sociology*, vol. 110, no. 1, pp. 198-230.

Marfleet, P. (2007) 'Refugees and History: Why We Must Address the Past', *Refugee Survey Quarterly*, vol. 26, no. 3, pp. 136-48.

Marselis, R. (2017) 'Prosthetic Memories of a Refugee Route' [Online]. Available at https://www.law.ox.ac.uk/research-subject-groups/centre-criminology/centreborder-criminologies/blog/2017/06/prosthetic (Accessed 29 May 2019).

Mayer, M. (2016) 'Germany's Response to the Refugee Situation: Remarkable Leadership or *Fait Accompli*?', *Newpolitik*, May, pp. 1-5.

McGrath, A. (2015) 'Deep Histories in Time or Crossing the Great Divide?', in McGrath, A. and Jebb, M. A. (eds) *Long History, Deep Time: Deepening Histories of Place*, Canberra, Australian National University Press, pp. 1-31.

McNevin, A. (2014) 'Forced Migration in Australia, New Zealand, and the Pacific', in Fiddian-Qasmiyeh, E., Loescher, G., Long, K. and Sigona, N. (eds) *The Oxford Handbook of Refugee and Forced Migration Studies*, Oxford, Oxford University Press.

Nail, T. (2016) *The Figure of the Migrant*, Palo Alto, Stanford University Press.

Neilson, B. (2010) 'Between Governance and Sovereignty: Remaking the Borderscape to Australia's North', *Local-Global Journal*, vol. 8, pp. 124-140 [Online]. Available at http://mams.rmit.edu.au/56k3qh2kfcx1.pdf (Accessed 29 May 2019).

Neumann, K. (2004) *Refuge Australia: Australia's Humanitarian Record*, Sydney, University of New South Wales Press.

———. (2009) 'Oblivious to the obvious? Australian asylum-seeker policies and the use of the past', in Neumann, K. and Tavan, G. (eds) *Does History Matter?: Making and debating citizenship, immigration and refugee policy in Australia and New Zealand*, Canberra, Australian National University Press, pp. 47-64.

———. (2015) *Across the Seas: Australia's Response to Refugees. A History*, Carleton, Black.

Niukko, K. (2009) 'The Concept of Landscape among Karelian Migrants in Finland', *Journal of Borderlands Studies*, vol. 2, no. 24, pp. 62-77.

Nora, P. (1989) 'Between Memory and History. Les Lieux de Mémoire', *Representations*, vol. 26, Spring, pp. 7-24.

Parker, N. and Vaughan-Williams, N. (2012) 'Critical Border Studies: Broadening and Deepening the "Lines in the Sand" Agenda', *Geopolitics*, vol. 17, no. 4, pp. 727-733.

Pezzani, L. and Heller, C. (2013) 'A disobedient gaze: strategic interventions in the knowledge(s) of maritime borders', *Postcolonial Studies*, vol. 16, no. 3, pp. 289-298.

Reggio, A. and Mittelstadt, M. (2018) 'Pushback to the Resistance: Criminalization of Humanitarian Actors Aiding Migrants Rises', *Migration Information Source* [Online]. Available at https://www.migrationpolicy.org/article/top-10-2018-issue-5-pushback-resistance-criminalization-humanitarian-actors-aiding (Accessed 29 May 2019).

Rodriguez, A., Mansoubi, M. and Okhovat, S. (2017) 'Unwelcome Visitors: Challenges Faced by People Visiting Immigration Detention', *Refugee Council of Australia Report*, vol. 2, August, pp. 1-28.

Serrano, M. (2018) 'How Europe Turned Compassion into a Crime', *Time* [Online]. Available at http://time.com/5433001/swiss-pastor-norbert-europe-compassion/ (Accessed 29 May 2019).

Sigona, N. (2018) 'EU migration deal, is it the answer?', *New Internationalist* [Online]. Available at https://newint.org//features/web-exclusive/30/07/2018/europe-migration-deal (Accessed 29 May 2019).

Smith, L. (2011) 'The "Doing" of Heritage: Heritage as performance', in Jackson, A. and Kidd. J. (eds) *Performing Heritage Research: Practice and Development in Museum Theatre and Live Interpretation*, Manchester, Manchester University Press, pp. 69-81.

Sturm-Martin, I. (2012) 'Migration: Europe's absent history', *Eurozine* [Online]. Available at www.eurozine.com/migration-europes-absent-history (Accessed 29 May 2019).

Tazreiter, C. (2015) 'Lifeboat Politics in the Pacific: Affect and the Ripples and Shimmers of a Migrant Saturated Future', *Emotion, Space and Society*, vol. 16, August, pp. 99-107. Available at http://www.sciencedirect.com/science/journal/17554586.

Tazzioli, M. (2016) 'Border Displacements. Challenging the Politics of Rescue between Mare Nostrum and Triton', *Migration Studies*, vol. 4, no. 1, March, pp. 1-19.

Tufekci, Z. (2018) *Twitter and Tear Gas: The Power and Fragility of Networked Protest*, New Haven, Yale University Press.

UNHCR Global Trends Report 2016 (2017) [Online] Available at www.unhcr.org/5943e8a34.pdf (Accessed 29 May 2019).

Van Mol, C. and de Valk, H. (2016) 'Migration and Immigrants in Europe: A Demographic and Historical Perspective', in Garcés-Mascareñas, B. and Penninx, R. (eds) *Integration Processes and Policies in Europe*, IMISCOE Research Series, Cham, Springer, pp. 31-55 [Online]. Available at https://link.springer.com/chapter/10.1007/978-3-319-21674-4_3 (Accessed 29 May 2019).

Weber, L. and Pickering, S. (2011) *Globalization and Borders: Death at the Global Frontier*, Basingstoke, Palgrave Macmillan.

Yurdakul, G. and zur Nieden, B. (2018) 'Introduction. Witnessing the transition: Refugees and migrants in transnational perspective', in Yurdakul, G., Römhild, R., Schwanhäußer, A. and zur Nieden, B. (eds) *Witnessing the Transition: Moments in The Long Summer of Migration*, Berlin Institute for Empirical Integration and Migration Research (BIM) [Online]. Available at https://edoc.hu-berlin.de/bitstream/handle/18452/19415/witnessing-the-transition.pdf?sequence=1 (Accessed 29 May 2019).

Flight

Refugees Once Again?
Rethinking the History of Ezidi Forced Migration and Displacement

Zeynep Türkyılmaz

Until Islamic State's latest genocidal attack in August 2014, Ezidis were one of the Middle Eastern communities least known to the rest of the world.[1] Indigenous Ezidi groups lived in the Ottoman and Persian Empires, yet exile and resettlement also took them to the Russian Empire during the nineteenth century. The emergence of nation states further dispersed and divided Ezidi communities across the borders of Syria, Iraq, Turkey, Georgia, and Armenia, with only the latter officially recognizing Ezidis as a distinct ethnic group and granting them citizenship rights. In Iraq, Syria, and Turkey – home to the majority of the Ezidis in the past – they have been doomed to *de jure* invisibility but also stigmatized both as *de facto* heretics and Kurds. Ironically, however, it was Islamic State's (hereafter IS) genocidal attack on the Shengal/Sinjar region of Ninewa (Nineveh) Governorate in northwestern Iraq in August 2014 that brought the community to the brink of annihilation but also abruptly ended the centuries-old obscurity, secrecy, and indifference that had kept the Ezidis veiled in invisibility.[2] The international community came to know them through dramatic images of their flight from the Shengal Mountains, with women and children desperately marching to survive, leaving the bodies of their loved ones behind, struggling with thirst, hunger, and extreme heat on the refugee route.

The experience of fleeing was devastating at the personal level, not sparing a single soul regardless of age, gender, or social status. The overall picture, however,

---

1   Although the community is known as Yazidis or Yezidis among outsiders, the term Ezidi is used here. The community itself favours this spelling. Further, the term Yazidi/Yezidi is often associated with Yazid ibn Muawiyah, the second caliph of the Umayyad dynasty. Increasingly, many community members thus refrain from this usage, which they deem misleading or even pejorative.
2   As in Ottoman times, the official name of the district under Iraqi administration is Sinjar, although it is more commonly referred to by the Kurdish toponym, Shengal, which is also the term that will be used here.

was even gloomier. According to the official propaganda magazine of IS militants, *Dabiq*, a group of Shari'ah students sent to study this community concluded that Ezidis were infidels (*mushrikun*) within the context of Islamic theology and law and that their very existence was something Muslims should question (*Dabiq*, 2014). IS took upon itself the task of totally eradicating Ezidis through mass killings, enslavement, rape, the sale of women and children, forced abortions, and forced Islamization. While they failed in their drive to fully exterminate Ezidis, the horrendous assault shattered the ethno-religious minority even in areas not within the immediate reach of the militants. This irreversibly altered life as they had known it until then.

There is little reliable data on the Ezidi population in the Shengal area prior to the assault: the last official census in Iraq dates from 1987 and the country has been a failed state since 2003, following the second invasion by the US-led 'Coalition of the Willing'. This is coupled with Ezidis' own desire to remain uncounted. Nevertheless, rough estimates range from 300,000 to 550,000.[3] Likewise unavailable are accurate data for the extent of the mass killings, the number who perished during the haphazard flight, and the number of abducted women and children still held by IS. It is estimated that during the course of a few months, there were as many as 7,000 casualties, with 5,000–6,000 captured, enslaved, or indoctrinated women and children (Omarkhali, 2016; Allison, 2016). But there are estimates that are even higher (PAX, 2016). Number crunching in and of itself is hardly consequential when it comes to crimes against humanity, but in this specific case, there is more or less a consensus within the international community that the damage exceeds the crime's statistical significance. An investigation conducted for the Office of the High Commissioner for Human Rights released in 2016, 'They came to destroy: ISIS Crimes Against the Yazidis', illustrates this point.[4] The investigators report that 'in [the occupation's] aftermath, no free Yazidis remained in the Sinjar region. The 400,000-strong community had all been displaced, captured, or killed' (OHCHR, 2016, p. 32). This concise observation rather strikingly captures the wholescale destruction and horror inflicted on the Ezidis in ways that absolute numbers cannot. This report constituted the foundations of United Nations Security Council Resolution 2379, adopted unanimously in September 2017, which recognized the

---

3 Citing the district mayor's office as its source, Iraq Food Security Cluster's 2017 report claims 93,000 households and 558,000 inhabitants in the Sinjar/Shengal district; the UN's Human Rights Council report mentions 400,000, whereas the UN's Inter-Agency Information and Analysis Unit [IAU] and Office for Coordination of Humanitarian Affairs [OCHA] estimates 237,073.

4 For details of UNSC Resolution 2379, see www.un.org/press/en/2017/sc12998.doc.htm. For the text of the Genocide Convention, see https://treaties.un.org/doc/publication/unts/volume%202078/volume-78-i-1021-english.pdf.

Ezidis' ordeal as a genocide and IS's accountability as its perpetrator. It also underscored the point that the genocide is not over and that it is an ongoing process.

This was not, however, the first time Ezidis suffered a massacre or were forced into exile. The communities claim to have survived 73 persecutions, which they call *ferman*, a noun derived from the Persian verb 'to order'. Historically, *ferman* became synonymous with decrees or edicts issued by the Ottoman sultan, the ultimate authority in the empire. In the late Ottoman and early Republican periods, however, the term came to be adopted by victim groups to differentiate state-sponsored extermination campaigns from other forms of persecution. It was therefore used to single out the culprits, as in the Armenian and Assyrian genocides of 1915 and the Dersim genocide of 1938.[5] Yet in the specific case of Ezidis, the term's use has not been limited to refer to persecution in the late imperial period or even to those attributable to the Ottomans: *ferman* denotes each pogrom endured by the community in the past, with the culprits ranging from early Islamic armies to Mongols. Indeed, many survivors' testimonies detailing IS crimes were filled with examples from and allusions to earlier accounts about the abduction of women, mass killing of men, desecration of holy sites, and experience of exile – memories orally transmitted from one generation to the next. Such evocation of trans-generational trauma may be taken as evidence of the Ezidis' long history of being persecuted. Yet the assault of 2014 has rendered the community more dispersed and distraught than ever, leaving many in uncertainty, struggling with how to find meaning and, more importantly, how to find a way out of their predicament. Photographs from the Shengal district – the religious, cultural, and demographic heartland of Ezidi life – substantiate this observation. The number of Ezidis who returned home did not exceed 90,000 for the entire Ezidi region. Even after the liberation of Shengal in November 2015, the number remained dramatically low – some 6,000 households. Around 300,000 Ezidis remained in IDP (internally displaced persons) camps, mostly within areas controlled by the Kurdish Regional Government (hereafter KRG), and another 90,000 people have crossed to Europe or gone to the US or Canada in search of new homes (Nadia's Initiative, 2018).[6] Displaced yet again, Ezidis are trying to re-establish their lives on the

---

5   Interestingly, Sunni Kurds also use the term *ferman* for the extermination of Armenians in 1915. On the memory of the Armenian genocide as a *ferman* among the Kurds of Diyarbakır, see the oral history project conducted by Adnan Çelik and Namık Kemal Dinç, Yüz Yıllık Ah!: Toplumsal Hafızanın İzinde 1915 Diyarbekir (İstanbul İsmail Beşikçi Vakfı, 2015). A song about the Dersim genocide, which illustrates the continued use of *ferman* in the Republican period, is available online (starting at 3:00): https://www.youtube.com/watch?v=kptsWZm3c_g.

6   On the return of the Ezidi refugees to their homes, see the report prepared by Nadia Mourad's initiative that provides detailed information. Another report prepared by REACH Initiative, a partner to the United Nations Operational Satellite Applications Programme (UNOSAT),

refugee routes, soul-searching and redefining their religio-cultural traditions in unfamiliar destinies and destinations.

It is within this specific context that the essay seeks to historicize Ezidi experiences as refugees from the Ottoman era up until the 2014 genocidal attack. Rather than listing them chronologically and denoting each one a *ferman*, this essay takes a diachronic approach to the study of Ezidi exile and forced migration, arguing that these spatial dislocations shed light on each discrete pogrom, something that is crucial for giving voice to a community muted by oppression and other factors. Yet the approach also allows us to capture something about the nature of Ezidi subjecthood at pivotal moments in history and to trace how subjecthood was shaped and redefined again and again through these violent episodes and encounters with political authorities, fanatical intruders, and unaccepting neighbours.

While it is important to emphasize that the Ezidis, historically, have indeed been targeted and persecuted more often than their neighbours, this essay's focus lies elsewhere. Instead of merely reiterating narratives of victimhood, it reflects on manifestations of Ezidi agency and the various forms of resistance Ezidis employed, specifically to fend off attack and avert persecution. Through a study of Ezidi refugee experiences, the essay insists on an analytic separation between the migration movements planned and implemented by the community by way of survival strategy and the forced deportations inflicted upon them. These have not always been mutually exclusive patterns. The essay argues, however, that tracing refugee routes is vital when it comes to contextualizing emerging ideological constructions and their praxis. Included among these are, for example, an all-encompassing imperial/national citizenship and then-novel technologies such as census-taking, conscription, and taxation that regulated Ezidi bodies and encroached upon their everyday lives. It is the contention of this essay that the genealogy of Ezidi experiences on the refugee and migration routes reveals how these mechanisms – particularly the introduction of equal and universal citizenship – have failed to grant Ezidis equal or impartial universal treatment as promised and claimed by the reforming political centres over the past two centuries. To the contrary, diffusion of these supposedly equalizing mechanisms has gradually led to Ezidi disempowerment, depriving them of their 'traditional' survival strategies and means of resisting, ultimately rendering them more vulnerable to their persecutors and even defenceless against exterminationist assaults.

This study is firmly grounded in historical methodologies that allow for the capture of those moments when Ezidis set off on the refugee routes as they appear in the archives. Methodologically and conceptually, it combines an historiographic

---

also confirms the dramatically low number of returns – 6,000 families to the Sinjar/Shengal region: 'Rapid Overview of Areas of Return (ROAR): Sinjar and Surrounding Areas', May 2018.

approach with an anthropological one. In addition to archival records of the previous *fermans*, survivors of the 2014 genocide left behind significant ethnographic accounts of their experiences, collected at the refugee camps right after the mass killings and their flight from the Shengal Mountains. Particularly detailed is the series of interviews carried out for over a year by a team of researchers at refugee camps at Diyarbakır, Siirt, and Batman, three predominantly Kurdish provinces.[7] Of the more than 100 interviews, twelve have been translated from Kurdish into Turkish and were published in 2017, while the rest have been made available to researchers by the Zan Institute in Diyarbakır (Dinç, 2017, p. 27). Other reports by NGOs, relief organizations, and individual researchers have also recorded the experiences of Ezidis. It should be noted that many Ezidis have shared intimate details about their identity, history, and the everyday life they left behind. They have described IS assaults and the trauma inflicted on them as a desperate cry for the international community's attention in the hope that this would save abducted children and women and provide a safer path than that of IDPs on a refugee route (OCHRC, 2016; Moradi and Anderson, 2016). There are ethical and technical complications involved in recording the stories of people who are suffering and at risk, yet such interviews provide valuable evidence of genocide as well as rich testimony to a haunting history filled with communal and personal loss. The documentation of the Shengal genocide is the first time in their entire history that Ezidis have allowed and received such public visibility. To contextualize the recent cataclysm, this essay draws on extensive archival research conducted in the Ottoman Archives in Istanbul as part of a larger research project covering three centuries of Ezidi life. Given the Ezidis' secrecy and the limits of the Ottoman state's capacity to monitor, register, and transform these communities prior to the nineteenth century, locating Ezidis in the official registers is no simple task. Gaps in the official record have thus been filled by referring to other sources ranging from orientalist novels and missionary reports to the travelogue of a seventeenth-century Ottoman explorer, Evliya Çelebi. While only some of these sources are cited here, collectively they are crucial for reconstructing the Ezidi lifeworld. This body of archival work has also informed the interpretive framework – what is referred to here as the three stages of Ezidi refugee routes. The historical and ethnographic approaches are thus put into dialogue in a sometimes anachronistic fashion that combines the often-hostile official record emanating from the political centres with the testimonies of the survivors, assembled through oral history and other ethnographic research.

---

7   In transition from the empire to republic, the province of Diyarbekir has experienced change both in its administrative borders and name. In 1937, during his visit to the city, Mustafa Kemal Atatürk renamed the city Diyarbakır, citing both the etymological obscurity of its previous name and rich copper resources. Throughout this text, Diyarbekir will be used for pre-1937 contexts and Diyarbakır will be reserved for the rest.

Cyclical and to the Highlands

In 1640, the celebrated traveller Evliya Çelebi described a military siege against Ezidis – an episode also listed by the community among the *fermans*. The attack was carried out by the governor of Diyarbekir, Melek Ahmed Pasha, in the Shengal Mountains, also known as Saçlı Dağı (literally Hairy Mountain) in reference to the Ezidi practice of men wearing long braids. This operation brought the Pasha's army, including 40,000 cavalrymen, to the arduous landscape of Saçlı Dağı in order to address the complaints of the city dwellers about the Ezidis, who they claimed were 'raid[ing] and plunder[ing] the villages of Mardin, swooping down from the mountain on merchants, and travellers, and committing highway robbery'. According to Çelebi, within the space of a week the 'Pasha's armies took 9,000 heads (that is killed or decapitated), with another 13,600 captives, women, men, girls, boys, and more gold, silver vessels and earrings, and rings, and caps and goblets and dishes and other booty, more than tongue could say or pen could write' (Dankoff, 1991, p. 172). Çelebi justified the military action on the basis of his beliefs about their creed:

> These were brave and plucky infidels. They all worship black dogs. In their villages, you never find a mosque. They know nothing of fasting, and prayer, pilgrimage and alms, and witness formula. All of them are wine bibbers, since they raise juicy grapes in their vineyards. Forever since the event of Kerbela, these people have been rich, and no king had ever conquered them before. (Dankoff, 1991, p. 173)

Interestingly, the story of Melek Ahmed Pasha's campaign was embedded within another story that was told by Çelebi twenty years later to the new governor of Diyarbekir, Firari Mustafa Pasha. He begged Çelebi to share the secret of his predecessor's success, someone who had managed to suppress the Ezidi, albeit briefly: '[O]n that merciless mountain live [...] Yezidis [...] "dog worshippers", worse than infidels, a band of rebels and brigands, and perverts, resembling ghouls of the desert, hairy heretic Yezidi Kurds, people who felt not the slightest fear or awe toward the commander' (Dankoff, 1991, p. 167). According to Çelebi, the Ezidi community had recovered: they once again enjoyed power over the highlands, challenged the authority of local governors, and conducted the business of robbing and plundering as they saw fit.

Even if we take into account Çelebi's oft-remarked tendency to exaggerate, he offers a striking counter-narrative about the Ezidis.[8] Rather than presenting further testimony to the persecution of the meek and powerless, he portrays Ezidis as fearless, daunting, and invincible as well as 'heretical' residents of the 'merciless'

---

8   On Evliya Çelebi's writing style, see Dankoff's article (2010) 'An Odyssey of Oddities: The Eccentricities of Evliya Çelebi', *Eurasian Studies*, vol. 8, pp. 97-106.

mountains. Like Çelebi's description implied, Ezidis of the seventeenth century indeed had more options and possibilities than has been assumed retrospectively. As a religiously non-conforming community living in a Muslim empire, Ezidis preferred to live in seclusion, out of easy reach of the state, mostly in rugged landscapes and surrounded by belligerent neighbours. Violence was thus not unknown to them, mostly on the receiving end but sometimes also as dispensers thereof. Throughout history, Ezidis have survived numerous exterminatory attacks by governing bodies and other local communities. The worst of these, however, would come with the twentieth century. Prior to that, the scope of the state's military, administrative, and ideological capabilities remained limited in the highlands. Borrowing anthropologist James Scott's eloquent formulation, these communities had mastered 'the art of not being governed' and thus enjoyed relative autonomy, self-rule, and the leeway to be non-conforming in the geographically inaccessible highlands (Scott, 2009, p. 156). As Çelebi's valuable, if exaggerated, account suggests, Ezidis' superior knowledge of the landscape, and the ease and speed with which they traversed it, provided an advantage in their encounters with hostile groups and over the Ottoman armies in particular. Other archival sources support this reading and suggest, moreover, that Ezidis came to be armed and confrontational out of necessity in this harsh environment. Given that bearing arms was a privilege granted only to Muslim subjects of the empire and Ezidis were not considered Muslims, their bearing arms attests to the complexities of coexistence on the local level and to the limits of Ottoman control over the highlands.

Along the same lines, it can be argued that it was because of the particularities of the highlands that the Ezidis developed a conscious mechanism for securing their own survival. This was based on a simple but crucial migration strategy – a cyclical play with altitude that involved ascending the mountains and hiding in areas beyond the army's reach when hostile forces posed a threat, attacking when they could, and then descending to resume normal life when the army withdrew. This kind of tactical transhumance proved an effective survival strategy for centuries. It was in fact practised not only against centralized armies, but deployed on a daily basis in the mountainous areas they traditionally inhabited. Life in this harsh region was regulated and conditioned by sporadic violence, where tribal feuds, mutual attacks on property, livestock, and the harvest were frequent. The community's survival depended on its ability to defend its members, reciprocate in kind, and deter potential invaders. Various documents in the Ottoman archives indicate that the Ezidi tribes were not passive subjects of attack by their neighbours – whether Muslim or Christian, Arab, Kurdish, or Nestorian – and they did not hesitate to mobilize and repel attacks or, at times, initiate retaliatory attacks, as was the case in their relationship with the Arab Shammar tribe.⁹ Historian Yavuz Aykan's research in the Amid [Ottoman Diyarbekir] court records demonstrates that among Ezidis, the politics of the highlands sometimes also transcended religious distinctions, enabling Ezidis to join forces with Sunni Kurds against a common enemy (Aykan, 2016). Along the same lines, Ezidi tribal chiefs also followed the patterns adopted by notables in other communities, often trying to secure favours from the Ottoman centre by underscoring their own ability to control the community, acting as powerbrokers both locally in inter-tribal relations and among the Ottoman, Russian, and Persian Empires, when possible.¹⁰ They were also politically astute, resisting state attempts to control matters relating to their identity, including socio-economic status, conscription, and taxation.¹¹ Moving between the highlands and lowlands did not always stave off persecution, nor was it always successful. But remaining in their historic homeland, enjoying close-knit social networks, and keeping to their sacred geography and close to places of worship were all factors that enabled them to recover and recuperate as a community, survive as a creed after each *ferman*, which the community registered in its collective memory through legends, stories, and songs (de la Bretéque, 2012; Gökçen, 2015).

Unilinear and Lateral

This time-honoured strategy of seeking refuge in the highlands began to fail in the second half of the nineteenth century after the implementation of the Ottoman centre's modernizing efforts known as Tanzimat reforms, beginning with the imperial decree of 1839. Census-taking, conscription, and taxation were the three most intrusive tools of the new Ottoman statecraft. Thanks to military modernization and technological innovations, the Ottoman state was now more visible at the empire's periphery, including in the highlands. Census-taking and conscription came with the imposition of Muslim identity, which began to threaten Ezidis' non-conforming religious structure and communal identity. With the Tanzimat reforms, conscription was a duty imposed on every Ottoman male subject, who in

---

9   The Prime Ministry's Ottoman Archives [hereafter BOA], based in Istanbul, holds documents relating to the empire for the entire period and includes nteresting details on such nonconforming communities. For a selection of documents on tribal feuds of the Ezidis, see BOA İE.DH 21/1941, 20/06/1118 [29/09/1706]; A.MKT.MHM281/54, 22/M/1283 [6 June 1863].
10   The patterns implied here are explored in Albert Hourani's seminal work on urban notables, particularly in the Ottoman Arab provinces: Hourani, A. (1993) 'Ottoman Reform and the Politics of Notables', in Hourani, A., Khoury, P. S. and Wilson, M. C. (eds) *The Modern Middle East*, Berkeley, University of California Press.
11   On the Ezidi notables, see BOA A.MKT 212/42, 17-08-1265 [08/07/1849]; HAT 376/20475, 29-12-1251 [16/04/1836]; İ.DH 760/61962, 25/11/1294 [01/12/1877].

return would be a citizen endowed with the rights and subject to the duties of the new era. Shortly after the proclamation of these reforms, however, an exemption was granted to members of non-Muslim communities, who were expected to pay a fee in lieu of service. While favoured by many, this new rule meant that Muslim and non-Muslim communities would continue to be differentiated from each other in terms of their rights and duties regarding census participation, conscription, and taxation. The model did not leave any room in the identity matrix of the polyglot, multi-ethnic, multi-religious empire for grey zones that would accommodate Ezidis and other non-conforming communities. The new census officials wanted not only to register as many people as possible, but also to assign them to the categories available on the forms. Theoretically, Ezidis could only be a derivation of Christians, Jews, or Muslims, yet given the realities of nineteenth-century imperial rivalry and the continued adherence of the Ottoman centre to Shari'ah law, the only option available to Ezidis and other non-conforming communities was to declare themselves Muslim, an option which was taken by some, but vehemently opposed by many.

Increased state capacity also meant greater mobility, longer expeditions, and a better equipped army, and consequently the highland altitude no longer offered the protection it once had. Relocating to higher ground began to fail the Ezidis as a tactic, making the outcome of military confrontations uncertain. Ottoman military encroachments were unbearable, as was harassment by officials, who attempted to conscript or Islamize Ezidis, which was connected with their seeking either favours from the centre or unaffordable bribes from the community.[12] As a result, Ezidis inhabiting areas close to the Ottoman-Russian borderlands opted to cross into the Russian Empire. Clearly demarcated borders were still a novelty, making borders porous for those with local knowledge of the mountain passes. Furthermore, tense Ottoman-Russian relations made it impossible for soldiers to chase the fugitives once they had crossed into the neighbouring state. Under these conditions, the new migration strategy had to be a lateral one: it was intended to be a cyclical and temporary strategy of relocating to avoid the conscription season. Members of the community would sometimes return after striking a deal with Ottoman officials for a reduced fee in exchange for exemption from service or because they were in possession of Russian citizenship, which allowed them to avoid conscription completely.[13] As the Ottoman administration enhanced its strategies for controlling the borders and population, particularly those groups marked as unruly and heretical, the cycles of lateral migration became ever longer, eventually becoming

---

12 For an example of bribery, see BOA A.MKT.UM 368/1, 27.S. 1276.
13 For a selection of documents on the initial cyclical nature of Ezidi escape to Russia, see BOA A.MKT.MHM 354/37, 07.Z.1282; A.MKT.MHM 359/15, 14.S. 1283; A.MKT.MHM 351/6, 27.L.1282; A.MKT.MHM 353/66, 28.Za.1282.

permanent. For the first time, this led to the extension of Ezidi settlements outside of their historic homeland. As a result, a significant Ezidi settlement emerged in Armenia which developed distinct ritual and identity markers that have, over time, come to distinguish this group from other Ezidi communities in the region (Açıkyıldız, 2014; Gökçen 2014). While saving some individuals from conscription and the pressure of converting to Islam, lateral migration across borders has gradually weakened the remaining Ezidi communities militarily and socially, possibly also creating frictions and widening divisions within the community. It has also rendered them suspect to the successor states of the empire, which see them as fickle for changing sides and forging alliances with the enemies of the Ottomans.

Lateral migration had already signalled to the Ezidis that the life they once knew was becoming less viable. The worst, however, was yet to come. The 1877-78 Russo–Turkish War resulted in an embarrassing defeat for the Ottoman Empire and significant losses on its eastern front and in the Balkans. Around the same time, the Armenian question emerged in the midst of the Ottoman struggle to secure control over its territory and subjects, reaffirming the European perception of the Ottomans as the 'sick man of Europe'. These factors increased pressure on the Ottoman centre, which resorted to a dual strategy. First, it was deemed necessary to enhance the empire's military competitiveness to serve as a deterrent and maintain the realm. Second, Ottoman leaders were convinced they needed to redesign ethno-religious coexistence in the empire. Paradoxically, they promised universal citizenship to restore order, while seeking to preserve Muslim superiority at all cost. In this context, two factors rendered the Ezidis, more than any other non-conforming community, the target of both local officials and policymakers in the imperial centre. First was the Ezidis' insistence on full citizenship with recognition as a distinct ethno-religious community, that is, independent of the recognized confessional categories of *millet*: the Greek Orthodox, Armenian, Catholic, Protestant, Muslim, and Jewish communities. Second was the unfortunate reality that they had been weakened by demographic losses resulting from the waves of migration to Russian Armenia. They were further weakened by changing power dynamics vis-à-vis neighbouring Muslim Sunni tribes and the Ottoman troops, which meant a loss of weapons and other means of fighting. Prior to the 1890s, Ezidis had to deal with violence that was punitive, short-term, or cyclical in nature, which caused suffering but ultimately allowed them to heal and regenerate as a community. After the 1890s, however, they were subject to new forms of violence that not only aimed to punish the community but also transform their creed, to resolve what officials termed the Ezidi question. Regardless of how small the community was, reforming Ottoman officials could not bring themselves to ignore the ills of ignorance, heresy, disobedience, and treachery, characteristics they believed were detrimental to the well-being of the empire and Islam. Thus, from this point on, all military interventions unleashed forms of violence that, even while killing people, sought to convert

Ezidis and quash Ezidism as an identity and creed.[14] In response, between 1890 and 1915, Ezidis fled from Mardin, Midyat, Viranşehir, and Batman in the north southwards to Shengal, in modern-day Iraq, and Afrin and the Kurdish Mountains in Syria to escape Ottoman exterminationist policies (Guest, 1993).

In 1915 in particular, Ezidis were subject to genocide together with Armenians and Assyrians, though their ordeal is hardly remembered outside of the community, which registered it as yet another *ferman*. In order to escape further slaughter and forced conversion, they trekked these arduous routes in despair, moving away from their homelands but to areas closer to the traditional Ezidi regions, again in the highlands. It is unclear whether they anticipated a return, but in the end, return was not possible. This refugee route remained unidirectional for at least a century, particularly after the creation of borders that divided the Ezidis among four nation-states, separating them firmly from each other. With the exception of Soviet Armenia, none of these nation-states granted them full citizenship rights, because they were deemed either Kurds or religious heretics or even both. According to researcher and journalist Eva Savelsberg, pressure continued to be exerted on Ezidis under the Iraqi monarchy. This took the form of land grabs, military repression, and enlisting them against Kurdish nationalist groups (Savelsberg et al., 2010). After the collapse of colonial monarchies, state structures were taken over by populist authoritarian regimes that supported their legitimacy through nationalist rhetoric. Equating de-colonization with Arabization, the new political elite treated non-Arab identities with suspicion and subjected them to assimilationist schemes. Ezidis were categorized this time as Kurds and included in these programmes. In Iraq we find further evidence of governmental anxiety about the highlanders. Saddam Hussein ordered the destruction of Ezidi villages in the highlands of Shengal and Sheikhan starting as early as the mid-1970s, forcing them to resettle at a lower altitude in newly created collective towns known as *mujama'at*. Saddam's methods and the consequences of his policies were little different from the late Ottoman ones. Village eradication and deportation resulted in radical depopulation. As a result of their enforced displacement, Ezidis became an urban population for the first time in their history, initially in these new settlements, but many of them also ended up in Europe. A reminder of having been deprived of their time-honoured survival strategies and proof of their history of disempowerment, these collective towns in the lowlands were what rendered them easier prey for IS some forty years later.

As the uneasy heir of its imperial past, Turkey continued to treat the remaining Ezidi population with suspicion. Up until 1980, there was still a significant number

---

14 Two massacres, one in 1892 and the other in 1909, were accompanied by forced conversions and abductions. These were particularly devastating for the Ezidi communities and produced sizeable populations of refugees and new Muslims.

of Ezidis, almost 80,000, living mostly in rural areas close to their places of origin. However, within a matter of only four decades, their numbers have been reduced to a mere 500 due to the dual pressures they have had to face. One of the policies that has been criticized by Ezidis is the lack of religious categorization on their identity card in the form of the dedicated box being either left empty or marked with an X, rendering them dangerously illegible (Yalkut, 2014, p. 28). While it is not possible to establish with certainty when and how this policy was devised, the X on their ID cards haunted Ezidis whenever they had to interact with any state office, from schools and healthcare providers to compulsory military service and birth registrations. Furthermore, their Sunni Kurdish neighbours, who harassed and abused them physically and psychologically while benefitting materially from their vulnerability, made life unbearably hard for the remaining members of the community (Yağız, 2014). The 1980 coup vowed to resolve the Kurdish question and suppress political demands. According to the generals, the Kurdish question was a foreign intrigue unfolding with the help of non-Muslim liaisons inside the country. Once again pointing a finger at the Ezidis, the coup intensified pressure on them and resulted in their mass migration.[15] Unlike the Kurdish or Alevi migration patterns, Ezidis consciously skipped the urban centres of Turkey, where they believed they would experience even more pressure to assimilate than in their hometowns. The most recent refugee route has thus led to Europe, particularly Germany and Sweden, both of which have been destinations for Ezidi migrants since the 1960s. While migration to Europe allowed Ezidis to enjoy greater safety, the communities are exposed to other pressures of assimilation. As put rather dramatically by one Ezidi migrant in Germany, who chose to be referred to as Hasan and who considered these waves of migration to be forced: '[F]orced migrations are [the] worst of all the suffering we have endured. For good or bad, they always come with assimilation. One day, they will say, once upon a time, there were a people called Ezidis' (Yağız, 2014, p. 118).

Cross-Continental and Diasporic

Under assault by Islamic State and betrayed by their Muslim neighbours and the armed forces of the Kurdish Regional Government, Ezidis have had no other option but to resort to their time-honoured survival strategies. First was a retreat into the mountains, where they passed the line beyond which IS forces would not be able to pursue them, saving many lives. The heat experienced during summer 2014 and the limited water resources meant this was a critical but only temporary

---

15   The same policy was applied to other groups that were, or at least were considered to be, Armenian converts who continued to live in the area.

solution. The second approach was to determine the best survival route to pursue. Some chose to descend to areas controlled by the KRG, areas still safe from IS; others decided to reverse the journey of their ancestors a century earlier, crossing the border into Turkey. Ezidis' testimonies after their arrival in Viranşehir, Midyat, Batman, and Diyarbakır make frequent reference to earlier flight. Ironically, some of these refugees were settled in the very villages inhabited by Ezidis before forced Islamization and flight from the 1915 genocide. Transcultural psychologist Jan Ilhan Kizilhan, who has been working among Ezidi women captured by IS, argues in an interview that 'apart from the current traumatization, the genocide by ISIS reactivated the Ezidi communal memory of earlier genocides and massacres. They experience a double or multiple traumatization, resulting in the conclusion that they are unable to defend themselves, and are bound to become victims of Islamic terror over and again' (Omarkhali, 2016, p. 153). Indeed, the interviews reveal that memories of earlier persecution have caused more despair than hope for the normalization of life in the near future, thus complicating the refugee experience even further. In a diary she kept during the exodus, 19-year-old Asya shared an inner conversation on belonging, homeland, and exile:

> Ezidis had lands, we were on these beautiful lands. Weren't these lands ours? We did not know that these lands were not ours. We never thought we would have to flee one day. In the old days, here in Diyarbekir, we had had lands, and we had to flee due to persecution. Here we are again, yet as refugees on the very lands that were owned by Ezidis once upon a time. We are always refugees, in Turkish as well as in other foreign cities. (Dinç, 2017, p. 353)

Some were reunited with relatives among the fewer than 500 Ezidis remaining in Turkey, only to witness the conditions to which Turkish Ezidis have long been subject and from which their ancestors had escaped. Naif, a 35-year-old Ezidi returnee, explained that his ancestors left Viranşehir for Shengal 85 years ago and that his uncles still had land with titles registered in their names. Muslim neighbours had appropriated the land, but despite repeated appeals, officials did not help them. Naif exclaimed:

> [I]f only we could take those lands back, we would stay here and not go to Germany. We had gone to Iraq, and we are back here again. We have no money and no language, [possibly meaning Turkish here] to fight, but they threaten to kill us. This time, we will leave the land of Arabs [possibly meaning Muslims] for good. (Dinç, 2017, pp. 194-95)

Another survivor, 33-year-old Neam, also referred to her ancestors' flight and stated plainly, 'It is rather futile to return to a place, if that place is hostile to you. My parents were from here, and they have escaped persecution. What is the use?' It remains to be seen whether in the long run these refugee routes will prove cyclical or unidirectional. In the interviews, however, many refugees express their unwillingness to return to their sacred and ancient homelands, where they no longer feel safe living with their Muslims neighbours:

> I will be honest with you. We do not believe that we can live in peace in any area ruled by Muslims for long. We would return to Shengal only and only if we are granted full autonomy and everything in Shengal is regulated and ruled by Ezidis. (Dinç, 2017, p. 200)

Most interviewees stressed that extending their migration route, this time to Germany and Sweden, was the most viable response to the fear of further persecution. A 41-year-old female interviewee who asked to remain anonymous said the following:

> We were in Turkey, they persecuted us, [a] surviving few went to Shengal, and multiplied there, and you see what happened to us now. This is why we are now on the route to Germany. We know that is not our homeland or patria, but we want to escape these infidels, we say, maybe there, we can end the fermans inflicted on us. (Dinç, 2017, p. 327)

Since 2014, 81,000 Ezidis have sought asylum in Germany, swelling their population in that country to more than 200,000, making it currently home to the second largest concentration of Ezidis after the KRG (ÊzîdîPress, 2018).

Conclusion

In 1908, right after the constitutional revolution in the Ottoman Empire, Ezidis suffered yet another pogrom that was initiated this time by prominent members of the local branch of the Committee of Union and Progress. While their first target was the ancien régime, epitomized in the figure of Ibrahim Pasha, chief of the Milli tribe and a symbol of the Tribal Troops that had been established under the Hamidian regime, soon enough Ezidis too became their victims. For the reformist elite, Tribal Troops in general, and Ibrahim Pasha in particular, embodied all of the evils of Abdulhamid II's despotic rule. Hüseyin Kanco, his aide, who converted from Ezidism to Islam in order to be eligible to serve in these sectarian troops, became the target of local volunteers and the army, who jointly plundered and burned down over fifty Ezidi villages and killed around 700 people, which provoked the first mass exodus of Ezidis in the early twentieth century (Kaiser, 2014). According to historian Hilmar Kaiser, it was the constitutional regime's first genocide. Documents also show that 150 women were abducted. Historians know the names of three of them because one of the girls was 12-year-old Zine, a cousin of Hüseyin

Kanco, who appealed on her behalf for mercy and for their return.[16] An official investigation began in due course. Two of the local abductors were volunteers from the Kurdish tribes who claimed that they had 'met' the women during the military operation. In their testimony, the women had apparently expressed their desire to be blessed with the glory of Islam, after which they 'voluntarily' married their abductors. In the investigation's report, it becomes clear that one of the women had already been married and that her husband survived the massacres; the other girl's father was killed in front of her. When the interrogator asked the women in the presence of two witnesses – the same individuals who had converted and married them – whether they had indeed come voluntarily, both said yes. Yet one of the women, in a heartbreakingly honest and straightforward fashion, said, 'I was taken captive, I was forlorn (sahipsiz). Even though he did not coerce me, I came by way of captivity and despair.'[17] For Ezidi women, being forlorn and captive more often than not also meant being Islamized and submitting to one's fate and accepting the rapist who may also have been the murderer of one's relatives. Once they had been Islamized, ethno-religious hierarchies of the empire, as well as local power dynamics, made the rescue of these women very unlikely. But even if rescued, their creed's very strict purity laws, which punish any form of sexual contact, rape or not, with excommunication, and the community's unwillingness to bend these rules often resulted in the community's refusal to receive 'fallen' women back into the religion.

This last refugee route, with all of its horrific scenes and appalling stories of abduction, rape, and enslavement, broke the silence over the double tragedy of women. Baba Sheikh, the spiritual leader of Ezidis in the Kurdistan Region, made an unprecedented move by declaring that Ezidi women who had been abducted and enslaved by IS were not to be excommunicated. To the contrary, he re-baptized and personally blessed them at Lalish – the most sacred site in the Ezidi tradition (George, 2015). This was intended to symbolize the fundamental transformation of the community after the latest genocidal attack – a way of coping with trauma and finding a way to recuperate. The international outcry has certainly been important in influencing this decision to bend and yield. Yet more decisive was the resilience of the survivor women who dared after the 2014 genocide to share their experiences of being kept captive, raped, tortured, enslaved, and sold. Being on the verge of extinction once again paradoxically loosened, if not totally broke, the community's control over the roles and acts deemed appropriate for Ezidi women, who empowered themselves against all odds and appeared as armed fighters, community builders, social workers, and representatives of the community in unprecedented

---

16 See BOA DH.MKT 2843/39, 25. Ca.1327 [14 June 1909] for Kanco's petition and the interrogation records for the two abducted women, their abductors, and witnesses.
17 See the minutes of the interrogation in BOA DH.MKT 2843/39, 25. Ca.1327 [14 June 1909].

numbers and ways. Figures like Nobel laureate Nadia Murad became the face of Ezidis not only as a community of survivors but also as a secretive group breaking their silence and revealing themselves to such an extent for the first time in their history. To reiterate, these testimonies not only aimed to help to rescue other Ezidis who are still held by IS, or who have been sold as slaves to others, but also to bring the culprits to justice and end the sexual violence that has been inflicted on Ezidi and other women in war situations. While Baba Sheikh's declaration and gesture at Lalish has been most welcome, and cherished as an example of spiritual generosity and compassion, it is important to note the Ezidi women's agency in bringing about this seemingly hopeful and encouraging development in the face of such evil and on the refugee routes. This essay might well have ended here had not events interrupted the editing process on 24 April 2019. On that day the Ezidi Spiritual Council issued a confusing decree that at first sounded like an extension of amnesty and blessing to the children born to Ezidi mothers as a result of rape, yet a few days later, a second announcement was made denying acceptance of these children as Ezidis after much uproar within the community (Otten, 2019). A news report that appeared on National Public Radio [NPR] revealed that the number of children born to fathers from IS has been estimated to be over one thousand, and some of the children have already ended up at orphanages (Araf, 2019). According to this report, some women volunteered to send their children to the orphanages, while others either do not know their children are now in orphanages or had their children brought to orphanages by someone else, being unable emotionally to do it themselves. This decision revealed the widening chasm among Ezidis on how to cope with such trauma, regenerate as a community, and revive Ezidi traditions for the first time since the 2014 genocide. It has the potential to promote further dialogue as well as divergence and fragmentation in the long run. Moral stigma attached to these children once again curbed the possibilities of hard-earned self-empowerment and deprived these traumatized Ezidi women of agency to decide for themselves and their children, by and large excluding women from this conversation for the time being.

These controversial decrees and the low rates of return to historical Ezidi homelands and sacred sites once again reminds us of the bigger picture. How will this broken community deal with the blow of the genocide, particularly considering the slow and inadequate response of local authorities and the international community? How will Ezidi women continue their lives after having been forced on refugee routes and left practically unaided to struggle for themselves and their community? What does it take to create a new normalcy after genocide at the personal, communal, and international levels? What do the transformations endured on the refugee routes and embraced by victims and communities entail for the future? While such despair confirms the desperate picture of massacres, destruction, and human suffering in the region, it also leaves us with broader questions about the possibility of rescuing what remains of ethno-religious, linguistic, and political plurality and co-existence in the Middle East without falling into the trap of essentializing these identities, sacrificing human rights for communal ones, and creating more victims, particularly on the basis of gender and class. We are prompted to ask whether peaceful coexistence has ever been and will ever be an option. For many Ezidis, still on the refugee routes, this is an irrelevant question – at least for now.

Bibliography

Açıkyıldız, B. (2010) *The Yezidis: The History of a Community, Culture and Religion*, London, I.B. Tauris.
Anonymous. (2014) 'The Revival of Slavery – Before the Hour', *Dabiq*, no. 4, pp. 14-17 [Online]. (Accessed 4 December 2015).
Arraf, J. (2019) 'In Syria, An Orphanage Cares For Children Born To Yazidi Mothers Enslaved By ISIS', *NPR*, 6 June [Online]. Available at https://www.npr.org/2019/06/06/729972161/in-syria-an-orphanage-cares-for-children-born-to-yazidi-mothers-enslaved-by-isis?t=1560720158663 (Accessed 8 June 2019).
Çelik, A., and Dinç, N. K. (2015) *Yüz Yıllık Ah!: Toplumsal Hafızanın Izinde 1915 Diyarbekir* [in Turkish], İstanbul İsmail Beşikçi Vakfı.
Dankoff, R. (1991) *The Intimate Life of an Ottoman Statesman Melek Ahmed Paşa (1588-1662) as Portrayed in Evliya Çelebi's Book of Travels (seyahat-name)*, Albany, State University of New York Press.
———. (2010) 'An Odyssey of Oddities: The Eccentricities of Evliya Çelebi', *Eurasian Studies*, no. 8, pp. 97-106.
Dinç, N. K. (2017). *Êzîdîlerin 73. fermanı: Şengal soykırımı*, Diyarbakir, Zan Enstitusu.
ÊzîdîPress, 'Zahl der Êzîden in Deutschland steigt auf über 200.000', *ÊzîdîPress*, 26 March [Online]. Available at www.ezidipress.com/blog/zahl-der-eziden-in-deutschland-steigt-auf-ueber-200-000/ (Accessed 26 March 2018).
George, S. (2015) 'Yazidi women welcomed back to the faith' [Online]. Available at https://www.unhcr.org/news/stories/2015/6/56ec1e9611/yazidi-women-welcomed-back-to-the-faith.html (Accessed 9 February 2019).
Gökçen, A. (2014) *Ediziler: kara kitap kara talih*, İstanbul, İstanbul Bilgi Üniversitesi Yayınları.
———. (2015) *Kadim bir nefes Ezidi ağıtları*, İstanbul, İstanbul Bilgi Üniversitesi Yayınları.
Guest, J. S. (1993) *Survival Among the Kurds: A History of the Yezidis*, London, Routledge.
Kaiser, H. (2014) *The Extermination of Armenians in the Diyarbekir Region*, İstanbul, İstanbul Bilgi University Press.
La Breteque, E. A. D. (2012) 'Voices of Sorrow: Melodized Speech, Laments, and Heroic Narratives among the Yezidis of Armenia', *Yearbook for Traditional*

Music, vol. 44, pp. 129-148 [Online]. Available at www.jstor.org/stable/10.5921/yeartradmusi.44.0129 (Accessed 28 September 2017).

Nadia's Initiative. (2018) In the Aftermath of the Genocide: Report on the Status of Sinjar [Online]. Available at https://nadiasinitiative.org/status-of-sinjar (Accessed 31 March 2018).

Inter-Agency Information and Analysis Unit [IAU], 'Ninewa Governorate Profile', March 2009 [Online]. Available at https://reliefweb.int/sites/reliefweb.int/files/resources/B622896799C0250EC125761200343844A-Full_Report.pdf (Accessed 28 March 2018).

Omarkhali, K. (2016) 'Transformations in the Yezidi Tradition after the ISIS Attacks: An Interview with Ilhan Kizilhan', *Kurdish Studies*, vol. 4, no.2, pp. 148-154.

Otten, C. (2019) 'A Broken Homecoming', *Foreign Policy*, 2 May [Online]. Available at https://foreignpolicy.com/2019/05/02/a-broken-homecoming-isis-rape-yazidi/ (Accessed 3 June 2019).

Savelsberg, E., Hajo, S. and Dulz, I. (2010) 'Effectively Urbanized: Yezidis in the Collective Towns of Sheikhan and Sinjar', *Études Rurales*, pp. 101-116 [Online]. Available at https://www.jstor.org/stable/41403604 (Accessed 5 February 2019).

Yağız, Ö., Uçak Erdoğan, E., Amca, D. Y. and Saydam, N. (2014) *Malan barkirin: evlerini yüklediler zorunlu göç anlatıları*, İstanbul, İthaki.

Yalkut, S. B. (2014) *Melek Tavus'un halkı: Ezidiler*, İstanbul, Metis Yayınları.

Right to Arrive
Topographies of Genocide, Flight, and Hospitality – Then and Now

Vanessa Agnew and Egemen Özbek

One hundred years ago, Syria was a destination for Armenians driven out of Ottoman Turkey during the genocide that claimed between 600,000 and more than one million lives. Those who survived headed for Aleppo and places further east, where they sought sanctuary. Today, the mass movement of people is occurring in the reverse direction, as refugees flee conflict and oppression in Syria, Iraq, and Afghanistan.

The conditions that gave rise to the genocide in the early twentieth century differ from those motivating conflict in the Middle East now. Unchanged, however, are the large numbers of people driven from their homes by war and persecution. Many of the displaced are eking out an existence in Turkey; others attempt to cross the Aegean and the Mediterranean to reach Western Europe. Yet others die along the way.

The movement of refugees across this broad topography – from the Middle East to Western Europe – reminds us of the historically unstable identities of hosts and strangers, persecutors and persecuted. Those who were once hosts may now be estranged; those who were once strangers may now have the opportunity to be hosts.

Right to Arrive takes inspiration from Immanuel Kant's late-eighteenth-century ideas in order to think through host/stranger relations, arrival and hospitality practices, notions of cosmopolitanism, and the mediating role of art – then and now. Kant argued that strangers are not automatically entitled to stay in a place. They are, however, entitled to be temporarily taken in, particularly if returning them to their homes would endanger their lives. This principle is encoded in international humanitarian law as the principle of non-refoulement. Shifting the emphasis from the obligations of the host to the rights of the stranger, Kant stressed that hospitality is not a philanthropic act, nor is the stranger's condition one of indebtedness. The right to arrive must be upheld because, regardless of his or her identity, the stranger enjoys a basic human entitlement to seek out others and cultivate cosmopolitan bonds. Only by upholding and enacting this right to arrive will perpetual world peace, *ewiger Frieden*, be achieved (Kant, 1977, p. 214).

Refugee Movement through Turkey

We are experiencing a global displacement crisis of unprecedented scale. According to United Nations High Commissioner for Refugees (UNHCR) data, there are 68.5 million forcibly displaced people worldwide. Forty million of these people are displaced internally within their own countries, while 25.4 million are officially classified as refugees, and 3.1 million as asylum seekers. More than 50% of the refugees are children. It is often assumed that high-income countries bear the brunt of the refugee crisis, yet 85% of the world's displaced people are hosted by developing countries. Turkey is currently the leading host of refugees in the world, followed by Uganda, Pakistan, Lebanon, and Iran (UNHCR, 2018a).

Since the second half of the nineteenth century, the Anatolian peninsula – roughly current-day Turkey – has seen waves of refugees and migrants (Blumi, 2013). Situated in close proximity to conflict-ridden and war-torn countries, and lying along trade routes connecting Africa, Asia, Europe, and the Middle East, its topography has long been criss-crossed by displaced people seeking refuge.

Turkey has been much impacted by the contemporary exodus from Syria. Since the beginning of the civil war, 5.6 million people have fled and 6.5 million are internally displaced (UNHCR, 2018c). Like the Ottoman Armenians internally displaced in the early twentieth century, present-day Syrians who relocate within Syria are not officially considered refugees. Those formally registered as refugees are hosted in neighbouring Turkey, Lebanon, Jordan, Iraq, and Egypt. At present, Turkey hosts 3.5 million refugees.

The lack of long-term prospects in host countries where refugees have found only temporary protection – combined with the desire for a better life – has prompted many displaced people to take to the Mediterranean, a major route for those trying to reach Europe. In 2015, the numbers of irregular migrants and asylum seekers attempting to reach Europe by sea peaked. Since then, approximately 1.6 million people have arrived by boat, with Greece, Italy, Spain, and Cyprus the main landing countries. Around 15,000 people are reported to have died or gone missing while attempting to reach safety (UNHCR, 2018b). The image of Alan Kurdi's body lying on a beach in western Turkey is still seared in public consciousness.

Although only a small proportion of the world's displaced head for Europe (Beauchamp, 2017), the EU is intensifying efforts to stem the flow. In March 2016, the EU reached a financial deal with the Turkish government to stop irregular migrants to Europe (Corrao, 2018). In consequence, Turkey has also been required to tighten its borders and minimize the number of refugees trying to reach the EU via the Mediterranean. Like Lebanon and Jordan, Turkey now restricts border crossings, so that thousands are trapped at border gates. Other Western countries have adopted a similar approach. Australia, for example, deters the arrival of refugees through mandatory detention and the offshore processing of asylum claims.

Attempting to prevent migration does not solve the issue for any party. Instead, it infringes upon people's legal right to seek asylum and prolongs the refugee's plight. In consequence, 'Protracted refugee situations have become the norm rather than the exception' (İçduygu and Şimşek, 2016, p. 60). As is also the case in some other European countries, Turkey has been hosting a substantial number of refugees for an extended period of time. There is increasing pressure on transit infrastructures and host countries' legal and operational frameworks, while public opinion is not always in favour of admitting and integrating refugees. These strains have long-term implications for democratic processes in Europe and elsewhere and contribute to policies that violate refugees' legal and moral right to arrive.

Worldly Possessions

'Worldly Possessions' explores the implications of reneging on the stranger's right to refuge and hospitality. These implications are epistemological, since failed encounters contribute to prejudicial forms of knowledge-making. They are also political, contributing to a Kantian state of 'perpetual war'. The installations make use of everyday objects such as children's board games, toy figures, and glassware to highlight the plight of civilians fleeing conflict. In the Brechtian sense, everyday objects constitute an alienated *mise-en-scène* for depicting refugee experiences. Plenitude is contrasted with scarcity, visibility with invisibility, and action with inaction. Conserved objects on display become metonyms for the preservation of life and the memorialization of loss.

'Kindertransport' uses the text message sent by Ahmed, a seven-year-old Afghan boy smuggled in a refrigerated lorry travelling from Calais to the UK in 2016: 'I need help, driver isn't stopping the car, no oxygen in the car. No signal. I am in the container. I am not joking. I swear by God.'

Linoleum printing – a handcraft medium with a restricted viewership – highlights disjunctions between, on the one hand, the ephemerality and limited impact of the refugee's plea for help and the urgency and exponential circulation of the message conveyed to a global audience, on the other. Historically specific modes of communication are hereby revealed to be central to the definition of who may belong and who may not. If war, sectarian conflict, poverty, and environmental degradation are the impetus for the global refugee crisis, media are one of its drivers.

Figure 3.1. Vanessa Agnew, Kindertransport, 2018, linoleum, mulberry paper.

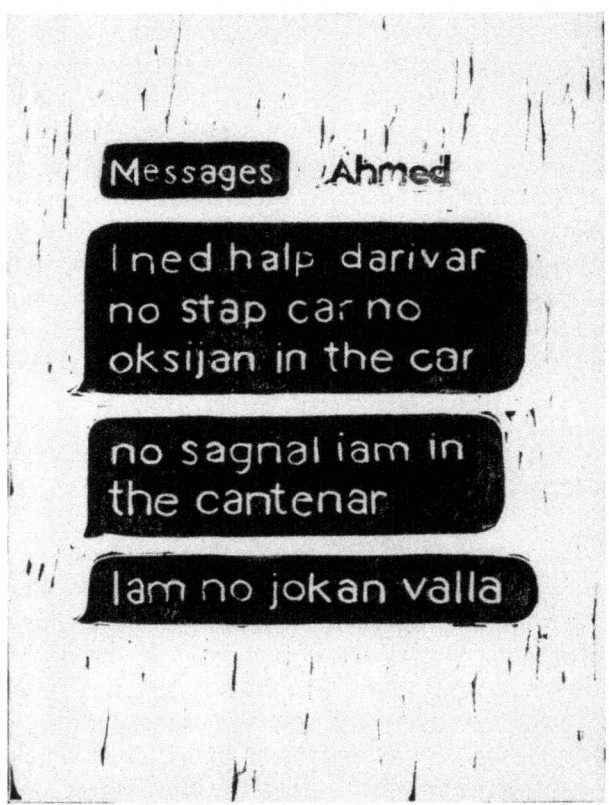

Source: Jobst von Kunowski.

Plaques set among cobblestones are inscribed with details of the refugee's search for a new home: *Habibullah A. wanted to live here DOB 1983 Fled Afghanistan 10.2015 Denied housing in Berlin on 20.7.2016*. The plaques speak to fantasies of a place where the streets are paved in gold. At the same time, the plaques recall Gunter Demnig's Stolperstein ('stumbling stone') Project, which upholds the memory of those expelled and murdered under National Socialism. 'Refugee Plaque' invokes the Nazi past to draw attention to the situation refugees face in Europe today. Refused rental contracts, refugees from predominantly Muslim countries are often consigned to inadequate emergency accommodation for long periods of time.

Figure 3.2. Vanessa Agnew, Refugee Plaque, 2016, granite, brass flashing.

Source: Jobst von Kunowski.

Second World War refugees are shown carrying their possessions and pulling a handcart – miniature figures arranged in spiral formation around the inside of a glass teapot. Their exilic journey occurs in full transparency, a plight visible within the context of ritualized daily life, represented by the accoutrements of tea consumption. As a result of this disjunction, the refugees' spiral course acquires an inevitability – it is a journey that lacks a *telos*. Without the possibility of arrival or hospitality, the refugees remain perpetual strangers.

Figure 3.3. Vanessa Agnew, Fleeing, 1945, 2015, glass teapot, model figures.

Source: Jobst von Kunowski.

Figure 3.4. Vanessa Agnew, Refugee Ludo, 2017, game set, modelling clay.

Source: Jobst von Kunowski.

Similar to the game Ludo, Mensch ärgere Dich nicht (Man, don't get annoyed!) is a popular German board game dating from the First World War. A player advances game pieces around the board through the roll of a die, winning when all his or her pieces reach 'home', but losing ground when an opponent's piece lands on his or her own. The installation transforms game pieces into refugee figures, whose abjection is reinforced by the arbitrariness of their enforced translocation. The frustration implied in 'Mensch ärgere Dich nicht!' raises questions about spectatorship and agency. While refugees are evaluated for inclusion or exclusion on the grounds of politically expedient criteria, the installation reinforces the substitutability of the individual within a system of refugee quotas. Further, it raises questions about current global refugee crises and the invisible hand of national and transnational bureaucracies.

Figure 3.5. Vanessa Agnew, Then and Now, 2017, acrylic box, backgammon set, brass plaque, prayer beads, coin, paper, mobile phone.

Source: Jobst von Kunowski.

A backgammon set and *tasbih* (a set of prayer beads) are overlaid with a 'night letter' (a death threat issued by the Taliban), invalid travel documents, a mobile phone, assorted currency from countries along the refugee route, and a worn photograph. The installation creates a palimpsest of everyday objects that reflects the changing reality of a refugee's life. Leisure and an orderly existence within a community have given way to a sense of insecurity, transience, statelessness, and fractured identity.

'Wanderlust Life Jacket' uses a found object – a life jacket abandoned by a refugee on a beach in Lesbos in 2016. Covered in souvenir travel patches from countries along the Balkan route, together with patches bearing aspirational slogans ('It's not the destination, it's the journey'), the installation highlights the difference in meaning of travel between people fleeing war and poverty and middle-

Figure 3.6. Vanessa Agnew, Wanderlust Life Jacket, 2017, life jacket, souvenir travel patches.

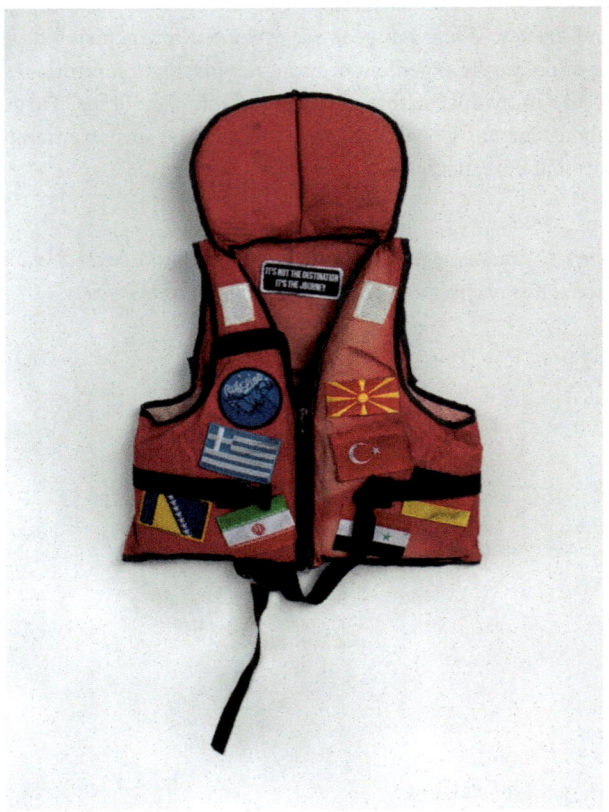

Source: Jobst von Kunowski.

class Westerners. The installation also highlights the discrepancy in opportunities for the young: self-realisation, adventure, and a self-congratulatory tone contrast with the struggle for mere survival. Moreover, the sheer volume of patches covering the jacket reinforces the length and arduousness of the journey undertaken by refugees, belying common assumptions about the ease with which people leave their homes.

The Concept of the Refugee against the Backdrop of the Armenian Genocide

The legal concept of the refugee dates to refugee flight and a genocide perpetrated one hundred years ago. There is a close relationship between ethno-religious separation, displacement, and genocide, since genocide may arise from what begins as 'a scheme to "remove" a group *en masse* from a particular locale' (Levene, 2011, p. 56). Around the turn of the century, the Ottoman government turned against a group of its own citizens, Armenians, perceiving them as a security threat and as an obstacle to the ethnic homogenization and Turkification of the country (Kévorkian, 2011, p. 244). The government ordered the deportation of Ottoman Armenians to a distant and hostile part of the empire, knowing full well that they would not survive at their destination (Suny, 2015, pp. 269-270; Dündar, 2011, pp. 276-277). The deportation was part of a genocidal calculus that sought to annihilate Ottoman Armenians through massacres, death marches, exposure to the elements, disease, and sexualized violence (Akçam, 2012, p. 193).

Survivors of the genocide became refugees within their own land and beyond. Yet their plight did not end with the conclusion of the First World War. 'The collapse of the repatriation provisions of the Treaty of Sèvres [which ultimately dissolved the Ottoman Empire], the multiple failures to establish an independent Armenian state, and the rise of Kemalist policies denying Armenians the right of return to their homeland and denaturalizing those living outside the borders of the newly constituted state' all deprived Armenians of state protection and made their refugeehood permanent (Watenpaugh, 2014, p. 168).[1] Surviving Armenians became stateless people in an emerging international refugee regime based on a nation-state system that consisted of entities which sought, above all, to protect their own sovereignty and to minimize refugee numbers. Under this new order, states erected barriers to asylum and created highly restrictive criteria that dictated who could receive refugee status (Gatrell, 2013, p. 53; Kushner and Knox, 1999, pp. 64-73).

By 1926, the number of refugees in Europe was estimated at 9.5 million, with another 20 million people internally displaced (Haddad, 2008, p. 99). In that decade, of all national communities, Armenians had the highest proportion of

---

1 Article 144 of the Treaty of Sèvres stipulated that 'the Turkish Government solemnly undertakes to facilitate to the greatest possible extent the return to their homes and re-establishment in their businesses of the Turkish subjects of non-Turkish race who have been forcibly driven from their homes by fear of massacre or any other form of pressure since January 1, 1914' (Martin, 2007, pp. 829-830). The same article annulled transactions undertaken since 1915 regarding 'abandoned properties' (*Emval-i Metruke*) and required the Turkish government to restore these movable and immovable properties to their owners, who were predominantly Ottoman Armenians (Onaran, 2013; Akçam and Kurt, 2012; Üngör and Polatel, 2011).

members of the community living as refugees (Haddad, 2008, p. 102). In the absence of reliable Ottoman population data, estimates of the number of Armenians who perished between 1915 and 1923 range from 600,000 to more than one million (Bijak and Lubman, 2016, p. 39). The League of Nations determined the number of stateless Armenians to be around 340,000 during the 1920s, a figure that does not include those who moved to the United States or resided in the Soviet Republic of Armenia (Watenpaugh, 2014, pp. 168-169). Hovanissian estimates that, as of 1925, some 275,000 Armenian refugees lived in the region that is now controlled by the current states of Syria, Lebanon, Palestine, Jordan, Egypt, Iraq, and Iran (quoted in Migliorino, 2008, pp. 31-32). Refugees also ended up in the Soviet Republic of Armenia, Bulgaria, Greece, Cyprus, the Balkans, Western Europe, the Americas, and Australia. Nonetheless, the League of Nations' comprehensive settlement plan for the Armenians was not very successful (Holborn, 1939, pp. 127-128). As late as 1937, Michael Hasson, President of the Nansen International Office for Refugees of the League of Nations, reported that thousands of Armenian families were still not permanently settled (Hansson, 1937).

The genocide and subsequent conflicts between Turkish-Muslim and Armenian groups were thoroughly gendered. Armenian adult males were perceived as threats to security and massacred immediately. Women and children were thought lesser threats and forced to participate in death marches from Anatolia to the Syrian desert (Rowe, 2011, pp. 152-153). Many died on these journeys or in massacres. Some survived the marches to become refugees at the margins of the empire; others survived as a result of forced assimilation. Between 100,000 and 200,000 women and children were incorporated into Muslim households (Bjørnlund, 2009, p. 34). For a long time, there was a profound silence about these women and children, since their experiences did not fit into clear-cut narratives of survival (Altınay and Türkyılmaz, 2011).

Ottoman Armenian women and children were taken from their homes and transferred to other locations within their own country. This was not merely a spatial relocation, but part and parcel of the genocidal policy (Sarafian, 2010). Armenian women and children had to convert, change their names and, in effect, relinquish their 'Armenianness' in order to survive. The forced assimilation of Armenian women and children complicates the concept of the refugee, since internally displaced people are not formally considered refugees. Those who remained in Ottoman-controlled territory could not draw on legal protections accorded to refugees, since they had not crossed an international border. They were deprived of the protection of the state to which they belonged and were at the mercy of those who captured or adopted them.

By the end of the First World War, Syria and Lebanon, now under French mandate, had become an important centre for Armenian refugees (Migliorino, 2008). Not only did this region have the highest concentration of refugees, but many humanitarian aid organizations worked there. The League of Nations and the French government ran settlement programmes for Armenian refugees in the territory (Gzoyan, 2014, pp. 92-101). In Syria and elsewhere, a large-scale campaign was established to support Armenian survivors (Rowe, 2011, p. 154). Armenian religious and secular organizations, such as the Armenian General Benevolent Union, led the campaign supported by the League of Nations through its multiple bodies, including the Office of the High Commissioner for Refugees, and the American group Near East Relief (Watenpaugh, 2010; Watenpaugh, 2014). As news of the persecution spread, other countries like Australia also took part in relief efforts. Organizations such as the Armenian Relief Fund and Friends of Armenia collected donations, sent funds and goods, and supported orphanages in Syria and Lebanon (Babkenian and Crispin, 2017). These efforts, which mark the emergence of modern humanitarianism, sought to help as many refugees as possible to survive, to rescue Armenian women and children who had been absorbed into Muslim households, and to return them to their families and communities (Maksudyan, 2015; Ekmekçioğlu, 2013; Watenpaugh, 2010).

The Armenian refugee situation also helped to set legal precedent. Throughout the interwar period, Armenian and other refugees fleeing the Ottoman Empire were at the centre of international legal thinking about refugeehood (Lochak, 2013). Together with the plight of Russians fleeing the Bolshevik Revolution and the ensuing civil war, the predicament of Armenian refugees was crucial in establishing refugee status as an internationally recognized legal category in the 1920s. Between 1920 and 1935, various measures were undertaken that aimed to provide refuge to those deprived of state protection. During this period, 'refugee' was defined in terms of membership of a specific group that had, for one reason or another, lost the protection of its own state. As Hathaway argues (1984, p. 358), this corresponded to the initial phase in a tripartite evolution in social and legal thinking about refugee status. First, Russian and then Armenian refugees were defined in this juridical and *ad hoc* way (Hathaway, 1984, p. 358). Then, between 1935 and 1939, a *social* approach to defining refugeehood dominated (Hathaway, 1984, p. 361). In this approach, refugees were defined as 'the victims of broad-based social and political upheaval, whether or not there were problems of international legal status' (Hathaway, 1984, p. 361). Membership in a targeted group continued to be a criterion of refugeehood (Hathaway, 1984, p. 370). And, according to Hathaway, from 1938 to 1950 refugee rights were further codified in international law, primarily in an individualized fashion through 'consideration of the relationship between a particular individual and his [sic!] State' (Hathaway, 1984, p. 370). The Holocaust and, subsequently, the Cold War were crucial contexts for defining the refugee against a backdrop of increasing geopolitical polarization (Goodwin-Gill, 2014, pp. 52-53; Moorehead, 2006, pp. 25-28).

Amidst the current unprecedented crisis of global human displacement, almost one hundred years after the emergence of the refugee as a legal concept, the international community still fails to adequately protect refugee rights. Refugee law is constantly flouted as states deny people the right to cross international borders – a legal requirement when applying for asylum (Haddad, 2008, p. 26). Moreover, the label of refugee has, since its inception, embodied numerous contradictions: it simultaneously undermines refugees' agency while according them individual rights (Haddad, 2008, pp. 34-39).[2] State and non-state actors rely on temporary responses rather than permanent solutions and insist on the possibility of refugees' 'safe return'. Increasing numbers of refugees are relegated, for ever-longer periods of time, to liminal spaces. There, they languish at the margins – if not completely outside – of our moral universe.

Armin T. Wegner (1886-1978)

Born in Wuppertal, Germany, Armin T. Wegner was a writer, poet, and human rights defender. At the beginning of the First World War, Wegner volunteered for military service and, in the spring of 1915, was assigned to the German medical mission to the Ottoman Empire under Trützschler von Falkenstein. Between April and August of 1915, Wegner was stationed in Istanbul, Rodosto, and Gallipoli, but that summer he fell ill with typhoid and was sent to Pera (Istanbul) to be treated at the German military hospital. During his stay there, Pastor Hans Bauernfeind informed him that Armenians were being deported. Later a Swiss merchant gave Wegner similar information. While on leave Wegner travelled as far as Konia to determine whether the rumours were true, before returning to Berlin (September–October 1915) to convalesce. With the disbandment of Trützschler von Falkenstein's mission in November of that year, Wegner joined the Sixth Ottoman Army under the command of Field Marshal Colmar von der Goltz. Von der Goltz was in Baghdad to organize troops at the front against the British forces. Here Wegner again fell ill and witnessed the death of von der Goltz from typhus. In the autumn of 1916, Wegner was recalled to Germany and travelled from Baghdad back to Berlin (Meier, 2011, pp. 155-158).

Wegner first learned of the deportation and killing of Ottoman Armenians during the summer of 1915 and travelled to Konia to witness this for himself (Meier, 2011, p. 156). Konia, which lay on the Berlin-Baghdad Railway, was the site of a concentration camp that had been established for Armenian deportees awaiting onward displacement by train (Kaiser, 1998, pp. 72-75). During wartime it was difficult to receive and distribute information about events in Asia Minor, since Ar-

---

2   For a discussion of terminology, see Maksudyan (2019) and Levin (2016).

menians and foreign missionaries were expressly prohibited from using the postal services. Soon missionaries' access to the telephone and telegraph was cut off as well, and the diplomatic missions of neutral states were banned from encrypting telegrams (Anderson, 2011, p. 204). When Wegner returned to Germany in September–October 1915, he contacted people who might have been able to help him to distribute information to the German public. This group included the editor-in-chief of the *Berliner Tageblatt* (Meier, 2011, p. 157). Wegner's efforts, however, were to little avail and he found it difficult to raise sufficient public awareness of the Armenians' predicament. Others whom he approached, including Johannes Lepsius, Paul Rohrbach, and Martin Rade, were already engaged in efforts to support Armenians. The theologian Lepsius had recently returned from an eye-opening visit to the Ottoman capital, where he met the Committee of Union and Progress leadership and registered its desire to solve the 'Armenian question' by any means. One of the first outcomes of Lepsius' efforts to draw attention to the genocide after his return was the publication of an anonymous article entitled 'The Extermination of a People' (*Die Ausrottung eines Volkes*) in the *Basler Nachrichten* in September 1915 (Hayruni and Hosfeld, 2017, pp. 233-34). Lepsius also informed his compatriots about the violence against Armenians in a piece published in the September-October issue of *Der Christliche Orient* (Kieser, 2011, p. 18). However, neither Wegner, nor Lepsius, nor anyone else was able to generate an effective platform for sharing news about the Armenian massacres.

Nevertheless, Wegner's findings contributed to a growing body of knowledge about the Ottoman exterminatory policies. Soon after the first deportations and massacres began, German consuls in the Ottoman territories sent detailed accounts about the annihilation of Armenians to the ambassador and to his superiors at the Foreign Office (Ihrig, 2016, pp. 105-138; Anderson, 2011, p. 205). As early as July 1915, the ambassador reported to the German chancellor, Theobald von Bethmann-Hollweg, that the Ottoman government was pursuing a policy of destroying the Armenian community (Anderson, 2011, p. 205; Hosfeld, 2005, p. 251). Later that year Johannes Lepsius, addressing the German Press Association, reported on the state of Armenians in the Ottoman Empire and relayed the conversation he had had the prior summer with Enver Pasha about the Armenians (Anderson, 2011, pp. 211-212).

There were other sources of information as well. The Ottoman government introduced the use of the railway to the history of modern genocide by deporting Armenians via sections of the Berlin-Baghdad Railway (Kaiser, 1998, p. 75). This meant that Franz J. Günther, the deputy general director of the Anatolian Railway Company, which operated the railway network in Asia Minor and Syria, had firsthand information about the massacres. In addition to protecting the company's Armenian skilled personnel and construction workers by resisting the Ottoman government's deportation orders, Günther sent many reports detailing the deportation and murder of Armenians to his superiors at the Deutsche Bank in Berlin, who then relayed this information to the Foreign Office. Other company employees also collected evidence. Although Cemal Pasha, commander of the Fourth Ottoman Army, had strictly prohibited photographing Armenians, the company's employees took pictures that attested to the genocidal policies of the government (Kaiser, 1998, p. 77).

Informing the public was seen as contravening German national interests since the German government did not want to risk breaking with its Ottoman allies over the fate of the Armenians (Hosfeld, 2005, p. 254). In response to the ambassador's demand that the Ottoman government be sanctioned for its anti-Armenian policies, Chancellor Bethmann-Hollweg clearly articulated the German position: 'Regardless of whether or not Armenians perish, our only goal is keeping Turkey on our side until the end of the war. In the event of a prolonged war, we will still very much need the Turks' (quoted in Hosfeld, 2005, p. 255, our translation). In keeping with this view, authorities at the Foreign Office suppressed news of the Ottoman crimes (Meier, 2011, p. 157). To make matters worse, those who tried to inform the German public about the genocide were denied a platform. As late as May 1916, the *Berliner Tageblatt* quoted the architect of the genocide: Talat Pasha claimed, in line with the official Ottoman position, that the Armenians were destroying the empire and that their deportation was thus a military necessity (Schaller, 2002, p. 529). In keeping with the instructions from Berlin, the German press proved willing to self-censor and largely avoided taking a critical stance against the Ottoman policies towards Armenians. The journalist Hellmut von Gerlach said that he learned about the Armenian massacres in a meeting with Wegner in October 1915 and had no difficulty confirming Wegner's reports among his colleagues. But, he added, this knowledge did not bring about change. On the contrary, 'Germany remained silent. Official censorship sealed our lips... So the best thing was to keep silent' (*Armin T. Wegner e gli Armeni in Anatolia*, 1996, pp. 49-50). Notwithstanding von Gerlach's claims, censorship was not watertight and, indeed, the German public had access to information in Dutch, French, English, Russian, and Swiss newspapers, which remained available. This has led historians to conclude that German elites did know about the Armenian genocide during the war (Anderson, 2011, p. 217). Even so, feeble talk about the genocide translated into neither an official condemnation nor a change of policy with regards to the extermination of Armenians.

Travelling to Baghdad in mid-November 1915 with von der Goltz's convoy, Wegner came into direct contact with deportees. They were there in the mountains that separate coastal Cilicia from the Anatolian plateau and the Arabian Peninsula, all along the Berlin-Baghdad Railway, and in the desert. Wegner knew what the marches signified. In a letter to Marga von Bonin dated 26 November 1915, Wegner concluded, 'Where? Where to? This is a route from which there is no coming back home' (1920, p. 20). While other members of the military convoy looked away, he deliberately sought out Armenian deportees in their camps. 'The Turks avoided these camps and denied their very existence. The Germans did not go to see them and acted as if they did not exist at all' (*Armin T. Wegner e gli Armeni in Anatolia*, 1996, p. 112). The following autumn, on his way back to Germany, Wegner visited deportation camps in Maden, Tibini, Abu Herera, and Rakka (Meier, 2011, p. 158). As part of a larger network of concentration camps in Syria and Mesopotamia, the camps constituted an important instrument of the genocidal campaign (Kévorkian, 2011, pp. 631-637). Wegner came to know two women, Beatrice Rohner and Anna Jensen, at the Aleppo orphanage.[3] Drawing on their assistance as interpreters, he was able to talk to orphans, access camps around Meskeneh and Aleppo, and record deportee testimonies (Meier, 2011, p. 158; Wegner, 1920, pp. 168-169). The camp at Meskeneh, like others, was a major way station on the deportation route, especially between spring 1915 and spring 1916, which constituted the height of the deportations. Thousands of Armenians tried to survive in the camps under conditions of terrible deprivation, disease, and fear (Mouradian, 2015, p. 44). Defying the ban on gathering information about the genocide, Wegner took photographs and collected eyewitness accounts (Balakian, 2015, pp. 95-96). He recorded eyewitness testimony in his diary, with some of these notes ending up in a chapter in his *Der Weg ohne Heimkehr, ein Martyrium in Briefen* (The Road of No Return Home, A Martyrdom in Letters), published in 1919. He also smuggled out petitions, documents, and letters, which he delivered to the US embassy in Istanbul (Meier, 2011, pp. 158-159).

In 1917, Wegner joined the editorial board of *Der Neue Orient* (The New Orient), which was controlled by the German Foreign Office. In the same year, he prepared a literary account of his time in Mesopotamia under von der Goltz. On 9 February 1918, he delivered a presentation to the Silesian branch of the *Deutsch-Türkische Vereinigung* (German-Turkish Society), illustrating the lecture with 108 lantern slides. Some of the images relating to the Armenian genocide were later used in a lecture titled *Die Austreibung des armenischen Volkes in die Wüste* (The Expulsion of the Armenian People to the Desert). Literary scholar Andreas Meier notes that even though Wegner used pictures depicting Armenian deportees in his lecture 'In Mesopotamia with von der Goltz', he stated that they were deportees of war, but he did not explicitly call them victims of genocide. Meier argues that Wegner came close to aligning himself with the official Turkish position justifying the expulsion, which blamed Armenians for betraying the empire. After the war, however, Wegner seems to have

---

3   Beatrice Rohner led an international rescue effort to support Armenians who survived the death marches and reached Aleppo. She was able to save more than a thousand children at an orphanage in the city (Kieser, 2014). In her study, Hilmar Kaiser showed that Rohner's work relied on an Armenian underground network led by the Reverend Hovhannes Eskijian, a network that attempted to establish safe havens and implement what Kaiser refers to as a 'program for Armenian national survival' (2002, 52).

revised this view, and in the 1919 *Austreibung* lecture he adopts an avowedly pro-Armenian stance (Meier, 2011, pp. 159-162).

Meier adds that it was only after the First World War that Wegner made a systematic study of the genocide and acquired a significant amount of factual information about the extermination of Armenians (2011, p. 163). A number of published accounts were available to him, including Johannes Lepsius's *Bericht über die Lage des armenischen Volkes in der Türkei* (Report on the Situation of the Armenian People in Turkey), published in 1916, Martin Niepage's *Ein Wort an die berufenen Vertreter des deutschen Volkes. Eindrücke eines deutschen Oberlehrers aus der Türkei* (The Horrors of Aleppo, as seen by a German Eyewitness), also published in 1916, and J. W. Ernst Sommer's *Das armenische Volk in Sage und Geschichte* (The Armenian People in Legends and History), published in 1917. The first product of Wegner's investigations – one that made his pro-Armenian stance public – was an open letter to US President Woodrow Wilson published on 23 February 1919 in the *Berliner Tageblatt*. In the letter, Wegner positioned himself as one of the few Europeans to have directly witnessed the annihilation of the Armenians and demanded justice for them (Payne, 2013, p. 28; Meier, 2011, p. 164).

Wegner continued his pro-Armenian advocacy in his public lecture *Die Austreibung des armenischen Volkes in die Wüste* (The Expulsion of the Armenian People to the Desert), which he delivered on 19 March 1919 at the Urania Society in Berlin. In addition to relying on his own field notes (albeit a small portion thereof), he drew on sources by Lepsius, Niepage, Sommer, and Paul Rohrbach, who published an edited volume titled *Armenien: Beiträge zur armenischen Landes- und Volkskunde* (Armenia: Contributions to Armenian Regional and Folklore Studies), in which he documented the persecution of Armenians. The result was a powerful narrative augmented by images (Meier, 2011, pp. 165-67). Meier emphasizes that Wegner's aim in this lecture, as well as in its subsequent versions, was less to provide an historically accurate eyewitness account than to influence German public opinion and to make a case for the Armenian cause (2011, pp. 167-68; Agnew and Konuk, 2020).

In adopting this approach, Wegner assumed the task of challenging German public opinion, which was ambivalent, if not hostile, towards Armenians. As historian Stefan Ihrig reminds us, post-war public attitudes were characterized by 'the interplay between information and whitewashing, accepting the charges of genocide and denying or justifying what had happened' (2016, p. 193). Such views remained strong during and after the trial of Solomon Tehlirian for the assassination of the exiled Talat Pasha in Berlin. There were many who blamed Armenians for engaging in fifth column activities and betraying the Ottoman government. In the preface written for the publication of the trial proceedings, Wegner challenged such views head-on, stating, '[A]nd all these fierce accusations which are being leveled against the Armenian people in order to find the guilty reason [*schuldige Ursache*] for these horrors in their own behavior cannot excuse what has been committed against them' (quoted in Ihrig, 2016, p. 280). Around this time, Wegner's position also shifted vis-à-vis German complicity in the genocide. Earlier iterations of the 'Expulsion' lecture exonerated Germany, but in the version he delivered in 1924 in Vienna, he assigned responsibility for the 'Armenian question', which had paved the way for genocide, to Germany and other signatories to the 1878 Berlin Treaty (Meier, 2011, p. 167).

Wegner's political advocacy was not limited to the Armenians and he continued to speak truth to power after the rise of National Socialism. On 11 April 1933, he published an open letter to Hitler protesting the persecution of Jews and requesting that Germany should be protected 'by protecting the Jews'. In other words, protecting the Jews was to protect Germany. 'Because', he added, 'even if Germany might be able to do without the Jews, she cannot do without her virtue. "There is only one true faith", wisely warns Immanuel Kant from the crypt of his hundred-year-old tomb, "even if there may be many different creeds." Keeping this doctrine in mind will allow you to understand also those you are now fighting. What would Germany be without truth, beauty, and justice?' (Wegner, 2015, pp. 157-158; English translation in *Armin T. Wegner e gli Armeni in Anatolia*, 1996, pp. 164-165). For this outspokenness Wegner was arrested, tortured, and incarcerated in several concentration camps (Hofmann, 1996, p. 1). Upon his release he fled Germany and went into exile. International recognition came in the 1960s, when Wegner received the title of 'Righteous Among the Nations' from Yad Vashem and the Order of Saint Gregory the Illuminator from Armenia (Yad Vashem, 2018; Khatchaturian, 2018). He died in Italy in 1978.

Armin T. Wegner's Images in *Right to Arrive*

Wegner's work is crucial, for it continues to counter the official and popular disavowal of and justification for the Armenian genocide by Turkey. Additional evidence for the genocide is to be found in the memoirs, diaries, letters, and other documents of the Committee of Union and Progress (CUP) leaders (Göçek, 2015; Adak, 2007). As critical biographies of the architects of the genocide come to be published, new light is shed on the genocidal calculus and on political continuities between the late imperial and republican periods (Kieser, 2018). Visual documentation of the Armenian genocide is limited because of Cemal Pasha's prohibition against photographing Armenian deportees and because of the technical challenges associated with photography at that time (Hofmann and Koutcharian, 1992, p. 54). As a result, there is no equivalent of the Holocaust's visual record or, to borrow Susan Sontag's phrase, a 'photographic inventory of ultimate horror' (1977, p. 19). Indeed, the Armenian genocide is characterized by the very paucity of images (Baronian, 2010, p. 207). The two most significant bodies of work are the collection of Near East Relief and that of Armin Wegner (Hofmann and Koutcharian, 1992, p. 54). The historical photographs in *Right to Arrive* are drawn from Wegner's collection, now held in the German Literature Archive in Marbach. He himself used the images in lantern slide lectures dealing with the plight of Ottoman Armenians, including in the lecture 'The Expulsion of the Armenian People to the Desert' in March 1919 in Berlin. Only a few images in Wegner's collection relate to the genocide per se; others are ethnographic images depicting Armenians and their ways of life. Some of the images included in *Right to Arrive* belong to the latter category.

Wegner did not leave detailed information about many of the images, and there is ongoing debate about provenance, dates, locations, and authorship. The captions used in *Right to Arrive* are drawn from Andreas Meier's edition of Wegner's slide lecture 'The Expulsion of the Armenian People to the Desert' (Meier, 2011, p. 93). It is known that Wegner took dozens of photographs during his deployment. Whether he photographed deportees on the way from Aleppo to Baghdad in 1915 is unclear. His diary, however, refers to pictures taken on the return trip from Baghdad to Constantinople the following year (Hofmann, 1996, pp. 10-11). Meier indicates that of the hundred-odd images used in the lecture, approximately one third can be attributed with some certainty to Wegner himself (2011, p. 108). Many of the photographs were taken at camps near Aleppo in 1916 and others *en route* (Hofmann, 1996, p. 11). Wegner smuggled slides back to Germany, but many did not withstand the heat and ravages of the journey (Wegner, 1920, p. 169). The surviving material seems to have been insufficient in creating the kind of impact he had had in mind. He thus looked to the existing photographic record in order to fill in the gaps, incorporating into his lecture images from other sources, including commercially available lantern slides from Theodor Benzinger's studio in Stuttgart and from Paul Rohrbach's work. Wegner also frankly conceded that some of the images depicted events that had occurred earlier (Meier, 2011, pp. 169-170). One such image appears in this exhibition under the caption 'Camp at the Anatolian Railway' (more on this image below). Favouring publicistic and literary approaches over strictly documentary ones, Wegner intended to illustrate rather than minutely record the Armenian experience (Meier, 2011, p. 170). At the time, this sparked controversy, with members of the public questioning the authenticity of some of the images used in the slide lecture. Later, Wegner's approach was seen to have jeopardized the credibility of his undertaking (Meier, 2011, p. 171). This does not mean that Wegner's work does not serve a vital historiographic function (Tamcke, 2011, p. 75). As an eyewitness to the atrocities, collector of survivor testimonies, and visual recorder of Armenian experiences, his work captures the horrors of the genocide and the predicament of the Armenians within the broader context of Armenian life in the Ottoman Empire (Agnew and Konuk, 2020). Though the record is incomplete, Wegner's collection provides some of the most powerful evidence of the genocide and flight that we have today.

Figure 3.7. Map of Turkey, ca. 1915; source: Wallstein Verlag, Göttingen.

Unattributed map depicting the Ottoman Empire and surrounding empires. Wegner appears to have marked Greater Syria, including locations such as the Syrian desert and cities, as the sites for which deported Ottoman Armenians were destined. Thousands ended up in camps that were visited and photographed by Wegner in 1915-1916.

Figure 3.8. Armenian Women; source: Wallstein Verlag, Göttingen.

Date, location, and authorship unknown. Wegner used the picture in an ethnographic fashion as a glimpse into the lives of Armenian women and to comment on familial relations. He also indicated that Armenians, like Jews, are 'the most scattered people on earth'.

Figure 3.9. Armenian Family Portrait; source: Wallstein Verlag, Göttingen.

Date, location, and authorship unknown. Wegner made use of an established tradition of family portraits, popular among Armenian and other communities in the empire, to emphasize the absence of Ottoman Armenians due to the deportations and genocide. These family portraits remain as shadowy reminders.

Figure 3.10. Burning Street; source: Armin T. Wegner, Wallstein Verlag, Göttingen.

Possibly Zeitoun (present-day Süleymanlı, a town in Kahramanmaraş Province, south-eastern Turkey). Wegner reports that the Armenian quarters in many cities were put to the torch and that there was widespread looting by Turks.

Figure 3.11. Abandoned Child, 1915–1916; source: Armin T. Wegner, Wallstein Verlag, Göttingen.

Location unspecified. During the deportations, children were often separated from their parents. Wegner notes that the children were sometimes taken into harems by Turks in order to convert them to Islam, while desperate parents searched in vain for their children.

Figure 3.12. After a Massacre, 1915–1916; source: Armin T. Wegner, Wallstein Verlag, Göttingen.

Unidentified town. Wegner reports that all that remained after the massacres were piles of half-clothed, unburied bodies abandoned behind a wall or in a deserted trench.

Figure 3.13. Corpses in the Desert, 1915–1916; source: Armin T. Wegner, Wallstein Verlag, Göttingen.

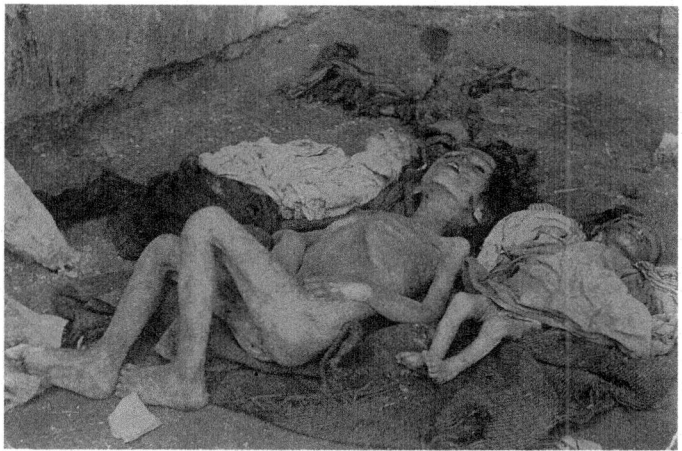

Possibly an Armenian deportation camp in Ottoman Syria. Wegner states that naked corpses lay all about, left in the open to be eaten by jackals. The horror of seeing starving, dying people could hardly be described, he adds. He witnessed children retrieving swallowed gold from the innards of their dead mothers and starving women forced to consume their own excrement or feed on their own dead new-born babies.

Figure 3.14. Refugees on the Coast, 1915–1916; source: Armin T. Wegner, Wallstein Verlag, Göttingen.

Refugees were driven to the Aegean coast, beyond the Sea of Marmara, where they often waited days for deportation. They were packed into small, unseaworthy fishing boats and sailed into the Gulf of İzmit. When a boat capsized, Wegner adds, the Turkish government considered it a welcome accident.

Figure 3.15. Armenian Mother Fleeing, 1915–1916; source: Armin T. Wegner, Wallstein Verlag, Göttingen.

Carrying a tent and poles, sleeping bag, and cooking pot, with her infant loaded atop the heavy bundle, this Armenian mother had been fleeing for two months, her husband slaughtered somewhere en route. In this manner, says Wegner, the mother and child laboured to cross the Amanus mountain pass towards the Syrian desert.

Figure 3.16. Camp at the Anatolian Railway; source: Wallstein Verlag, Göttingen.

Contested date – possibly after the 1909 massacres in Cilicia, courtyard of the German-Levant Cotton Company in Adana (Krikorian and Taylor, 2015).[4] Wegner reports that streams of people carried bundles and pushed their belongings in handcarts while others were deported on the Anatolian rail system. By the time he travelled to Baghdad via Aleppo in 1915, refugee numbers at the railway station had swelled to 50,000.

---

4   This image predates the genocide, as reported by Abraham D. Krikorian and Eugene L. Taylor on the Armenian News Network/Groong. A photograph of the same scene, but cropped differently, is included in Ernst Jäckh's *Der aufsteigende Halbmond: Beiträge zur türkischen Renaissance*, Berlin, Buchverlag der 'Hilfe', facing p. 110, published in 1911.

Figure 3.17. Delousing, 1915–1916; source: Armin T. Wegner, Wallstein Verlag, Göttingen.

Camp for Armenian deportees in Ottoman Syria. Never would he forget, Wegner says, the images of desperation and suffering that confronted him in the camp. 'You are German', someone called out to him, 'and you Germans are allied with the Turks. How is it possible that your chancellor allows such a crime to occur? So, it's true that you yourselves wanted it to happen?' He could give no reply. 'But imagine', he adds, 'if tens of thousands of our own people were suddenly crammed together on a bare patch of earth; what efforts we wouldn't go to, to alleviate their slightest need.' The shadow cast on the subjects is possibly that of the photographer and witness himself.

Bibliography

Adak, H. (2007) 'Ötekileştiremediğimiz kendimizin keşfi: 20. yüzyıl otobiyografik anlatıları ve Ermeni tehciri', *Tarih ve Toplum: Yeni Yaklaşımlar*, no. 5, pp. 231-253.

Agnew, V. and Konuk, K. (2020) 'The Difficulties of Witnessing: Armin T. Wegner's Lantern Slide Show on the Armenian Genocide', in Jolly, M. and de Courcy, M. (eds) *The Magic Lantern at Work: Connecting, Witnessing, Experiencing and Persuading*, London, Routledge, pp. 176-194.

Akçam, T. (2012) *Young Turks' Crime against Humanity: The Armenian Genocide and Ethnic Cleansing in the Ottoman Empire*, Princeton and Oxford, Princeton University Press.

Akçam, T. and Kurt, Ü. (2012) *Kanunların Ruhu: Emval-i Metruke Kanunlarında Soykırımın İzini Sürmek*, İstanbul, İletişim.

Altınay, A. G. and Türkyılmaz, Y. (2011) 'Unravelling Layers of Silencing: Converted Armenian Survivors of 1915', in Singer, A., Neumann, C. and Somel, S. A. (eds) *Untold Histories of the Middle East: Recovering Voices from the 19th and 20th Centuries*, London and New York, Routledge, pp. 25-53.

Anderson, M. L. (2011) 'Who Still Talked about the Extermination of the Armenians? German Talk and German Silences', in Suny, R. G., Göçek, F. M. and Naimark, N. M. (eds) *A Question of Genocide: Armenians and Turks at the End of the Ottoman Empire*, Oxford and New York, Oxford University Press, pp. 199-218.

Armin T. Wegner e gli Armeni in Anatolia, 1915: Immagini e testimonianze = Armin T. Wegner and the Armenians in Anatolia, 1915: Images and testimonies, 1996, Milano, Guerini e Associati.

Babkenian, V. and Crispin, J. (2017) 'Australia's Armenian Story', *Inside Story*, 6 April [Online]. Available at https://insidestory.org.au/australias-armenian-story/ (Accessed 17 August 2018).

Balakian, P. (2015) 'Photography, Visual Culture, and the Armenian Genocide', in Fehrenbahc, H. and Rodogno, D. (eds) *Humanitarian Photography: A History*, New York, Cambridge University Press, pp. 89-114.

Baronian, M.-A. (2010) 'Image, Displacement, Prosthesis: Reflections on Making Visual Archives of the Armenian Genocide', *Photographies*, vol. 3, no. 2, pp. 205-223.

Beauchamp, Z. (2017) '9 Maps and Charts That Explain the Global Refugee Crisis', *Vox*, 30 January [Online]. Available at https://www.vox.com/world/2017/1/30/14432500/refugee-crisis-trump-muslim-ban-maps-charts (Accessed 12 August 2018).

Bijak, J. and Lubman, S. (2016) 'The Disputed Numbers: In Search of the Demographic Basis for Studies of Armenian Population Losses, 1915-1923', in Demirdjian, A. (ed) *The Armenian Genocide Legacy*, Basingstoke and New York, Palgrave Macmillan, pp. 26-43.

Bjørnlund, M. (2009) '"A Fate Worse Than Dying": Sexual Violence during the Armenian Genocide', in Herzog, D. (ed) *Brutality and Desire: War and Sexuality in Europe's Twentieth Century*, Basingstoke and New York, Palgrave Macmillan, pp. 16-58.

Blumi, I. (2013) *Ottoman Refugees, 1878-1939: Migration in a Post-Imperial World*, London, Bloomsbury.

Brubaker, R. (1995) 'Aftermath of Empire and the Unmixing of Peoples: Historical and Comparative Perspectives', *Ethnic and Racial Studies*, no. 18, pp. 189-218.

Corrao, I. (2018) 'EU-Turkey Statement & Action Plan', *European Parliament Legislative Train Schedule towards a New Policy on Migration*, 20 July [Online]. Available at www.europarl.europa.eu/legislative-train/theme-towards-a-new-policy-on-migration/file-eu-turkey-statement-action-plan (Accessed 10 August 2018).

Dündar, F. (2011) 'Pouring a People into the Desert: The "Definitive Solution" of the Unionists to the Armenian Question', in Suny, R. G., Göçek, F. M. and Naimark, N. M. (eds) *A Question of Genocide: Armenians and Turks at the End of the Ottoman Empire*, Oxford and New York, Oxford University Press, pp. 276-284.

Ekmekçioğlu, L. (2013) 'A Climate for Abduction, A Climate for Redemption: The Politics of Inclusion during and after the Armenian Genocide', *Comparative Studies in Society and History*, vol. 55, no. 3, pp. 522-53.

El-Hage, B. (2007) 'The Armenian Pioneers of Middle Eastern Photography', *The Jerusalem Quarterly*, no. 31, pp. 22-26.

Gatrell, P. (2013) *The Making of the Modern Refugee*, Oxford and New York, Oxford University Press.

Goodwin-Gill, G. S. (2014) 'The International Law of Refugee Protection', in Qasmiyeh, E. F., Loescher, G., Long, K. and Sigona, N. (eds) *The Oxford Handbook of Refugee and Forced Migration Studies*, Oxford and New York, Oxford University Press, pp. 51-59.

Göçek, F. M. (2015) *Denial of Violence: Ottoman Past, Turkish Present and Collective Violence against the Armenians, 1789-2009*, Oxford and New York, Oxford University Press.

Gust, W. (2011) 'Armin T. Wegners Vortrag "Die Austreibung des armenischen Volkes in die Wüste"', in Wegner, A.T. *Die Austreibung des armenischen Volkes in die Wüste: Ein Lichtbildvortrag*, Meier, A. (ed), Göttingen, Wallstein Verlag, pp. 193-210.

Gzoyan, E. (2014) 'The League of Nations and Armenian Refugees: The Formation of the Armenian Diaspora of Armenia', *Central and Eastern European Review*, vol. 8, no. 1, pp. 83-102.

Haddad, E. (2008) *The Refugee in International Society: Between Sovereigns*, Cambridge and New York, Cambridge University Press.

Hansson, M. (1937) 'The Refugee Problem in the Near East', *Journal of the Royal Central Asian Society*, vol. 24, no. 3, pp. 397-410.

Hathaway, J. C. (1984) 'The Evolution of Refugee Status in International Law: 1920-1950', *International and Comparative Law Quarterly*, vol. 33, no. 2, pp. 348-380.

Hayruni, A. and Hosfeld, R. (2017) 'Johannes Lepsius und die armenische Frage im Beziehungsgeflecht des Weltkriegs', in Pschichholz, C. and Hosfeld, R. (eds) *Das Deutsche Reich und der Völkermord an den Armeniern*, Göttingen, Wallstein Verlag, pp. 217-243.

Hofmann, T. (1996) *Armin Wegner*, Yerevan, National Academy of Sciences of the Republic of Armenia Institute-Museum of Armenian Genocide.

Hofmann, T. and Koutcharian, G. (1992) '"Images that Horrify and Indict": Pictorial Documents on the Persecution and Extermination of Armenians from 1877 to 1922', *Armenian Review*, vol. 45, nos. 1-2, pp. 53-184.

Holborn, L. W. (1939) 'The League of Nations and the Refugee Problem', *The Annals of the American Academy of Political and Social Sciences*, vol. 203, no. 1, pp. 124-135.

Hosfeld, R. (2005) 'Deutsche Realpolitik', in *Operation Nemesis: Die Türkei, Deutschland und der Völkermord an den Armeniern*, Köln, Verlag Kiepenheuer und Witsch, pp. 263-272.

İçduygu, A. and Şimşek, D. (2016) 'Syrian Refugees in Turkey: Towards Integration Policies', *Turkish Policy Quarterly*, vol. 15, no. 3, pp. 59-69.

Ihrig, S. (2016) *Justifying Genocide: Germany and the Armenians from Bismarck to Hitler*, Cambridge, Harvard University Press.

Kaiser, H. (1998) 'The Baghdad Railway and the Armenian Genocide, 1915-1916: A Case Study in German Resistance and Complicity', in Hovannisian, R. G. (ed) *Remembrance and Denial: The Case of the Armenian Genocide*, Detroit, Wayne State University Press, pp. 67-112.

———. (2002) *At the Crossroads of Der Zor: Death, Survival, and Humanitarian Resistance in Aleppo, 1915-1917*, in collaboration with Luther and Nancy Eskijian, Princeton and London, Gomidas Institute.

Kant, I. (1795) 'Zum ewigen Frieden. Ein philosophischer Entwurf', in *Werke in zwölf Bänden*, volume 11, Frankfurt a.M., Suhrkamp Verlag (this edition 1977).

Kévorkian, R. (2011) *The Armenian Genocide: A Complete History*, London, I.B. Tauris.

Khatchaturian, Z. (n.d.) 'Armin T. Wegner – Biography', ArmenianHouse.org [Online]. Available at http://armenianhouse.org/wegner/bio-en.htm (Accessed 29 October 2018).

Kieser, H. L. (2011) 'Johannes Lepsius: Theologian, humanitarian activist and historian of Völkermord. An approach to a German biography (1858–1926)', in Briskina-Müller, A., Drost-Abgarjan, A. and Meissner, A. (eds) *Logos im Dialogos: Auf der Suche nach der Orthodoxie*, Berlin, Lit.

———. (2014) 'Beatrice Rohner's Work in the Death Camps of Armenians in 1916', in Semelin, J., Andrieu, C. and Gensburger, S. (eds) *Resisting Genocide: The Multiple Forms of Rescue*, Oxford, Oxford University Press, pp. 367-382.

———. (2018) *Talaat Pasha: Father of Modern Turkey, Architect of Genocide*, Princeton and New York, Princeton University Press.

Krikorian, A. D. and Taylor, E. L. (2015) 'Bringing a Photograph into Clearer Focus: Update to a Library of Congress' Bain News Service Collection Photo', *Armenian News Network/Groong*, 12 October [Online]. Available at http://groong.usc.edu/orig/ak-20151012.html (Accessed on 15 February 2019).

Kushner, T. and Knox, K. (1999) *Refugees in an Age of Genocide: Global, National and Local Perspectives during the Twentieth Century*, London, Frank Cass.

Levene, M. (2011) 'The Tragedy of the Rimlands, Nation-State Formation and the Destruction of Imperial Peoples, 1912-48', in Panayi, P. and Virdee, P. (eds) *Refugees and the End of Empire: Imperial Collapse and Forced Migration in the Twentieth Century*, Basingstoke and New York, Palgrave Macmillan, pp. 51-78.

Levin, A. K. (ed) (2016) *Global Mobilities: Refugees, Exiles, and Immigrants in Museums and Archives*, London, Routledge.

Lochak, D. (2013) 'Qu'est-ce qu'un réfugié? La construction politique d'une catégorie juridique', *Pouvoirs*, no. 144, pp. 33-47.

Marsoobian, A. T. (2017) *Reimagining a Lost Armenian Home: The Dildilian Photography Collection*, London, I.B. Tauris.

Maksudyan, N. (2015) 'Üç Kuşak Üç Katliam: 1894'ten 1915'e Ermeni Çocuklar ve Yetimler', *Toplum ve Bilim*, no. 132, pp. 33-49.

———. (2019) *Exodus after World War I: Production of Lives and Knowledge in Exile.* Conference proposal. Freie Universität Berlin and Centre Marc Bloch, 26-27 September.

Martin, L. (ed) (2007) *The Treaties of Peace, 1919-1923*, New York, Lawbook Exchange.

Meier, A. (2011) 'Nachwort', in Wegner, A.T. *Die Austreibung des armenischen Volkes in die Wüste: Ein Lichtbildvortrag*, Meier, A. (ed), Göttingen, Wallstein Verlag, pp. 153-192.

Migliorino, N. (2008) *(Re)constructing Armenia in Lebanon and Syria: Ethno-Cultural Diversity and the State in the Aftermath of a Refugee Crisis*, New York, Berghahn Books.

Moorehad, C. (2006) *Human Cargo: A Journey Among Refugees*, London, Vintage Books.

Mouradian, K. (2015) 'The Meskeneh Concentration Camp, 1915-1917: A Case Study of Power, Collaboration, and Humanitarian Resistance During the Armenian Genocide', *Journal of the Society for Armenian Studies*, no. 24, pp. 44-55.

Onaran, N. (2013) *Osmanlı'da Ermeni ve Rum Mallarının Türkleştirilmesi (1914-1919): Emvâl-i Metrûkenin Tasfiyesi-I*, İstanbul, Evrensel Basım Yayın.

Özendes, E. (1998) *Abdullah Frères: Ottoman Court Photographers*, İstanbul, Yapı Kredi.

———. (2008) 'Ottoman Empire: Asia and Persia (Turkey, the Levant, Arabia, Iraq, Iran)', in Hannavy, J. (ed) *Encyclopedia of Nineteenth-Century Photography*, London and New York, Routledge, pp. 1034-1037.

Payne, C. (2013) '"A Question of Humanity in its Entirety": Armin T. Wegner as Intermediary of Reconciliation between Germans and Armenians in Interwar German Civil Society', in Schwelling, B. (ed) *Reconciliation, Civil Society, and the Politics of Memory: Transnational Initiatives in the 20th and 21st Century*, Bielefeld, transcript Verlag.

Panayi, P. (2011) 'Imperial Collapse and the Creation of Refugees in Twentieth-Century Europe', in Panayi, P. and Virdee, P. (eds) *Refugees and the End of Empire: Imperial Collapse and Forced Migration in the Twentieth Century*, Basingstoke and New York, Palgrave Macmillan, pp. 3-27.

Refugee Solidarity Network (n.d.) 'Refugees & Asylum in Turkey' [Online]. Available at https://www.refugeesolidaritynetwork.org/about-refugees-in-turkey/ (Accessed 8 August 2018).

Rowe, V. (2011) 'Armenian Women Refugees at the End of Empire: Strategies of Survival', in Panayi, P. and Virdee, P. (eds) *Refugees and the End of Empire: Imperial Collapse and Forced Migration in the Twentieth Century*, Basingstoke and New York, Palgrave Macmillan, pp. 152-72.

Sarafian, A. (2001) 'The Absorption of Armenian Women and Children into Muslim Households as a Structural Component of the Armenian Genocide', in Bartov, O. and Mack, P. (eds) *In God's Name: Genocide and Religion in the Twentieth Century*, New York and Oxford, Berghahn Books, pp. 209-21.

Schaller, D. J. (2002) 'Die Rezeption des Völkermordes an den Armeniern in Deutschland, 1915-1945', in Kieser, H. L. and Schaller, D. J. (eds) *Der Völkermord an den Armeniern und die Shoah = The Armenian Genocide and the Shoah*, Zürich, Chronos Verlag, pp. 517-555.

Shaw, W. M. K. (2009) 'Ottoman Photography of the Late Nineteenth Century: An "Innocent" Modernism?', *History of Photography*, vol. 33, no. 1, pp. 80-93.

Sontag, S. (1977) *On Photography*, New York, Farrar, Straus and Giroux.

Suny, R. G. (2015) *"They Can Live in the Desert but Nowhere Else": A History of the Armenian Genocide*, Princeton, Princeton University Press.

Tamcke, M. (2011) 'Armin T. Wegner: Augenzeuge des Völkermords an den Armeniern', in Wernicke-Rothmayer, J. (ed) *Armin T. Wegner: Schriftsteller, Reisender, Menschenrechtsaktivist*, Göttingen, Wallstein Verlag, pp. 74-80.

UNHCR. (2018a) 'Figures at a Glance' [Online]. Available at www.unhcr.org/figures-at-a-glance.html (Accessed 8 August 2018).

———. (2018b) 'Mediterranean Situation' [Online]. Available at https://data2.unhcr.org/en/situations/mediterranean (Accessed 8 August 2018).

———. (2018c) 'Syria Emergency' [Online]. Available at www.unhcr.org/syria-emergency.html (Accessed 3 August 2018).

———. (n.d.) 'Mediterranean Situation' [Online]. Available at https://data2.unhcr.org/en/situations/mediterranean (Accessed 8 August 2018).

United States Holocaust Memorial Museum (2018) 'The Armenian Genocide (1915-16): In Depth – Photograph', *Holocaust Encyclopedia* [Online]. Available at https://encyclopedia.ushmm.org/content/en/gallery/the-armenian-genocide-1915-16-in-depth-photographs (Accessed 21 November 2018).

Üngör, U. Ü. and Polatel, M. (2011) *Confiscation and Destruction: The Young Turk Seizure of Armenian Property*, London, Bloomsbury Publishing.

Watenpaugh, K. D. (2010) 'The League of Nations' Rescue of Armenian Genocide Survivors and the Making of Modern Humanitarianism, 1920-1927', *The American Historical Review*, vol. 115, no. 5, pp. 1315-1339.

———. (2014) 'Between Communal Survival and National Aspiration: Armenian Genocide Refugees, the League of Nations, and the Practices of Interwar Humanitarianism', *Humanity: An International Journal of Human Rights, Humanitarianism, and Development*, vol. 5, no. 2, pp. 159-181.

Wegner, A. T. (1920) *Der Weg ohne Heimkehr. Ein Martyrium in Briefen*, 2nd ed, Dresden, Sybillen Verlag.

———. (2011) *Die Austreibung des armenischen Volkes in die Wüste: Ein Lichtbildvortrag*, Meier, A. (ed), Göttingen, Wallstein Verlag.

———. (2015) 'Die Warnung: Sendschreiben an den deutschen Reichskanzler Adolf Hitler', in Esau, M. and Hofmann, M. (eds) *Rufe in die Welt: Manifeste und Offene Briefe*, Göttingen, Wallstein Verlag, pp. 149-158.

Yad Vashem (n.d.) 'Armin T. Wegner' [Online]. Available at https://www.yadvashem.org/righteous/stories/wegner.html (Accessed 29 October 2018).

Acknowledgements

Right to Arrive draws on work done by Vanessa Agnew under the auspices of a 2017 Visiting Research Fellowship on the theme of 'The Question of the Stranger' at The Humanities Research Centre, The Australian National University. The ensuing exhibition, co-curated by Vanessa Agnew and Egemen Özbek, with Annette An-Jen Liu, was held at the PROMPT Gallery, The Australian National University, 2-22 September 2018. The authors and curators gratefully acknowledge the support of the following:

Kader Konuk, Chair, Institute of Turkish Studies/Director, Academy in Exile, University of Duisburg-Essen

Academy in Exile, University of Duisburg-Essen/KWI/Forum Transregionale Studien

Institute of Turkish Studies, University of Duisburg-Essen

Wallstein Verlag, Göttingen

PROMPT Gallery, The Australian National University

Martyn Jolly, Head, Photography and Media Arts, School of Art and Design, The Australian National University

Paul Pickering, Director, Research School of the Humanities and the Arts, and the Australian Studies Institute, The Australian National University

William Christie, Director, Humanities Research Centre, The Australian National University

The Dean's Office, School of Humanities, University of Duisburg-Essen

Andrea F. Bohlman, Department of Music, University of North Carolina at Chapel Hill

Jason O'Brien, Technical Officer, School of Art and Design, The Australian National University

Wiktoria Konvent, Graphic Artist, Wrocław

Jobst von Kunowski, Photographer of 'Worldly Possessions' installations, Berlin

Sefâ Agnew, Berlin

Elze Rimkute, Essen

Olivia Ozbek, Essen

Telling

Hunted Scholarship
How Fugitive Ideas Change the World

Ngũgĩ wa Thiong'o

In their beginnings, ideas which have changed the world profoundly were fugitives.[1] There is the example of the early Christians hiding in catacombs so they could voice their beliefs, or the flight of Mohammed from Mecca to Medina. Scientific ideas too. After the Roman Catholic authorities indexed Copernicus' book, *On the Revolution of the Heavenly Spheres*, and later Galileo's *Dialogue Concerning the Two Chief World Systems*, the ideas in the books lived on, but as fugitives. And Giordano Bruno's books were not only indexed but he, the author, lost his life for refusing to deny the fugitive ideas they carried.

But the title of this talk concerns hunted scholars and scholarship of my title. How on earth did I come up with this hunting business? I should have said 'haunted' instead of hunted, for there is something ghostly about the numerous invisible forces that repressive authorities unleash to stalk unwanted scholars and their scholarship.

It was in my hotel in Mexico City for the Zócalo Book Festival in September (2017) that I woke up to how I may have come to the title. Sometime in June, I mentored Abigail Uribe, an English major from Berkeley, then on SURF (Summer Undergraduate Research Fellowship) at UC Irvine. She wanted to work on the literature of incarceration, but, given the time, we settled on the topic of language and confinement; for a text, she came up with *How to Tame a Wild Tongue* (1987) by Gloria Anzaldúa. I was new to Anzaldúa's work, but the image of taming the wild tongue intrigued me and reminded me of Giordano Bruno, whose tongue was wild enough to respond to the sentence of death with defiance: 'You may be more afraid to bring that sentence against me than I am to accept it.' The Roman Catholic authorities responded to the defiance by stripping Giordano Bruno naked and tying his tongue before burning him at the stake. They had to physically tame the wild

---

1   This is the text of the keynote address given at the Scholars at Risk (SAR) conference held to celebrate the launch of the UC Irvine-SAR program at the University of California, Irvine, on 20 October 2017. A shorter version appeared as 'HUNTED SCHOLARSHIP: How Fugitive Ideas Change the World' in *Index on Censorship*, vol. 47, no. 03 (2018).

tongue of the heretic. All this may have stolen into my consciousness and gave me the title of my talk today.

We do not hunt or tame domestic animals. We hunt wild ones. With 'hunted' scholarship, I am thinking of it as that which a ruling or a conquering authority deems wild, or not domesticated by official limits and prescriptions. The authority actively hounds the scholar, seizes her work or both. Unfortunately, hunting down scholars or artists and their work is not just a metaphor. It has happened too many times in diverse societies and histories; it often begins with a given authority prohibiting, say, a song, a painting, a book, or any offending script, and then following the censure with cursing the author of the unwanted. We have the example of the Catholic *Index Librorum Prohibitorum* from 1559 to 1966, which in its early years resulted in the indexed books going up in flames and the cursed authors in prison, exiled, or dead.

Throughout the British rule in Kenya from 1895 to 1963, the colonial state regularly banned the songs and even dances it deemed defiant. The ban was not very successful because people would simply vary the dance moves or hum the melody without voicing the offending words. The state also banned books of poetry in African languages and followed this with jailing the offending parties.

Banning and burning books deemed to harbour dissent and heresy has been a constant theme in the history of ideas: from the book burnings and burial of scholars by the potentates of ancient China to the burning of Mayan books by the conquering Spaniards in the sixteenth century to the Berlin book bonfires of Nazi Germany. Hordes of zealots hunted down the offending scripts and manuscripts, ferreting them out of their hiding places in shelves at home or in public spaces, and, with triumphant cries and gestures of victory, throwing them into the flames. Leave it to Bertolt Brecht to bring out the touch of irony in the burning of books in his poem 'The Burning of the Books' (1939):

> When the Regime commanded that books with harmful knowledge
> Should be publicly burned and on all sides
> Oxen were forced to drag cartloads of books
> To the bonfires, a banished
> Writer, one of the best, scanning the list of the Burned, was shocked
>   to find that his
> Books had been passed over. He rushed to his desk
> On wings of wrath, and wrote a letter to those in power,
> Burn me! he wrote with flying pen, burn me! Haven't my books
> Always reported the truth? And here you are
> Treating me like a liar! I command you!
> Burn me!

Actually, hunting down the producers, eliminating them altogether à la Giordano Bruno, may be deemed the more effective approach because, if successful, it would end the source of those dangerous ideas altogether. Nearly every country has cases of writers and intellectuals who have met just such an end or who have had to flee their own countries to seek refuge elsewhere to avoid a similar fate. Being hunted down by one's own state is an experience bitter to swallow. But as long as one is not finally run down by knife, bullet, or poison, the fighting spirit of the hunted can generate creative outputs that thwart the intentions of the hunter. Some of these creations may come to impact the world in big and small ways. So, any efforts which help in the survival of the script, the book, and the producer, can and do contribute to the collective good. To come to the aid of a fleeing scholar, to shelter a fugitive idea, is to help possibilities that add to our being. It is to give home to hope.

    I want to illustrate the crucial role of the helping hand in the survival of hunted scholarship with a short chronicle of my own experience as the hunted. In 1968, a group of us at the University of Nairobi called for a change and the re-organization of the teaching of literature, advocating the centring of African, Caribbean, African-American, Asian, and Latin American literatures with European literatures, including English, in that order. This would turn out to be the earliest major challenge to the dominance and assumed centrality of English national literature in the post-colony and one of the earliest steps towards what would now bear the name of post-colonial theory and studies. Admittedly our title, 'On the Abolition of the English Department', was provocative, but it was certainly not a call for the abolition of English or English literature. But this did not deter the then Attorney General, who, from the premises of Parliament, accused us of wanting to abolish Shakespeare. Actually, Shakespeare was quite safe.

    A year later (1969), I resigned from the University of Nairobi in protest against government infringement upon academic freedom, which I then defined as free circulation of ideas.[2] I did not think it was the task of the state to decide who of the guests invited by the student body could or could not speak at the university. I was without a job. My old university, Makerere, then extended a helping hand and offered me a one-year writing fellowship. Another helping hand was Northwestern University, which offered me a position as Visiting Associate Professor of English and African Studies. So, from Makerere, Uganda, I went to Evanston, Illinois. The period between 1969 and 1972 became my first experience of exile. But it was self-imposed, and I did not feel any hounds of the state behind me.

    It was a productive mini-exile. I published *Homecoming* (1972), which would turn out to be the first major work of literary and cultural criticism published in East Africa. I then returned to Nairobi in 1972 and rejoined the department, now reorganized and renamed Department of Literature. I became chair. One of my

---

2   'On the carpet' interview with Peter Darling, in *Sunday Nation*, 16 March 1969.

concerns was always how to make literature and scholarship actively relate to the general society in some way. I did not want to see the literature that I loved being confined to a gated community, or what we called the ivory tower. I wanted the department and the university to be an integral part of the living social organism. In my memoir, *Dreams in a Time of War* (2010), I have celebrated the moment I discovered that written words could also sing. I dream of the university as a market place of clashing ideas, but of ideas that sing, dance, and move. In my letter of resignation, I had argued that that 'a young developing country in fact needs this conflict of ideas much more than an older country with a tradition of conservative ideas'.[3] Now I was back to the same university of a young country.

We tried many innovations, among them, public lectures open to all and traveling theatre, which meant our students taking theatre to the people, performing in villages and towns during the long vacations, and eventually, some of us relocating to Kamĩrĩĩthũ village to work in community theatre directly. But there were consequences.

At midnight on December 1977, armed police raided my house in Limuru, Kenya, confiscated copies of the playscript of *Ngaahika Ndeenda/I will marry when I want*, whose performance the government had earlier stopped. So, on January 1, 1978, I found myself in a maximum security prison, no longer the chair and Professor of Literature at the University of Nairobi, but a man without a name, a number. For the first three weeks or so, I was under internal segregation, which meant that the other political prisoners in the same block could not talk to me or sit by me. I remember distinctly the moment when a sympathetic warder whispered to me about the formation of a Ngũgĩ Defence Committee in London. That fact alone – that there were people out there doing something about my fate – was a shot of good hope from the bow of international solidarity.

Prison was meant to silence me. But it was during my one-year confinement that I wrote a novel in Gĩkũyũ. I wrote *Caitaani Mũtharabainĩ* (translated into English as *Devil on the Cross*) on toilet paper, which was the only writing material available to me. This would turn out to be the first modern novel in the Gĩkũyũ language. But even then, its publication in 1982 led to the publisher losing his finger to a machete attack following months of telephone threats to deter him from publishing the work. I may also add that it was during the same year of incarceration that I thought more intensely about the politics of language, especially the unequal power relationship between English and African languages and about the psychological bonds that language had on the intellectuals and intellectual production of the for-

---

[3] 'It would be a pity if in a young developing country, ideas are not allowed to collide. A young developing country, in fact, needs this conflict of ideas much more than an older country with a tradition of conservative ideas.' From 'Interview', *Sunday Nation*, 16 March 1969.

merly colonized. These thoughts would years later lead to my book, *Decolonizing the Mind* (1986).

When, in December 1978, I was released from prison following the death of the first president, Jomo Kenyatta, his successor, Daniel arap Moi, would not allow me to resume my old job at the university or take up another position in any of the colleges in the country. My work in community theatre was stopped, with the televised destruction of Kamīrīthū by armed police. The relentless hunting had started. In 1982, I was in London for the launch of *Devil on the Cross*, the novel on toilet paper, and *Detained* (1981), my memoir of prison, when I got information about a very 'red carpet' welcome waiting for me on my return home. I found myself in exile, this time real forced exile, living mainly in London.

This was the period when I experienced the real life of a scholar without a home. I did not have a residency permit, I was on a visiting visa, and so every time I left the country of my exile, I always dreaded the moment of return. Always being detained at Heathrow airport. Questions. Explanations. The dread of going out; the dread of coming back. And yet my work with the London-based Committee for the Release of Political Prisoners in Kenya demanded that I move in and out of the country of my exile.

It became worse when my passport expired. Now I had no papers at all. Ghana gave me a helping hand and for many years I traveled on a Ghanaian passport. But this did not end the questionings at Heathrow. Eventually Britain did give me a residency permit. Yale University extended another helping hand in 1989 with an offer of a regular Visiting Professorship of English and Comparative Literature.

One day during my first term at Yale, I went to the library to look at Kenyan newspapers. I read some headlines: The Moi government was accusing me of being in Sudan organizing a communist party. It's only recently via declassified documents that I learned the extent to which the Moi government was obsessed with me. In an article carried in the *Sunday Nation* of Kenya, April 23, 2017, the author, Odhiambo Opiyo, who read the declassified material of the period, recounts the details of this obsession. Looking back, I can see the hunting was more intense than I had sensed at the time. I could see the sequence. I got the 'red carpet' warning in June 1982. That was why I did not return to my home land. On November 12, 1984, the Kenyan High Commissioner to London, Benjamin Kipkulei, called on the British Secretary of State to complain that I was receiving 'more attention than I deserved'. The government also complained to the British High Commission/Embassy in Kenya about my being employed by the Islington Council in London. Actually, it was not really employment. It was a one-year writer's residency. Opiyo cites another letter from the British Embassy/High Commissioner in Kenya to J.R. Johnson, a senior official at the Foreign and Commonwealth Office in London, in which he claimed he was being told by the government 'that the only thing on the President's mind that hurts our image is the presence and activities of Ngugi'.

Opiyo also tells of a two-hour meeting in January 1985 between President Daniel arap Moi and Sir Geoffrey Howe, the British Secretary of State for Foreign and Commonwealth Affairs in Margaret Thatcher's government, to discuss trade and diplomatic matters between the two countries. According to the writer, 'it was the President's concern over the activities of Kenyan academic and writer Ngugi wa Thiong'o, who was living in exile in London, that dominated the meeting'.

In another dispatch, Moi accused me of conducting propaganda among Kenyan students in the UK and planning to start a communist party, and demanded that Britain 'reject any visa extension application by the Kenyan academic and force him to relocate to another country'. The accusations I was reading about in Yale Library in 1989 thus had their basis in a web of fabrications designed to make Britain deny me sanctuary. I was really grateful that the UK did not accede to Moi's demands.

There were other incidents, including one in 1990, when Zimbabwe Intelligence detained Moi's armed agents outside the door of my hotel in Harare during a UNICEF-sponsored conference on solidarity with Mozambique children, victims of the then horrendous war between the government and rebel groups. Moi demanded I be expelled from Zimbabwe, and when the government refused, he recalled the official Kenyan delegation. These actions were haunting and hunting and trying to hound me out of any sanctuary.

It was during my years of exile in London between 1982 and '89 that I wrote and published my second novel in Gĩkũyũ: *Matigari* (1986). Matigari, a fictional character, is an ex-freedom fighter who goes about the country, asking questions only about Truth and Justice. Readers oralized the literary and so talked about the figure and his questions about truth and justice. The Moi regime thought the character a real living person and issued a warrant for his arrest. Realizing that he was a fiction, they banned the novel instead and for many years, Matigari, both the novel and the character, existed only in English translation, abroad. I was in exile, and my book was in exile too.

It was during the same years that I published *Decolonizing the Mind* (1986), a development of those thoughts about unequal power relationships between languages that I had conceived in prison. The book was based on lectures I gave at Auckland University, New Zealand. The passion some readers sense behind the polemics had its roots in the circumstances under which I first worked out the ideas that I then coded into formal lectures and then, finally, into a book.

Last May (2017) in Johannesburg, South Africa, over two thousand people, faculty, students, lawyers, and members of Parliament, came to hear me talk on the topic 'Secure the Base: Decolonize the Mind'. In Cape Town and the Eastern Cape, I was met with similar crowds. A few months later, I was back and talked in Pretoria and the northern part of the country to similarly enthusiastic but attentive listeners. This is because the idea of decolonizing institutions is currently at the centre of political debate in the country. Elsewhere, decolonial studies and decolonial aesthetics seem to be an emerging field.

I was in the middle of writing this paper in my hotel room in Mexico City when I got an email from my publisher telling me that the *Observer* of London had chosen *Decolonizing the Mind* as one of '100 Political Classics' that shaped the modern world. I felt a little teary, for, despite the years in between, I could not help but go back to my prison cell in 1978.

The story of my life as the hunted would not be complete without mentioning the parallel pressure on my family – the raids on my house in Kenya at rumours of my secret return. When, for the first time in 23 years of exile, in 2004, I returned to the country for the launch of *Mũrogi wa Kagogo/Wizard of the Crow* (2006), in Gĩkũyũ, a novel that I wrote during my years in the USA, mostly at UC Irvine, my wife and I were brutally attacked in our Nairobi hotel and we barely escaped with our lives. This happened eleven days before the book's publication and the launch. The publisher, the same one who once lost his finger to a machete attack for my prison novel, still went ahead with the launch as scheduled. The English version later won the 2006 California Gold Medal, putting it in the company of Steinbeck's novels *Tortilla Flat* and *In Dubious Battle*, which won it in 1933 and 1937, respectively.

My case is not unique in Kenya, Africa, and the world. Hunted scholarship and art are realities in history yesterday and today, as we have seen. In my book, *Penpoints, Gunpoints, and Dreams* (1998), I have argued that 'authority' and 'author' share the author part. But one authors laws and the other ideas. Both use words to do so. The difference is that a scholar uses words to ask questions; authority uses words to issue answers. Scholars don't confuse fact with fiction. They separate fiction from fact to arrive at truth. Authority infuses truth with falsehood to turn its own fiction into fact. The scholar uses the pen to win arguments. Authority uses the sword to force a win. Haunt, hunt, and hound. Jail, kill, or force the scholar to flee. Wherever scholars are deemed defiant to the prevailing authority, they are at risk, and they face the three alternatives of prison, death, or exile. Obviously the third is the better option. But even then, the hounds of hunting authority are after them, and when they fail, they take out it on the ideas. Ban their ideas; burn their books.

By the very nature of their trade, using words to force a different look at whatever seems obvious, given, and settled, scholars and artists will always find themselves haunted by fear or hunted by the hounds of an intolerant authority. The question is then one of refuge and sanctuary for their lives and ideas. Living, they can always tell the tale. This is where a helping hand can mean so much for the scholar at risk. A hand that enables the scholar to live is truly a friend in both need and deed.

My first book, after I learnt to read, was the Bible, the *Old Testament*, mostly. Among many of its magical stories was one I found truly imbued with wonder.

According to the Book, a Hebrew mother, Jochebed, fearing that her male child might be slaughtered, puts him in a basket and hides it among the reeds in the Nile. A baby fugitive. Bithis, Pharaoh's daughter, finds him, rescues him, and brings him up in the palace as her own. I am talking about Moses, the future author of the Ten Commandments, and the father of the three Mosaic religions of the book – Judaism, Christianity, and Islam – which have changed the world and continue to impact our lives today.

Thus, Egypt was among the first of the ancient civilizations to host fugitive lives. The same book also tells of the flight of infant Jesus for sanctuary in Egypt. Ethiopia has also played the role of rescuer of holders of what others then saw as dangerous ideas: King Negash gave sanctuary to the family or followers of Mohammed, who arrived at Aksum, in flight from their persecutors.

Whether these stories are rooted in fact, in myth, or in exaggeration, they do talk of workers in ideas who find a helping hand, which enables ideas that later impact the world. We do have examples within more recent centuries. Karl Marx was forced out of Germany and emigrated to Paris in 1820. At the end of 1848, he was expelled from France and sought refuge in Brussels. Later he moved back to Paris and was expelled in 1849 and sought refuge in London, where he turned the British Library into his second home. Thus, Britain and the British Library have joined Egypt and Ethiopia in giving a home to hunted scholars and their fugitive ideas.

Whatever position one may take on Marxism, there is no doubt about the impact of Marxist ideas on political, economic, social, and literary theories. New York gave sanctuary to the Frankfurt School of Social Research and the scholars associated with it, Adorno among them. They and their scholarship have had an immense impact on critical theory. Joseph Conrad was not personally hunted down by the Tsarist empire that controlled Poland in the nineteenth century, but he was a product of hunted scholars, his father and mother. His poet father was jailed, and Conrad's childhood was spent with his parents in forced exile from their beloved Poland. Though it was France which first gave the French-speaking Conrad refuge, eventually the country denied him permission to continue his stay. Britain gave him sanctuary. Conrad had to learn English at the age of nineteen. But look at the impact of his work on English literature and even on writing from the postcolonial worlds of Asia, Africa, and Latin America.

We can tell from these cases the loss it would have been had these scholars not have found a helping hand and a sanctuary. I am sure the world has lost thousands who, given the chance to live and breathe, would have given equally to the world. We should be grateful to all those who enabled these producers of ideas to survive. We must also be grateful to those who have helped rescue intellectual products at risk from the fires of willful destruction waged by political and religious zealots.

Imagine all the history, poetry, inventions, mathematics, astronomy lost to the world through the burning of the library at Alexandria. Alas, we have only names and titles to tease us about the loss: Berossus' *Babylonaica* (circa 281 BCE), the major work of Sappho (circa 612-570 BCE), Hero of Alexandria (circa 10-70 CE), Hypatia (circa 370-415 CE), and Aristarchus of Samos (circa 310-230 BCE). There are similar losses of the pre-Columbian history of Mesoamerica through the zealotry of the Spanish missionaries in the sixteenth century who incinerated the Mayan texts. We can be thankful for the rescued *Popol Vuh* of the Quiche Maya, and also of fragments of Sappho's poetry:

> Although they are
> only breath, words
> which I command
> are immortal.

The call to rescue is a call to give shelter to those who might contribute to this immortality. We are called upon to follow in the footsteps of those countries, institutions, and individuals who rescued hunted scholars from death and hunted scripts from destruction and hence contributed to the wealth of our cultures. Saviours of scholars at risk will then be in the tradition of the Pharaoh's daughter who once rescued the child Moses from drowning among the reeds. In the process, she also rescued a big idea.

As a writer and scholar who owes so much of his life and work to helping hands, known and numerous unknowns, I am so glad that UC Irvine has become part of the world-wide network Scholars at Risk in support of hunted scholars and scholarship.

Antaram's Journey

Nazan Maksudyan

My great-grandmother, Antaram Abrahamian (later Boghossian), was the strongest woman I have ever known (Fig. 5.1). She was without doubt the head of the household; she worked incessantly all day, slept very little, lovingly provided for her two daughters, their children (her grandchildren), and even her great-grandchildren, yet she never complained about her responsibilities nor did she ever leave something unfinished, and she always had the best sense of humour. Like my father, I used to call her *medzmama* (literally 'grandmother' in Armenian). Yet it was not only our prerogative as her descendants to call her this. Neighbours, friends, and acquaintances who were not kin also called her *medz*: 'big' or 'great'. As a child I wondered why. Later, I thought it was maybe because they noticed and respected her authority, her endurance, but most of all her stamina. In the end, she was the one who resisted wilting in a cruel world that orphaned her and the one who had the courage and strength to start life anew...

Antaram was from Çengiler, then a large and prosperous village close to the town of Pazarköy, in the vicinity of the city of Bursa, in western Anatolia. Çengiler was a large village of 5,000 inhabitants, with a clear Armenian majority.[1] The main agricultural product was olives. But a variety of skilled crafts, such as blacksmithing, leatherwork, coppersmithing, tinsmithing, and goldsmithing, were also practised. In fact, Çengiler was an important centre of sericulture and silk weaving, the most important industry in Bursa and its surroundings. The village was known for its silk workshops, which employed several hundred workers, and its steam-driven wheels, which numbered 500 to 600 across all the workshops in the village.

In 1913, the members of several community organizations, the Intellectual Society, the Students' Union, the Theatre Society, the Athletes' Society, and General Construction founded a cooperative in order to fund small businesses and artisans. It was meant to act as a neighbourly bank. In addition to fund-raising, the

---

1   For detailed information on the economic, social, and cultural life of Çengiler, see Derebeyian, S. *Houshamadian Chengileri Hayots', 1528-1923* [Memorial volume of the Armenians of Chengiler, 1528-1923], Paris, P. Elekian, 1973.

Figure 5.1. Antaram at her home in İcadiye, with her beloved cigarette in hand, 1970s.

Source: The author's family archive.

cooperative constructed a building, in which a great number of commodities were sold. The cooperative changed the village to a great extent. Trade flourished and customers poured into Çengiler to shop. Around 1914, the village exported more than 2,000 kilograms of raw silk annually to Marseille, Lyons, Milan, and London by way of this cooperative, which local craftsmen had founded to secure supplies and encourage sales. These were glorious days for the villagers. They invited notable members of the Armenian community, including intellectuals. Nazaret Daghavarian,[2] Siamanto,[3] and Gomidas Vartabed[4] all visited Çengiler before 1915.

Antaram was born there in 1901, her parents' first and only daughter, who followed three elder brothers. She would soon have a younger brother as well, who she would later wish had been a sister instead.

In August 1914 the military's general mobilization very quickly drained the village households of their young men. But there is no record of any particular problems occurring until late May 1915, at which point, house searches and arrests began. The official objective behind these was to induce the population to hand over its weapons to the authorities.

Starting in July 1915, news of deportations began circulating in the village, especially thanks to the presence of American missionaries in the village, who had operated educational institutions in the area since the 1860s. These rumours did not prompt the general population to take any action. But one of Antaram's elder brothers, Hagop, had already migrated to Bulgaria shortly after the 1908 Revolution. His in-laws had been wary of the situation since the Hamidian massacres of 1895-96. When they decided to move their business from Edirne to Plovdiv, Hagop moved along.

The deportations reached Çengiler on 4 August 1915. The village was surrounded by 2,000 soldiers and gendarmes under the leadership of Haci Alaeddin, the Committee of Union and Progress's temporary delegate and a member of Pazarköy's Ittihadist club, and Abdülhamid Bey, the military commander in Bursa, who had been charged with carrying out the deportation in Çengiler.[5] According to missionary accounts, some families succeeded in refusing to submit or leave for some time.

In these unfortunate days, Antaram was a young girl of about fourteen. If it had not been for the war, she might even have been married. American women

---

2   Nazaret Daghavarian (b. 1862 in Sebastia, d. 1915 in Ayaş) was an Armenian doctor, agronomist, and public activist, and one of the founders of the Armenian General Benevolent Union (AGBU). He was one of the victims killed on 24 April 1915.
3   Atom Yarjanian (Ատոմ Եարճանեան), better known by his pen name Siamanto (Սիամանթօ) (1878–1915), was an influential Armenian writer, poet, and national figure from the late nineteenth century and early twentieth century. He was killed by the Ottoman authorities during the Armenian Genocide.
4   Soghomon Soghomonian, commonly known as Gomidas (Կոմիտաս) (26 September or 8 October 1869–22 October 1935), was an Armenian priest, composer, choir leader, singer, ethnomusicologist, music pedagogue, and musicologist. Many consider him to be the founder of modern Armenian classical music. He experienced a mental breakdown after witnessing the horrors of the Armenian Genocide.
5   For detailed information on the deportations in Çengiler, see Kévorkian, R. (2011) *The Armenian Genocide: A Complete History*, New York, I. B. Tauris, pp. 561, 569, 589.

missionaries wrote in the 1870s that most of the girls in the area were married at twelve, and seldom was a girl still unmarried after the age of fifteen.[6]

Decades later she would still recount how the family first reacted to the news about *tehcir* (the central order for 'forced deportation'). As everyone was busy packing up the most necessary items in advance of their departure, her mother, Maryam, suddenly disappeared. A short while later, they started to hear the harsh noise of glass being smashed. When they and her father, Abraham, followed the noise down to the cellar, they saw the mother hurriedly throwing dozens of jars of marmalade, pickles, and other conserved food to the floor. Her father felt revulsion at the sight of his wife's fury and started shouting at her, calling her crazy (*khent*). Then, Maryam calmed down for a moment and said with absolute conviction: 'Do you think we will ever be able to come back to this place? Do you think we will ever see our house again? Do you think we will have another winter to eat these? We are going to leave nothing behind, nothing for the enjoyment of those responsible for our misfortune and loss.'

Sadly, she was right. After a short exchange with the local notables, the gendarmes forced around one thousand two hundred families onto the road, accompanied by an escort. All Çengiler families, including the Abrahamians, were forced to leave their homes. They were not allowed to take any moveable assets with them. They started off on a long and uncertain journey which would end, for those who managed to survive, in Syria.

About 100 men were kept behind in the village in order to transport the Armenians' belongings to the church, where they were divided up among peasants, soldiers, and gendarmes. After that, the village was methodically plundered and put to the torch. These 100 men were then led from the village under guard and slaughtered.

Çengiler was entirely emptied, it was like a ghost town. It was like a corpse with no blood in its veins. Its vibrant economy, its lively cultural life had been extinguished, stolen. Its future had been disrupted forever. And its past has been forever distorted. The village of Çengiler was literally effaced from the map of Turkey as part of the conscious policy of suppressing and silencing the Armenian presence both geographically and in the social memory of the new nation-state. Like thousands of other place names – of cities, towns, villages, squares, and streets – the name of Çengiler was changed, becoming Sugören.

At the very beginning of the journey, only one hour's march away from the village, the men were separated from the convoy and executed on the banks of a river near Barzudağ. Antaram's father and one of her older brothers were killed right away. Since her mother, like undoubtedly many of the others, quickly realized

---

6   Women's Board of Missions (2013 [1872]) *Life and Light for Heathen Women*, vol. 2, reprint, London, Forgotten Books, pp. 304-305.

that the lives of male family members were in danger, she decided to dress her youngest son, Antaram's little brother, as a girl in the hope of saving his life.

Finally, the three *women* of the Abrahamian family – Antaram, her mother Maryam, and her younger brother disguised as a girl – started their long journey from Çengiler towards Der Zor in the company of their fellow villagers, sharing their misery. The sources at our disposal do not provide us with an exact number of deportees who travelled by foot. A survivor reports that the 11,000 people in his convoy, including natives of Balıkesir, Bandırma, Bursa, Gemlik, Adapazarı, Yalova, and Çengiler, had to walk all the way to Konya because the trains had been requisitioned by the army. Maybe Antaram was in that convoy, as she repeatedly recounted that she had walked all the way.

Holding tightly to one another, they continually prayed their number would not diminish any further. Unfortunately, their prayers were in vain. Early in the journey, soldiers realized that there was something peculiar about Antaram's little *sister*. When they got closer and started to push and pull at his clothes, it soon became obvious that this was actually a boy dressed as a girl, with quite short hair under the scarf that had been put around his head. Despite the resistance and lamentation expressed by his mother and sister, they pulled him from the convoy and killed him before their very eyes. Not long after that, Maryam passed away, a result of the exhaustion and starvation suffered along the way, together with the unbearable agony of seeing her son slaughtered. Antaram was ultimately left on her own in the convoy that followed the route to Bursa, Eskişehir, Konya, Pozantı, Adana, Aleppo, and finally, Der Zor.

Curiously, and in keeping with the meaning of her name, 'unfading', Antaram was the only one to reach the refugee camps in Der Zor, in Syria. At the time, one of her older brothers was in Bulgaria, while another brother, the one who had settled in Istanbul a couple of years earlier, was tormented by the lack of news from his family. How my great-grandmother lived and survived in the camps as a 15-to-16-year-old orphan remains a mystery to us since she hardly spoke about it (Fig. 5.2).

There are a number of plausible scenarios, and all of them might be equally true. We know that survivors in those circumstances attempted all of these strategies. She could have stayed in an orphanage, though her age would have been a bit of an impediment. But we know that older girls were also accepted in order to help in the running of the institution. It is also probable that she stayed with her fellow villagers, who would have provided the only familiar link to the life and world that she had left behind forever. This larger community (how large, we do not know) might have acted as a saviour and protected her. They might have camped together, moved from one shelter to the other, stayed close in the refugee camps. Like the rest of the entire camp population, she must have suffered from disease, starvation, and unremitting hardship. She might have even become one of the em-

Figure 5.2 Armenian genocide orphans, place and date unknown.

Source: The author's family archive.

ployees of the Ottoman state factories established in the Syrian cities of Homs and Hama, ironically taking part in the war effort in support of those who caused her misery. She might have spent some time with Muslim families, which she may have experienced as a form of shelter or, just as likely, a prison. Oral histories and memoirs from the time are full of accounts of the 'adoption' of child survivors. Still, most faced precarious circumstances marked by exploitation, unpaid hard labour, forced conversion, and relentless physical and sexual abuse.

Whatever the case, she was definitely one of the tens of thousands of Armenian survivors in Der Zor, and she was forced to stay there until the end of the war.

When their de facto imprisonment in the middle of the desert came to an end with the armistice in 1918, she, like many other survivors who were stuck in either Der Zor or Mosul, continued to follow the road to Basra. In one of the few fortunate instances in this heartbreaking story, Antaram's loneliness came to an end in this city: she married my great-grandfather, Hmayak Boghossian. How he ended up in Basra likewise remains an untold history. Hmayak was always silent on the subject.

In 1915, my great-grandfather Hmayak was around 18 years old, as the year of his birth was registered as 1313 (1897). He was from Shadakh (Çatak), in the south of the city of Van, one of the biggest of the ancient Armenian urban centres at the farthest edge of eastern Anatolia. As a young man, he most likely took part in the resistance in the city against Ottoman military forces in charge of deportation and massacres. The city was able to successfully defend itself for some time, nevertheless almost the entire population was killed. But Hmayak was among the Armenians from the villages surrounding Van who managed to escape and take refuge in Iraq, which was under British occupation. Many of these escapees from Van took shelter in a large refugee camp in Bakuba, near Baghdad. Hmayak spent the war years in the camp until leaving for the port town of Basra in 1919 as part of a large wave of exiles looking to be repatriated.

The result was that both of my paternal great-grandparents found themselves in Basra in 1919. They were around 20 years of age, or perhaps a little older. They had spent the last four years separated from their 'homes', on the road, in the desert, in various shelters or refugee camps, and they had no family or relatives. How did these two strangers who both found themselves in an unknown place meet and end up getting married? Was it love? Did they feel close to one another because of their shared experiences? Was it arranged by the Armenian clergy in the city as a form of creating means of support and promoting the survival of destitute, rootless, needy survivors? All of these played a part, and the newly married couple were among those who were repatriated by the British from Basra.

With gratitude in her voice, my great-grandmother used to say, 'The British put us on a boat and brought us to Istanbul'. She was both fortunate and strong. She survived the deportations and the genocide; she endured years of homelessness and poor conditions in refugee camps; she suffered maltreatment, malnutrition, and possibly molestations, harassment, even worse. Yet it was only the prospect of re-establishing contact with a sense of 'home' that made her believe that she was alive, that she had a life to live. Apart from the intellectuals that were sent to their deaths on 24 April 1915, the Armenians of Istanbul had been exempted from the massacres and/or deportations. Antaram thought she would be able to reunite with at least one living member of her family: her brother, Sahak.

In late 1919, the young couple reached Istanbul, which was then under British occupation (Fig. 5.3). Sahak welcomed his now grown-up sister and her husband. He took them into his house in İcadiye, a large Armenian neighbourhood in Üsküdar, on the Asian coast of the city. He also made them partners and associates in his butcher shop. Thanks to Sahak, they settled down, earned a living, and built a family. Antaram lived in the same spot for the rest of her entire life. She gave birth, saw her daughters married, rejoiced at the arrival of her grandchildren, and then her great-grandchildren. Her entire family lived in the same neighbourhood, within walking distance from her house. It must be an inherited trait that has led my parents to live in the same house into which they first moved after getting married in 1977 – only one block away from my great-grandparents' old butcher shop (Figs. 5.4, 5.5, 5.6).

Figure 5.3. The young couple, Antaram and Hmayak, managed to build a new life for themselves in the 1920s in Istanbul.

Source: The author's family archive.

Figure 5.4. Antaram with her daughters Sona and Maryam at their house door, 1940s.

Source: The author's family archive.

As someone who had undertaken a journey of so many kilometres all alone – though she may have been physically accompanied by many who shared her fate – Antaram chose not to move an inch from her house in Istanbul for the rest of her eighty-odd years of life. She never saw, nor showed any desire to see, her hometown, Çengiler, again, though it was only two hours away. She never went to visit her brother and his family in any of the cities in which they lived: Plovdiv (Bulgaria), Beirut, and Los Angeles. She did not join her husband when he visited Soviet Armenia to see part of his family after decades of longing for a reunion. She even resisted going to the European side of the city, since she did not want to set foot on a boat crossing the Bosphorus. Who can blame her? She had ample legitimate reasons for avoiding even the thought of a new journey.

After all, what made her happiest was growing strongly rooted fruit trees in her garden so that she could make jars and jars of marmalade for the coming winter.

Figure 5.5. Antaram holding the hand of the author's father, Vartan, on his first school day, 1958.

Source: The author's family archive.

Figure 5.6. Antaram and the author, 1980.

Source: The author's family archive.

Walk past the vines, past the orchards[1]

Meltem Gürle

'The train is delayed', said the woman.
'Let's go and have a beer.'
    The man lifted his bag off the floor and slung it over his back. With his other hand he grabbed the handle of the trolley. His jacket hung limply from his arm. His shirtsleeves were rolled halfway to his elbow. The woman's hands were empty. She was wearing a light summer dress and her hair in a careless bun at the nape of her neck.
'The usual place?' she asked.
'The usual place', he replied. 'We can still hear the announcements there.' He started walking with long, confident steps.
    They crossed from one end of the station to the other. There were only two platforms. Arrivals and departures. When they first settled in this small town, they thought this was a good thing. Their guests would never get lost. Not that they had many guests. Only a few people. And nobody stayed for long.
    They followed a young woman pushing a pram. On the way to the exit, they heard the announcement again. A woman's voice apologized at length for the delay.

                ***

'What was that again?' asked the man once they'd sat down at the pub.
'They found a bomb', said the woman. 'It must be somewhere close to the rails. A team is working on it.'
'One from the war?'
    The woman nodded, but the man did not see her. 'They always give some reason for the delays', he said digging in his backpack for cigarettes. 'Everything happens for a reason here.'
'When you know the cause of events, there is a sense of relief', she responded. 'The information makes it easier to wait.'
'Thus spake Zarathustra!', said the man and placed the cigarette between his lips.

---

[1]   This essay was first published in *The Yale Review*, 2019. Available at https://yalereview.yale.edu/walk-past-vines-past-orchards. Republished with permission.

'Did you have to light one now? We just got here.'
'I haven't lit it yet', said the man and struck a match. 'And for *your* information', he added, inhaling the smoke, 'I am not relieved when I know the cause of events. Not one bit.'

He looked for the waiter. The place seemed deserted. *It's roasting hot*, he thought, *people must be hiding inside*. There was an old couple a few tables away. The man was holding half a glass of beer. The woman had folded her small wrinkled hands in her lap.

'*Zwei Kölsch, bitte*', he heard his wife asking in her deep, melodious voice.

The waiter was a young man with short blond hair, which he had combed very neatly to one side. On one of his cheeks was a birthmark in the shape of Australia. They didn't serve *Kölsch*, he informed her, offering instead, '*Weizen, Pils, oder Alt?*'

'*Dann nehmen wir Alt*', replied the woman.

'You should let me order some time', the man said. 'I need to practice my German.' He puffed another big cloud of smoke into the air.

'Please don't start again', she sighed. 'Your German is fine.'

'You always forget', he continued, '*Kölsch* is the beer from the *other* side. In Düsseldorf, it's *Alt*. Don't you know the joke? In Köln people hate *altbier* so much that they remove the ALT tab in their laptops.'

'Goodness', said the woman, 'that's so lame!'

'I know', said the man.

'Why "the other side"?'

'They were part of the Roman Empire. The *Kölsch*. The Romans didn't get this far, though.'

'Shame for the Romans', laughed the woman. 'They don't know what they're missing.'

'You're also Roman', the man said, kissing her hand. 'From Eastern Rome.'

'The Roman Empire collapsed.' She took her hand back and reached for the menu. 'Do you want something to eat?'

'Do you think we should?', he said. 'What's the time?'

'The greatest distance between two places.'

'Don't make things more difficult than they actually are.' The man took a deep breath. His cigarette was burning his fingers. He threw the butt away.

'But things *are* difficult.'

'Come on, tell me the time', he said with a quirky smile. 'All right, then. *What watch?*'

'Almost five.'

'Such watch!'

She laughed, appreciating the *Casablanca* reference. The deep lines around her mouth softened.

'I don't think we have time to eat', he said. 'The train may come any moment.'

He looked at the other couple again. They weren't talking. The old woman held the handles of her purse as though preparing to leave. Her fingers were crooked with arthritis. Her companion had a growth on his bald head, maybe a benign tumor. *Nobody dies here*, the man thought. *They get old but they don't die. They just get smaller and smaller.*
'They go together', the woman was saying.
'Who, dear?'
'The old couple in *Casablanca*. They leave together.'
'So did we', said the man.
The woman did not answer.
The blond waiter brought the beers. The man paid the bill. He left a generous tip.
'*Danke, mein Freund*', he said to the waiter. '*Gerne*', said the boy. The Australia on his cheek flared up and became bright red.
'You should not really say that', said the woman, after the waiter left. 'They'll take it the wrong way.'
'What did I say?'
'Nothing, dear. It's not a big deal. How long will you be in Berlin?'
'I thought I could stay at Cemil's for a couple of days. Then I'm off to Istanbul.'
'Off to Istanbul', the woman echoed. Then took a sip from her beer.
'I forgot to tell you', the man went on, 'I had a dream the other night. I was kicked out of the university.'
'You don't say!'
'It was much worse than in real life', he said, ignoring her comment. 'I was back to school. I was looking for my office and I couldn't find it. I walked around the whole campus, checking every corner. There was not a single trace of me. It was like I had disappeared from the face of the earth. Can you imagine?'
'And it was like he had disappeared from the face of the earth', said the woman. Then she dipped a finger in the beer to fish out a leaf that had fallen into the glass.
'You dream a lot, too', he said.
'Do I?'
'Yes, you do. You talk in your sleep.'
'Really? What do I say?'
'You sang an Ahmet Özhan song the other night.'
At this, the woman spurt beer through her nose. The thought of her singing that cheesy song! They laughed together. The couple at the next table looked at them disapprovingly.
'It's nerves', said the woman, wiping tears from her cheeks. She dabbed the beer stains on her dress. Her chest was still moving up and down with silent laughter.

'*When you left, my soul shed a burning bright flame*', the man sang in a baritone voice. He closed his eyes and raised the cigarette pack to his mouth like a microphone.

'No, wait!', said the woman still laughing. 'We have to part your hair in the middle, like this.' She reached out and stuck his hair to his forehead.

'Go ahead', he teased her, 'wipe your beer hands on my face!'

'Tell me the truth! Was I really singing that song?'

'Does it matter what song it was? You were singing in your sleep.'

The woman's reply disappeared in the rattling noise of a goods train passing by. A whistle blew somewhere far off. The old man sitting at the next table looked at his watch and signaled to the waiter for the bill.

'You know what I'm thinking?', asked the man after the train had passed.

'What?'

'We could buy a small piece of land. Somewhere on the Aegean. A few olive trees. Or a small vineyard. You love vines. I'm just saying. Whichever you like.'

The woman looked at her hands in distress.

'We don't have to stay in academia, you know. We could have another life, another future.'

The woman was silent.

'Like in the poem. *Walk past the vines, past the orchards...*'

'Cemal Süreya's poem?'

'Yes. You like that poem, don't you?'

'Walk past the orchards, past the parks, the bridges', she corrected him.

'Right', said the man, 'your memory is better.'

'There are no vines', said the woman. She turned her head away from him. Her lips were trembling.

'Yes, dear', said the man. 'I got it wrong.'

The old couple paid and left. They leaned on each other slightly as they walked to the station. *They are leaving together*, the man thought.

'The train is coming', said the woman. 'I just heard the announcement.'

'It is coming, yes', said the man.

'We have to go', said the woman.

'Chop, chop!', said the man.

They did not move. The man played with the handle of the trolley. He pulled and pushed it again.

'Are you really leaving?' The woman's voice was coarse, and she was staring at a beer stain on the table.

'Let's not go back to square one', said the man. 'We've been through this.'

'How can you go!'

'On an airplane.' When she looked at him with unbelieving eyes, he imitated the fake joy of the jingle, 'Turkish Airlines, globally yours?'

The woman did not smile. She tried to scrape the stain on the table, in vain. She pulled a coaster over it and placed the empty beer glass on the coaster.
'What if they don't let you leave the country again?'
'Then you can fly home to me', the man replied.
'I can, yes', said the woman.
'When?'
'Later.'
'How much later?'
'I don't know', said the woman, 'I'm teaching now. When classes are over', she pushed the chair and stood up, 'Later'.

***

The platform was becoming busy. They stood at the very end without touching each other. Under the sun, the rails bent like golden snakes and disappeared in the distance.
'Look, there's a bright light over there', the man said, pointing to the rails. Then he put his arms around the woman and pulled her towards himself.
    The woman tried to clear her throat. She hid her face in his chest.
'You totally misunderstood that poem', she said finally, 'It is not like you said. Not like that at all.'

> Walk past the orchards, past the parks, the bridges;
> It's a shame I never learned that love needs tending.
>
> Make love, traveller, say your big words and leave;
> Cliffs will unite the high hills without bending.
> *— from 'Make love, traveller', by Cemal Süreya*
>
> Translation: Meltem Gürle

Re-Rooting

German Literary Responses to the 'Migrant Crisis'
Space and the Colonial Past in Jenny Erpenbeck's *Gehen, ging, gegangen* (2015) and Bodo Kirchhoff's *Widerfahrnis* (2016)

Christiane Steckenbiller

Jenny Erpenbeck's novel *Gehen, ging, gegangen* (2015) and Bodo Kirchhoff's novella *Widerfahrnis* (2016) were both published at the height of the so-called European 'migrant crisis' (de Genova, 2017, p. 2), at a time when media coverage was dominated by stories of rising death rates in the Aegean and Mediterranean and the arrival of thousands of people on the shores of Europe and, above all, in Germany. But as postcolonial scholars Koen Leurs and Sandra Ponzanesi (2018) point out, what was being labelled a 'crisis' in the summer of 2015 had already been a normal state of affairs for some time. For years large numbers of migrants had been living outside of their countries of origin, often in substandard refugee camps in Jordan, Turkey, Pakistan, and Lebanon ('Ten countries', 2016). In 2015, as increasingly large numbers of people started to make the perilous journey west and north, Western media and members of the European public started employing a 'desensitizing and rather cynical rhetoric' (de Genova, 2017, p. 2). Instead of acknowledging that this was 'a crisis experienced by individual human beings of all ages and walks of life who [were] forced to flee their homes' only to be met 'with hostility, criticism, and rejection upon arriving', the situation came to be characterized as a 'crisis' for Europe (Leurs and Ponzanesi, 2018, p. 7).

It is this theme – the arrival of non-European Others and their reception, which in Germany ranged from a 'culture of welcome/hospitality' (Karakayalı, 2019, p. 191) to xenophobia and racism, as well as more ambiguous responses – that was taken up by German authors Jenny Erpenbeck and Bodo Kirchhoff.[1] Their prompt liter-

---

1 In Germany, the positive attitude towards refugees was labelled *Willkommenskultur*, a 'culture of welcome' or 'hospitality', which, according to sociologist Serhat Karakayalı, was evident as early as 2011 and reached a peak in 2015. That year thousands of citizens donated food and clothing, joined volunteer organizations and demonstrations, accompanied refugees to appointments, helped out with bills, translated forms, and gave German lessons.

ary responses to the 'long summer of migration' (Bock and Macdonald, 2019, p. 3) received significant attention from critics: Erpenbeck was shortlisted for the prestigious German Book Prize in 2015, while Kirchhoff took home the award in 2016, which some critics called a 'mistake' (Cordsen, 2016, n.p.). Both literary texts received mixed reviews. Erpenbeck's novel was criticized for its oversimplification of the topic and its characters, particularly the way in which the individual stories of refugee characters seem to blend into one other (Biller, 2015; Magenau, 2015). On the other hand, it was applauded for its critique of German refugee policies and bureaucracies and the 'political ignorance and endemic chauvinism' with which German politicians and bureaucrats responded to forced migration (Magenau, 2015). Kirchhoff's novella, in turn, was criticized for its 'paternalistic' approach to the topic of migration and its 'antiquated machismo' (Cordsen, 2016) but was admired in other quarters for attending to the pressing political questions of the day (Krekeler, 2016; Platthaus, 2016).

Erpenbeck and Kirchhoff touch upon another issue that has received less literary critical scrutiny. In the wake of the events of 2015, some scholars have begun to theorize migrant mobilities and border crossings in terms of appropriating space (de Genova et al., 2018; de Genova, 2017; Garelli and Tazzioli, 2017). Human geographer Nicholas de Genova (2017), for instance, asserts that migrants and refugees, in leaving their home countries, are 'exercising their elementary freedom of movement, thereby appropriating mobility, transgressing the border regime and thus making spatial claims' (p. 17). He understands contemporary forms of migration management – including border policing and asylum policies enforced by the European Union – as responses to such spatial claims, responses that impose geographical restrictions on the right of migrants to move and settle within the EU. As will be explored in this essay, a spatial reading of migration provides a fruitful means to consider Erpenbeck's novel and Kirchhoff's novella afresh. Both works carefully attend to geography – the urban topography of Berlin in Erpenbeck, and roads, borders, the city of Catania, Sicily, and the Mediterranean Sea in Kirchhoff. At the same time, the texts thematize the spatial practices associated with migration and the everyday navigation of the city. These practices – walking, pausing, or temporarily residing in particular places – might be considered examples of ordinary people occupying or asserting claims over space. State and social responses to migration – the militarization and policing of borders and other spaces and the distribution of migrants within a city or across the European Union – emerge, in contrast, as forms of spatial control.

As will be shown here, *Gehen, ging, gegangen* and *Widerfahrnis* thematize competition over space, but they also treat colonial history, a topic which has not featured prominently in critical assessments of these two works. Early in Erpenbeck's novel, Richard, the German white male protagonist, stumbles on the concept of 'bureaucratic geometry' while reading about the consequences of German colonialism (p.

49).² He was prompted to pick up a volume on the subject by an interaction he had with a heterogeneous group of African asylum seekers. This book on the imposition of colonial order provides Richard with a much-needed vocabulary for making sense of what he observes around him. Specifically, it gives him tools for reflecting on current refugee policies and what he comes to think of as hegemonic spatial practices, or the ways in which power is wielded through controlling access to and use of space. Richard's new awareness about the organization and control of space – in this case Berlin – allows the reader, by extension, to understand spatial management as a direct continuation of colonialist thought and practice. In Kirchhoff's novella, the allusions to colonial history are not immediately obvious. Like *Gehen, ging, gegangen*, *Widerfahrnis* draws attention to the ways in which space – here the city of Catania and the Mediterranean border zone – is navigated, organized, and controlled. There are no direct references to colonial history, but the colonial past emerges in the form of repressed fears and anxieties that are triggered by the white male protagonist's encounter with a young female refugee. Postcolonial critics have recently argued that refugees and migrants 'whose mobilities may be productively understood to appropriate the space of Europe ... most commonly originate from places across Africa, the Middle East, and Asia that were formerly the outright or de facto colonies of European masters' (de Genova, 2017, p. 18). As such, many individuals are not fleeing from a place that is positioned outside of or completely unconnected to Europe. This suggests an analytic perspective that considers mass displacement to be directly related to historical or continuing practices of colonialism. In Kirchhoff's novella, the young female refugee remains nameless and readers learn nothing about the country she left behind. This allows for a symbolic reading of the encounter between her and the protagonist as emblematic of Europe's confrontation with its own 'undigested colonial history' (Gilroy, 2016, p. xi).³

---

2   The quotes from Erpenbeck's novel are taken from the English translation *Go, Went, Gone* (2017). The translations from Kirchhoff's novella and all other translations are the author's, unless otherwise indicated.
3   According to the UN Refugee Agency, 'refugees' are 'persons fleeing armed conflict or persecution' ('UNHCR viewpoint: "Refugee" or "migrant" – Which is right?'). Migrants, on the other hand, 'choose to move not because of a direct threat of persecution or death, but mainly to improve their lives by finding work, or in some cases for education, family reunion, or other reasons' ('UNHCR viewpoint: "Refugee" or "migrant" – Which is right?'). 'Asylum seeker' describes someone who intends to seek sanctuary in another country. According to the UN, asylum is 'the right to be recognized as a refugee and receive legal protection and material assistance' ('What is a refugee'). As political scientists Heaven Crawley and Dimitris Skleparis maintain, however, none of these terms can fully capture individual experiences. Such categories risk homogenizing and simplifying the day-to-day realities of those on the move or newly arrived. Often, people are 'trapped in the space between "refugee" and "migrant"' (p. 51), or their status changes. This essay uses 'refugee' and 'asylum seeker' when the context

Erpenbeck's novel and Kirchhoff's novella thus invite a reading that spatializes and historicizes current developments and situates the contemporary experience of refugeeism and forced migration within the historical context of colonialism. In the respective works, Berlin and the Mediterranean emerge as richly imagined sites of forgotten histories, repressed desires, and contested inclusion. This calls attention to what has been referred to as the 'after-effects' (Hall, 1996, p. 248) of colonialism and the 'lingering colonial past' (Gilroy, 2016, p. xvi). The two literary texts call attention to the ways in which such after-effects inform attitudes and policies in the 'postcolonial present' (Bhambra, 2016, p. 188), which includes intricate mechanisms of marginalization, obstruction, amnesia, and erasure. In Erpenbeck's novel, Richard's friendship with young male refugees from various African countries enables him to recognize the shortcomings of German integration policies, the contemporary German state's refusal to come to terms with its colonial past (and by extension, the similar refusal by its two predecessor states) and the ways in which current policies must be seen as a continuation of colonial as well as National Socialist and post-unification policies related to space. Kirchhoff's novella, on the other hand, positions its protagonist as a more problematic character, suspicious, evasive, and self-centred. The fact that the encounter with the female refugee in Catania is depicted as a deeply unsettling experience and as a threat to the protagonist's male identity invites a wide variety of critical readings of the novella. This encounter may be viewed as symbolic of Europe's confrontation with colonial history, and the protagonist's hostile and chauvinist attitudes may prompt readers to critique exclusionary practices of border policing and migration management. Building on scholarship in postcolonial studies and cultural geography, this essay focuses specifically on the way the texts imagine and represent space in the form of cities, squares, streets, monuments, and border zones and examines how Erpenbeck and Kirchhoff grapple with the twin challenges of mass displacement and colonial history. In their thematization of power relations and oppression, the texts also pose the question of how literature might intervene in current political discussions.

---

and individual circumstances clearly warrant their use. In Erpenbeck's novel, the African men are referred to as 'Flüchtlinge' ('refugees'). It is also specified that the men are seeking asylum, even if, according to the Dublin Regulation (see 'What is the Dublin Regulation'), they are ineligible to apply for asylum in Germany but need to do so in the EU member state in which they first registered, which is Italy in their cases. Kirchhoff, on the other hand, avoids using the terms 'migrant' or 'refugee' yet it can be assumed that the individuals encountered in the text are 'refugees'. Accordingly, this essay uses the term 'refugee' in the discussion of Kirchhoff's novella. The term 'migrant' is used when the context is unclear and to describe people on the move more generally.

Spatial Logics of Exclusion, Erasure, and Control in Erpenbeck's *Gehen, ging, gegangen*

In *Gehen, ging, gegangen*, the protagonist Richard, professor emeritus of classics at Humboldt University in the former East Berlin, tries to come to terms, first, with his retirement and, then, with the opaque asylum policies of the European Union, the German government, and, at the local level, the Berlin Senate. The novel is set in 2014, one year before the so-called migration 'crisis' of 2015, at a time in which increased migration to Europe was already evident and public mobilization in the form of protest marches and a protest camp on Oranienplatz, a square in Berlin, had already begun. Given the prominence of the topic in the media, it is striking that Richard is at first completely unaware of contemporary developments. The novel traces Richard's learning process (Janzen, 2018) as he befriends a group of asylum seekers, young men from Chad, Ghana, Libya, Mali, Niger, and Nigeria, and learns about their individual stories and places of origin while simultaneously reading up on colonial history and contemporary politics. Literary critic Brangwen Stone (2017) notes that Richard's own life is marked by experiences of violence, loss, and escape. He fled with his parents from Silesia to Berlin at the close of the Second World War and, as an adult, has watched his familiar world disappear with the fall of the Berlin Wall. According to Stone, these personal experiences of loss and exile help both Richard and the reader to empathize with and better understand the experiences of recent newcomers. Richard is also acutely aware of the atrocities perpetrated by the Nazis. Critics have applauded the novel precisely for this interweaving of personal stories and historical references (Janzen, 2018). Richard redefines his own worldview even if he remains fundamentally prone to racist, chauvinist, Eurocentric, and Germano-centric attitudes (Ludewig, 2016; Steckenbiller, 2018). Monika Shafi (2017), also interpreting the novel to be about social transformation, highlights its thematization of citizenship, borders, and nationhood. These critics argue that the novel may offer an ethical response to the events of 2015. Stefan Hermes (2016), in contrast, remains sceptical about the text's pedagogical focus and tone, which, according to him, precludes critical engagement with the consequences of colonialism and the everyday realities of the African men, who remain stereotypically cast as victims. Critics have highlighted the novel's concern with spatiality, in particular places of learning like schools and classrooms (Janzen, 2018) and sites of hospitality, like Richard's own home (Shafi, 2017). Existing critical assessments of the novel have not sufficiently connected these two concerns, namely the way in which colonial, National Socialist, and post-war histories and contemporary experiences are woven into the spatial fabric of Berlin and how they relate to larger German and EU institutional frameworks.

The novel's concern with spatiality and processes of erasure and marginalization are evident from its first pages, which are set by the lake next to Richard's house. He cannot 'avoid seeing the lake when he sits at his desk' (Erpenbeck, 2017, p. 5), and although it is 'placid' (p. 4) on its surface, the lake harbours a tragic history. 'They still haven't found the man at the bottom', Richard says, adding that '[he] died in a swimming accident' (p. 5). The lake's ability to hide or erase what has happened recalls anthropologist and historian Ann Stoler's (2016) reminder that the 'imperial effects' (p. 3) of colonialism in the present are not always 'self-evident' or 'in easy reach' for contemporary observers. By addressing right from the novel's beginning the ways in which appearances can be misleading, the text draws attention to that which is hidden, invisible, erased, absent, or, quite literally, submerged under water or buried underground. The drowned swimmer in the lake foreshadows another topic that Richard will confront soon enough, the deaths of thousands of migrants trying to cross the Mediterranean. But above all, the image of the lake calls attention to the ways in which past events keep resurfacing in the present.

Complex Locations of Power

Richard's first encounter with the male refugees occurs in a context that reveals, so to speak, those things that are hidden beneath the surface. The reader first encounters the refugees as Richard crosses Alexanderplatz, a prominent square in the part of the city that was East Berlin, where he walks right past a group of protesters. The narrator describes Richard as being preoccupied with other things, specifically, the fate of Polish Jewry during the Holocaust. From imagining the catacombs beneath the square that, as his archaeologist friend told him, were used to store and sell goods during the Middle Ages, his thoughts drift to similar tunnels in Rzeszów, Poland, where he and his wife once spent a holiday. During the war, Richard recalls, residents would seek shelter underground. 'Later, in the time of fascism, Jews took refuge here until the Nazis hit on the idea of filling the subterranean passageway with smoke' (p. 12). Richard, distracted by the memory of the Holocaust, overlooks the men protesting at the square because he is in no position to perceive them. The square is a space he knows well and that he navigates with ease as part of his daily routines (Shafi, 2017). Places are imbued with social, cultural, political, and historical meanings that are organized along axes of power, including race, ethnicity, class, and gender (Ahmed, 2007; Mahler and Pessar, 2001; Massey, 2005) that determine who does or does not belong. Individuals may be rendered hyper-visible if they are metaphorically out of place. But visibility depends on who is looking, and despite the cardboard signs that read 'We become visible' (Erpenbeck, 2017, p. 18), Richard will not take notice of the group of refugee activists until later that night when he turns on the evening news and the protest is catapulted right into his living room.

A later scene in the novel reverses the roles played by Richard and the asylum seekers. The scene highlights the way in which context determines whether or not individuals can assert control over space and therefore experience a sense of belonging, as opposed to being controlled and restricted in their mobility and actions. With Karon from Ghana, Richard visits a small shop in a neighbourhood, perhaps Kreuzberg or Neukölln, that he does not normally frequent. By now, Richard has gotten to know the men and is more than familiar with the legal obstacles they face and the general precariousness of their situation. Overcome by a sense of helplessness with regard to the fact that Karon and the other men are ineligible to apply for asylum in Germany, Richard has decided that he wants to support Karon financially by buying a piece of property in Ghana for the family Karon left behind. This, the reader learns, is only the second time in his life that he considers buying real estate. On the previous occasion, right after the collapse of the German Democratic Republic (GDR), he had felt overwhelmed by the process of acquiring property 'in this strange land his country had suddenly become' (Erpenbeck, 2017, p. 224). Now Richard needs to venture into even stranger territory. Passing a kebab shop and a place selling mobile phones, he and Karon enter a shop that seems to transport them into a different world:

> They cross the threshold, but what counts here as inside and outside? It's foggy in the room, or smoky, so Richard is only gradually able to make out his surroundings. On stakes all around the room, braids have been tied, and he sees strange fruit piled up high in wooden bowls, some with thorns, some with transparent skin, some look like eggs, others like meat. The fruit is arranged as if around an altar, and in the middle of the room an African woman, her hair in wild disarray, sits on a three-legged stool, before her in the linoleum floor is a crevice from which vapors are rising. (p. 225)

Richard is puzzled by the fact that he has to toss the money necessary for the transaction – three thousand euros in cash – into the crevice in the floor. After this, another man hands Karon a piece of paper with numbers that Karon must convey to his mother in Ghana. Richard observes: 'Here in this place, Karon knows his way around, and for a moment he's no longer a refugee, he's a man like any other' (p. 226). It is suddenly Richard who feels out of place. But he also feels strangely out of time, imagining that the doorbells 'no doubt tinkled during the first postwar years every time a German housewife left the shop with her purchases' (p. 226). The bells remind Richard of an earlier time in the GDR, possibly his childhood. But the sound would also be familiar to other Germans his age who grew up in West Germany. The bells thus represent something shared by residents of the former East and West. But whatever the sounds shared through time, this particular neighbourhood itself, located in the Western part of the city, remains startlingly unfamiliar to him. He clearly is an outsider in this space where East and West strangely overlap and which today is filled with curious objects and marked by Ghanaian customs and rituals that Richard has difficulties comprehending.

Hegemonic Spatial Practices

Like the lake outside Richard's house and the central square of Alexanderplatz, the shop illustrates the mechanisms by which the novel continuously interweaves the past with the present. What is striking is the way geographical places are brought together in this space too. Richard imagines the shop being located above a passageway that links Germany with Africa. He envisions the woman passing the money 'directly to Ghana by the shortest possible path, through the Earth's curved crust' (p. 227). Richard's fantasy, which includes exoticized descriptions of the shop interior, is suggestive of an orientalist or colonialist mode of thinking that reduces other cultural contexts to stereotypes. This is not the only time the novel calls attention to such ways of thinking. While collecting information about the countries the asylum seekers left behind, Richard not only learns more about colonial history and its repercussions in the present, but he is also forced to reassess aspects of his own life, in which he can now discern the imprint of colonial thought and practice. There is, for example, a book Richard refers to as '*Negerliteratur*' (p. 23, italics in original) from 1951 that he pulls off his bookshelf without further elaboration, leaving it to the reader to wonder whether it is a scholarly volume, a textbook, a work of literature, or something else entirely. And there is a copy of *Hatschi Bratschi's Hot Air Balloon*, a popular children's book from the early 1900s. Richard can no longer simply pass over the books' mentions of 'bush spirits' and a 'cannibal boy' (Erpenbeck, 2017, p. 24), respectively, or ignore the colonialist thinking that shaped them. Both books explicitly juxtapose a perceived European superiority with an assumed African backwardness. In the former, Richard reads that the 'land of the bush spirits' is empty, vacant, and devoid of history and '[u]nder the earth there is only more earth. What comes after that, no one knows' (p. 24). Richard can no longer ignore the assumption that other regions are empty and primitive, assumptions that legitimized the colonial enterprise. This calls to mind the distinction between a static and a progressive approach to space theorized by the feminist geographer Doreen Massey (2005). According to Massey, a static approach refuses 'to acknowledge [a space's] multiplicities, its fractures and its dynamism' (p. 65); it simplifies space just as Africa is in the book Richard revisits. A progressive approach, in contrast, recognizes space to be always in flux, always becoming and dynamic, as multi-layered and rich in constantly shifting realities, narratives, memories, and cultural, historical, and political meanings – as is reflected in the novel's depiction of Berlin. It is only later, as he learns more about colonial history and the cultural, political, and historical contexts the asylum seekers have left behind, that Richard will shift to a progressive approach, recognizing the regions, countries, cities, and villages whence his acquaintances came as comparably complex and multifarious.

Richard soon comes across another example of a static approach to ordering and organizing space, this time in Berlin. After attending a community meeting in Kreuzberg, Richard finally visits Oranienplatz, the site of a large protest encampment (Bhimji, 2015; Landry, 2016). Here he reflects on the Huguenots, refugees from France who in the late 1600s were the first settlers in the area (Göktürk et al., 2007, p. 5), before his thoughts turn to events from his own life. He recalls, for instance, how he and his late wife used to take long walks here, engrossed in conversations about Peter Joseph Lenné, the Prussian landscape architect who made considerable changes to the neighbourhood. Richard realizes that Germany probably still had colonies when Lenné was engaged in his work here. This prompts him to recall that the German word for 'colonial goods', *Kolonialwaren*, 'was still visible in weathered script on some East Berlin facades as recently as twenty years ago' (Erpenbeck, 2017, p. 36). Oftentimes '*Kolonialwaren* and WWII bullet holes might adorn the very same storefront', and he further reflects on the fact that many of those buildings used to display cardboard signs advertising fruit and vegetables with an acronym familiar to multiple generations of East Germans: 'OGS', *Obst Gemüse Speisekartoffeln*, or 'fruit, vegetables, and potatoes'. All of those diverse layers of meaning disappeared after German reunification when 'the West', as Richard emphasizes, 'started renovating everything' (p. 37). As is evident from Richard's observations, the West, which here is a metonym for the unified German nation-state, incorporated the GDR by partially erasing physical reminders of the former East.

The city is revealed to be multi-layered, a palimpsest of successive historical and political configurations, in which Richard not only uncovers or rediscovers memories of German colonialism and East German socialism but also recognizes the mechanisms by which such memories have been repressed or deliberately erased. Cultural theorist Fatima El-Tayeb (2016) has argued that the conceptualization of contemporary Germany as postcolonial, post-fascist, and post-socialist makes visible the intricate ways in which German society, and north-western Europe more generally, has systematically been constructed as the 'neutral norm' (p. 39). This 'norm' defines diverse Others, including 'the socialist East and the colonial subject' (p. 39), through contrast with itself. She argues that defining certain subjects and their histories as 'Other' authorized the unified German nation-state to incorporate the former GDR and willfully erase its history and reconstruct the city. The Nazis, too, reshaped Berlin by erecting buildings in the typical National Socialist style and renaming prominent streets and squares, thus inscribing a vision of racial superiority into the cityscape. In her study, El-Tayeb asks how such practices live on in contemporary Germany and continue to legitimize the exclusion of Europe's racialized Others in the present (pp. 39-40). Erpenbeck's novel, too, seems to suggest that previous forms of control have a lasting effect in determining oppressive and exclusionary practices today.

These practices are also informed by more recent developments. In response to the Berlin Senate's decision to close the Oranienplatz protest camp and move its residents to refugee centres dispersed across the city, Richard notes: 'For a year and a half, anyone who wanted to could speak with the refugees ... But the moment they signed an *agreement*, it became necessary to administer them' (Erpenbeck, 2017, p. 49, italics in original). Marxist geographer David Harvey (2012) finds cities at the centre of a twenty-first-century neoliberal politics that, in attempting to regulate and exercise power over space, 'often seeks to reorganise urban infrastructure and urban life with an eye to the control of restive populations' (p. 117). This regulating impulse is evident in the policies enacted by the Berlin Senate and the agreement it reached with the refugees. But Richard wonders whether the decision to move the refugees, supposedly in order to 'preserve the Africans' safety', is not in fact a cover-up:

> The colonized are smothered in bureaucracy, which is a pretty clever way to keep them from political action. Or was it just a matter of protecting the good Germans from the bad Germans, sparing the Land of Poets the indignity of being dubbed the Land of Killers once more? (Erpenbeck, 2017, p. 49)

Juxtaposing the 'Land of Poets' and the 'Land of Killers', the narrator traces a lineage not just from German intellectual traditions to National Socialism but also from colonial practices to Nazi ideology and, finally, to present-day policies. Subordinating and managing populations through the control of space – the occupation, expropriation, or legal acquisition of space and the subsequent authority to organize its use – is not a method only employed by contemporary neoliberal states, but by colonial powers, the National Socialists, and the unified German nation-state, too, first in incorporating the former East Germany and now in relation to recently arrived refugees. The novel may be read as a warning about contemporary German refugee policies and EU law, particularly the Dublin Regulation, which requires asylum applications be processed in the first EU member state through which applicants enter ('What is the Dublin Regulation'). Richard will later recognize this regulation to be the key obstacle to the refugees' successful integration in Germany. The institutions described in the novel, particularly the Berlin Senate and the government of the Federal Republic of Germany, are revealed to be heirs to the colonial and National Socialist regimes, continuing, in some measure, their violent and dehumanizing legacies by exercising neo-colonial practices in the present.

Mechanisms of Power and Control in Kirchhoff

While Richard recognizes and re-evaluates the violent nature of past and present institutions in *Gehen, ging, gegangen*, the characters in Kirchhoff's novella fail to reach comparable insights. In contrast to the rich historical references in Erpenbeck's novel, *Widerfahrnis* is distinguished by its striking lack of historical detail, its methodically constructed ambiguity, and narrative restraint. Although allusions to colonial histories are woven into the text, it takes an observant reader to recognize them and incorporate them into a reading of the novella as a critique of colonial and neo-colonial practices. The protagonist, Reither, a white German man and a former publisher, betrays no interest in learning about the past or about the migrants or refugees he encounters. Both he and his travel companion, Leonie Palm, with whom he has only recently become acquainted, set out on what appears to be a rejuvenating and liberating journey south to Italy but which is in fact an attempt to cope with their own problems – aging, disease, regret, loneliness, and death. The novella pairs these personal anxieties with contemporary politics as the two holidaymakers encounter migrant travellers throughout their trip. Critics have read the novella as juxtaposing Western affluence with the deprivations experienced by refugees (Kämmerlings, 2016) or the 'bliss of love' with 'refugee suffering' (Moritz, 2016). They have pointed to the novella's 'didactic potential' given its emphasis on 'fundamental human experiences' and 'the confrontation with humans in need of help' (Theele, 2018, p. 64), while others note the characters' shocking disinterestedness with regard to the refugees (von Sternburg, 2016). This essay's analysis also finds that Kirchhoff treats contemporary politics in, as one critic has written, a 'painfully paternalistic way' (Cordsen, 2016). Reither's approach to current events and his relationships with other characters – most importantly with women of varying backgrounds – are shaped by a mix of chauvinism, entitlement, and sense of European superiority. From the start, the novella frequently refers to the fact that Reither is a former publisher who decided which books would be published and which authors included and who dictated the title and cover design of individual works. In addition, the novella highlights mechanisms of control and regulation by emphasizing its own constructedness. Reither's reflections on his former profession are paired with contemplations on processes of writing and storytelling, which oftentimes seem to relate to the novella itself. From the beginning, the text cements an image of Reither as someone who is used to being in control of not only his own narrative, but those of others too. Accordingly, he serves to focus readers' attention on power hierarchies and mechanisms of control, regulation, and exclusion. After the two travellers arrive in Sicily, their final destination, they meet a young female refugee, who emerges as a proxy for the non-European Other. Her mere presence at Europe's outer border makes visible the imbalance of power between Europe and its Others and the fears and anxieties prompted by the presence of refugees. Postcolonial scholar Paul Gilroy (2016) has recently attributed the emergence of such fears in contemporary Europe to the rise of nativism, populism, and the far right.

As Erpenbeck did in her novel, *Widerfahrnis* emphasizes how individuals negotiate the spaces of their everyday lives differently depending, for instance, on social status and access to resources. The novella juxtaposes the seemingly unrestricted movement of the two main characters, who hold EU passports, with the restricted, policed, clandestine, and often deadly paths taken by refugees. Huddled together as an anonymous mass by the side of the road, the nameless migrants in this novella are presented in a manner that is in stark contrast to the way the male refugees are described individually in Erpenbeck's novel. Massey (2005), Harvey (2012), and Gilroy (2016) have stressed that the experience of space is shaped by race, class, gender, and other social structures as well as by free-market capitalism and exclusionary policies. Refugees' mobility is restricted by spatial control, containment, and segregation, both before and after they have applied for asylum, whereas tourists are able to travel freely and openly and easily traverse national borders. In the novella, too, the protagonists travel unimpeded past refugee characters 'at the margins' (Platthaus, 2016), on the side of the road and on an Italian island at the southern edge of Europe. The novella reduces the refugee crisis, including its causes and effects, to a topic of marginal significance, which reflects how the topic is first introduced in Erpenbeck's novel. Stoler (2016) notes how 'unruly' colonial histories are sometimes 'safely sequestered on the distant fringes of national narratives' while at other times they 'trample manicured gardens' (p. 122). In Erpenbeck's novel it is Richard's own garden, the lake outside his house, and, by extension, the city of Berlin that prompt him to begin to recognize the pressing challenges posed by mass displacement as they relate to space and colonial history. This realization is missing in Kirchhoff's novella, in which the topic of refugeeism is deliberately suppressed and relegated to the margins even as it reappears in the lives of the protagonists, until they are eventually forced to confront this political issue, albeit in Italy instead of in their home country, Germany.

Europe's Periphery

From the beginning, the novella makes numerous references to mobility, transit, forced migration, and Southern Europe. Italy, in particular, the protagonists' destination and place of first arrival for many refugees, is construed as a site of romantic longing and new possibilities. Italy has long held a particular fascination for the educated German middle classes (Richter, 2009; Theele, 2018), but it is also a place that harbours repressed desires and uncomfortable pasts. 'This story that still breaks his heart … how would he have started it?' (Kirchhoff, 2016, p. 5), Reither wonders at the very beginning, highlighting his own agency in crafting and relaying that story whilst also hinting at a lack of agency for those experiencing hardships and heartbreak. Equally cryptic and ambiguous is the mention of 'Spuk' (p. 5), worries, ghosts, or, in Reither's words, 'the world, all its misery' (p. 5), which he tries to block out by opening a bottle of wine from Apulia. It is fitting that the bottle is the last one in his house, given that Italy is the last place where he saw his former lover. Still agonizing over that break-up, Reither is even more troubled by thoughts of the daughter they never had, an uncomfortable past that keeps punctuating the present. The reader soon learns that his neighbour, Leonie Palm, is also dealing with personal challenges, mourning her daughter's suicide and fighting the early stages of cancer. Aster, the Eritrean woman working at the reception desk of their residential complex, has an equally heart-breaking story, which is relayed by Marina, her Bulgarian co-worker. According to her, Aster recently fled from Eritrea in a strenuous journey (p. 40) that included three months in Sudan and a stay in Khartoum, where she worked as a maid to save money for the rest of the trip and where her landlord repeatedly raped her. After fleeing Khartoum and spending eleven days at sea, she arrived in Catania, Sicily's second largest city, located on its eastern coast. The narrator relays this story in passing as Reither and Leonie are getting ready to leave, first to drive south more generally, then expressly to Italy. Reither is strikingly dismissive of the two non-German women, treating them in a patronizing way and making condescending comments about their looks and behaviour. Leonie seems to mention Aster's story only to encourage Reither and herself in their own attempt to set out on their journey. 'Our Aster didn't give up either as she was fleeing' (p. 41), she remarks, vastly understating the differences between a recreational road trip taken by two white Germans and the harrowing experiences of forced migration. Italy, home to 'escape stories' of all sorts (p. 43), occupies a special place in the novella: a place of arrival and new beginnings; a place to come to terms with personal crises or past mistakes; and a place to finish mourning and fall in love.

It is unsurprising then that it is precisely in Catania, a place that the novella has already introduced as fraught with meaning, that the two protagonists encounter a young female refugee. This encounter serves as an uncanny reminder not only of personal experiences of loss, bereavement, and haunting, but also of Europe's repressed colonial heritage and its neo-colonial present. It is also an example of the ways in which migrants' claims to space are viewed in terms of spatial disobedience, especially in the wake of the events of 2015 that saw a rise in polarized political rhetoric. In this episode, Reither and Leonie meet a young girl who travels with them for a few days and who, from the very beginning, is depicted in explicitly hierarchical, racialized, and sexualized terms. When Reither first sees the girl, for instance, he does so from a vantage point of power and privilege. Looking down from a high balcony, he spots her pressed against the facade of a building, where she would have blended in with the narrow alleyway were it not for her 'torn red dress' (p. 123). Bewildered by the girl's appearance, Reither immediately believes her to be 'loitering' or 'hanging around' (pp. 123-124). His judgement carries criminal, sexual, and racial connotations, in line with the way much contemporary political rhetoric stigmatizes migrants as outsiders, criminals, deviants, or even terrorists (de Genova et al., 2018, p. 247). Reither later even labels the young woman a 'stray' and a 'tramp' (Kirchhoff, 2016, pp. 128-129). He calls her 'die Kleine' in his head ('the little one', p. 128) or uses the personal pronoun 'es', referring to 'das Mädchen' (the girl), which is gendered neuter in German. Such neutering and infantilizing underscores the unequal power relations that mark this interaction. Although he initially tries to brush off the encounter, the young woman will not go away, but keeps reappearing at intimate moments: as Reither and Leonie are strolling through the city, sitting down for dinner in a restaurant, returning to their apartment, and again after they have spent their first night together. In the woman's presence, Reither feels a discomfort that soon gives way to feelings of guilt and paranoia. 'Now we are committing a criminal act' (p. 166), he says, for instance, when the girl climbs into the car with them, voicing his anxieties about the legal consequences for themselves for facilitating her crossing of the border. The girl thus appears as a 'boundary figure', the kind of figure who, according to McClintock (1994), represents 'a crisis in male imperial identity' (p. 26, p. 27). A character who remains nameless, she triggers a whole assortment of fears and anxieties relating to migration and border management. Kirchhoff's work extends this notion of male identity crisis to a crisis in modern European identity. The young woman exercises her right to move around the city. Yet from the beginning, Reither perceives her as an intruder and therefore as someone who is illegitimately appropriating space.

The Policing of Contemporary Borders

If Reither's attitude reveals a crisis in modern European identity triggered by the threat posed by the non-European Other, the encounter with the female refugee might also be considered to symbolize Europe's confrontation with its colonial past. This notion is reinforced by the references to Sicily's complex history, to former empires and patterns of invasion and forced settlement. When Reither and Leonie see the young woman for the first time together, they are contemplating the symbol of the city of Catania, the black elephant and Egyptian obelisk erected at one of the city's most central squares, a sculpture that dates back to the Roman period but also hints at Muslim control of the city. Marvelling at this symbol, Reither is unusually curious. The 'little black elephant', 'abandoned by its parents' or 'war booty on display' (Kirchhoff, 2016, p. 125), he wonders to himself as the girl reappears right in front of him. Reither's thoughts foreshadow Leonie's decision to take the girl with them, as if she were a piece of property, an abandoned creature, or an artefact to be looted. But the black elephant, for Reither, also seems to be a symbol of conquest and violence, a notion reinforced by other physical reminders of former ruling powers. Strolling through the narrow streets of the city, for instance, Reither keeps noticing the Arabic script, sometimes painted bright red, that adorns old storefronts. These letters, he says, resemble 'small swords, hooks and splashes of blood' (p. 163). Reither cannot read Arabic and therefore the words have no meaning beyond what he perceives to be their threatening nature, their ability to conjure a history of violence that has no actual referent in the reality of the novella.

The physical traces of a former occupying power, however, call attention to the complex histories of conquest and contact in the Mediterranean and link these earlier instances to contemporary forms of contact. Located at the crossroads of conflicting colonial interests (Norwich, 2015), Sicily sits near the centre of the Mediterranean, which Chambers (2008) characterizes as a complex site 'where the Occident and the Orient, the North and the South, are ... entangled in a cultural and historical net cast over centuries, even millennia' (p. 3). Morocco, Libya, and Albania, all places Reither speculates may be the girl's country of origin (Kirchhoff, 2016, p. 129), are part of this hybrid and transitory space. To the perceptive reader, Reither's reflections invoke French, Spanish, and Italian spheres of interest, in addition to former Arab dynasties and the ancient empires of Rome, Greece, and the Ottomans. These associations attest to the overlapping histories of the region but also highlight the ways in which borders and states are always changing. For Reither, however, the physical remnants of Arab rule in Sicily only intensify the discomfort caused by the presence of the young woman. For him, the alien letters invoke violence in contexts and places foreign to him, whether related to Islam or conflicts in places whence refugees are fleeing.

An 'intricate site of encounters and currents' (Chambers, 2008, p. 32), the Mediterranean is also a border zone characterized by the diffuse violence of migration management and policing authorized by the European Union. The novella illustrates such mechanisms of control, regulation, and exclusion vis-à-vis Reither, who is personally invested in stopping the young woman from crossing the Mediterranean Sea. The presence of the non-European Other is portrayed as physically dangerous and life-threatening when Reither cuts himself in interacting with the girl, first on the can of Coke he opens for her at dinner and then on her pendant as he tries to prevent her from leaving the car when they are on the ferry. Reither's pain makes physical the shock or crisis caused by the presence of the refugee who has arrived at Europe's shores. But it also alludes to a trauma more deeply rooted in the European psyche, which Gilroy (2006) defines as the 'multilayered trauma – economic and cultural as well as political and psychological – involved in accepting the loss of the empire' (p. 99). Rather than working through such crises and accepting such losses and the discomforts associated with them, which here overlap with Reither's regrets regarding his own past, Reither evades having to deal with such circumstances. 'Not wanting the child was one of the mistakes of his life' (p. 93), Reither acknowledged earlier, referring to the daughter he never had. Now he seems to make a similar mistake by symbolically attempting to prevent the young woman from entering the European mainland. For Reither, the woman's exercise of her freedom of movement is a violation of his own sense of who is allowed to move freely and who belongs in this space. The young woman disappears and readers are left with Reither's failure to recognize the complexity of the situation: the inability to counteract the 'historical amnesia' (de Genova, 2016, p. 78) with regard to colonial history as well as the hostility and rejection refugees frequently face when entering the European border zone.

This cannot be counterbalanced by a later episode in which Reither invites a Nigerian man, who comes to Reither's aid and tends to his wounds, and the man's wife and child to drive back north with him. Reither's generosity and sudden awareness of the precarious circumstances faced by the three individuals from Nigeria does not make up for the hostility with which he treated the young woman earlier. Furthermore, the Nigerian man – the novella even reveals his name, Taylor – serves an altogether different purpose. Reither, whose right hand is injured, needs Taylor to help him drive his car. With Reither in the driver's seat and Taylor in the passenger seat, they manoeuvre the car together through the Italian harbour town. Yet it is still Reither who drives and who refuses to relinquish control. By mere chance they spot Leonie at the train station where Taylor had stored a piece of luggage in a locker. Leonie had abruptly gotten out of the car on the ferry to look for the young refugee woman. Now she informs Reither that she saw the woman leave the ferry. From there, however, she has disappeared without a trace, and Leonie, too, decides to continue her journey without him. Rather than offering any sense of 'catharsis' – for Reither or for the reader – as some critics have claimed (Platthaus, 2016), the ending stands as a bleak reminder of Europe's administrative, political, and economic dominance, perceived cultural superiority, troubling surveillance and security policies, and practices of control and exclusion.

Conclusion

Gehen, ging, gegangen and *Widerfahrnis* address the mass displacement of refugees, the challenges posed by forced migration, and the ways in which white-majority German culture interacts with non-Europeans. Both texts call attention to echoes of colonial history and the daily struggles faced by refugees in Germany and in Italy. Individuals occupy and navigate complex spatial locations differently depending on their social status, nationality, race, ethnicity, gender, and access to resources. Refugees' experiences are presented as varying articulations of claiming space, which tend to be met by efforts aimed at controlling, containing, and preventing such forms of spatial appropriation or disobedience. In addition, both works highlight the ways in which echoes of the colonial past can be discerned in contemporary politics. In *Gehen, ging, gegangen*, Richard, who is at first shockingly uninformed about current events and Germany's colonial legacy, starts as a result of his experiences to eagerly consume the news, peruse legal documents, and learn more about Germany's colonial past. His rigorous engagement with the history and politics of his own country leads him to identify structural similarities between colonial practices, National Socialism, and policies enacted by various (West) German and European institutions. *Widerfahrnis* similarly calls attention to exclusionary practices with respect to migrants and refugees, but here Reither is himself implicated in sharing a desire to curb the influx of newcomers and prevent them from entering Europe. Critics have accurately described Kirchhoff's novella as 'paternalistic' (Cordsen, 2018), but its approach also offers 'didactic potential' (Theele, 2018, p. 64). The reader might therefore interpret Reither's actions as emblematic of various containment strategies enacted by the EU, enabling criticism of the character's actions to serve as criticism of precisely such strategies. The encounter with the non-European Other, a female refugee, possibly from one of Europe's former colonies, symbolizes Europe's refusal to confront its colonial history, something that has been systematically repressed, erased, or whitewashed (El-Tayeb, 2011, pp. 8-14). Rather than accepting or working through this repressed past, Reither chooses to preserve the status quo.

The two texts thus construe mass displacement and colonial history as a particularly German but also European phenomenon and invite a reading that recognizes mass displacement and colonial history as interrelated, a subject taken up in the scholarly literature. Erpenbeck's novel is set in Berlin but also makes ample references to EU-wide policies. While Kirchhoff's novella is set predominantly in Italy, it must be read as a German experience, given its two German protagonists and the centrality of Italian travelogues within the German literary tradition. Literary and cultural theorists including Colpani and Ponzanesi (2016) and Gilroy (2016) insist that 'Europeans need to confront the effects of colonization and decolonization on the European space itself in order to better understand contemporary political struggles and move toward alternative modes of cohabitation in Europe' (Colpani and Ponzanesi, 2016, p. 6). These two works, by incorporating discussions of EU policy or shifting the setting to other parts of Europe, namely Italy, do just this, expanding the focus from a German perspective to a more broadly European one.

Responding to injustices and bringing about social and political change might seem an impossible task. Yet Erpenbeck's novel seems to encourage action, hospitality, and resistance. The German original, published in 2015, includes a call for donations, including information on where readers can contribute funds. Kirchhoff's novella, too, seems to propose that empathy, compassion, and critical self-reflection go a long way, not just when it comes to current conflicts and divisions within Europe but also with respect to personal happiness and self-fulfilment. The character of Reither might be unlikable, but a critical reading of his actions may promote 'cultural and ethical competence' (Theele, 2018, p. 64). Finally, both texts participate in a larger conversation that positions historical knowledge and the awareness of cultural difference as the key to a more inclusive future. According to Gilroy (2016):

> The political movements that have vowed to stop Europe's supposed Islamification and made a target out of immigrants, refugees, and sans-papiers are overwhelmingly populist in character. They are fueled by austerity, precariousness, anxiety, and fear, but they rely upon a deficit of historical information about Europe's colonial and imperial past ... Historical information is thus more important than ever, even, or perhaps especially, where it can promote the possibility of 'working through' the past. (pp. xiii-xiv)

One of the most important tasks in the years to come might well be to combat such 'managed ignorance' (p. xiv) – whether engineered by governments, political movements, or individual actors – and in doing so make this world a more hospitable place.

Bibliography

Ahmed, S. (2007) 'A Phenomenology of Whiteness', *Feminist Theory*, vol. 8, no. 2, pp. 149-168.

Bhambra, G. K. (2016) 'Whither Europe?', *Interventions*, vol. 18, no. 2, pp. 187-202.

Bhimji, F. (2016) 'Visibilities and the Politics of Space: Refugee Activism in Berlin', *Journal of Immigrant & Refugee Studies*, vol. 14, no. 4, pp. 432-450.

Biller, S. (2015) 'Gestrandet in der Warteschlaufe', *Neue Züricher Zeitung*, 10 October [Online]. Available at https://www.nzz.ch/feuilleton/buecher/gestrandet-in-der-warteschlaufe-1.18627304 (Accessed 31 May 2019).

Bock, J. and Macdonald. S. (2019) 'Making, Experiencing and Managing Difference in a Changing Germany', in Bock, J. and Macdonald, S. (eds) *Refugees Welcome? Difference and Diversity in a Changing Germany*, New York, Berghahn, pp. 1-38.

Chambers, I. (2008) *Mediterranean Crossings: The Politics of an Interrupted Modernity*, Durham, Duke University Press.

Cordsen, K. (2016) 'Keine gute Wahl. Deutscher Buchpreis für Bodo Kirchhoff', *BR.de*, 18 October [Online]. Available at https://www.br.de/radio/bayern2/sendungen/kulturwelt/deutscher-buchpreis-bodo-kirchhoff-kommentar-100.html (Accessed 31 May 2019).

Crawley, H. and Skleparis, D. (2018) 'Refugees, Migrants, Neither, Both: Categorical Fetishism and the Politics of Bounding in Europe's "Migration Crisis"', *Journal of Ethnic and Migration Studies*, vol. 44, no. 1, pp. 48-64.

De Genova, N. (ed) (2017) *The Borders of 'Europe': Autonomy of Migration, Tactics of Bordering*, Durham, Duke University Press.

———. (2016) 'The European Question: Migration, Race, and Postcoloniality in Europe', *Social Text*, vol. 34, no. 3, pp. 75-102.

De Genova, N., Garelli, G. and Tazzioli, M. (2018) 'Autonomy of Asylum? The Autonomy of Migration Undoing the Refugee Crisis Script', *South Atlantic Quarterly*, vol. 117, no. 2, pp. 239-65.

El-Tayeb, F. (2011) *European Others: Queering Ethnicity in Postnational Europe*, Minneapolis, University of Minnesota Press.

———. (2016) *Undeutsch. Die Konstruktion des Anderen in der postmigrantischen Gesellschaft*, Bielefeld, transcript.

Erpenbeck, J. (2015) *Gehen, Ging, Gegangen*. Munich, Knaus.

———. (2017) *Go, Went, Gone* (trans. S. Bernofsky), New York, New Directions Books.

Garelli, G. and Tazzioli, M. (2017) 'Choucha beyond the Camp', in de Genova, N. (ed) *The Borders of 'Europe': Autonomy of Migration, Tactics of Bordering*, Durham, Duke University Press, pp. 165-84.

Gilroy, P. (2016) 'Europe Otherwise', in Ponzanesi, S. and Colpani, G. (eds) *Postcolonial Transitions in Europe: Contexts, Practices and Politics*, London, Rowman & Littlefield International, pp. xi-xxv.

———. (2006) *Postcolonial Melancholia*. New York, Columbia University Press.

Hall, S. (1996) 'When Was the "Post-Colonial"? Thinking at the Limit', in Chambers, I. and Curti, L. (eds) *The Post-Colonial Question: Common Skies, Divided Horizons*, London, Routledge, pp. 242-60.

Harvey, D. (2012) *Rebel Cities: From the Right to the City to the Urban Revolution*, London, Verso.

Hermes, S. (2016) 'Grenzen der Repräsentation. Zur Inszenierung afrikanisch-europäischer Begegnungen in Jenny Erpenbecks Roman *Gehen, ging, gegangen*: Afrika schreiben/writing Africa', *Acta Germanica: German Studies in Africa*, vol. 44, no. 1, pp. 179-191.

Janzen, M. (2018) 'Berlin's International Literature Festival: Globalizing the Bildungsbürger', in Bauer, K. and Hosek, J. R. (eds) *Cultural Topographies of the New Berlin*, New York, Berghahn, pp. 272-93.

Kämmerlings, R. (2016) 'Bodo Kirchhoff im Interview: Der Deutsche Buchpreis als Erlösung', *Die Welt*, 18 October [Online]. Available at https://www.welt.de/kultur/literarischewelt/article158864331/Der-Preis-war-eine-unheimliche-Erloesung.html (Accessed 20 March 2018).

Kirchhoff, B. (2016) *Widerfahrnis*, Frankfurt, Frankfurter Verlagsanstalt.

Krekeler, E. (2016) 'Die Liebe und die Krise siegen über den Wahn', *Die Welt*, 17 October [Online]. Available at https://www.welt.de/kultur/literarischewelt/article158843254/Die-Liebe-und-die-Krise-siegen-ueber-den-Wahn.html (Accessed 31 May 2019).

Landry, O. (2015) '"Wir sind alle Oranienplatz!" Space for Refugees and Social Justice in Berlin', *Seminar: A Journal of Germanic Studies*, vol. 51, no. 4, pp. 398-413.

Leurs, K. and Ponzanesi, S. (2018) 'Connected Migrants: Encapsulation and Cosmopolitanization', *Popular Communication*, vol. 16, no. 1, pp. 4-20.

Ludewig, A. (2016) 'Jenny Erpenbecks Roman Gehen, Ging, Gegangen (2015). Eine zeitlose Odyssee und eine zeitspezifische unerhörte Begebenheit', in Hardtke, T., Kleine, J. and Payne, C. (eds) *Niemandsbuchter. und Schutzbefohlene: Flucht-Räume und Flüchtlingsfiguren in der deutschsprachigen Gegenwartsliteratur*, Göttingen, Vandenhoeck & Ruprecht, pp. 269-85.

Magenau, J. (2015) 'Ein Stückchen Acker in Ghana', *Süddeutsche Zeitung*, 30 August [Online]. Available at https://www.sueddeutsche.de/kultur/longlist-zum-deutschen-buchpreis-ein-stueckchen-acker-in-ghana-1.2627330 (Accessed 31 May 2019).

Mahler, S. and Pessar, P. (2001) 'Gendered Geographies of Power: Analyzing Gender Across Transnational Spaces', *Identities*, vol. 7, no. 4, pp. 441-59.

Massey, D. (2005). *For Space*, London, Sage.

McClintock, A. (1994) *Imperial Leather: Race, Gender and Sexuality in the Colonial Contest*, London, Routledge.

Moritz, R. (2016) 'Zwei fahren nach Sizilien, der Liebe entgegen', *Neue Züricher Zeitung*, 29 September [Online]. Available at https://www.nzz.ch/feuilleton/buecher/bodo-kirchhoffs-novelle-widerfahrnis-zwei-fahren-nach-sizilien-der-liebe-entgegen-ld.119284 (Accessed 31 May 2019).

Norwich, J. J. (2015) *Sicily: An Island at the Crossroads of History*, London, Random House.

Platthaus, A. (2016) 'Bodo Kirchhoffs "Widerfahrnis": Vier Tage eines neuen Lebens', *Frankfurter Allgemeine Zeitung*, 23 September [Online]. Available at www.faz.net/aktuell/feuilleton/buecher/rezensionen/rezension-zu-bodo-kirchhoffs-widerfahrnis-14432276.html (Accessed 20 March 2018).

Richter, D. (2009) *Der Süden: Geschichte einer Himmelsrichtung*, Berlin, Wagenbach.

Shafi, M. (2017) '"Nobody loves a refugee": The Lessons of Jenny Erpenbeck's Novel "Gehen, Ging, Gegangen"', *Gegenwartsliteratur*, vol. 16, pp. 185-208.

Steckenbiller, C. (2019) 'Futurity, Aging, and Personal Crises: Writing About Refugees in Jenny Erpenbeck's *Gehen, ging, gegangen* (2015) and Bodo Kirchhoff's *Widerfahrnis* (2016)', *German Quarterly*, vol. 92, no. 1, pp. 68-86.

Stoler, A. L. (2016) *Duress: Imperial Durabilities in Our Times*, Durham, Duke University Press.

Stone, B. (2017) 'Trauma, Postmemory, and Empathy: The Migrant Crisis and the German Past in Jenny Erpenbeck's *Gehen, Ging, Gegangen* [*Go, Went, Gone*]', *Humanities*, vol. 6, no. 4, 88, pp. 1-12.

'Ten Countries Host Half of World's Refugees' (2016), *Al Jazeera*, 3 October [Online]. Available at https://www.aljazeera.com/news/2016/10/ten-countries-host-world-refugees-report-161004042014076.html (Accessed 31 May 2019).

Theele, I. (2018) 'Vom Sturz in die Menschlichkeit. Bodo Kirchhoffs Novelle *Widerfahrnis*', *Der Deutschunterricht*, vol. 1, pp. 58-66.

'UNHCR Viewpoint: "Refugee" or "Migrant" – Which Is Right?' (2016), *UNHCR*, 11 July [Online]. Available at https://www.unhcr.org/news/latest/2016/7/55df0e556/unhcr-viewpoint-refugee-migrant-right.html (Accessed 26 June 2019).

Von Sternburg, J. (2016) 'Bodo Kirchhoff: "Widerfahrnis"', *Frankfurter Rundschau*, 31 August [Online]. Available at www.fr.de/kultur/literatur/shortlist-2016-bodo-kirchhoff-widerfahrnis-a-313065 (Accessed 20 March 2018).

'What Is a Refugee?' (2019), UNHCR [Online]. Available at https://www.unrefugees.org/refugee-facts/what-is-a-refugee/ (Accessed 26 June 2019).

'What is the Dublin Regulation?' (2015), openmigration [Online]. Available at https://openmigration.org/en/analyses/what-is-the-dublin-regulation/(Accessed 29 July 2019).

Teaching with Grief
An Exploration of Politics, Pain, and Power in *Monsieur Lazhar*

Hande Gürses

> 'We are all refugees from our childhoods. And so we turn, among other things, to stories. To write a story, to read a story, is to be a refugee from the state of refugees.'
> (Mohsin Hamid, *How to Get Filthy Rich in Rising Asia*)

On an ordinary day, on an ordinary school's ordinary courtyard, students play their ordinary games during recess. Simon, one of the pupils, rushes inside the building when his friend Alice reminds him that it is his turn to bring the milk into class on that particular day. Simon picks up the crate of milk and heads towards the classroom but stops short; through the glass panel of the classroom's door he sees the lifeless body of his teacher, Martine Lachance, hanging from the ceiling. In shock Simon drops the crate, the cartons split open, spilling milk on the floor. From that moment on, nothing is ordinary and, like the milk on the floor, the violence and unpredictability of life seeps into the cracks of even the most ordinary lives. The impact of the opening scene of *Monsieur Lazhar* does not derive from the tragic incident it depicts, but rather stems from the juxtaposition of the ordinary with the extraordinary. The image of the lifeless body of Martine Lachance is followed by the image of spilt milk on the floor. This opening scene sets the tone for the rest of the film as it powerfully conveys the ways in which the ordinary may be interrupted by the most unexpected turn of events. The film, while telling the story of an asylum seeker from Algeria, thus precludes a reading that is limited to a particular geography or identity but rather invites awareness of a common human ground from which pain, joy, and grief are shared.

Directed by Philippe Falardeau, *Monsieur Lazhar* is a 2011 French-Canadian film that tells the story of Bashir Lazhar, an Algerian asylum seeker who is trying to build a new life in Montréal. When a position teaching French opens up mid-semester at a local elementary school, Bashir applies for the job, appropriating his late wife's résumé as his own. The class to which he is assigned has been struck by tragedy: it was their teacher, Martine Lachance, who committed suicide by hanging herself in the classroom. Brought together under these traumatic circumstances, Bashir, a foreigner still awaiting asylum, with a tragic story of his own, and his students embark on an unanticipated journey of healing, a collective catharsis that will eventually provide an avenue for Bashir and for the students to regain a sense of belonging and self.

Monsieur Lazhar is adapted from Évelyne de la Chenelière's 2002 play *Bashir Lazhar*, a one-act solo performance. The heteroglossia that the film creates by introducing multiple characters allows for new and unexpected connections to be made. One such connection, between the main character, Bashir Lazhar, and his student Simon, based on their shared experiences of trauma and guilt, establishes an intriguing parallel between the displaced asylum seeker and his guilt-ridden student. Simon, as is revealed later in the film, had expressed his irritation with his late teacher Martine Lachance when she had kissed him while she was helping him with his studies. It is insinuated that this incident made public by Simon may have prompted Martine Lachance's suicide, which clearly resulted in Simon feeling guilty.

Bashir's feelings of guilt, on the other hand, stem from the death of his wife and two children, who were victims of an arson attack the day before they were scheduled to escape Algeria to join him in Canada. The parallel established in *Monsieur Lazhar* between Bashir and Simon through the shared feelings of guilt invites viewers to reconsider the power dynamics that exist within the classroom between teacher and student. It is through this reconsideration that the film suggests an analogy between the child and the asylum seeker. This essay will discuss how the film's use of visual and textual language prompts a reconsideration of power structures. By focusing on the power dynamics within the classroom, the essay will explore both the broader political implications of subverting power dynamics and the healing and liberating potential of teaching with vulnerability.

Bashir & Simon & Other Ghosts

The title of the play, *Bashir Lazhar*, underwent a name change when de la Chenelière's work was adapted for the big screen, becoming *Monsieur Lazhar* in Falardeau's film. This re-naming echoes an important aspect of the refugee experience by mimicking a migratory move along with a redefinition of identities. The experience of displacement strips the refugee of previously held titles and identities that were meaningful predominantly with respect to their social communities. One of the few determinants that the refugee might hold on to is their proper name. Once in a new country with a distinct culture and language, the refugee's name, while being the only familiar component of their identity, might end up being a source of alienation within the context of the new social community.

The play's title, *Bashir Lazhar*, captures the experience of displacement by presenting only a proper name, without any additional determinants. The title 'Monsieur Lazhar', on the other hand, indicates formality and context with the addition of the French form of address. The film title's omission of the given name has implications beyond being a merely aesthetic choice. Appearing on its own, the name Bashir Lazhar might not be immediately registered within a social context. As a form of address, the word 'monsieur' introduces Bashir Lazhar into the social structure as an active member. It allows Bashir Lazhar to be addressed in formal contexts, including his workplace and the courtroom. While the inclusion of the formal 'monsieur' hints that the undocumented asylum seeker is recognized as a member of society, it also adds distance and formality. Bashir Lazhar's interactions in Canada are limited to the official settings and formal contexts in which he is addressed as 'monsieur'; he does not have any intimate relationships in which he would be addressed simply by name. He has no close friendships, no family members who would call him by his name. There is the possibility of an exception later in the film when his colleague Claire, who shows a romantic interest in Bashir, invites him over for dinner. Claire insists they drop the formal French form of address 'vous' and adopt instead the informal 'tu'. In the ensuing scenes Bashir reverts to 'vous' by accident, constantly making his discomfort visible. His resistance towards using the informal 'tu' is indicative of a lack of intimacy. While Claire is trying to establish familiarity and a connection with her colleague, Bashir, aware of the absence of any real intimacy, prefers to keep a distance. This is also partly due to the fact that he is hiding a truth that would compromise his position at the school were it to become known.

The significance of the name is made evident in the first scene of the film where we encounter the protagonist. Following the teacher's suicide, Bashir decides to present himself at the director's office as a possible replacement for the remainder of the semester. As he introduces himself to the school's director, Madame Vaillancourt, Bashir is forced to deny multiple identities and claim many more. The director makes an immediate assumption regarding Bashir's profession when he first enters her office, believing him to be a journalist interested in the details of the suicide. Given the circumstances, the director's assumption is plausible. For Bashir, however, this marks the beginning of a process of multiple negations. Without letting Bashir explain, the director makes yet another assumption, asserting that he must be a parent of one of the students. Given the tragic event, we understand that there have been frequent visits from parents to the director's office. When she enquires, 'You are the father of...?', Bashir explains that he is 'not anyone's father'. The original French – 'je suis père de personne' – could alternatively be translated

'I am the father of no one'. The text of the play has a slightly different version: 'Non, je ne suis le parent d'aucun élève. Je ne suis pas un parent d'élève' (de la Chenelière, 2011, p. 16). The English translation would be 'No, I am not the parent of any student. I am not a parent of a student.' The double entendre is evident in both versions. Bashir's response is factually correct within the context in which it is uttered, but it also contains a poignant reference to the loss of his children and the redefinition of his identity as a father through this loss.

Bashir eventually manages to explain the reason for his visit: he introduces himself as a schoolteacher with nineteen years of experience at a school in Algeria. It is revealed later in the film that it was Bashir's late wife who was a schoolteacher, while Bashir was a former public servant who ran a restaurant, most likely because he had been forced to leave public service during the Algerian Civil War. In order to overcome bureaucratic hurdles, Bashir lies, saying that he is a Canadian permanent resident, a status that would allow him to legally work as a teacher. Bashir thus adopts the fake identity of a teacher and a permanent resident in order to be accepted into the social structure of his host country and to gain a legitimate status. The only identity that is actually accurate within the context of this exchange, his fatherhood, is defined by the absence of his children. As is the case for many forcibly displaced people, Bashir reinvents himself with these new identities to fill the void that is left in the wake of all the loss that he has experienced.

When the director finally addresses him, she confuses his first and family names, calling him 'Monsieur Bashir'. Familiar with the Biblical homonym 'Lazare', Madame Vaillancourt misidentifies 'Lazhar' as his first name, converting Bashir to his family name. When Bashir corrects her, stating that the correct form is Monsieur Lazhar, he baptizes himself with a new identity. The scene in which Bashir and the director first meet is more than an exchange of names, given the asymmetrical power relation between the two. The next scene in which Bashir is introduced involves the students and is governed by an entirely different set of power dynamics. As Bashir enters the classroom to meet his students, he introduces himself by writing his name – Bashir Lazhar – on the blackboard. Before he has a chance to utter it out loud, one of the students, Alice, raises her hand to ask about the origins of the name. Unlike the director, who was interested in other aspects of Bashir's identity, such as his relationship to the school's students and his profession, the students are more curious about his origins. Bashir's explanation of what his first and last name mean – Bashir means bearer of good news – is followed by a repartee among the students, who sarcastically start calling him 'Bashir Bazaar'. The spontaneous reaction of the students stands in contrast to the tense response by the director, who, while trying to hide her confusion, prevented Bashir from revealing who he really is. In his encounter with the students, however, Bashir is able to make known his Algerian origins. He is thus able to present an identity that does not need to be concealed with social attributes.

Having introduced himself, Bashir moves on to take attendance. We are presented with an extended scene in which the students say their names in turn and Bashir writes each down, making sure that he has the correct spelling. Bashir's meticulous recording of the names echoes the students' own interest in his name. The encounter between the students and Bashir is devoid of other distinctive categories of identity as it merely relies on the exchange of names. While Bashir is the teacher who occupies a position of power, in this initial encounter where names are exchanged, he appears to be on equal terms with his students. Visually this analogy is highlighted by the depiction of Bashir sitting at his desk with his name on the blackboard behind him. This image of him foregrounds a parallel between Bashir, a refugee who has been removed from other social relations that previously defined his identity, and the students: all have been reduced to their names alone. His posture at his desk and his notetaking make him barely distinguishable from the students. Without the protection that titles offer, Bashir exposes his own childlike vulnerability.

Figure 8.1. Bashir taking attendance.

Source: Still from *Monsieur Lazhar*.

The following scene draws a narrower parallel between Bashir and one specific student, Simon. Simon's name, which means 'listen', further emphasizes the connection between the two characters, since Simon is the one who needs to listen to the 'good news' brought by Bashir. Their initial encounter however, is marked by tension. While Bashir is busy taking attendance, Simon snaps a picture of him with his camera. Bashir asks Simon not to take his picture without permission, but his sudden angry outburst exceeds what would be expected of a teacher under the circumstances. Bashir's reaction may be explained by the fact that, as an asylum seeker, he fears any evidence that might compromise his position at the school. While photographs represent a potential threat to Bashir, they represent an emotional outlet for Simon, since the camera was a gift from the late Martine Lachance. While this initial encounter causes friction, photographs later become the common thread linking Simon and Bashir by virtue of their connection to death.

In *Camera Lucida* (1981) Roland Barthes establishes a link between photography and death, identifying death as photography's '*eidos*' (Barthes, 1981, p. 15). Drawing on this insight, literary scholars Eduardo Cadava and Paola Cortés-Rocca point out the ghostly constitution of the photograph, both for its subject and its object:

> What survives in a photograph, what returns in it, is therefore always also the survival of the dead, the appearance of a ghost or phantom. This is why, within the space of the photograph, the dead always are alive, and the alive always are dead without being dead. (Cadava and Cortés-Rocca, 2006, p. 23)

For both Bashir and Simon, the spectral presence emanating from the photographs of his family and of the late Martine Lachance, respectively, constitutes a source of ambiguity and uncertainty. Unable to leave the ghostly presence of the dead behind, they exist in a state of troubling limbo. It is in that state of displacement that Simon and Bashir find a common ground.

The photograph Simon took of his teacher, Martine Lachance, becomes an uncanny object following her suicide. The photograph shows Martine Lachance standing in front of her classroom desk, suggesting that Simon must have taken it without warning, just as he later would to Bashir. She is wearing a blue dress and is looking at the book in her hands; she has a calm and content expression. The complexity of Simon's connection to the photograph *qua* object becomes evident by his evolving reaction to it throughout the film. Immediately following her death, we see Simon trying to get rid of this photograph by offering it to Alice as a gift. Troubled by its uncanny quality, Simon wants to dispose of the ghostly presence that is embodied in the photograph. His attachment to the photograph, however, reappears later in the film. When a fellow student tries to steal the photograph, Simon retaliates by physically attacking him. Simon's changing attitude is also reflected in the photograph, which has been altered to show Martine Lachance with angel wings and a rope drawn above her head. This manipulation reflects Simon's struggle to make sense of his teacher's suicide. The angel wings reveal an attempt to alleviate the crude reality of death through the more serene image of an angel.

The photograph that he once wanted to get rid of becomes an object of emotional value for Simon once he manually alters it. The change can be explained

Figure 8.2. Photograph of Martine Lachance with hand-drawn wings and rope above her head.

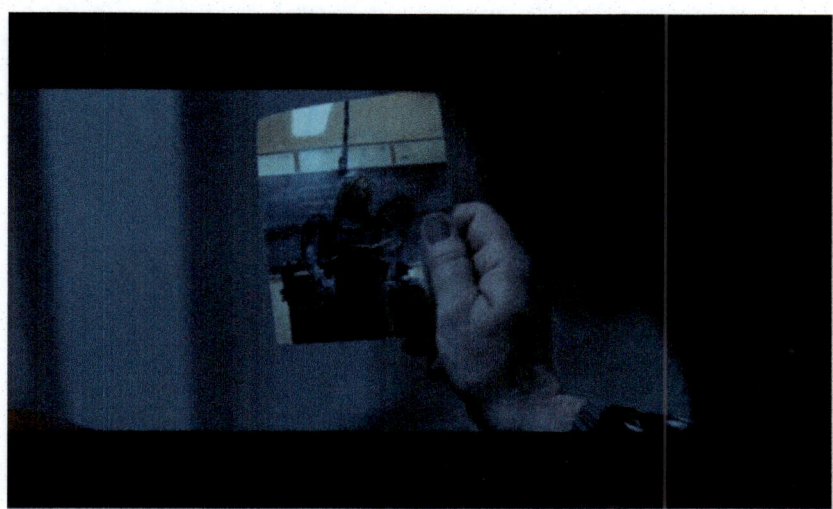

Source: Still from *Monsieur Lazhar*.

by the difference between the stillness of the photograph and the movement that is introduced by Simon's drawings. Simon's drawings subvert the uncertain space between life and death by introducing movement, life from the present. Barthes explains, '[T]he photograph's immobility is somehow the result of a perverse confusion between two concepts: the Real and the Live: by attesting that the object has been real, the photograph surreptitiously induces belief that it is alive' (Barthes, 1981, p. 79). The movement of Simon's pen aims to suspend the confusion that the image generates by invoking the spectral presence of the late Martine Lachance. It is by drawing on the photograph that Simon gains control over this ghostly presence that keeps haunting him.

Bashir's feelings of guilt are similarly communicated through photographs, reinforcing the parallel between Simon and Bashir. In the box sent from Algeria containing his late wife's belongings, Bashir finds a framed photograph of his wife and his two children. The subjects' pose and the size of the photograph are almost identical to that of Martine Lachance, only this time the subjects are looking straight at the camera, aware of the fact that they are being photographed. We can even see that Bashir's wife is smiling.

In this instance the immobility of the photograph is conveyed through the frame, which implies that the photograph was meant to occupy a specific place

Figure 8.3. Bashir looking at the framed photograph of his wife and children.

Source: Still from *Monsieur Lazhar*.

in a specific household. It denotes a stable life in which this photograph could be exhibited at a fixed location and would be relevant to the people looking at it. Referring to a time when all of the family members were alive, happy, and together, the photograph itself stands in stark contrast to Bashir's new reality marked by instability. As a refugee who has lost his home, family, and identities, Bashir is unsettled by the photograph's reference to a time of order and stability. In order to eliminate the discrepancy between his own experience at the present moment and the memories conveyed by the photograph, he removes the photograph from its frame, thereby allowing it to exist in a new reality where it will be exposed to the effects of passing time.

It is by removing the frame that Bashir allows the photograph to mimic an experience of displacement. Without the protection of the frame, the photograph becomes vulnerable, like Bashir, to the degrading effects of being uprooted. It now has creases from being folded and will most likely soon show other signs of wear and tear. It conveys the impact grief and displacement have on Bashir.

The significance of the stillness of photographs becomes even more evident when it is presented in juxtaposition with the moving images of film. In one elaborate scene, Falardeau depicts the students having their class photographs taken. This not only reinforces the analogy between the students and Bashir as subjects of authority, but it also confronts the viewer with a contrast between the stillness

Figure 8.4. Bashir holding the photograph, this time without the frame.

Source: Still from *Monsieur Lazhar*.

of photographs and the moving images of film. The scene opens with students' headshots being captured, with each student standing in front of the camera and looking straight ahead.

This sequence of headshots disrupts the dynamics of the film as it presents still images of the students posing in front of the camera. The film's viewers assume the position of the person behind the camera taking the photographs. By having the students look straight at the camera to create a moment of immobility, Falardeau transforms the moving images of the film into still photographs. Until this point, the viewer has occupied the role of passive observer. Once the actors in the film start looking into the camera, however, the viewer is no longer able to uphold the position of onlooker, becoming instead an active agent. By positioning the viewer behind the camera that takes the photographs, Falardeau invites the viewer to experience the uncanny and ghostly feelings that Simon and Bashir experienced while looking at the photographs. The viewers are implicated in the experience of the ghostly immobility produced by these still images. Comparing cinema and photography, Roland Barthes describes the difference between the impact of the screen and the frame as follows:

> Yet the cinema has a power which at first glance the Photograph does not have: the screen (as Bazin has remarked) is not a frame but a hideout; the man or woman who emerges from it continues living. (Barthes, 1981, p. 55)

Figure 8.5. Headshot of Simon.

Source: Still from *Monsieur Lazhar*.

While the moving image of cinema creates a sense of reality in which figures are not fixed but have a life beyond the scene, the photograph offers a more limited experience of life. The unsettling impact of the consecutive still images derives mainly from this shift from cinema to photography. The illusion of a continuous life is disrupted with the introduction of photography, with this disruption taking the viewer from the comforts of an illusion into the sphere of unsettling and raw reality. Thus death ceases to be a *theme* of the film and becomes a stark reality that confronts the viewer.

Following the sequence of individual shots, the viewer is presented with the class photograph. It invites the viewer back into the realm of moving images as the viewer is no longer behind the camera, but looking from a vantage point next to the photographer. The scene's two cameras are joined by a third, Simon's camera, with which he takes a photograph of the photographer.

The subversive visual impact of this scene derives from its self-reflexivity and is evocative of Diego Velázquez's painting *Las Meninas* (1656). The painting depicts several royal members of the Spanish court, with Velázquez working on a painting while looking directly at the viewer. Behind Velázquez is a mirror that reflects the king and queen as if they were standing behind the viewer of the Velázquez painting. This painting, the epitome of the politics of representation, illustrates the undermining of a singular sovereign power as the ultimate creator, instead display-

Figure 8.6. Class photo with Bashir.

Source: Still from *Monsieur Lazhar*.

ing the numerous facets and processes of representation. Rather than a singular artist who holds authorial power, there are multiple agents, including the viewer, who contribute to the production of meaning. In *Monsieur Lazhar* the figures who contribute to the creation of multiple representations and meanings include, in addition to the film's director Philippe Falardeau, the photographer taking the class photograph, Simon creating his own photograph of the experience, and the viewer observing these different creative processes.

Literary critics Marianne Hirsch and Leo Spitzer highlight the crucial ideological role school photographs play, especially during times of uncertainty:

> School photographs thus do more than certify a step in the trajectory of ideological incorporation. They also instantiate the institutional process that interpolates the individual into a group identity. As such, the instrument that creates them – the camera with which they are taken – both documents and participates in the process of socialization that integrates children into the dominant worldview. (Hirsch and Spitzer, 2014, p. 257)

While the school photograph promotes a group identity that brings Bashir and the students together, it also invites the viewer to assume a different position from that of a distant observer. The scene therefore operates in two opposing directions, very much like *Las Meninas*, blurring the line that separates the viewer from the scene that is being depicted. The upheaval that the students experience following the death of their teacher and the uncertainty that Bashir experiences as an asylum seeker are momentarily reversed by this group photograph, which allows them to find certainty and belonging. Hirsh and Spitzer suggest that 'the group sameness and the uniformity of pose desired in class photos – features consciously shaped during the photography's preliminary setup – tend to impede but not altogether eliminate the possibilities of subversion by individuals in the class. Subjects may try to fool around before or even while the photos are being taken' (Hirsch and Spitzer, 2014, p. 257). As this class photograph is being taken, the students decide that rather than uttering the conventional phrase 'cheese', they will say 'Bashir' in defiance of the school administration's authority and in celebration of their new teacher. Although the photograph does not capture this sound, the film's viewers are granted access to this auditory dimension. Cadava and Cortés-Rocca note that the photograph occupies a liminal space in which it 'exists between life and death, the past and the present, interiority and exteriority, body and image, and subject and image. It opens onto a future whose lineaments are not yet known, even if what can be known enables us to delineate the contours of the horizon and limit of death' (2006, p. 27). Viewers of *Monsieur Lazhar* are called to this threshold between the moving image and the stillness of the photographs by this unusual utterance. The photographic capture of the enunciation of Bashir's name, like the mirror reflection of the king and queen in *Las Meninas*, allows for a subversion of authorial power.

Stories of Pain, Pleasure, and Power

The analogy between Bashir and the students is also maintained through their embrace of the liberational power of language. Right at the beginning of the film a striking difference becomes apparent regarding how people refer to the teacher's death. At a meeting with the students and their parents, the school's director emphasizes the importance of expressing emotions yet refers to the suicide in a vague manner herself. She states that they 'will go through this together', without articulating what 'this' is. She announces that Julie, the school psychologist, will help them 'talk about what happened last Thursday'. Her persistent avoidance is contrasted with the raw and straightforward language used by the students. Seeing that one of the students in the class stares at a specific point on the ceiling, Bashir demands an explanation, to which another student offers a disturbingly candid response: 'That's where Martine hanged herself.' The school director's unwillingness to use unsettling words like 'death' or 'suicide' upholds the pretence of protecting the students from trauma, yet it is precisely her refusal that prevents the students from freely expressing their sorrow, pain, shock, and anger.

The students' desire to talk about the incident becomes more apparent when Alice, as part of her homework, writes an essay about the violence of Martine Lachance's death and her own struggle in making sense of this violence. Impressed by the force of her words, Bashir takes the essay to the director and asks for permission to distribute it to the other students in the school so that they can start a conversation about their shared experience. As someone suffering from trauma himself, Bashir identifies the potential impact of telling stories, implicitly recognizing that storytelling 'sutures the psychic wounds caused by … traumatic event[s]' (Kabir, 2014, p. 65). The school director, however, refuses his request and claims that the text is too violent. She is apparently intimidated by the subversive quality of Alice's text and the unpredictable outcome were it to reach a wider audience. For Bashir, in contrast, the text mirrors his own experience of displacement and insecurity. He appreciates it not only for its content, but also for the uncertain potential that it holds. Although the director claims to be in favour of dialogue and healing, she is apprehensive about any potential threats to the status quo and consents only to a conversation in which she is in control.

This attitude is also adopted by figures of authority in the courtroom where Bashir's asylum case is heard. The use of language within the legal context aims to minimize any unwanted dissemination of meaning and operates within a highly structured and predetermined process, so much so that in preparing Bashir for his appearance, his lawyer provides him with the specific words he needs to use in order to win the case. The spatial layout of the courtroom scene is reminiscent of a classroom, only in this instance Bashir is seated like a student and is subject to the authority of the judge. The scene opens with Bashir staring at signs on the wall which indicate that eating and using a phone are not allowed in the room. While the signs themselves are not unusual in such a context, they are significant in the film since they invite a semiotic reading of the scene. As Bashir tries to present his case – which ought to be as straightforward as the courtroom signs – he finds it increasingly difficult to communicate his life experience. The metaphorical signs he uses to narrate his experience do not deliver the message as simply as the signs on the wall deliver theirs.

The judge interrogating Bashir remains unconvinced by Bashir's assertion that he experienced threats to his life. Bashir concedes that there is no documentation proving that the death threats in Algeria were directed at him specifically – the legal criterion for being granted asylum – and the fire that killed his family is dismissed by the judge on the grounds that the entire building was set on fire. Noting that Bashir fled the country when it was his wife who had received threats, the judge demands to know why he 'abandoned' his family. The use of the word 'abandon' takes Bashir by surprise, as he never conceived of his departure for Canada in such terms, believing instead that he was coming in advance to prepare for the eventual arrival of his family. In shock, Bashir responds: 'I didn't abandon them.' The

Figure 8.7. Bashir looking at the signs inside the room where his asylum case is heard.

Source: Still from *Monsieur Lazhar*.

word 'abandon' thus conveys different meanings for the two people using the word whereas the signs on the wall convey a meaning that is unambiguous. The image of a phone crossed out – the signifier – refers to a signified that communicates a uniform meaning, whereas the verb 'to abandon' signifies different experiences for the judge and for Bashir. In other words, Bashir's experience might be described by others with the word 'abandon', whereas for Bashir his departure to Canada to prepare for the arrival of his family, was anything but abandoning.

In an attempt to understand what happened, the judge asks Bashir to tell him 'the facts', indicating his belief in a language that corresponds perfectly to experience. Bashir sets out the events in a factual manner, in chronological order. The narrative he is asked to share in this space of sovereign power requires that he not depart from the predetermined system of signification. Bashir is required to use certain words and expressions in order to provide legitimacy to his experience within the legal context. In the classroom on the other hand, there is an opportunity for a more creative narrative to emerge.

For both Bashir and his pupil Simon a narrative that promotes healing becomes possible, as they are able to create their own narratives. In Simon's case, the cathartic moment arrives as the result of a series of unpredictable occurrences. While Bashir is reading aloud from a text, Abdelmalek, another student in the class, is instead reading a magazine. Coming across an unfamiliar word, Abdelmalek asks what it means. While Bashir is annoyed by this interruption to the flow of his class, he responds and explains that the word 'défenestrer' means to be thrown out of the window. This digression allows for a moment of spontaneity that invites vulnerability. A conversation on death and suicide ensues, eventually culminating in Simon's outburst. Simon finally speaks up about his motives behind his behaviour towards Martine Lachance and enquires in tears, 'It's not my fault?' When Bashir hugs him, repeating that it is not his fault, it is both Simon and himself that he is consoling and reassuring.

The closing scene of the film presents a healing narrative for Bashir when he reads out his own fable, inspired by those of Jean de la Fontaine. The fable tells of the tragic death of Bashir's family through an allegorical story about butterflies. While both the fable and the narrative presented in court depict the same events, it is the fable that allows for an exploration of feelings regarding the nature of the experience and thus for the possibility of healing. Similar to the photographs, the fable provides a haunting experience of temporality in which it becomes impossible to distinguish between life and death, past and present, truth and fiction. And it is by moving into that liminal space that both the students and Bashir find comfort in the embrace of Simon and Bashir.

Conclusion

Monsieur Lazhar presents the tension between stability and movement in visual, linguistic, and political contexts through the figure of the refugee. The film explores the aesthetic, pedagogical, political, and psychological implications of the tension that emerges in the juxtaposition of the ambiguity and potential inherent in the experience of liminality with the sovereign determination to achieve certainty and stability. Both the figure of the child and the figure of the refugee, coming up against distinct forms of authority, are deprived of their agency and are required to restrict their narratives to predetermined forms. It is the integration of the figure of the refugee into that of the teacher that makes *Monsieur Lazhar* innovative. By bringing together these two figures, the film explores how the classroom may be a space for exploring uncertainty.

In departing from the curriculum, Bashir does not emphasize the teaching of facts but rather exhibits the stamina and courage needed to tread uncharted territory. As a refugee who has lost many of the attributes that previously constituted his identity, Bashir, with his students, discovers the potential held by storytelling. Like bodies that migrate and young children who grow, language has the potential to move in unpredictable ways, to defy authority, and to experience vulnerability. The traumas experienced by Bashir and his students make them open to change and to the possibility of change. As Shoshana Felman and Dori Laub explain, 'There is a parallel between this kind of teaching (in its reliance on the testimonial process) and psychoanalysis (in its reliance on the psychoanalytic process), insofar as both this teaching and psychoanalysis have, in fact, to *live through a crisis*. Both are called upon to be *performative*. ... Both this kind of teaching and psychoanalysis are interested ... in the capacity of their recipients to *transform themselves* in function of the newness of that information' (Felman and Laub, 1992, p. 53).

Monsieur Lazhar shows how, even under the most unusual circumstances, only teaching that transcends the straightforward transmission of knowledge can become a tool for the transformation of the individual. Bashir's experience of displacement translates itself into a willingness to explore the potential inherent in the displacement of meaning through language. As images, stories, words, and other forms of signification are allowed to go beyond the boundaries of stability, there develops a potential for meaning that flows in unpredictable ways. Bashir's experience of displacement and the loss of identities transforms itself into an infinite potential for new meanings.

Bibliography

Barthes, R. (1981) *Camera Lucida*, Toronto, Farrar, Straus and Giroux.
Brown, E. and Phu, T. (eds) (2014) *Feeling Photography*, Durham and London, Duke University Press.
Cadava, E. and Cortes-Rocca, P. (2006) 'Notes on Love and Photography', *October*, no. 116, pp. 3-34.
Caruth, C. (ed) (1995) *Trauma: Explorations in Memory*, Baltimore and London, The Johns Hopkins University Press.
———. (1996) *Unclaimed Experience: Trauma, Narrative and History*, Baltimore and London, The Johns Hopkins University Press.
De la Chenelière, E. (2011) *Bashir Lazhar*, Montréal, LEMÉAC.
Felman, S. (ed) (1980) *Literature and Psychoanalysis: The Question of Reading: Otherwise*, Baltimore and London, The Johns Hopkins University Press.
Felman, S. and Laub, D. (eds) (1992) *Testimony: Crises of Witnessing in Literature, Psychoanalysis, and History*, New York, Routledge.
Hamid, M. (2014) *How to Get Filthy Rich in Rising Asia*, New York, Riverhead Books.
Hirsch, M. and Spitzer, L. (2014) 'School Photos and Their After Lives', in Brown, E. and Phu, T. (eds) *Feeling Photography*, Durham and London, Duke University Press, pp. 252-272.
Kabir, A. J. (2014) 'Affect, Body, Place', in Beulens, G., Durrant, S. and Eaglestone, R. (eds) *The Future of Trauma Theory: Contemporary Literary and Cultural Criticism*, New York, Routledge, pp. 63-76.

Monsieur Lazhar (2012) Directed by Philippe Falardeau [Film]. Chicago, Music Box Films.

Nail, T. (2016) *Theory of the Border*, New York, Oxford University Press.

———. (2018) 'Political Centrality of the Migrant', in Karakoulaki, M., Southgate, L. and Steiner, J. (eds) *Critical Perspectives on Migration in the Twenty-First Century*, Bristol, E-International Relations Publishing, pp. 15-27.

Sedgwick, E. K. (2003) *Touching Feeling: Affect, Pedagogy, Performativity*, Durham and London, Duke University Press.

Sontag, S. (1977) *On Photography*, Toronto, Farrar, Straus and Giroux.

Looking

Calais's 'Jungle'
Refugees, Biopolitics, and the Arts of Resistance

Debarati Sanyal

Before their destruction by the French state, the informal camps of Calais, called 'the jungle' by its inhabitants (from the Farsi term jangal, for forest), stood in close proximity to the city, its port complex, and the Eurotunnel. These tents and shacks were the precarious dwellings of refugees from Syria, Afghanistan, and Iraq, but also from Eritrea, Sudan, Ethiopia, Libya, Somalia, Egypt, Chad, Pakistan, Bangladesh, Kurdistan, and Iran. The demolition of the jungle dispersed these refugees across France, in shelters, detention centres, and other encampments, such as the state-funded camp of Grande Synthe or makeshift camps in the streets of Paris. Yet many, including unaccompanied minors, are returning to Calais, since it remains the shortest clandestine route to Dover and the United Kingdom, where family and community ties, employment opportunities, including jobs on the black market, a familiar language, and until recently, a higher rate of asylum acceptance seem to promise more hospitable conditions.[1]

Since the closure of Sangatte refugee camp in 2002, several jungle camps have coalesced in Calais and been dismantled by the state. Before its destruction in October 2016, the 'new jungle camp', built on a former toxic waste dump in the outskirts

---

1   In 2015 France granted asylum to less than 22 per cent of its applicants. 'France: Country Report', Asylum Information Database (AIDA), last modified 24 February 2016, www.asylumineurope.org/reports/country/france/statistics. A note on terminology: technically, an asylum seeker becomes a refugee once s/he is granted asylum on the basis of a well-founded fear of persecution. The United Nations High Commissioner for Refugees (UNHCR) recommends distinguishing between refugees fleeing war or persecution and migrants who move for reasons not included in the legal definition of the refugee (see Adrian Edwards, 'UNHCR Viewpoint, "Refugee" or "Migrant" – Which is Right?', UNHCR: The UN Refugee Agency, 11 July 2016, www.unhcr.org/ 55df0e556.html). But if the broader definition of a refugee is a person in flight from wars and disasters, it should also encompass so-called migrants fleeing economic destitution, ecological devastation, and/or intolerable conditions in countries deemed 'safe', none of which can be separated from political factors. This essay refuses to parse differences between forms of persecution; it therefore designates those in flight as refugees, and as asylum seekers when such people focus their quest on asylum.

of Calais, was a fortified space of deterrence and detention, with routine administrative procedures of harassment, incarceration, deportation, and destruction. A large police presence, composed of the gendarmerie mobile and riot police (the CRS, or Compagnies Républicaines de Sécurité), was deployed to contain 'undesirables'. The path from the jungle to the ferry terminal was lined with surveillance cameras and walled by twenty-nine kilometres of chain-link fences and triple-coiled razor wire.

Figure 9.1. *(Top) Calais – the fence. (Bottom) Calais – the container camp.*

Source: Léopold Lambert, February 2006. By permission of Léopold Lambert.

The ground around the tunnel's entry was flooded to block access, while helicopters regularly patrolled the area. As Eric Fassin and Marie Adam observed, such fortifications sought to implement ghettoization as a form of securitarian governmentality, where the objective was the containment, deterrence, and displacement of refugees, since outright expulsion would violate their rights (Fassin and Adam, 2015). After the eviction of autumn 2016, the United Kingdom paid 2.7 million euros to build an 'anti-intrusion' concrete wall in order to secure trucks headed for the port.

The security measures taken in Calais's jungle have been couched in humanitarian rhetoric and enfolded into the logic of protection and care. Before the jungle's destruction, the state built a camp with shipping containers by day, while the police tear-gassed men, women, and children by night (Fig. 9.1, bottom). This seamless juxtaposition of compassion and repression illustrates humanitarianism's production of what Miriam Ticktin calls 'casualties of care' (Ticktin, 2011).[2] In spring 2016,

---

2 See, as well, Ticktin, M. (2016) 'Calais: Containment Politics in the "Jungle"', *Funambuliste*, vol. 5, pp. 28-33. The choice of shipping containers was symbolic at many levels. Not only did it

an estimated 3,500 occupants were initially evicted by order of Calais's prefecture, and state authorities razed the southern zone of the jungle.[3] France's then minister of the interior, Bernard Cazeneuve, euphemistically termed the destruction of the southern zone an evacuation, 'a humanitarian stage of intervention' (une étape humanitaire), conducted with 'respect for the dignity of persons', to protect them from 'indignity, the mud, and the cold' (l'indignité, la boue, et le froid) (French Ministry of the Interior, 2016). Video footage of this evacuation recorded in the name of dignity and salubrity showed bulldozers razing the makeshift shelters under heavy police protection, while tear gas and water guns were fired at protesting refugees. Several months later, Cazeneuve designated the destruction of the jungle and the eviction of close to 10,000 refugees as a 'humanitarian duty' conducted in the name of protection, shelter, and care, une mise à l'abri (Favre, 2016). Not only is such doublespeak symptomatic of hypocrisy, wherein humanitarian language masks securitarian violence, but it also constitutes the aporia of border security practices, which positions 'the "irregular" migrant as both a security threat and threatened life in need of saving' (Vaughan-Williams, 2015, p. 95).[4]

Calais's former jungles offer a reflection in miniature of the imbrication of repression and compassion in Europe's escalating border 'crisis'.[5] The European Union's controversial refugee deal with Turkey in spring 2016 legitimated what amounts to pushback operations or refoulement in the name of saving lives from the perils of human trafficking and Mediterranean crossings. Sending back 'all new irregular migrants' who land on Greek shores to Turkey, in exchange for Syrian asylum seekers held in Turkish detention centres, at the ratio of one illegitimate body to one deemed legitimate, is a measure that violates international laws banning collective expulsions (European Council, 2016). In response to the threat of mass migration, the EU has, in some sense, outsourced its borders to the external frontiers of Turkey, an increasingly authoritarian state that paradoxically may gain access to the EU as a result of a deal requiring its exteriority to it. Borders are not only materialized as walls or fences partitioning territories; they also function as

---

reduce (racialized) refugees to the status of packaged things, as Ticktin argues, but it also materialized the state's desire to ship them off.

3   Philippe Wanneson has provided an invaluable resource as to the shifting demographic data of the Calais bidonville (slum) and the state interventions within it with his blog Passeurs d'hospitalités (https://passeursdhospitalites.wordpress.com), launched in March 2012.

4   This essay is indebted to Vaughan-Williams's lucid overview of current theoretical approaches to the border.

5   For a trenchant critique of the rhetoric of 'crisis' in the context of refugees and migrations, see Heller, C., De Genova, N., Stierl, M., Tazzioli, M. and van Baar, H. (2016) 'Europe/Crisis: New Keywords of "the Crisis" in and of "Europe"', in De Genova, N. and Tazzioli, M. (eds) Europe at a Crossroads, no. 1 [Online]. Available at http://nearfuturesonline.org/europecrisis-new-keywords-of-crisis-in-and-of-europe-part-2/.

pre-emptive membranes that selectively filter and regulate the movement of bodies by means of new technologies. This dislocation of borders is similarly visible in France, where the Le Touquet Treaty (2003) moved the British border and immigration checkpoints to hexagonal France, and France moved its own borders to checkpoints in mainland Britain. The construction of the 'Great Wall of Calais' funded by the United Kingdom continued this politics of border expansion, as does the ongoing use of carbon dioxide probes, sniffer dogs, and X-ray scanners by British immigration officials to check trucks crossing the channel for human cargo.

The convergence of securitarian management and humanitarian care in the encampment of refugees has a long history. Even before World War II, Hannah Arendt observed that the exiled and stateless, as lives that simultaneously threaten and are threatened, were doomed to camps: 'Apparently, nobody wants to know that contemporary history has created a new kind of human being – the kind that are put into concentration camps by their foes and internment camps by their friends' (Arendt, 2007, p. 265). For several theorists of the refugee experience, contemporary border practices materialize a state of exception that finds its historical emblem in the Nazi camp. Sites as diverse as Guantánamo Bay, airport waiting areas, cross-border zones like Calais or Ceuta, and other spaces of detention, processing, or transit are addressed as zones of exception that strip the human subject of rights, as crucibles for the production of 'bare life' (Giorgio Agamben), 'human waste' (Zygmunt Bauman), 'undesirables' (Michel Agier) or the 'living dead' (Achille Mbembe).[6] Agamben's view of Auschwitz as a paradigm for such sites has been particularly influential. For him, there exists 'a perfectly real filiation' between 'internment camps, concentration camps, and extermination camps' (Agamben, 2000, pp. 15-28). The camp, as 'hidden paradigm of the political space of modernity', is 'the pure, absolute, and impassable biopolitical space'; its emblem is the refugee, naked life stripped of political and juridical value, existing only in its unconditional capacity to be killed by sovereign power (Agamben, 1998, p. 123).

This conception of the camp as a paradigm for political space, in which biopolitics, or the politics of life, turns into thanatopolitics, or the politics of death, and its corollary view of the refugee as 'bare life', can be seen to converge with humanitarian reason. As Didier Fassin has argued, in recent decades the political right to protection enshrined by asylum has been replaced by an appeal to moral sentiments such as compassion and empathy. Humanitarian governmentality, it follows, relies on the asymmetries of compassion rather than the reciprocities of justice and equal rights. When they are not dismissed as economic migrants or reviled as potential threats, asylum seekers are frequently positioned as 'speechless emissaries' whose

---

6   I do not mean to suggest that these thinkers approach subjects and spaces of abjection in identical terms. The enumeration merely highlights how such designations emphasize life's vulnerability, rather than resistance, to biopolitical capture.

wounds speak louder than the words they say (Malkki, 1996). In the words of a Bangladeshi refugee I interviewed in Paris, 'We have to show that we are victims, pure victims.' Humanitarian reason capitalizes on trauma, suffering, and victimhood, reducing refugees to supplicant bodies in need of intervention and protection. It yields an impoverished view of asylum seekers' subjectivity, narratives, and political energies, in a preemptive gesture of exclusion from equal citizenship.

I am suggesting that we currently witness a convergence between biopolitical theory and humanitarian reason, both of which pivot upon figuring the refugee as 'bare life' and as apolitical, speechless victim. As Calais's destruction illustrates, humanitarian reason is but the obverse of securitarian management, which views refugees as terrorist threats, sexual predators, mass invaders, or otherwise inassimilable others. Both humanitarian and securitarian approaches, however opposed in intention, envision the irregular migrant as a body to be saved, contained, policed, moved around, encamped, kept out, or expelled – in short, as a body to be managed.

A purely negative biopolitical analysis of bodies in motion – one that essentializes categories like 'bare life' or the subaltern, and totalizes modes of sovereignty – risks colluding with this imbrication of humanitarian protection and securitarian management in the policing of borders. As refugee encampments proliferate at the borders of Europe and elsewhere, excessive analytical focus on biopolitical capture and the poignant essentialism of 'bare life' may blind us to alternate subjectivations, potential 'lines of flight', and ephemeral solidarities within these 'borderscapes'.[7] We need heuristic tools that help unravel the strands of surveillance and control composing the contemporary border regime, while remaining attentive to modes of becoming, perseverance, even resistance within it.

While it is urgent that we think through the continuities between historical forms of detention and confinement as we seek to understand the operations of contemporary borders, paradigms from the past may not be supple enough to account for their violence, nor for how such violence is negotiated, eluded, or resisted. Instead of reducing the heterogeneity of contemporary camps to the singular paradigm of Auschwitz, despite evident differences between self-organized refuges, shantytowns, and other encampments at borders, but also humanitarian camps, open-air sites of detention, or closed offshore sites like Guantánamo, we

---

7   By 'biopolitical capture' I mean the subjugation of bodies and lives through technologies of control, in this case, through the border regime's dispositifs. I borrow 'lines of flight' from Gilles Deleuze and Félix Guattari, and my use of borderscape comes from Prem Kumar Rajaram and Carl Grundy-Warr, who 'use the concept "borderscapes" to emphasize the inherent contestability of the meaning of the border between belonging and nonbelonging ... zones of abjection are not without resistance': Rajaram, P. K. and Grundy-Warr, C. (eds) (2007) *Introduction to Borderscapes: Hidden Geographies and Politics at Territory's Edge*, Minneapolis, University of Minnesota Press, p. xxviii.

should envisage them in their diversity and adapt our conceptual frames accordingly. After all, even concentration camp survivor David Rousset, who coined the concept of 'the concentrationary universe' in postwar France, did not fix Buchenwald into a paradigm that infinitely repeats across time, nor did he essentialize history into the repetition of an identical catastrophe. Instead, the concentrationary (le concentrationnaire) circulated in the political culture of France and its colonies as a metaphor to illuminate new or ongoing forms of terror with partial or asymmetrical links to the Nazi past. Rather than assuming that sites of detention and containment are structured by an identical matrix and rehearse the biopolitical operations of the past, we need figures attuned to the mutations of form that power and resistance take over time.

This essay explores what nuance recent visual representations of Calais bring to the theorization of borderscapes as camps and to contemporary views of the refugee as 'bare life', as passive object of humanitarian intervention, and as active threat to be policed or pushed out. How do cultural forms such as cinema or photography frame the figure of the refugee and provide a symbolic platform for those denied the right to appearance and movement in traditional conceptions of the polis? The hospitality of visual form can offer 'small acts of repair' to the dehumanizing violence of border practices (Hirsch and Spitzer, 2016). Yet, perhaps more urgent than the gesture of symbolic reparation, or 'visual asylum', is art's capacity to give more complex accounts of the conditions and constraints of a refugee's politicization. Aesthetic forms open supple and reflexive frames for envisioning modes of capture and flight both past and present. Representations of borderscapes offer heuristic figures that remain on the move, thus conveying the lived itineraries and symbolic resources of those in flight. These figures give visible and audible form to the singularities of refugees' experience, sometimes by challenging normative conceptions of what it means to appear and to have a voice in traditional conceptions of the polis. In other words, experimental visual forms can reconfigure our understanding of what it means to see and be seen beyond the regime of visibility, recognition, and control we witness in borderscapes such as Calais.

In what follows, I suggest that *Qu'ils reposent en révolte*, a recent French documentary on Calais's encampments, challenges the border's securitarian logic, exposes its humanitarian conceits, and hosts alternate political subjectivations. My reading considers forms of resistance not only in the film's visual poetics but also in its subjects' testimonies and practices. These arts of resistance are not the exclusive province of cultural representation, for they are wielded by refugees seeking room for manoeuvre within the repressive apparatus of the contemporary border. Both the documentary and its subjects invoke disparate histories of racialized violence to render intelligible the operations of flight and capture in the jungle. This gesture decentres the paradigm of the Nazi camp and pries open its assumption of total biopolitical capture. I then turn to the dialectic of invisibility and visibility characterizing refugees' resistance to securitarian/humanitarian management and show how their resistance is supported by the visual frames of cinema and photography. Such arts of disappearance and appearance are political, in Jacques Rancière's understanding of the term, insofar as they disrupt the partition of bodies that governs a given regime of representation and rights.

Ecologies of Belonging, Memories of Violence: *Qu'ils reposent en révolte*

Qu'ils reposent en révolte: Des figures de guerre I is an experimental documentary by film director Sylvain George. From 2006 to 2009, when the French state last razed the jungle, the director filmed refugees in Calais in what was initially conceived as the first installment in a trilogy on migration and the global neoliberal order, with projected sequels in the encampments of Greece and the Spanish autonomous cities Ceuta and Melilla, in North Africa. George's films include *Les Éclats: Ma gueule, ma révolte, mon nom* (2011), also set in Calais; the poetic and experimental newsreel *Vers Madrid: The Burning Bright* (2012), on the Indignados protest movement in Madrid's Puerta del Sol; and, most recently, *Paris est une fête: un film en 18 vagues* (2017), a cinematic poem that juxtaposes the itinerary of an unaccompanied foreign minor in Paris under the state of emergency with the waves of social movements that followed the 2015 terrorist attacks. A genre-defying thinker, poet, and filmmaker with a strong background in philosophy, political theory, and activism, Sylvain George is committed to framing migrants and refugees, neither through the victimology of trauma nor the asymmetries of humanitarianism, but through the lens of politics: 'The migrants are not victims but people, they are political subjects. ... Men and women who fight and cannot resolve themselves to passively accept the violence of the State. They fight with their own strength and resources, and draw and promote at the same time, different visions of the world, as real, as necessary.' He later adds, 'I see them as political subjects who, for reasons of their own and that I find legitimate, decide to trace their line of flight' (George, n.d.).

George's meditation on borders and lines of flight explicitly gestures to the work of Walter Benjamin, himself a refugee who committed suicide at the Spanish border while fleeing Occupied France. (George wrote a master's thesis on Benjamin's concept of allegory, a telling choice for his practice as a documentary filmmaker who moves back and forth between archive and poesis.) As we shall see, his film's visual atmospherics channel Benjamin's poles of melancholic contemplation and insurrectional charge, while specific sequences invoke the philosopher's ruminations on memory, allegory, the trace, and the archive. *Qu'ils reposent en révolte* (May they rest in revolt) also borrows its title from a postwar poem by Henri Michaux that celebrates the posthumous remembrance of rebellion: the memory of s/he who rests in revolt remains alive, 'In what suffers, in what seeps/In what seeks and does not find ... In one who harbors fever within/Who cares not a whit about walls' (Michaux, 1972, pp. 104-105).[8] Filmed in elegiac black and white, George's film is similarly an ode to the memory of transient, invisible warriors, an archive of precarious yet uncontainable life.

The formal experimentations in *Qu'ils reposent en révolte* – including techniques of over- and underexposure, mid- to low-angle shots of people's faces, jump cuts, and fade-outs – create a singular visual poetics of migration that is at once meditative and incendiary. Stretching across two and a half hours of viewing time, the film follows none of the traditional conventions of documentary narrative. No voiceover organizes the progression, nor do we hear George speak. Instead, the camera meanders through various Calaisian sites: the public park, the seafront, the water pump at the riverbank where refugees wash, the town centre with its monumental belfry, the industrial port, the encampments, a soup kitchen, a medical station. We encounter refugees who take a moment to share a piece of their story – where they are from, why they flee, who they left behind, how they feel. In sharp contrast to the partition of spaces and bodies orchestrated by the disciplinary viewpoint of state authorities, George's cinematic gaze is deeply immersed in the perspective of its subjects, in shots taken from unexpected angles and mobile perspectives: a divergence firmly established in the documentary's opening sequence, unfolding in a manicured public park in Calais under heavy police surveillance. Refugees are hunted down, rounded up, and taken away in vans, as George's camera traverses the park's fences, bushes, and walls with deliberate fluidity. The next sequence opens in the same lush setting, with the camera tilted upward and filming leafy treetops in a slow, vertiginous rotation as we hear the strains of a song. The perspective descends to three young refugees singing and clapping. Over several minutes, we witness close-ups of each face and its flicker of emotions – nostalgia, shyness, pleasure. The camera cuts to a tree's foliage whispering in the breeze, then returns to the men singing against the leafy backdrop, then finally rests its upward-tilted gaze on one of the youths as he sings about Ethiopia, his own gaze raised toward an undisclosed point on the horizon (Fig. 9.2).

Rather than a fixed, frontal close-up of the refugees' faces, the spectator witnesses and participates in an oblique relay of gazes. George's predilection for low- to mid-angle shots tilts our own gaze at an angle so that we are not looking at refugees, but rather toward them. This visual movement toward the other conveys an ethos of proximity rather than capture, a solidarity that remains mindful of the difference between the camera's unrestricted movement and the restrictions of those beheld, even as it conveys the refugees' flight from home toward an 'elsewhere'. All the while, the oblique approach of the low- to mid-angle shot resists

---

8   Note that Sylvain George translates the singular form of Michaux's title into a plural, collective subject of rebellion.

Figure 9.2. *Song of Ethiopia.*

Source: Still from *Qu'ils reposent en révolte: Des figure de guerres I*.

the camera's potentiality as a technology of capture and leaves open the possibility of escape from the cinematic frame: after the song, the men duck away from the camera to attempt their clandestine crossing, throwing parting words over their shoulders: 'Thank you, now, we are ready for loss!'

The environment that emerges from George's cinematic apparatus is a palimpsest of different time scales: long close-ups of rock formations gesture toward geological time; the ebb and flow of ocean tides evoke marine cycles; long shots of trees covered in foliage, then barren, then laden with snow convey the cycle of seasons. The Judeo-Christian frame is conjured in the opening shot of Mount Sinai and the references to Exodus interspersed throughout the film. Our own time of the Anthropocene and of global capital is visible in shots of giant illuminated ferries crossing the channel and audible in the soundtrack's ever-present rumble of trucks carrying goods across the border. The camera limns this temporal superimposition with a lyricism that gestures toward figuration without ever settling into anthropocentric correspondence.

Of course, there are resonances between Calais's bodies in exile and the shifting environment of living and nonliving things registered by the film: sea foam buffeted by the winds trembles on the beach; a feather briefly rests on its ethereal embankment, the trace of its quill facing erasure by the tide (Fig. 9.3). In a metallic sky, a cloud in the shape of a bird is followed by a seagull's flight. Yet these images are not placed in an anthropomorphic logic of reflection where the natural world affirms or negates the human experience of migration. Rather, the camera weaves multiple elements of Calais's borderscape into an ever-shifting tapestry in which living organisms, atmospheric phenomena, the elements, and inanimate things are in constant, nonhierarchical interaction (as in the echoes between whispering foliage and a refugee's song). In this ecology, no body or thing is out of place. To cite Sylvain George, 'Patches of ice, insects, spiders, stone statue with eyes gnawed by time, a can of cola, a sunset radiating, bird feathers, the belfry of the town center of Calais, immigrants and onlookers, police: all are in close communication with each other as an environment' (Kuener, n.d.).[9]

Figure 9.3. *Feather on sea foam.*

Source: Still from *Qu'ils reposent en révolte* (00.19.00).

Even as the camera conjures this ecology of belonging and its multiple points of communication, however, the montage deliberately produces effects of irony and counterpoint that re-inject divisive historical forces into the borderscape. The film ends with the destruction of this iteration of the jungle in 2009 under Eric

---

9   George situates his cinematic practice and its ethos of multiplicity within Deleuze's concept of immanence: 'On this plane of immanence, categories and hierarchies no longer apply, they yield to intensities produced by the shock of encounters, or the contemplation of the event. An encounter, as infinite as it might be, is an event, and for those who try to look at it, life is a permanent encounter.' See George, S. (2014) 'Ne pas savoir d'où cela vient, où cela va', *Débordements*, 6 November [Online]. Available at www.debordements.fr/spip.php?article306.

Besson, who at the time held the controversial, short-lived position of 'minister of immigration, integration, national identity and co-development' (Ministre de l'immigration, l'intégration, l'identité nationale et le développement solidaire). The title disclosed the state's assumption of tensions between these categories, which were amalgamated into a single office, while couching the securitarian regulation of labor flows from the global south in the humanitarian rhetoric of 'development in solidarity'.[10] *Qu'ils reposent en révolte* shows us Besson, like Cazeneuve this year, qualifying the camp's destruction as a humanitarian measure that protects migrants from human traffickers and spells 'the end of the law of the jungle' (la fin de la loi de la jungle). We watch tents crushed by bulldozers, the police clash with refugees and activists, unaccompanied minors lined up for deportation, unwanted bodies forcibly pushed out. In the aftermath of this eviction, the camera contemplates the deserted jungle's wreckage, pausing on a sign that reads 'hunting prohibited', a scrap of paper that bears the words 'forget fingerprints in other states and give us asylum in France, but not such asylum as it is'. We see the remnants of tents in the bulldozers' wake, precarious dwellings built out of the debris of global capital and its false promises: a piece of cardboard advertising social lodging, a torn poster exhorting the joys of thrift ('Je me simplifie la vie, je fais des economies'), a canvas bag sporting an Air France logo, the packaging from a Goodyear tyre. The camera lingers on a shoe half buried in the sand and crawling with bugs (Fig. 9.4).

The intensity of George's cinematic gaze on the trace, the remnant, the afterlife of things, recalls Benjamin's figure of the nineteenth-century rag-picker who picks up what the city discards and commits it to memory, a figure crucial to postwar reflections on mass disappearance.[11] It is also reminiscent of the concentrationary aesthetic developed by poet and Mauthausen camp survivor Jean Cayrol, who authored the screenplay for Alain Resnais's classic documentary on Nazi deportation, *Night and Fog* (1955). This concentrationary or Lazarean aesthetic was the correlative of Rousset's concentrationary universe I evoked earlier; its inspiration was the figure of the survivor, likened to Lazarus arisen from the dead. The Lazarean project resurrected the remnant and committed the anonymous to memory, with the aim to 'restore life, so that a shoe lost in a garbage can may be part of our legacy. The concentrationary taught me to leave nothing aside. Man lives on in his remains' (Cayrol, 1982, p. 110). *Qu'ils reposent en révolte* similarly frames a visual archive of ghostly presences still palpable in the material traces left behind.

---

10   For an incisive critique of this office, see Thomas, D. (2013) *Africa and France: Postcolonial Cultures, Migration, and Racism*, Bloomington, Indiana University Press, pp. 65-70.

11   See, for instance, Patrick Modiano's narrative pursuits of the disappeared in postwar Paris (for example, in his book *Dora Bruder*), frequently figured in relation to the Baudelairean poet as visionary and chiffonier.

Figure 9.4. Shoe half buried in the sand.

Source: Still from *Qu'ils reposent en révolte* (2.23.08).

Yet if the testimonial poetics of Calais's camp in this documentary bear traces of the Nazi camps, other histories of detention and racialized violence are conjured and coalesce with this memory, forming a palimpsest, a 'coexistence of sheets of past' within the cinematic image (Deleuze, 1989, p. 122). In one sequence, a young man recounts his chaotic itinerary from Turkey while striding down railroad tracks flanked by barbed-wire fences, as the camera turns to follow a seagull's unfettered flight and we hear its cries. The train tracks and barbed wire recall iconic scenes, from Resnais to Claude Lanzmann and beyond, of train journeys leading to concentration and death camps. The upward tilted camera hurtles past a silhouette splayed on the barbed wire above the tracks, clothing left behind by a refugee who was probably caught in its spikes (Fig. 9.5). This fleeting evocation of a body hanging off a fence conjures visual memories of detainees electrocuted in Nazi camps, yet the dangling shape simultaneously evokes the 'strange fruit' of American lynching – a history acoustically fleshed out on the soundtrack by free-jazz pioneer Archie Shepp that George had chosen for a previous version of the documentary.[12] But the absence of an actual body on Calais's fence – at once a reminder of the differences

---

12   Archie Shepp's 'Rufus (Swung, His Face At Last To The Wind, Then His Neck Snapped)' comes to mind. Sylvain George refers to the various objects left behind by the migrants of Calais's jungle as 'strange fruit' and mentions the importance of Archie Shepp's music for his film (conversation with the director).

between these regimes of racialized terror and a trace of their allegorical continuity – twists this image of biopolitical capture into a figure of flight.

Figure 9.5. Clothing on barbed wire fence.

Source: Still from *Qu'ils reposent en révolte* (00.21.58).

Other scenes of refugees bearing witness to their own dehumanization similarly echo testimonies of Nazi camp survivors, while gesturing toward the legacies of colonialism and slavery. These accounts of dehumanization are all the more haunting for their emergence from within the city and port of Calais, signaling the extent to which spaces of extremity that the European postwar imaginary primarily associated with the Third Reich are folded into the everyday life of a Western (neo)liberal democracy. A refugee conveys this abjection within the polis in piercing terms: 'I give my life to cross this storm, the desert, the sea, ok? But I came in Europe. I didn't lose my life in the Mediterranean Sea and the Sahara Desert. I lose my life here, the city ... it's a matter of time.' Another stark testimony to Calais as a death-world within the city emerges after a long tracking shot of graffiti that depicts scenes of war and destruction. A faceless voice describes the refugee's condition as the suspended animation of a living death: 'Comme ci comme ça, fifty-fifty, so-so, not dying, not living, I exist, I no exist, in between the tombs in between, not human being, not animal, in between.' We do not see the man's face, only his gesturing hand, which signals this indescribable in-betweenness, or indistinction, between life and death, humanity and animality, while cheerless laughter punctuates his words.

These accounts of existential spectrality, of flickering between life and death, man and beast, make it tempting to read the exiled in Calais through a purely negative paradigm of biopolitics turned zoopolitics, exercised on bare life as sheer animality. Yet even if such utterances attest to the grim precarity of a refugee's condition, their expression as testimony decisively refutes the analogy between the refugee and 'bare life', drawn by Agamben and theorists in his wake, who view the asylum seeker as an avatar of the Muselmann, or detainee at the threshold of extinction in Auschwitz.[13] It is one thing to articulate the conditions of 'bare life', such as the slippage from human to inhuman, or the unstable threshold between existence and non-existence. It is quite another to embody this condition. There is an abyss between being the Muselmann, who for Auschwitz survivor Primo Levi embodied abjection beyond speech, and expressing this condition of abjection.

If contemporary refugee testimonies reverberate with those from the Nazi camps, they simultaneously and explicitly evoke other legacies of dehumanization, in particular those of colonialism and slavery: the evocation of abject spaces nested within the polis recall Frantz Fanon's colonial city, 'a compartmentalized world, a world divided in two ... inhabited by different species' (2004, p. 5). Further, if we consider that 'the plantation is one of the bellies of the world', the afterlife of slavery, as necropolitics or 'the subjugation of life to the power of death', continues to shape contemporary zones inhabited by 'the living dead' (Glissant, 1997, p. 40; Mbembe, 2003, p. 40). The racialized histories of terror and dehumanization brought to bear on the so-called 'refugee crisis' are inextricably entwined and therefore irreducible to the Eurocentric prism of the Nazi camp, which itself, as Aimé Césaire, Fanon, and Arendt have taught us, is not a unique locus of biopolitics but requires historical rethinking in relation to sites such as the plantation and the colony.

Calais's jungle may be designated as a camp or theorized as a state of exception that produces bare life, but *Qu'ils reposent en révolte* pictures it as an unstable zone of traversal between political and 'bare' life, biopower and necropolitics, resistance and abjection, city and camp. It is a place where bodies, in all their clandestine 'out of placeness', nevertheless create, construct, and persevere in their attempt to survive, remain in place or stay on the move. These are 'political subjects' who draw from the knotted symbolic resources of the past in their resistance to the contemporary border's regime of surveillance and control.

---

13   For example, David Farrier recognizes the perils of likening asylum detention to the extermination camp, but nevertheless considers such parallels worth pursuing, insofar as both the asylum seeker and the Muselmann are 'exemplary in incarnating the point in which the human slides into the inhuman' (65); 'biopower and necropower ... converge in both the asylum seeker and the Muselmänner' (65) so that 'both asylum seeker and Muselmann embody a form of limit situation, analogous to the state of exception' (66). Farrier, D. (2011) *Postcolonial Asylum: Seeking Sanctuary Before the Law*, Liverpool, Liverpool University Press.

Bodily Arts of Resistance

My reading has sought to illuminate how *Qu'ils reposent en révolte*, in both its form and contents, resists the state's partitioning of space, time, and bodies in Calais's jungle. The visual allusions to slavery, colonialism, and the Final Solution track continuities between the past and the present while preserving the particularity of Calais's borderscape and challenging the refugee's figuration as mute 'bare life'. If the film may be understood as an art of resistance – resistance to the surveillance gaze, to state disciplinary technologies, to biopolitical capture – in a similar vein, the refugees it documents practice their own arts of resistance, both in their testimonies and upon their bodies. The most powerful – and disturbing – illustration of bodily resistance is the erasure of fingerprints. For migrants within the Eurozone, fingerprint mutilation by means of razors, fire, or acid is an attempt to escape the reach of Eurodac, the database that collects and manages the biometric data of asylum seekers and illegal entrants into the European Union. As one technological arm of the Dublin regulation, requiring that refugees lodge an asylum claim in the first EU country they enter (often Italy or Greece), the Eurodac database ensures that migrants who cross additional borders after being fingerprinted are returned to the previous country.[14] Destroying their skin, as they would their papers, the subjects of these passages in George's film paradoxically reveal themselves becoming unclassifiable, illegible, even invisible.

In the first of two sequences on fingerprint mutilation, we witness anonymous hands brandishing a plastic razor and applying its blade onto finger pads in a swift curving motion that shaves off slivers of skin (Fig. 9.6). A young man's face suddenly surges into the frame. With blazing eyes and a bitter twist to his lips, Temesghen, from Eritrea, exclaims (Fig. 9.7):

> Survive! We have to survive in Europe. This is virus, HIV virus you know, this is virus in Europe [brandishing his hand]. If it was possible to cut this one and throw it and bring another hand, I was doing that. But it is not possible. Just burning my hands. I don't know what happens to my hand. They are making us slaves, you know, slaves of [their] own country, by this fingerprint. They destroy our life. We can't go. We can't change our life [the sound is muted, his head turns in slow motion, face drawn in a grimace of disgust].

---

14   Databases in Europe's information system that form the 'digital border' also include the Schengen Information System (SIS), storing information on visas in order to flag illegal immigrants as they arrive in the Schengen Area (the Schengen Agreement of 1985 abolished internal border controls between its signatories and instituted a common visa policy; the Schengen Area now includes 26 countries). Other databases regulating movement within the EU are False and Authentic Documents Online and the Visa Information System.

Figure 9.6. Fingerprint mutilation by razor.

Source: Still from *Qu'ils reposent en révolte* (00.40.00).

Figure 9.7. Temesghen, 'They are making us slaves'.

Source: Still from *Qu'ils reposent en révolte* (00.42.48).

The mute slow motion and fade to black on which this scene concludes is visually reminiscent of Benjamin's concept of history as 'petrified unrest', time sunk into rigor mortis, eternal movement that knows no development. It is the stalled time of border encampments. Yet far from assuming the position of supplicant victimhood assigned by humanitarian reason, Temesghen embodies the rebellion celebrated in the documentary's title. He voices the rumble of *rogne*, the 'cheerless humor of the rebel' that Walter Benjamin ascribed to the stalled rage of poets and revolutionaries.[15]

Temesghen's designation of his own dark hands as 'HIV virus ... in Europe' is an accurate ventriloquism of contemporary rhetoric on the migrant as figurative and literal contagion; it reflects xenophobic discourses in Europe and the United States that dehumanize irregular migrants through the rhetoric of swarms, infections, vermin, plagues. The virus has a long history as a figure for the Western state's contamination by various racialized others deemed inimical to its values: a figure in anti-Semitic rhetoric during World War II, designating the Jewish population as an oriental plague that migrates across the oceans to infect Europe, it has re-emerged in current discourses as fundamentalist Islam's contagion, a primary vector of which is the viral diffusion of internet jihadi propaganda sites. The contagion evoked both then and now is not simply signifying the contamination of a body politic by foreign values. It is quite literal, as we see in the medicalization of borders and fear mongering about 'irregular' immigration as an infectious threat. Temesghen powerfully conveys how the border defending 'Fortress Europe' functions like an immune system, both in the epidemiological and symbolic senses.[16] Framed by George's cinematographic poetics, Temesghen's analysis illuminates and resists the new technologies of information management and topographies of surveillance that unfurl the tentacular reach of what Roberto Esposito has termed the 'immunitary dispositif' of contemporary societies of control. In Esposito's words:

> This immunitary *dispositif* is ... the coagulating point, both real and symbolic, of contemporary existence. ... The fact that the growing flows of immigrants are thought (entirely erroneously) to be one of the worst dangers for our societies also suggests how central the immunitary question is becoming. Everywhere we look, new walls, new blockades, and new dividing lines are erected against

---

15 That is to say, Charles Baudelaire and Louis-Auguste Blanqui. Benjamin, W. (1999) *Arcades Project* (trans. H. Eiland and K. McLaughlin), Cambridge, MA, Harvard University Press, pp. 329, 332.
16 'Fortress Europe', in its post-Second World War understanding, and specifically in the aftermath of the Schengen Agreement, designates the system of patrols, detention, and regulations in place to defend Europe's external borders against migrants and refugees. In common parlance, it describes the hardening of European policies and attitudes against immigration.

> something that threatens, or at least seems to, our biological, social, and environmental identity. It is as if that fear of being even accidentally grazed has been made worse, that fear that Elias Canetti located at the origin of our modernity in a perverse short circuit between touch (tatto), contact (contatto), and contagion (contagio). The risk of contamination immediately liquidates contact, relationality, and being in common. ... What is important is inhibiting, preventing, and fighting the spread of contagion wherever it presents itself, *using whatever means necessary*. (Esposito, 2013, pp. 59-60, my italics)

Temesghen's response to these 'new walls, new blockades, and new dividing lines', both material and digital, is self-mutilation as an enactment of 'the right to disappear'.[17] For the allusion to his hands as 'HIV ... in Europe' also suggests that the unique self that is imprinted on these fingers, attached to these hands, is itself the virus requiring eradication. An instrument of touch and contact that short-circuits into a vector of contagion, this hand that the young man would cut off and throw away if he could, must be disfigured beyond recognition. The destruction of a 'self' in its official biopolitical inscription, as digital marker of identification, is the price of survival and flight toward another becoming. As a challenge to the border's immunitary paradigm with its practices of detection, displacement, and expulsion, Temesghen invokes an autoimmune crisis, in the form of severing one's hand or cutting away fingerprints. The fantasy of self-amputation and the practice of erasing fingerprints are a subversive mimicry of state violence, where the will to circulate confronts the state's blockade, in turn 'using whatever means necessary'.

The production of illegibility by means of razors, fire, sandpaper, or battery acid is a political tactic devised in resistance to the biopolitical dispositif that manages bodies and polices frontiers. As we see in Calais, these frontiers are increasingly virtual even as, paradoxically, they act upon and intrude on the human body's biology itself: consider the carbon dioxide probes or heartbeat detectors used to determine human cargo on trucks. The body becomes a zone recorded, mapped, and traversed by technologies of management and governance. For Esposito, the human body's penetration by technologies has taken unprecedented proportions:

> The world, in all its components – natural and artificial, material and electronic, chemical and telematics – ... penetrates us in a form that eliminates the separation between inside and outside, front and back, surface and depth: *no longer content merely to besiege us from the outside, technique has now taken up residence in our very limbs*. (Esposito, 2011, p. 147, my italics)

---

17 'The right to disappear' is Maurice Blanchot's formulation. Blanchot, M. (1987) 'Michel Foucault as I Imagine Him', in *Foucault/Blanchot* (trans. J. Mehlman), New York, MIT Press, pp. 61-110.

If technique has 'taken up residence in our very limbs', most visibly in biometric controls, resistance must alter those same limbs. While Temesghen rages against the border's immunitary dispositif, the camera cuts to his companion, who calmly, pedagogically, explains that the mutilation of fingerprints is a technique crafted in resistance to the techniques implemented by the European Union to restrict migrants' mobility: 'Because, you know, all European have their system for circularization of our fingerprint in order to know where you arrive and where you will go. And where the European nations have their techniques, we have our techniques to be hide our fingerprints.' A disposable razor and a red-hot screw are invoked as weapons that mirror the EU surveillance databases and their transnational reach. As incommensurable as these techniques may be, the claim underscores the impossibility of reducing refugees to abjection or bare life; they must be recognized as resourceful subjects struggling to affirm their right of mobility in order to 'change their future', as Temesghen puts it.[18] The make-do tactics documented by these cinematic scenes show refugees as political beings who, in George's words (evoked earlier), 'fight with their own resources and draw different visions of the world'. Their practices or techniques, exercised to transform their own bodies into unreadable hieroglyphs, offer the fleeting glimpse of an affirmative biopolitics in which the power over life wielded by border controls cedes to the power of life to evade them. A vitalist view of the priority of the irregular migrant's movement glimmers through the biopolitical paradigm of total capture.

As the film shows, the symbolic touchstone for those in Calais's camp is not the concentrationary universe but the memory and temporality of colonialism and slavery: 'They are making us slaves, you know, slaves of [their] own country, by this fingerprint.' Temesghen historicizes biometric prints as an update on the branding of slaves, where disposable racialized bodies are held hostage by one territory. In George's film, the symbolic significance of slavery for those who seek to elude biometric capture is further developed in the second sequence on fingerprint mutilation. A close-up of a crackling fire plunges viewers into a strange rite, the significance of which is not immediately grasped. We discern small screws attached to wire stems, heated to incandescence in the flames as we hear the cry of seagulls, eruptions of laughter, hisses of pain, and untranslated exclamations. We only

---

18   In a commentary on this scene, Jacques Rancière evokes 'a certain equilibrium between the mutilation of bodies and the vision of these beings' capacity to paint themselves, sculpt themselves, tattoo themselves in order to escape the logic of identification, as if what the film showed was a double capacity of bodies, on the one hand the capacity to travel, to move through all stages, on the other this capacity to transform themselves, to find a response that is a painful response, expressed as painful.' Rancière, J. (2011) 'Savoir où l'on place l'intolérable dans nos vies', interview with C. Fouteau and J. Confavreux, *Mediapart*, 16 November 16 [Online]. Available at https://www.mediapart.fr/journal/france/151111/ jacques-ranciere-savoir-ou-lon-place-lintolerable-dans-nos-vies.

gradually come to realize that we are witnessing the searing away of finger-prints by hot screws. 'I say this is our tradition. They did it to our great grandfathers', jokes a faceless voice to a chorus of hoots and guffaws, while we watch anonymous dark fingers grow striated with white marks, then outstretched hands bearing scars of disquieting beauty (Figs. 9.8-9.9). As we witness the methodical application of hot screws to flinching fingers, the same faceless voice continues, joined by other voices:

> FIRST VOICE: Now we are not going to wait somebody to pain me, I will pain ourselves. The fire ... [sucking sound of pain].

> PERHAPS ANOTHER VOICE: Inch Allah . . [fragment of song]; Africa unite!

> FIRST VOICE: Too much, very very painful, but what can we do? We have to [exclamation of pain]. What can we do? What can we do, what can we do what can we do [rueful groan]. Anyway, it shall stop one day. I believe that one day Africa will become Europe and Europe will become Africa.

> ANOTHER VOICE: This is our pray.

> ANOTHER VOICE: Yah, this is our prayers. One day we shall see Europeans migrating to Africa to look for a job. Shame on Europe.

> CHORUS OF VOICES: Africa, unite, Africa proudest! Africa proudest! Africa unite!

'Now we are not going to wait somebody to pain me, I will pain ourselves', says the anonymous voice with grim humour. The oscillation in pronouns from singular to plural (we, me, I, ourselves), the alternations of his voice with the laughter, hisses, and exclamation of others, in languages that are not translated in the film's subtitles, produce a choral voicing, intimations of a collectivity to come. The same voice repeats, again with a kind of jovial resignation, that the burning screws are 'very very painful, but what can we do? What can we do?' As the faceless narrator goes on to anticipate that future in which 'Africa will become Europe and Europe ... Africa', we hear the fragment of a song and exclamations of 'Africa unite!'[19] While

---

19 The reversal of Europe and Africa is the central conceit of Abdourahman Waberi's 2009 novel, *In the United States of Africa* (trans. D. and N. Ball), New York, Bison Books.

Calais's 'Jungle' 179

Figure 9.8. Fingerprint mutilation by burning.

Source: Still from *Qu'ils reposent en révolte* (00.44.36).

Figure 9.9. Scarred hands.

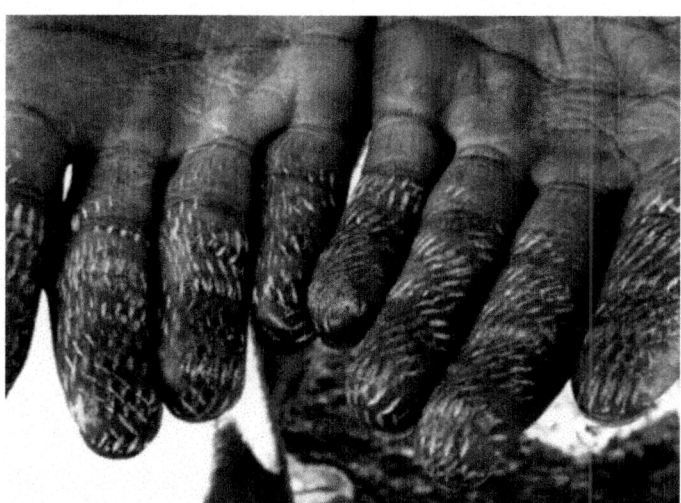

Source: Still from *Qu'ils reposent en révolte* (00.47.10).

the crackling fire heats up these new miniature irons and their paradoxical promise of fugitivity, global memories of slavery and colonialism fuse with the present of postcolonial migration, flickering toward a transnational liberation to come. This temporal conjunction within Calais's flames visually recalls Benjamin's dialectical image, in which past and present are disruptively illuminated in a flash.[20]

For George, the evocation of slavery in this scene is not symbolic, but utterly material, for the contemporary politics of migration and its biometric controls 'literally' brands migrants, marking their bodies within a European economy of recognition and forcing them to brand themselves in response: 'This is no longer an image. An image, to brand oneself with hot iron? ... It isn't simply a metaphor' (George, 2012). Yet if today's digital imprints are analogous to the branding of slaves by hot iron, their concealment by burning is a strategy of counter-branding, a self-tattooing in resistance to the border's dispositif. The violence once inflicted by slave owners to mark their property ('I say this is our tradition') is now self-inflicted by slavery's descendants in order to deterritorialize themselves, in what could be seen as a contemporary form of marronnage or fugitivity. The inscription of racial violence is made visible as a white scar on dark skin, enhanced by the black and white image. Yet this mark of enslavement is redrawn as the threshold of a line of flight.[21]

The rights of the stateless are predominantly framed as a right to be seen and heard, a right to appear in public space. An Arendtian view of rights hinges on the right to action and to speech in the public realm that is the polis, that is to say, 'the space of appearance in the widest sense of the word, namely, the space where I appear to others as others appear to me' (Arendt, 1998, p. 198). In contrast to the logic of recognition implicit in discourses of rights, however, the erasure of fingerprints is not conducted in the name of a right to be seen, but in the name of a right to disappear. The reduction of recognizable, politically qualified, and hence containable and deportable life, to what might be seen as illegible, 'bare' life – a body that cannot be identified as belonging to any state, or indeed to any (registered) name – is precisely what constrains the violence of sovereign power. In the current landscape of migration and statelessness, claiming one's right to have rights, which for many means staying on the move, involves strategically claiming the right to disappear, the right to a naked, yet politically charged, life at the threshold of what counts as human, unprotected, and undetected by the state.

---

20 This is entirely in keeping with Sylvain George's intention: 'The fixed image is an attempt to capture something fleeting, to extract layers of emotion and reality, and to create some dialectical links between the present and the past': 'Welcome to Calais: Sylvain George and the Aesthetics of Resistance'.
21 I am inspired here by Michelle Koerner's 2011 essay, 'Lines of Escape: Gilles Deleuze's Encounter with George Jackson', *Genre*, vol. 44, no. 2, pp. 157–80.

The Right to Disappear

The 'right to disappear', for Maurice Blanchot (by way of Michel Foucault), is constitutively denied under modernity's regime of surveillance and control, which finds its origins in seventeenth-century techniques for containing the plague. The containment of a literal virus forms the blueprint for today's immunitary borders:

> How did we learn to fight the plague? Not only through the isolation of those stricken, but through a strict parceling out of the contaminated space, through the invention of a technology for imposing order that would later affect the administration of cities, and, finally, through meticulous inquests which, once the plague had disappeared, would serve to prevent vagrancy (the right to come and go enjoyed by those of little means) and *even to forbid the right to disappear, which is still denied to us in one form or another*. (Blanchot, 1987, p. 84, translation modified, my italics)[22]

The 'right to disappear' invoked by Blanchot back in the 1980s, with reference to the birth of immunitary borders, is all the more pertinent today within the overlapping systems of surveillance, control, and filtering that compose the digitized Fortress Europe. Refugees who resort to erasing their fingerprints may find symbolic and imaginative resources within the past, in such tropes as slavery's legacy and the figure of the fugitive or the maroon. But their 'techniques' speak to an acutely contemporary grasp of what Michael Hardt and Antonio Negri diagnose as the current security regime, with its imperatives of visibility and capture, and its criminalization of those in flight:

> All you can do is flee. Break your chains and run. Most often, flight involves not coming out into the open but rather becoming invisible. Since security functions so often by making you visible, you have to escape by refusing to be seen. Becoming invisible, too, is a kind of flight. The fugitive, the deserter, and the invisible are the real heroes (or antiheros) of the struggle of the securitized to be free. (Hardt and Negri, 2012, p. 38)

As moving targets of a global security regime and its humanitarian alibis, refugees who erase their fingerprints participate in a wider struggle for mobility, where 'the right to disappear' is tactically seized to elude a border regime that blocks and

---

22 For a compelling discussion of Blanchot's 'right to disappear' in the context of the global War on Terror and the emergence of the citizen as target, see Goh, I. (2006) 'Prolegomenon to a Right to Disappear', *Cultural Politics*, vol. 2, no. 1, pp. 97-114. Goh designates the escalation of visual technologies and surveillance in the state's management of life and death as 'photobiopolitics'.

encamps in the name of protection. Without seeking to generalize 'data disappearance' as the only path to survival and safety, its strategic use can effectively elude the surveillance and control of technological borders.

Proponents of the 'autonomy of migration' theorize the tactical agility of bodies on the move, in sites such as Calais, in precisely this vein. The heuristic model of autonomous migration departs from the assumption of sovereign power's total capture of life toward a vitalist account of migrant agency that traces the priority of movement over control and encampment ('Escape comes first!') (Papadapoulos et al., 2008, pp. xv, 42-83).[23] The autonomy of migration perspective valuably attends to the subjective and social aspects of migration, the 'world-making' powers of migrant itineraries, and the challenge that border crossings pose to the very structure of the nation-state. In this view, the migrant becomes an unruly figure of excess and resistance to the borders and coordinates of the sovereign state. Dimitris Papadopoulos and Vassilis Tsianos qualify tactics such as burning papers, mutilating fingerprints, and other creative strategies of disappearance as Deleuzean forms of becoming imperceptible that, within the context of migration, challenge the ubiquitous politics of representation, rights, and visibility, thereby undoing the humanist regime of subjects and citizenship. A strategy of disidentification such as fingerprint mutilation is 'a voluntary "de-humanization" in the sense that it breaks the relation between your name and your body. A body without a name is a non-human human being; an animal which runs. It is non-human because it deliberately abandons the humanist regime of rights' (Papadopoulos and Tsianos, 2008, p. 227). From the autonomy of migration perspective, then, the migrant is the harbinger of a politics beyond the exclusions of representation, visibility, citizenship, and (human) rights.

In its focus on agency and resistance, the autonomy of migration perspective poses an important challenge to the humanitarian and securitarian reduction of refugees to bodies that must be managed. Yet the celebration of anonymity and disappearance remains a perilous gesture, given the tragically embodied reality of these terms in the mass grave that is the Mediterranean Sea. By the same token, even as we recognize the cunning and creativity of refugees as they cross borders, the priority of mobility over control cannot be assumed when so many are migrating in response to intolerable forms of control, and whose flight is arrested by camps proliferating on Europe's shores. In addition, it is difficult to assume the temporal priority of migrants' movement given the border's preemptive filtering

---

23 For a lucid overview of the 'autonomy of migration' model, see Nyers, P. (2015) 'Migrant Citizenships and Autonomous Mobilities', *Migration, Mobilities and Displacement*, vol. 1, no. 1, pp. 23-39.

of 'risky' bodies through the increasingly sophisticated technology of biometrics.[24] Even if techniques of resistance such as fingerprint mutilation continue to be practised by the exiled in sites like Calais, Europe's unparalleled anxiety about potential routes of terrorist infiltration that materialized in France's ongoing state of exception is compromising such room for manoeuver.

In short, just as we must remain wary of paradigms that immobilize the refugee into the essentialism of 'bare life', we must also take care not to essentialize the migrant's imperceptible mobility in heroic terms. Conceptualizing the im/mobility of those on the move requires figures, rather than paradigms, to mediate between autonomy and control, agency and capture, strategic imperceptibility and the claim to representation, tactics of subversion and the discourse of rights. 'Becoming imperceptible', or having the right to disappear, is not opposed to but on a continuum with the need to appear, become visible, remain in place, or, indeed, claim a place. Refugees may tactically disappear to remain on the move. Yet they also join together to form provisional communities during their itineraries, becoming visible as bodies within a common space, however constrained, from which they claim the right to have rights. As a point on the itinerary toward the United Kingdom, Calais's former jungle exemplifies how the most transitory of habitations can also become the material site of politics, how refugees confronting the most abject of conditions nevertheless endure, come together, resist, and organize. The perseverance, resistance, and creativity harboured in these borderscapes assume many forms, from strategic invisibility to tactical visibility.[25]

The Right to the Image

Approaching Calais's jungle as a zone of political virtuality on a continuum with biopolitical capture yields insight into what Vicki Squire, in dialog with Engin Isin and Kim Rygiel, has termed 'the critical inhabitation of abject spaces' (Squire, 2009, p. 147). The encampments of Calais may be 'abject spaces', in Isin and Rygiel's formulation, 'spaces in which the intention is to treat people neither as subjects (of

---

24 For a concise analysis of how biometric databases reduce migrants' room for manoeuver, see Scheel, S. (2013) 'Autonomy of Migration Despite Its Securitisation? Facing the Terms and Conditions of Biometric Rebordering', *Millienium: Journal of International Studies*, vol. 41, no. 3, pp. 575–600.
25 A bracing illustration of the right to disappear exercised through visible mobilization took place in Vienna, in 2012, when refugees protested against their encampment and demanded both the right to freedom of movement and the right to data sovereignty. Their manifesto read, 'If you don't meet our demands, then please delete our fingerprints from your databases and let us move on. We are entitled to our future.' See Kuster, B. (2013) 'Erase them! The image as it is falling apart into looks' [Video]. Available online at https://vimeo.com/59932817.

discipline) nor as objects (of elimination), but as those without presence, without existence, as inexistent beings, not because they don't exist, but because their existence is rendered invisible and inaudible'. Yet 'it is precisely in this difference that abject spaces are not spaces of abjection but spaces of politics' (Isin and Rygiel, 2006, p. 184). Indeed, collective actions such as Art in the Jungle, a festival in November 2015 during which refugees, migrants, activists, and artists cocreated art installations, even gesture toward the possibility of a creative inhabitation of abject spaces. Recent mobilizations in Calais have drawn unprecedented media attention to France's 'ghettoization' of undesirables in the name of hygienic compassion. Yet they also have made visible the ways in which this camp, ghetto, shantytown, or jungle was a vibrant city-in-the-making, harboring sites of gathering and sustenance (termed *lieux de vie* or sites of life) such as kitchens, restaurants, mosques, schools, churches, an office of legal counsel, even a library called 'Jungle Books'.

In the spring that preceded its destruction, Calais's jungle became a world stage, even a global spectacle, with particular media focus on the fate of unaccompanied minors seeking to reunite with family in Great Britain. Activists, aid workers, volunteers, artists, and media personalities from all over Europe formed 'bordering solidarities', to borrow another concept from Rygiel, participating in the promise of 'a tentacular collective oeuvre built despite the barbed wires and mud ... a city-world'.[26] Earlier that year, when the police issued an ultimatum for the jungle's evacuation in preparation for the destruction of its southern zone, refugees, migrants, and activists mobilized in protest and drew up the following manifesto (Fig. 9.10):

> We, the united people of the Jungle, Calais, respectfully decline the demands of the french Government with regards to reducing the size of the jungle.
>
> We have decided to remain where we are and will peacefully resist the government's plans to destroy our homes.
>
> We plead with the french authorities and International Communities that you understand our situation and respect our fundamental human rights.

The designation of disparate individuals cohabiting in a space as 'we, the united people' conjured into existence a people at once deterritorialized from the state

---

26 For a rich account of how such alliances contribute to transforming sites of detention into sites of contestation, see Rygiel, K. (2011) 'Bordering Solidarities, Migrant Activism and the Politics of Movement and Camps at Calais', *Citizenship Studies*, vol. 15, no.1, pp. 1-19.

and yet embedded within its borders. As we saw, the jungle's law/lessness was considered intolerable to French state authorities at the time of its prior demolition in 2009, when Eric Besson declared, 'The law of the jungle cannot last eternally on this territory of the French Republic.' Yet it is from within the new jungle that refugees ushered themselves into collective being through the language of the law and the rhetoric of human rights. This language was used to make perceptible bodies that have been deemed irregular and out of place, while pointing out the exclusion of such bodies from the universal rights incarnated by the French state. 'The united people of the Jungle, Calais' symbolically regularized and politicized themselves by dint of their ephemeral belonging to an encampment conjoined with a city. The capitalization of both camp and city underscored the continuity and contiguity of these spaces, even situating the jungle as the capital of Calais.[27] The collective self-designation of the jungle's inhabitants as a 'united people' staged a provisional 'becoming perceptible', but in terms that refused (and continue to refute) the dichotomies that govern the political sphere of appearances: statelessness/citizenship, illegality/legality, jungle/sovereign territory, camp/polis. To be sure, the plea's rhetorical tactics did not halt the bulldozers' course. Nevertheless, something shifted in this performative evocation of a different kind of body, space, belonging, and community. The misplaced articulation of rights opened up the very category of citizenship to critical, even creative, inhabitation.

In order to illustrate how such instances of appearance, which remain on a continuum with disappearance tactics, challenge and re-imagine the border regime, I turn to a photograph taken at the threshold of Calais's jungle before its destruction. In December 2015, Youssef, a sixteen-year-old boy from Sudan, was killed by a truck in a hit-and-run collision as he attempted to access the Eurotunnel. (Such deaths are a regular occurrence in Calais, yet their public mourning is prohibited under the state of emergency's ban on gatherings.) In response to Youssef's death, 'the united people of the Jungle, Calais', composed of refugees, migrants, and international activists, organized a silent march in his memory, bearing signs such as 'Our Destiny Here is Unknown', 'We are humans, not dogs', and 'Borders are Killing us'. The riot police (CRS) were stationed at the camp's entrance to block the marchers' procession toward the city of Calais. There is no small irony in the fact that the protestors' bodies were halted in their movement underneath a highway bridge on which vehicles generally pass with unfettered mobility. The heavily fenced and now walled highway leads to the port two kilometres away, illustrating the differential filtering of goods, services, and bodies under the current border dispositif.

A photo essay by Marie Magnin published in the pages of *Libération* captioned the wordless confrontation between the protestors and the police not as a stand-

---

27   My thanks to Églantine Colon for this point.

Figure 9.10. 'We, the united people of the Jungle, Calais'.

> We, the united people of the Jungle, Calais, respectfully decline the demands of the french Government with regards to reducing the size of the jungle.
> We have decided to remain where we are and will peacefully resist the governments plans to destroy our homes.
> We plead with the french authorities and the international communities that you understand our situation and respect our fundamental human rights

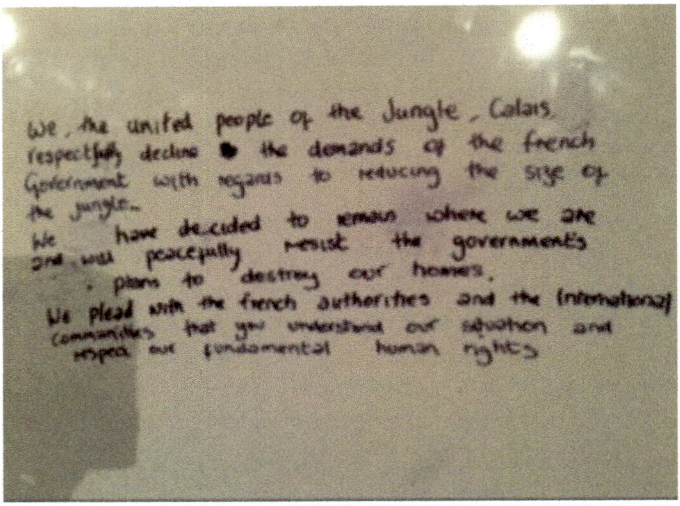

Source: Nick Gutteridge.

off between undesirable bodies at the threshold of their allocated zone and the armed forces seeking to contain them, but as a calm face-to-face encounter (Fig. 9.11). According to Ariella Azoulay, photography is the product of an infinitely re-actualizable encounter between photographer, photographed subject, and camera. The photographic image has the capacity to arrest the state's divisive perspective and nourish alternate visions of governance, thus conjuring a citizenry without borders:

> A civil discourse is ... one that suspends the point of view of governmental power and the nationalist characteristics that enable it to divide the governed from one another and to set its factions against one another. When disaster is consistently imposed on a part of the whole population of the governed, civil discourse insists on delineating the full field of vision in which disaster unfolds so as to lay bare the blueprint of the regime. (Azoulay, 2012, pp. 2-3).

This alternate field of vision opens up relationality between citizens and noncitizens within a given regime and invokes their fundamental partnership in a shared world. The image has the capacity to instantiate 'a civil space – the citizenry of photography – within whose borders the photographed subjects fight for their rightful place by means of the photograph and the space of appearance' (Azoulay, 2012, p. 51).

Figure 9.11. 'Dans le calme, le face-à-face entre migrants et CRS'.

Source: Marie Magnin.

How might Azoulay's vision of photography, as exposing a regime's immunitary blueprint and as an alternate scene of appearance, help us read the march for Youssef? The blueprint of France's securitarian regime is made visible as a stark confrontation between bare life and sovereign bio-power: unarmed protestors are blocked at the border of a camp on French territory, laying bare the division between camp and city, between the concentrationary space of the jungle and the polis of Calais.[28] Yet life, however exposed, is never altogether 'bare', nor is it an indivisible or absolute biopolitical substance. It is always already suffused with differences such as race, gender, religion, and class, qualifying a body as 'human, not quite human, and non-human' (Weheliye, 2014, p. 43). With her choice of black and white photography, Marie Magnin, like Sylvain George, underscores the racialized violence of this encounter between lawlessness and the law within a state whose official republican discourse prohibits any discussion of race.

The photograph is a cropped version of another wide-angle shot disclosing the larger scale of this confrontation with the state's machinery of containment. The cropped version, however, singularizes the encounter between protest and power while displaying the glaring asymmetries of this 'face-to-face': the exposure of protestors' faces – the metonym of the individual par excellence – contrasts the serial uniformity of the riot police, whose reflective shields, plastic visors,

---

28 On the relationship between Foucault's biopower and Agamben's sovereign power, see Squire, *The Exclusionary Politics of Asylum*, p. 151.

helmets, and shoulder and elbow pads form a gleaming shell around them. Perhaps this asymmetry explains the anxious set of the older officer's face. Despite his protective plastic layers, he appears perturbed: his lips are pursed, his jaw pugnacious. His expression may betray an awareness that no polycarbonate shield can defend against the moral damage of inflicting force on undefended life – unless it is simply fear. In any case, it is in stark contrast with the quiet defiance of the protestors, whose bare hands hold up a banner, their gazes intent, their faces exposed yet composed, the grain of their skin visible.

Yet even as this encounter discloses an absolute separation between naked flesh and militarized carapace, noncitizen and citizen, vulnerability and force, the officer is exposed as well, albeit in fragments: an ear, the sliver of jaw, and the nape of the neck escape his helmet, visual reminders of our common vulnerability to violence even as the scene stages the spectacular inequity of this vulnerability's distribution. Still, the participants remain visually bound by their common corporeal condition. They are also bound by the text on the creased banner, illegible to us but reflected back in fragments on the shields of the riot police. If the shield seems to virtually throw the words back into the protestors' faces, the illegible letters nevertheless weave the subjects and their place into a common semiotic field, as does the graffiti on the wall, enigmatic hieroglyphs at the jungle's entry.[29] The photographer appears to stand in the middle of the encounter, inscribing the viewer at the seam between statelessness and state power. As viewers of this image from Calais, 'we' are inevitably implicated in the conditions of its making, for, as Azoulay reminds us, 'the central right pertaining to the privileged segment of the population consists in the right to view disaster – to be its spectator' (Azoulay, 2012, p. 1). The embodied encounter we observe at the threshold of Calais's camp is thus at the same time a powerful scene of reading, self-inscription, and interpellation.

In the march for Youssef, refugees came out of the jungle not as furtive illegals who attempt to cross borders at night, or as fugitives whose bodies are subjected to biometric inscription and decoding, but as silent plaintiffs who stood upright and bore the text of their grievances. Significantly, these were not addressed to any particular nation-state, but to the supranational bodies of Europe and the United Nations. Although we cannot see it in this photograph, the banner held by the refugees carries the following questions: 'Today Youssef, tomorrow who?'; 'Europe, do you hear our call from Calais?'; 'Where is the United Nations in all this?'; and, finally, 'Living is illegal?'. The concluding interrogation conveys the tension we currently witness at Europe's borders between law and life: law experienced not as protection but as deterrence and containment, and life as the right to survival and mobility until sanctuary has been secured rather than assigned; law as the total capture and

---

29 The graffiti may be by EMC, a French graffiti crew.

management of life by the operations of sovereign and biopower, whether physically manifested by a line of armed officers or in virtual form as biometric data, and the sheer aliveness that perpetually eludes capture. Such aliveness may tactically disappear to remain in motion or coalesce into a collective body to stay in place.

The collective mobilization captured by this photograph, occurring from within the abjection and perceived rightlessness of the jungle's border, in the form of bodies stopped in their movement, is precisely what Jacques Rancière calls politics. Politics is what disrupts the boundary between so-called bare life and politically qualified life; it stages 'a dispute over what is given and about the frame within which we see something as given' (Rancière, 2010, p. 69).[30] Such dispute performs equality and belonging from within inequality and exclusion, as when those who apparently have no legitimate voice enact the right to be heard, and when those who are unseen seize the right to the image and find material support in visual frames fashioned by themselves and others. These claims to be seen and heard from the border of the camp dismantle the very binaries by which bodies-in-flight are being figured: 'bare life' versus speaking agent, abjection versus agency, illegality versus citizenship, jungle versus polis. As refugees continue to be envisioned in France and elsewhere through the reductive and related poles of contained threat on one hand and pure victimhood and object of compassion on the other, what these visual productions illuminate is something different: the traces of political subjects on the move.

Bibliography

Agamben, G. (1998) *Homo Sacer: Sovereign Power and Bare Life* (trans. D. Heller-Roazen), Stanford, Stanford University Press.

———. (2000) 'Beyond Human Rights', in *Means Without Ends: Notes on Politics* (trans. V. Binetti and C. Cassarino), Minneapolis, University of Minnesota Press.

Agier, M. (2008) *Gérer les indésirables: Des camps de réfugiés au gouvernement humanitaire*, Paris, Flammarion.

Arendt, H. (1998) *The Human Condition*, Chicago, University of Chicago Press.

———. (2007) 'We Refugees', in Kohn, J. and Feldman, R. H. (eds) *The Jewish Writings*, New York, Knopf Doubleday.

---

30 For a powerful analysis of migrant activism in Calais through the lens of Rancière's dissensus, see Millner, N. (2011) 'From "Refugee" to "Migrant" in Calais Solidarity Activism: Re-staging Undocumented Migration for a Future Politics of Asylum', *Political Geography*, vol. 30, no. 6, pp. 320-28.

Azoulay, A. (2012) *Civil Imagination: A Political Ontology of Photography* (trans. L. Bethlehem), London, Verso.
Bauman, Z. (2003) *Wasted Lives: Modernity and Its Outcasts*, Oxford, Oxford University Press.
Blanchot, M. (1987) *Michel Foucault as I Imagine Him*, New York, Zone Books.
Cayrol, J. (1982) *Il était une fois Jean Cayrol*, Paris, Seuil.
Deleuze, G. (1989) *Cinema 1: The Time-Image* (trans. H. Tomlinson and R. Galeta), Minneapolis, University of Minnesota Press.
Esposito, R. (2011) *Immunitas: The Protection and Negation of Life* (trans. Z. Hanafi), Cambridge, Polity.
———. (2013) 'Immunization and Violence', in *Terms of the Political: Community, Immunity, Biopolitics (Commonalities)*, New York, Fordham University Press.
European Council/Council of the European Union (2016) 'EU-Turkey Statement, 18 March 2016' [Online]. Available at www.consilium.europa.eu/en/press/ press-releases/2016/03/18-eu-turkey-statement/.
Fanon, F. (2004) *The Wretched of the Earth* (trans. R. Philcox), New York, Grove Press.
Fassin, E. and Adam, M. (2015) 'Calais, jungle d'Etat', *Libération*, 23 April [Online]. Available at http://ww.liberation.fr/france/2015/04/23/calais-jungle-detat_1261872.
Favre, H. (2016) 'Bernard Cazeneuve: "Ce démantèlement est un devoir humanitaire pour notre pays"', *La Voix du Nord*, 23 October [Online]. Available at www.lavoixdunord.fr/63970/article/2016-10-23/cazeneuve-ce-demantelement-est-un-devoir-humanitaire-pour-notre-pays.
French Ministry of the Interior (2016) 'Discours de M. Bernard Cazeneuve', 22 February [Online]. Available at www.interieur.gouv.fr/Le-ministre/Interventions-du-ministre/22.02.2016-Discours-de-M.-Bernard-Cazeneuve-au-Mans.
George, S. (2102) 'Burning Fingers', *Independencia*, 18 August [Online]. Available at www. independenciarevue.net/s/spip.php?article621.
———. (n.d.) 'Q & A: Sylvain George' [Online]. Available at http://desistfilm.com/q-a-sylvain-george/.
Glissant, E. (1997) *Poetics of Relation* (trans. B. Wing), Ann Arbor, University of Michigan Press.
Gutteridge, N. (2016) 'Calais Migrants Pen Note to Block Jungle Camp Revamp Fearing It Will Affect UK Asylum Bids', *Express*, 13 January [Online]. Available at www.express.co.uk/ news/world/634103/Calais-migrants-block-French-raze-Jungle-camp-fear-affect-UK-asylum-Britain.
Hardt, M. and Negri, A. (2012) *Declaration*, New York, Argo Navis.
Hirsch, M. and Spitzer, L. (2016) 'Small Acts of Repair: The Unclaimed Legacy of the Romanian Holocaust', *Journal of Literature and Trauma Studies*, vol. 4, no. 1/2.

Kuener, J. (n.d.) 'Welcome to Calais: Sylvain George and the Aesthetics of Resistance', *Cinemascope*, vol. 47 [Online]. Available at http://cinema-scope.com/cinema-scope-magazine/interviews-welcome-to-calais-sylvain-george-and-the-aesthetics-of-resistance/.

Isin, E. and Rygiel, K. (2006) 'Abject Spaces: Frontiers, Zones, Camps', in Masters, C. and Dauphinée, E. (eds) *Logics of Biopower and the War on Terror*, Basingstoke, Palgrave Macmillan.

Magnin, M. (2015) 'Marche pour Youssef, mort à Calais', *Libération*, 6 December [Online]. Available at https://www.liberation.fr/france/2015/12/06/marche-pour-youssef-mort-a-calais_1418642.

Malkki, L. H. (1996) 'Speechless Emissaries: Refugees, Humanitarianism, and Dehistoricization', *Cultural Anthropology*, vol. 11, no. 3, pp. 377-404.

Mbembe, A. (2003) 'Necropolitics', *Public Culture*, vol 15, no. 1, pp. 11-40.

Michaux, H. (1972) 'Qu'il repose en révolte', in *La Vie dans les plis*, Paris, Gallimard.

Papadopoulos, D. and Tsianos, V. (2008) 'The Autonomy of Migration: The Animals of Undocumented Mobility', in Hickey-Moody, A. and Malins, P. (eds) *Deleuzian Encounters: Studies in Contemporary Social Issues*, Basingstoke, Palgrave Macmillan.

Papadopoulos, D., Stephenson, N. and Tsianos, V. (2008) *Escape Routes: Control and Subversion in the Twenty-First Century*, London, Pluto Press.

Qu'ils reposent en révolte: Des figure de guerres I (2015) Directed by Sylvain George. First release 2010 [DVD]. Paris, Noir Productions.

Rancière, J. (2010) *Dissensus: On Politics and Aesthetics* (trans. S. Corcoran), New York, Bloomsbury Academic.

Squire, V. (2009) *The Exclusionary Politics of Asylum*, Basingstoke, Palgrave Macmillan.

Ticktin, M. (2011) *Casualties of Care: Immigration and the Politics of Humanitarianism in France*, Berkeley, University of California Press.

Vaughan-Williams, N. (2015) *Europe's Border Crisis*, Oxford, Oxford University Press.

Weheliye, A. G. (2014) *Habeas Viscus: Racializing Assemblages, Biopolitics, and Black Feminist Theories of the Human*, Durham, NC, Duke University Press.

Refugee Trajectories
Post-1945 Refugee Management and the Implications of Demography as a Field

Aslı Iğsız

More than 90 years after the massive Greek–Turkish population exchange, Greece and Turkey are implicated in yet another mass human displacement.[1] The 1923 exchange severed the ties of about one and a half million Greek Orthodox and Muslims to their homes. The first internationally ratified and executed forced migration, the 1923 exchange set a precedent, providing a legal basis for 'demographic engineering' in nation-states and becoming an international reference point for other population transfers and partition plans (Özsu, 2015).[2] Today, the route once taken by Greek Orthodox and Muslims to and from Turkish and Greek Aegean shores is again an active site of relocation: refugees are trying to cross from Turkey to Greece on a daily basis and, since the signing of the controversial agreement between the European Union and the Turkish government in 2016, most of those who make it to Greece are routinely 'returned' to Turkey (European Council, 2016). Unlike the subjects of the exchange of 1923, these 'returned' are not considered 'nationals' who are being sent to territories where they presumably 'belong'. Rather, EU officials appear to index refugees as surplus members of undesirable groups to be kept outside the external borders of the EU so as to uphold the fluidity of its internal borders – the Schengen Area (Timmermans, 2015; European Commission, 2016).

Within this framework, the European Union designated Turkey a country that is key to the EU's ability to solve its 'refugee problem' (Hahn, 2015) and thereby 'end the flow of irregular migration from Turkey to the EU' via Greece (European Commission, 2017). In a speech delivered in Brussels on 13 November 2015, Frans Timmermans, the first vice-president of the European Commission, emphasized

---

1   See Greek-Turkish readmission Protocol in relation to migration in European Council (2016) 'European Council Conclusions, 17-18 March 2016', 18 March [Press Release].
2   See also Mazower, M. (2009) *No Enchanted Palace: The End of Empire and the Ideological Origins of the United Nations*, Princeton, Princeton UP; Nathan-Chapotot, R. (1949) *Les Nations Unies et les Réfugiés: Le Maintien de la Paix et le Conflit de Qualifications Entre l'Ouest et l'Est*, Paris, Editions A. Pedone, pp. 72-76.

the importance of Turkey in this endeavour. According to Timmermans, permitting the continued flow of refugees into the EU would strain relations among the Schengen states; 'there is', he added, 'no solidarity that does not have a core of self-interest in it' (Timmermans, 2015). Consequently, measures had to be taken, Timmermans asserted, that would ensure the effective management of the crisis to preserve this solidarity within the EU. The controversial EU–Turkey Statement of 18 March 2016 was geared towards achieving this result. A year later, the European Commission announced that 'irregular arrivals' to the EU had dropped by 97 per cent thanks to Turkey's commitment (European Commission, 2017). This commitment effectively turned Turkey's borders into a barrier that sealed off Europe to refugees. Figures in the EU and national governments decided that ensuring mobility within the European Union required that the flow of refugees to the EU be stopped as a matter of political necessity.

On 15 April 2016, a month after the EU–Turkey Statement was signed, Ban Ki Moon, then secretary-general of the United Nations, announced that the world was 'facing the biggest refugee and displacement crisis of our time', adding, 'Above all, this is not just a crisis of numbers; it is also a crisis of solidarity' (Secretary General, 2016). Comparable in scale to the mass displacement wrought by the Second World War, contemporary refugeeism is often referred to in terms of a crisis. The notion of crisis entails a temporary condition, a disruption within a given context because of a threat to public safety and/or property (Sellnow and Seeger, 2013, p. 4). The threat posed to the refugees who flee their home countries because of conflict and violence is evident. However, it is unclear what threat the European Union faces other than demographic concerns such as the arrival of 'undesirables'. To counter that perceived threat the EU has allocated billions of euros to Turkey to keep the refugees away.[3]

Accounts about or from refugees in Turkey refer to housing and social opportunities funded by that allocation, but they speak to racism and discrimination too. In addition, it appears that Turkish officials instrumentalize refugees in order to portray the Turkish government as a humanitarian patron (Crisis Group, 2018; Günaydın, 2019). Turkey might have agreed to host the Syrian refugees, but the Turkish authorities do not appear to consider them to be desirable candidates for permanent settlement in Turkey.

This essay addresses the implications of the 'undesirable' in demographic terms, with a focus on displacement. Specifically, I will revisit the two decades after the Second World War, during which demographic engineering and mass deportation

---

3 See the European Commission's press releases 'EU-Turkey Cooperation: A €3 billion Refugee Facility for Turkey', dated 24 November 2015, and 'EU Facility for Refugees in Turkey: The Commission Proposes to Mobilize Additional Funds for Syrian Refugees', dated 14 March 2018.

of minorities was systematized as a solution for peace, a new international human rights legal architecture was built, and the fields of eugenics and demography converged to epistemologically legitimize the configuration of the 'undesirable'.

Refugee Trajectories and the Regulation of the Undesirable

Refugee trajectories, a term that I use in the title of this essay, does not solely denote the physical routes that the displaced follow in an attempt to escape violence and rebuild their lives elsewhere. 'Trajectory' also implies a pattern in approaching the displaced in terms of 'desirables' and 'undesirables'. This pattern is notable in demographic redistribution and deportation, and in the configuration of the unwanted.

The legal precedent set by the 1923 Greek–Turkish population exchange has arguably contributed to the systematization of so-called population transfers, in particular the 'settlement' of the desirable and the undesirable at the end of the Second World War (Özsu, 2015; Yıldırım, 2006; Aktar, 2000). Some examples include the 1945 Potsdam Agreement and the partitions of India and Palestine in 1947 and 1948, respectively (Mazower, 2009). Today, thanks to important work on international law and the protection of minorities, we have a better understanding of interwar and post-war displacement. What is missing is a more focused, critical analysis of the post-1945 demographic production of knowledge and its implications for population management generally and for the 'undesirables' in particular. I have traced the politics of expertise in population management elsewhere by focusing on the formation of a European refugee association and the studies presented to it following the Second World War (Iğsız, 2018, pp. 41-72). I have discovered that some eugenicists in Italy and Germany – former supporters of fascism or those who rose to prominence under fascist rule – moved into population studies and contributed to the study of refugees in the decade after the Second World War. Their influence was widespread, reflected not least in their collaboration with Turkish scholars and eugenicists. More research on this subject is necessary to fully unravel the political implications of demographic production of knowledge at the time,[4] particularly with regard to refugees and displacement.

Whereas political ideology – such as nationalism – and the use of law have been widely examined in the scholarly literature on displacement,[5] the political impli-

---

4   For more on demography and demographic production of knowledge in connection to policy, see Greenhalgh, S. (1996) 'The Social Construction of Population Science: An Intellectual, Institutional, and Political History of Twentieth-Century Demography', *Comparative Studies in Society and History*, vol. 38, no. 1, pp. 26-66.
5   See Özsu's *Formalizing Displacement* and Mazower's *No Enchanted Palace*.

cations of demographic knowledge production has received less critical attention. The rise of demography as a significant field of study coincided with post-war 'demographic engineering' efforts and population transfers. Demographic production of knowledge during this period offers important pointers for scholars examining policies regarding refugees. My objective here, then, is to briefly explore the work of some prominent demographers and eugenicists in post-war Western Europe and Turkey and consider the intersections of the two fields – eugenics and demography – as a productive site to question the implications of the 'undesirable' as a demographic category. Some of the paradigms from that time have resurfaced in contemporary xenophobic discourses, if not practices.

In the hands of some politicians in liberal democracies today, including the United States and Italy, xenophobic discourses are being translated into contentious policies such as building walls or criminalizing humanitarianism.[6] Reports on the violation of 'the legal obligation to provide assistance to any person at distress at sea'[7] as well as the criminalization of humanitarian aid to refugees through its reclassification as 'human trafficking' raise questions about the implications of being human and the value of human life today.

Demography and Eugenics: A Brief Overview

Demography and eugenics are generally addressed as two distinct fields of study. The field of demography is commonly traced to the British economist Thomas Malthus (1766-1834) and his work on population growth in relation to the availability of resources, which stipulated the importance of controlling reproduction for welfare (Petersen, 1999). Eugenics, on the other hand, is traced to Sir Francis Galton (1822-1911), who coined the term in 1883 (Galton, 1883, pp. 24-25; Gillham, 2001). Galton, a Victorian scientist and cousin of Charles Darwin, defined eugenics as the science to improve stock. He was concerned with heredity and intelligence as well as breeding 'high quality' genus (Galton, 1869). Eugenics and demography share an interest in numbers, with one focused more on the 'quality' and 'improvement' of the genus and the other on control over the numbers. Both deploy statistical data,

---

6   A quick search on the subject reveals a plethora of news reports on arrests related to helping migrants.
7   Heller, C., Pezzani, L. and Studio, S. (2012) *Report on the Left-To-Die Boat*, Forensic Oceanography/European Research Council Project 'Forensic Architecture', p. 9 [Online]. Available at https://content.forensic-architecture.org/wp-content/uploads/2019/06/FO-report.pdf . A more recent case involves the German captain Carola Rackete's vessel Sea-Watch 3 and Italian authorities in 2019: see, for example, BBC (2019) 'Italy Migrants: Rescue Ship Captain Arrested at Lampedusa Port', *BBC News*, 29 June [Online]. Available at https://www.bbc.com/news/world-europe-48809134.

and when it comes to the regulation of numbers, it almost always matters whose numbers are to be controlled.

Eugenics and demography converged early on. In 1891, Galton addressed the demography section of the International Conference on Hygiene and Demography in London and raised questions about heredity and fertility (Hodgson, 2015). At the turn of the twentieth century, eugenicist concerns with the composition and quality of the population had gained traction and were manifested in different ways. For example, in the United States 'an active immigration restriction movement allied itself with those expressing eugenic fears' and who opposed 'inferior' Eastern and Southern European immigrants who 'degenerated' the high quality of the Anglo-Saxon and Northern European genus (Hodgson, 2015, p. 177). Following Galton's logic that the increase in numbers of the lower stock endangered the high-quality stock of the upper classes, members of the immigration restriction movement argued that growth in the number of the 'inferior' was the cause of a decrease in fertility rates of the 'superior' (Hodgson, 2015, p. 177; Hodgson, 1991).

Eugenicist experiments and scientific racism in the interwar years and during the Second World War are well documented.[8] Often associated after the war with Nazi policies, eugenics as a field gradually fell from grace, while demography became a popular area of study. Eugenicist concerns were by no means confined to European fascism, nor did eugenics disappear with the end of the Second World War. As I briefly address below, eugenicist approaches found a niche in demographic research. Concomitantly, statistics developed as a major field to collect data on birth and death rates, ageing, and changes to populations as well as the composition of a population.

One of the leading figures in statistics is Italian statistician Corrado Gini (1884-1965), perhaps best known for developing the Gini coefficient to calculate income inequality. Widely acknowledged as a key figure in the fusion of fascism, eugenics, and demography, Gini was a supporter of Mussolini and fascism in Italy before and during the war (Gini, 1927). He developed his own theories of migration and race, was instrumental in establishing a refugee association in post-war Europe, and published widely on demography. He also collaborated with Turkish social scientists and eugenicists and was invited to Turkey in 1950 to establish the Statistics Institute at Istanbul University (Iğsız, 2018, pp. 34-70, 91), where he also taught a course on demography.[9] Gini's lectures covered demography and population den-

---

8   See, for example, Soloway, R. (1995) 'World War II and the Population Question', in *Demography and Degeneration: Eugenics and the Declining Birthrate in Twentieth Century Britain*, Chapel Hill, The University of North Carolina Press, pp. 312-335; Barkan, E. (1992) *The Retreat of Scientific Racism: Changing Concepts of Race in Britain and the United States Between the World Wars*, Cambridge, Cambridge University Press.

9   Istanbul University Press published these lectures in French: Gini, C. (1952), *Démographie et Sociologie* [Demography and Sociology], Istanbul, Istanbul University Press.

sity, the question of class and population increase, and migration and the infusion of young blood into an underpopulated country.

The topics of Gini's lectures corresponded with post-war demographic concerns. In the decade immediately following the Second World War, the reconstruction of war-torn Western Europe meant that underpopulation and the need for a labour force were dominant demographic concerns. Demographic composition was another concern: minorities were targeted as 'threats' to peace and stability; mass population transfers ensued (Mazower, 2009). Anxiety over the composition and numbers of the population informed settlement policies. Post-war national reconstruction efforts in war-torn countries necessitated statistical data collection that would then be translated into population regulation policy.

This political climate had an impact on the institutionalization of demography. Between 1945 and 1967, a number of centres and institutions of demographic research were established across Europe and the United States (Hodgson, 2015, pp. 177-178). In 1945, the National Institute of Demographic Studies (INED) was founded in France, and in 1946 it started publishing the journal *Population* in French and English.[10] Also in 1946, the United Nations established its 'Population Division' under its Department of Economic and Social Affairs, seeking to streamline demographic data collection and methods.[11] The journal *Population Studies: A Journal of Demography* was inaugurated in 1947 in London. In the United States, Princeton University pioneered demographic research, and between 1951 and 1967, sixteen American universities opened population research centres (Hodgson, 2015, p. 178). Istanbul University's invitation to Gini to teach a course on demography and to found its statistics institute in 1950 might be considered within this broader framework.

In addition to the institutionalization and mainstreaming of demography as a field of study, mass population transfers – which legal historian Umut Özsu calls 'demographic engineering' – marked the decade after the end of the Second World War. The founding of the United Nations in 1945 and the regulation of international law coincided with the post-war refugee crisis in Europe. In addition, several newly independent nation states emerged after the war following rapid decolonization. Of these, India is a significant case with respect to both local and international demographic engineering. Locally, the partition of India generated a mass population displacement that led to demographic redistribution, altering the composition of the population. Internationally, especially in the United States, there was also a concern that 'less developed' new countries like India would reproduce faster than

---

10 Institut National d'Études Démographiques. https://www.ined.fr/en/.
11 See 'About United Nations Population Division', *United Nations Department of Economic and Social Affairs: Population Division*. Available at https://www.un.org/en/development/desa/population/about/index.asp.

those in the so-called free world (Hodgson, 2015, pp. 177-178; Greenhalgh, 1996, pp. 38-46). 'Third World' became a common term to refer to these countries.

This term was coined in 1952 by one of the leading figures in French demographic research, Alfred Sauvy (1952, p. 14).[12] Drawing a parallel between the (mostly) non-aligned countries in the Cold War and the French 'Tiers état' – the third estate that denominates the common people as distinct from the nobility and the clergy – Sauvy identified the 'less developed' as the 'Third World'. It was used to refer to the 'non-industrialized' countries, most of which were recently decolonized and aligned with neither the Soviet Union nor the so-called free world.

In the 1950s and 1960s, demographers in the United States utilized funding from the Rockefeller and Ford Foundations to convince politicians in the 'Third World' to develop birth control policies (Hodgson, 2015, pp. 177-178; Greenhalgh, 1996, pp. 38-46). The Ford Foundation was particularly interested in population control and funded most of this work. Concerns with the increase in numbers of the 'wrong kind' was not unique to the United States. In an international refugee conference organized in Istanbul in 1954, Gini called attention to the demographic pressure 'coloured' peoples put on 'European overseas possessions' – meaning colonies (Iğsız, 2018, p. 46). He warned his audience that the numbers of 'coloured peoples' increase more rapidly than the populations associated with 'Western Civilisation'. He added that the 'white peoples' behind the Iron Curtain also reproduced at a higher rate than those in the West, and that these two non-Western groups might join forces in future given their shared antagonism to the so-called 'free world' in the Cold War.

Gini is one of the most well-known of the number of individuals who combined eugenics and demography in his work. It is hard to know to what extent he and other scholars who had previously supported fascism, or figures such as Karl Valentin Müller (1896-1963), who believed in breeding quality workers belonging to a Nordic superior race and controlling the numbers of inferior groups, revised their previously held beliefs after the war (Iğsız, 2018, p. 52). This question is pertinent, as both Gini and Müller were part of a European refugee association and conducted research on post-war refugees. It is certain, however, that eugenics – promoting biologized solutions to social matters while considering the population to be a site of improvement (such as proposing birth control, as opposed to economic, political, or social policies, as a remedy for unemployment) – did not disappear after the Second World War. Many scholars working in the field of eugenics directed their expertise towards demography and population research, with a focus on refugees.

---

12   For more, see Shohat, E. and Stam, R. (2012) *Race in Translation: Culture Wars Around the Postcolonial Atlantic*, New York, NYU Press.

One was Sir Julian Huxley (1887-1975), a British evolutionary biologist, who was named the first director-general of the United Nations Educational, Scientific and Cultural Organization (UNESCO).[13]

In *Unesco: Its Purpose and Its Philosophy*, Huxley pushed for UNESCO to pursue eugenicist work, even if it had fallen out of favour by that time:

> Whereas variety is in itself desirable, the existence of weaklings, fools, and moral deficients [sic!] cannot but be bad. It is also much harder to reconcile politically with the current democratic doctrine of equality. In face [sic!] of it, indeed, the principle of equality of opportunity must be amended to read: 'equality of opportunity within the limits of aptitude.' [...]
>
> To adjust the principle of democratic equality to the fact of biological inequality is a major task for the world, and one which will grow increasingly more urgent as we make progress towards realising equality of opportunity. To promote this adjustment, a great deal of education of the general public will be needed as well as much new research; and in both these tasks Unesco can and should co-operate. This does not mean, of course, that Unesco should aim at labelling, docketing, or dragooning humanity. It means that it should encourage all studies and all methods which can be used to ensure that men find the right jobs and are kept away from the wrong jobs – to ensure that individuals find outlets satisfying to their temperament, and work appropriate to their talents, while at the same time ensuring that society is not overburdened with people in positions for which they are inadequate or, still worse, which they are likely to abuse.
>
> Biological inequality is, of course, the bedrock fact on which all of eugenics is predicated. But it is not usually realised that the two types of inequality have quite different and indeed contrary eugenic implications. The inequality of mere difference is desirable, and the preservation of human variety should be one of the two primary aims of eugenics. But the inequality of level or standard is undesirable, and the other primary aim of eugenics should be the raising of the mean level of all desirable qualities. While there may be dispute over certain qualities, there can be none over a number of the most important, such as a healthy constitution, a high innate general intelligence, or a special aptitude such as that for mathematics or music.
>
> At the moment, it is probable that the indirect effect of civilisation is dysgenic instead of eugenic; and in any case it seems likely that the dead weight of genetic stupidity, physical weakness, mental instability, and disease-proneness, which already exist in the human species, will prove too great a burden for real progress to be achieved. Thus, even though it is quite true that any radical eugenic policy will

---

13   For more on Huxley's eugenicist thought, see Weindling, P. (2012) 'Julian Huxley and the Continuity of Eugenics in Twentieth-century Britain', *Journal of Modern European History*, vol. 10, no. 4, pp. 480-499.

be for many years politically and psychologically impossible, it will be important for Unesco to see that the eugenic problem is examined with the greatest care, and that the public mind is informed of the issues at stake so that much that now is unthinkable may at least become thinkable (1946, pp. 20-21).

Here Huxley stresses that biological differences encompass differences of aptitude. The avowed eugenicist further insists that the more UNESCO succeeds in redistributing educational opportunities, the more such biological differences will inhibit human progress. His main concern is human advancement, and he considers successful matching of aptitude with the right job as key for 'progress'. Huxley's approach clearly aligns eugenicist thinking with UNESCO's agenda.

At the same time, Huxley was instrumental in formulating and revising the earlier drafts of UNESCO's *The Race Question*.[14] UNESCO spearheaded efforts to end scientific racism and sponsored the 1950 Statement on Race to debunk 'scientific research' on racial hierarchies (Iğsız, 2018, pp. 73-74). Collaborating with anthropologists like Claude Lévi-Strauss and Ashley Montagu – the student of influential anthropologist Franz Boas, who promoted the study of culture instead of race – UNESCO offered institutional support to refuting theories of racial hierarchies. In line with these efforts, Huxley advocated the use of the term 'ethnicity' instead of the biologically charged notion of race. However, this did not stop Huxley from outlining a eugenicist agenda to discuss biological differences when he was the director-general of UNESCO.

Ambivalence towards biologized approaches to humankind was common in the decade after the end of war. The institutionalized mobilization against scientific racialism was advocated concurrently with aspirations to continue to improve the human genus. Under the auspices of UNESCO, ethnicity and culture were promoted as alternative notions to race. Yet it remains an open question as to whether this shift in terminology was really divorced from assumptions about bloodlines and biologized essences (including moral character and criminal 'disposition') that were presumably transmissible from one generation to the next. Huxley's endorsement of eugenics and assumptions about biologized hierarchies, while pushing for a reconsideration of 'race', is a case in point.

This ambivalence should be taken into account when viewing the rise of demography as a field of study after the Second World War. Eugenics, like race, might have been tarnished by the Nazi's scientific racism and atrocities, and scholars might have gradually dropped the notion of eugenics in favour of demography and population studies, but the extent to which eugenicist paradigms were discarded remains questionable. Eugenics and demography are clearly intertwined in post-war

---

14   *The Race Question*, Unesco Programme, vol III, 1950.

scholarship.[15] This is not to suggest that all demographers were fascists; rather, the field's main tenets were, to some extent, coterminous with the interests of fascism and eugenics.

Human Capital and the Undesirable

In 1966, French demographer Sauvy acknowledged that 'acceptable or not', eugenicist 'plans to improve the human race opened the way to qualitative demography' (Sauvy, 1969, pp. 509-510). This meant that the quantitative character of demography, the use of statistical data such as birth and death rates, was expanded to include the composition of the population as well as concerns to improve its quality. Migration, displacement, and the adaptation and assimilation of migrants were some of the important demographic research categories that emerged. Other important categories included family, women raising children, and the cost of 'producing men', which involved the cost of training, the expected subsequent (labour) output, and the cost of prolonging his life (Sauvy, 1969, pp. 233-247).

Within the epistemological matrix of demography, the value of human life is contingent upon productivity and ability to contribute to the economy. Those unable to contribute in this way and who therefore do not constitute 'human capital' are considered undesirable. Sauvy is not alone nor the first to articulate this approach. Others, including Gini, raised questions about 'human capital' in relation to the labour force of migrants and refugees. Gini identified the migrants and refugees in terms of human 'capital', a term that construes the displaced as labour-ready bodies whose training has already been funded by the country of origin and who thus constitute a potential gain for the host country (Iğsız, 2018, pp. 41-72). Though he may not have used the same words, Gini did in fact also address that which Sauvy called the 'cost of producing men'.

Precarious and vulnerable migrants, who for the most part did not have comparable exchange value, were likely to be denoted 'undesirable' refugees by a recipient country. At the 1954 international convention in Istanbul of the European Association for the Study of the Refugee Problems, Walter Schätzel, a scholar of international law, explained that most states did not want the group of refugees who were often referred to as a 'social burden' (*bagage social*) (Iğsız, 2018, pp. 51, 53). Schätzel's use of 'social burden' resonates with Huxley's earlier designation of specific groups as a 'deadweight for the society'. In his work on refugees, Karl Valentin

---

15   For an earlier example of how these fields have been entwined in the case of Turkey, see Gökay, F. K. (1934) 'Milli Nüfus Siyasetinde (Eugenique) Meselesinin Mahiyeti' [The Nature of the Issue of Eugenics in National Population Policy], *Ülkü: Halkevleri ve Halkodalari Dergisi*, vol. 3, pp. 206-213.

Müller also underlined the importance of categorizing refugees according to their vocation and ability to work, so that they would not feel like a 'deadweight for the society' (Iğsız, 2018, p. 51).

In the context of refugees, the so-called social burden thus included those who could not be easily employed – orphans, criminals, the anti-social, sickly, and elderly – who would today, for the most part, be referred to as the precarious (Iğsız, 2018, pp. 51, 266). The configuration of the precarious as 'undesirables' and potential criminals, who are deemed difficult to employ, creates a stark contrast with the notion of refugeehood. A refugee by definition is precarious and precisely because of this precarity, humanitarian assistance is necessary. The importance of expressing solidarity with the displaced was underlined in such forums, but it is clear that refugees were assigned a place in hierarchies according to their labour capacity and vocation, and not just according to their racial, linguistic, cultural, and religious backgrounds.

In the post-war environment, when deportation of minorities and partition were promoted as peace-making measures and when international human rights were considered to be more a matter of protecting individuals than minority groups as a whole, it was no longer enough to be 'a designated group of displaced and stateless persons to have access to asylum protection' (Cohen, 2011, p. 54). Displaced persons were individually screened for eligibility, except for Holocaust survivors, who bypassed individual screenings (Cohen, 2011, pp. 54-55). According to the new international human rights law, everybody had the right to seek asylum, but not the right to automatically be granted asylum (Cohen, 2011, p. 57). Concomitantly, French international jurists argued that the 'West' was picking and choosing individuals from masses of refugees and displaced persons (Nathan-Chapotot, 1949, pp. 72-76).

In 1949, Sauvy wrote that after the war both the Soviet Union and the United States 'opposed any initiative that would give substance to international solidarity' and that the international atmosphere favoured this outcome:

> In nations that are in the process of being formed, nationalism calls for a period of self-absorbed isolation; in advanced nations, anxiety to protect the labor market and sometimes also preoccupations with race induce great caution about immigration or even lead to a closed-door policy. In contrast to the flow of goods and of capital, where at least intentions toward greater international rapprochement do manifest themselves, national sovereignty in the matter of immigration, more than ever, rules supreme. (Sauvy, 1949)

Sauvy gestures to differences between the flow of goods, capital, and people. Concerns with race and labour clearly have an impact on the configuration of the 'undesirable'.

Following its founding in 1949, the Council of Europe decided to approach refugee problems as overpopulation because of their presumable similarities (Iğsız, 2018, p. 49). Gini, for one, agreed with this approach, stating that in post-war Italy there were mostly 'national refugees' – descendants of Italians arriving from the former colonies or others whom he considers to be affiliated with Italy, while the others were international refugees, whom he deems guests (Gini, 1954, pp. 21-23). Gini argued that refugees contributed, together with high birth rates in Italy, to the problem of overpopulation. Coupled with post-war unemployment, this situation created tension in economic life and politics, he claimed. Be that as it may, it is clear that the national refugees, whom Gini likens to the Greek–Turkish population exchangees who were relocated in their 'own country', were in Italy to stay, while the international refugees were temporarily hosted there.

Labour and race, then, have long been entwined in the configurations of social and physical mobility and used to demarcate the limits of solidarity. These limits demonstrate how racialized paradigms and labour concerns were embedded in political anxieties articulated in the terms and categories of demography. Demographic knowledge production appears to be deployed to legitimize demographic policy. The category of the 'undesirable' is a resilient one, and the same list of the 'useless' and the 'criminal' reappears in Sauvy's influential book on population studies published in French in 1966:

> Physical organisms eliminate unwanted toxins and dangerous or useless bodies in order to preserve their life and their good working order. Human society too tends to eliminate unwanted members, either useless or dangerous, more or less discreetly, more or less unintentionally. The useless ones are those who cannot contribute to the economic or social life: the old, the ill, the invalids, the unwanted new born etc.; the dangerous ones are the criminals, the degenerate, the antisocial, the madmen, or even sometimes the political enemies, the members of other races or other religions. They can be eliminated directly, by murder, expulsion, exclusion; or with hypocrisy, through bad treatment, refusal of care, even abandonment. (Sauvy, 1969, pp. 341-347)[16]

The 'useless' are those deemed unemployable, with no exchange value as 'human capital'. Sauvy's example serves as a reminder that economic productivity plays a key role in administering a given social order. Under 'dangerous', Sauvy categorizes political dissidence alongside racial, religious, and other differences. Sauvy's categorization of the undesirable as a group that can be excluded or expelled recalls demographic engineering projects such as the Greek-Turkish population exchange, post-war mass population transfers, and the partition of India, whereby the states

---

16   The book was originally published in French in 1966 under the title *Théorie Générale de la Population*.

in question removed undesirables through expulsion or limiting the admission of refugees.

Conclusion

In January 2016, the Turkish government made a move to 'benefit' from the qualified labour force of Syrian refugees by granting them limited employment authorization (Çetingüleç, 2016). Later newspaper headlines claimed that the most qualified and educated refugees were already 'taken' by Europe (*Milliyet*, 2016). In May 2016, the International Monetary Fund praised Germany for opening its doors to a limited number of Syrian refugees on the grounds that Germany needs new members of its labour force to compensate for its ageing population (IMF, 2016). Concerns with 'human capital' in relation to the displaced are clearly intact, as is the practice of choosing refugees for resettlement individually, at least in the EU context.

Instead of automatically qualifying for asylum because of persecution and hardship, Syrian refugees' right to asylum is secured with billions of euros paid to Turkey by the EU, which, in the form of a number of member state governments, declared the refugees to be 'undesirable'. Given the contemporary dynamics, there is reasonable ground to ask whether those same governments would take the same stance had these refugees been 'white'. In the United States, the Trump administration's migration policy not only places children in cages, but it also racially targets migrants. Trump's description of the convoy of refugees as 'very bad people' reproduces racist eugenicist paradigms that deploy a biologized essence to explain moral character. Race and labour are resilient categories that have long informed demographic policies of inclusion and exclusion, and they resurface today in political discourses and policies that raise yet again questions about what it means to be human.

Post-war international conceptions of human rights, with all of their limitations and problems in practice, conceptualized the human being as a subject worthy of dignity and endowed with rights. The fact that those who today seek to help refugees – whose lives are at risk – are criminalized and charged with human trafficking crystallizes a disturbing reconfiguration of who belongs to the category of human: the refugees are not counted among the human beings who are worthy of dignity and whose basic human right is the right to life. The criminalization of humanitarianism demonstrates that refugees are objectified, considered subhuman, reduced in their worth to their bodies along – as trafficking is usually a crime that entails smuggling human beings for exploitation or slave labour.

Xenophobic discourses routinely conceive of refugees and migrants as undesirable, large numbers of whom will dilute the stock of the white residents of the countries to which they are moving. Alt-right groups like Identity Evropa in the United States, which recently renamed itself the American Identity Movement, lament the dilution of white American ties to Europe.[17] Similarly to the active migration restriction movement of the 1930s, the current political administration's policies in the United States appear to empower these groups that are hostile to migration.

Demographic concerns over numbers, fears of the hyper-reproductivity of those from the 'Third World', and racialized reconfigurations of hierarchies of being human all continue to echo post-war demographic production of knowledge. In a rare instance of subjecting demographic production of knowledge in Germany to criticism, Susanne Schultz argues that demography has been presented as *the* science, leaving no room for the consideration of other perspectives on social issues in the country (2015). This approach to demography may not be as new as she seems to believe, as this essay argues. In fact, demographic anxieties and categories resurface unapologetically in 'Western' liberal democracies today both in xenophobic political discourses and state policies regarding displacement.

Anthropologist Susan Greenhalgh has discussed how demography is often perceived to be a highly methodical but non-theoretical field that is closely related to politics and policy-making organizations (1996, pp. 26-33). This may be why demographic production of knowledge is not questioned in the same way as demographic engineering projects themselves, as these critiques focus on actions taken as opposed to their epistemic foundations. There is a need for more critical research on demographic policies and epistemologies. This work might incorporate theoretical insights from a number of different fields, but scholars need to consider biopolitics in relation to demography – not only as population policy and regulation but also as a field of population study. The role played by the positivistic language of post-war demographic research needs to be interrogated in relation to demography's presentation as *the* science.

French philosopher Michel Foucault insisted that 'truth' was not an abstract term to be found 'out there', but something embedded in institutional and social frameworks of power (1980, pp. 109-133). Following this, it could be argued that every social context has its own 'régime of truth' – its 'general politics' of truth – that is, the types of discourse configured as true, the tools one deploys to identify statements as truth, and the techniques and procedures accorded value in the acquisition of truth. Universities and armies are just two of the multiple institutions that contribute to the production of truth. The field of demography, which as detailed above plays a key role in the configuration of the undesirable, is another example of these institutional processes. Demographic production of knowledge finds its echo both in policy and in public discourse, which, instead of questioning

---

17   https://www.americanidentitymovement.com/about/

the logics of exclusion, focuses on demographic concerns with the numbers of the 'wrong kind'.

As mentioned above, demography is both population regulation and a field of population study. Today, contemporary population management, especially in regard to displacement and biometrics, is the subject of numerous works on biopolitics – the regulation of populations in terms of bodies and numbers. Bringing post-war concerns with demography in conversation with contemporary scholarship on refugees, displacement, and humanitarianism organized around the concept of biopolitics is an important step towards interrogating the implications of post-war demographic epistemes.[18] Most scholars working on displacement and borders today engage biopolitical paradigms, but only rarely does such work draw links between contemporary biopolitics and post-war demographic production of knowledge on refugees.

Rethinking régimes of truth pertaining to demography and mobility with a critical eye on the past might help us to see the inconsistencies, anxieties, and contradictions embedded in the configuration of the 'undesirable'. This configuration has long informed humanitarian engagements with the displaced. Tracing these epistemic and political trajectories with respect to refugees and patterns of demographic concerns might help us to question structural discrepancies in the management of crises, past and present, and unravel the implications of being human.

Bibliography

Aktar, A. (2000) *Varlık Vergisi ve Türkleştirme Politikaları*, Istanbul, Iletişim Yayınları.

Çetingüleç, M. (2016) 'Turkey Grants Syrians Right to Work, but Is It Too Little, Too Late?', *Al Monitor.* 26 January [Online]. Available at https://www.al-monitor.com/pulse/originals/2016/01/turkey-syrian-refugees-granted-right-to-work.html.

---

[18] Ticktin, M. (2006) 'Where Ethics and Politics Meet: The Violence of Humanitarianism in France', *American Ethnologist*, vol. 33, no. 1, pp. 33-49; Pinkerton, P. (2019) 'Governing Potential: Biopolitical Incorporation and the German "Open-Door" Refugee and Migration Policy', *International Political Sociology*, vol. 13, no. 2, pp. 128-144; Davitti, D. (2018) 'Biopolitical Borders and the State of Exception in the European Migration "Crisis"', *European Journal of International Law*, vol. 29, no. 4, pp. 1173-1196; Fassin, D. (2001) 'The Biopolitics of Otherness: Undocumented Foreigners and Racial Discrimination in French Public Debate', *Anthropology Today*, vol. 17, no. 1, pp. 3-7; Estévez, A. (2014) 'The Politics of Death and Asylum Discourse: Constituting Migration Biopolitics from the Periphery', *Global, Local, Political*, vol. 39, no. 2, pp. 75-89; Bargu, B. (2017) 'The Silent Exception: Hunger Striking and Lip-Sewing', *Law, Culture and the Humanities*, pp. 1-28.

Cohen, G. D. (2011) 'The "Human Rights Revolution" at Work', in Hoffmann, S. L. (ed) *Human Rights in the Twentieth Century*, Cambridge, Cambridge University Press.

Crisis Group (2018) 'Turkey's Syrian Refugees: Defusing Metropolitan Tensions', Report No. 248, 29 January [Online]. Available at https://www.crisisgroup.org/europe-central-asia/western-europemediterranean/turkey/248-turkeys-syrian-refugees-defusing-metropolitan-tensions.

European Commission (2016) 'Refugee Crisis: Back to Schengen', 4 March [Commission Announcement].

European Commission (2017) 'EU-Turkey Statement One Year On', 17 March [Press Release].

European Council (2016) 'European Council Conclusions, 17-18 March 2016', 18 March [Press release]. Available at https://www.consilium.europa.eu/en/press/press-releases/2016/03/18/european-council-conclusions/.

Foucault, M. (1980) 'Truth and Power', in *Power/Knowledge: Selected Interviews and Other Writings, 1972-1977*, New York, Pantheon Books, pp. 109-133.

Galton, F. (1869) *Hereditary Genius: An Inquiry into Its Laws and Consequences*, London, MacMillan.

———. (1883) *Inquiries into Human Faculty and Its Development*, London, MacMillan.

Gillham, N. W. (2001) 'Sir Francis Galton and the Birth of Eugenics', *Annual Review of Genetics*, vol. 35, pp. 83-101.

Gini, C. (1927) 'The Scientific Basis of Fascism', *Political Science Quarterly*, vol. 42, no. 1, pp. 99-115.

———. (1954) '570,000 National and International Refugees in Italy', *Integration*, vol. 1, pp. 21-23.

Greenhalgh, S. (1996) 'The Social Construction of Population Science: An Intellectual, Institutional, and Political History of Twentieth-Century Demography', *Comparative Studies in Society and History*, vol. 38, no. 1, pp. 26-66.

Günaydın, E. (2019) 'Antalya: Gazipaşa plajlarında Suriyeli mülteci yasağını belediye başkanı veto etti' [Antalya: Mayor vetoed the ban of Syrian refugees in the beaches of Gazipaşa], *Euronews*, 11 June. https://tr.euronews.com/2019/06/11/antalya-gazipasa-plajlarinda-suriyeli-multeci-yasagini-belediye-baskan-veto-etti.

Hahn, J. (2015) 'Remarks by Commissioner Johannes Hahn on the EU's support for Western Balkans, Turkey and neighbourhood in addressing the challenges of refugee crisis', 17 September [Speech].

Hodgson, D. (1991) 'The Ideological Origins of the Population Association of America', *Population and Development Review*, vol. 17, no. 1, pp. 1-34.

———. (2015) 'Demography: History Since 1900', in Wright, J. D. (ed) *International Encyclopedia of the Social & Behavioral Sciences*, 2nd edn, vol. 6, Oxford, Elsevier, pp. 176-181.

Huxley, J. (1946) *UNESCO: Its Purpose and Its Philosophy*, Preparatory Commission of the United Nations Educational, Scientific and Cultural Organization.

Iğsız, A. (2018) *Humanism in Ruins: Entangled Legacies of the Greek-Turkish Population Exchange*, Stanford, Stanford University Press.

IMF (2016) 'Germany: Staff Concluding Statement of the 2016 Article IV Mission', International Monetary Fund statement. 9 May [Online]. Available at www.imf.org/external/np/ms2016/050916.htm.

Mazower, M. (2009) *No Enchanted Palace: The End of Empire and the Ideological Origins of the United Nations*, Princeton, Princeton UP.

Milliyet (Anon.) (2016) 'Eğitimli Suriyelileri Almanya kaptı' [Germany Caught Well-Educated Syrians], *Milliyet*. 4 March [Online]. Available at www.milliyet.com.tr/dunya/egitimli-suriyelileri-almanya-kapti-2203923.

Nathan-Chapotot, R. (1949) *Les Nations Unies et les réfugiés: Le maintien de la paix et le conflit de qualifications entre l'Ouest et l'Est*, Paris, Editions A. Pedone.

Özsu, U. (2015) *Formalizing Displacement: International Law and Population Transfers*, Oxford, Oxford University Press.

Petersen, W. (1999) *Founder of Modern Demography: Malthus*, New Brunswick, Transaction Publishers.

Sauvy, A. (1952) 'Trois mondes, une planète', *L'Observateur*, vol. 118, 14 August.

———. (1969) *General Theory of Population*, New York, Basic Books.

———. (1990) 'Alfred Sauvy on the World Population Problem: A View in 1949', *Population and Development Review*, vol. 16, no. 4, pp. 759-774.

Schultz, S. (2015) 'Reproducing the Nation: The New German Population Policy and the Concept of Demographization', *Distinktion: Journal of Social Theory*, vol. 16, no.3, pp. 337-361.

Secretary General of the United Nations (2016) 'Refugee Crisis about Solidarity, Not Just Numbers, Secretary General Says at Event on Global Displacement Challenge', 15 April [Press Release].

Sellnow, T. L. and Seeger, M. W. (2013) *Theorizing Crisis Communication*, West Sussex, Wiley and Blackwell.

Timmermans, F. (2015) 'Speech of First Vice-President Frans Timmermans at "Prague European Summit" Conference', 13 November [Speech]. Available at http://europa.eu/rapid/press-release_SPEECH-15-6079_en.htm.

Yıldırım, O. (2006) *Diplomacy and Displacement: Reconsidering the Turco-Greek Exchange of Populations, 1922-1934*, New York, Routledge.

Suffering and its Depiction through Visual Culture
How Refugees are Turned into Enemies and Figures of Hatred: The Australian Case

Claudia Tazreiter

Introduction

The resurgence of neo-nationalist or, indeed, turbo-nationalist sentiment, rhetoric, and policies is evident in many parts of the world, often manifest as apparent reactions to the arrival or presence of refugees, asylum seekers, and irregular migrants. The United Nations High Commissioner for Refugees (UNHCR) documents the number of refugees and displaced persons at 68.5 million in early 2019 – a number unprecedented since the end of the Second World War (see https://www.unhcr.org/en-au/figures-at-a-glance.html). This essay is interested in the manifestations of bordering practices targeting the most vulnerable migrants and border crossers, refugees, and asylum seekers. Bordering practices incorporate spatial, territorial, imaginative, psychological, affective, and political components (Mezzedra and Nielsen, 2013). Despite the multifarious, heterodox manifestations of 'border' in the contemporary world, as has been noted by many researchers, when it comes to the most needy and vulnerable migrants, nation-states' reactions to attempted border crossings or arrivals by refugees and asylum seekers reflect the adoption of a war footing, with rhetoric and interventions premised on the state facing an invasion. This war-like approach is used by states to justify giving themselves licence to remove, incarcerate, and punish refugees for their mode of arrival and for simply being present – as is the case, I argue, across the EU, North America, and Australia. This development is of great concern not only with respect to the rights of refugees, but also for the societies that wreak havoc through the adoption of such policies and arrangements.

Many states have responded to refugee flows with policies and practices that deter, detain, and deport asylum seekers, refugees, and other persons labelled 'irregular migrants', justifying this punitive response with rhetorical and emotive assertions of fear and danger. This essay explores artistic, visual, and filmic interventions by asylum seekers, refugees, and others who take exception to state practices. These interventions seek to document and recount refugees' own stories, to give voice to those who would otherwise be silenced through their entanglement with contemporary politicized processes in which nation-states are de-territorialized and re-territorialized, making and unmaking the idea of 'sovereign spaces' as territories for certain authorized members through the exclusion of others.

The focus here is on asylum seekers and refugees responding to the violence in the 'sovereign spaces' of detention centres. These spaces have been created specifically as part of Australia's practice of 'off-shore' detention and the processing of asylum seekers on the Pacific island nation of Nauru and on Manus Island, Papua New Guinea. This examination of these responses will begin with a brief consideration of the creation of these spaces as 'spaces of disappearance' (Tazreiter, 2018) before turning to several key artistic and narrative interventions that tell stories very different from the dominant governmental rhetoric.

The visual and artistic work considered here, which narrates and documents asylum seekers and refugees who are subject to state 'capture' and subsequently to a type of 'disappearance', lends itself to an analysis of a politics of resistance as well as one of reimagining the world. On the one hand, the politics of protest, resistance, or dissent is understood as a politics focused on the state, with advocating changes to state policy being the key driver (Tazreiter, 2010; Rosenberger, 2018). In this essay the focus will not be on policy change and advocacy for 'reform' in this traditional sense. It is instead social change or transformation that is of interest here, particularly that which comes about through the affective impact of visual cultures, particularly in their artistic, filmic, and photographic forms. The affective realm is felt through the body and also expressed through emotions (Tazreiter, 2015). This essay asks what impact affective visual forms of communication have on diverse publics' understanding of the circumstances faced by refugees.

The next section will evaluate the concept of outsider alongside contemporary refugee status. This is followed by a discussion of the context in which refugees arrive and are received in Australia. With this conceptual and contextual overview in place, chosen case studies of intervention, advocacy, and the sharing of the refugee voice through visual cultures are examined.

The contemporary refugee and outsider status

Borders have territorial as well as temporal and metaphysical manifestations. The physical territory encapsulating a nation-state as a sovereign space is easily visualized in the concrete, physical manifestation of walls, fences, border guards, and detention centres that dominate in the twenty-first century. However, the nation-state border and its historical legacy of defining members and limiting access to non-members through citizenship also generates psychological barriers manifest in social attitudes to those seeking to cross national borders, such as asylum seekers, refugees, and other 'irregular migrants'. In a different manner, the Mediterranean Sea forms a barrier to irregular migrants seeking to enter Europe through the sea corridor from North Africa, notably Libya. In Australia, irregular migrant arrivals – asylum seekers – face a new kind of 'border of disappearance' whereby the legal excision of Australian territory and off-shore removals have resulted in a hybridized form of border (Tazreiter, 2018). Asylum seekers wanting to invoke Australia's protection obligations under the Refugee Convention are sent to the small island nation of Nauru or to Manus Island, Papua New Guinea, where they are detained while their claims are assessed. This policy continues amid an information blackout ordered by the Department of Home Affairs that prevents Australian media from receiving information about attempted boat arrivals and 'push backs'. In early May 2019 a boat of Sri Lankan asylum seekers landed on Christmas Island but were forcibly returned to Sri Lanka. The news was only released to the Australian public in early June after the federal election held on May 18.[1] As will be discussed in more detail below, Australia's approach to refugees and asylum seekers has some unique and perhaps remarkable characteristics, but it also fits a pattern across the affluent parts of the world in which new borders and boundaries are created with respect to migrants and particularly to the most vulnerable among them. These borders are of the psyche and imagination as much as they are tangible borders on land crossings or at air and sea ports.

The 'border of disappearance' is a construction of the Australian state that is unique in that it renders refugees and asylum seekers physically 'removed' from the Australian mainland, where they seek to lodge a protection application, and psychologically disappeared to the general population of Australia through the rhetorical and legal shields of media and information blackouts and the long-standing demonization of asylum seekers and refugees (Tazreiter, 2017). Despite this double disappearance, the stories, voices, and faces of the detained make themselves heard and visible – even to those who are most vocal in wanting refugees to disappear. The concept of haunting introduced by Avery Gordon is apt in this context (2008). Gordon uses the language of haunting to convey an experiential modality to assist in understanding organized force, abusive systems, and their impacts on everyday life – impacts felt not only by the oppressed, but by wider society and the bystander. The themes of disappearance and haunting re-emerge later in this essay in the context of visual interventions by Behrouz Boochani, a refugee detained on Manus Island, and his collaborators.

In migration studies, the border relates to the gate-keeping role of the state, yet the concept simultaneously does the cultural work of sifting and sorting af-

---

[1] https://www.abc.net.au/news/2019-05-30/asylum-seekers-sent-back-to-sri-lanka-from-christmas-island/11163526

filiations, loyalties, and social ties built across generations and often in defiance of the geographically fixed spatiality of the nation-state. Properly seen, the border is polysemic: a coextensive concept that is physical, metaphysical, and relational (Mezzadra and Neilson, 2013). The multiplicity of types of bordering practices and imaginaries mitigates a linear analysis of migrant experiences (Tazreiter, 2004, 2015, 2017). The border relates as much to markets and human subjectivities as it does to ways of being in the world, which carry values and histories through the embodied self, or to the outline of the nation-state, with borders labelled most potently in recent political rhetoric as the sites of 'crisis migration'. The multiple meanings and policy implications of the border are manifest in migrant experiences and suffering (Sontag, 2013). An analysis of the border as membrane introduces an additional level of complexity to theorizing the border (Bauböck, 2015; Tazreiter et al., 2016), as do considerations of the border as paper barriers created through bureaucratic exclusion and as a 'non-place' or extra-territorial zone (Augé, 1992). It is not only the physical barrier of the border that mediates the opportunities for entry and access to rights, it is also the complex layers of law and of politics.

The Australian context:
An immigrant nation with a punitive refugee policy

Before examining case studies of visual interventions in more detail, it is worth considering the broader context of Australian refugee policy. The history of Australia's refugee policy and the country's treatment of asylum seekers and irregular migrants exists within an immigrant 'settler society' (Dauvergne, 2015) built on waves of immigration since British colonization 230 years ago. Ethnic, cultural, and linguistic diversity are key aspects of contemporary Australian life. Up to forty per cent of the population are first- or second-generation immigrants. Notwithstanding this long history as an immigration nation, Australia's approach to asylum seekers is widely considered by researchers, intergovernmental organizations such as the UNHCR, and human rights activists to be uniquely punitive. The harshest treatment is applied to asylum seekers arriving by boat. The year 1992 marks the start of the mandatory and indefinite detention of all asylum seekers as 'unauthorized arrivals'. Asylum seekers, as well as those designated refugees at the end of a legal assessment procedure, have been systematically dehumanized and labelled undeserving 'queue jumpers' who will destabilize the orderly Australian immigration system (Juss, 2017; Tazreiter, 2004).

Although Australia has a long history of settling refugee and humanitarian entrants who come through a pre-determined resettlement system, in recent decades refugee arrivals have generated high levels of anxiety and fear in the country. The degree of public debate over the arrival and reception of asylum seekers, the pointed political pronouncements, and copious media coverage are all incommensurate with the actual scale of asylum arrivals and their impact on the domestic population. At various points over the past two decades, even the anticipation of asylum arrivals has led to feverish public debate and anxieties about being swamped and overwhelmed by unwelcome and uninvited newcomers. The reality is that there is a small, yet steady arrival of asylum seekers, both by boat and by air, alongside a much more significant 'humanitarian' intake of refugees and people in 'refugee-like' situations who are selected for entry and resettlement in Australia.[2] As a country of immigration, Australia has a long history of proactive selection of immigrants according to specific categories that align with visa classes, such as skilled immigrants, family reunion immigrants, humanitarian and refugee immigrants, and, more recently, short-term migrant workers. The state and government, which are intent on controlling immigration, do not deal well with spontaneous arrivals that disrupt this orderly approach to immigration (Tazreiter, 2004).

One development that is especially pertinent to the argument presented here is that since 13 August 2012, asylum seekers arriving in Australia by boat without authorization (a valid visa) have been subject to 'offshore' or 'third country' processing on Nauru or Manus Island in Papua New Guinea (PNG). Australia first introduced 'offshore processing' in Nauru and PNG in 2001 under a plan called the 'Pacific Solution'. Offshore processing was suspended under the Labor government of Prime Minister Kevin Rudd in late 2007. It was resumed under the new Labor government of Prime Minister Julia Gillard in August 2012 and has continued under successive conservative Liberal-National coalition governments ever since. Offshore processing means that asylum seekers are forcibly transferred to Nauru or PNG and undergo a process to determine refugee status in those countries. This policy has received considerable negative scrutiny both within Australia and internationally as a breach of human rights standards and the spirit of the 1951 Refugee Convention.

Notably, since 2013 the conservative governments under Prime Ministers Abbott and Turnbull have also imposed a culture of secrecy and silence within the Australian Department of Immigration and Border Protection (now called Home Affairs), with little information officially available to journalists, lawyers, and the Australian public. The conditions and day-to-day circumstances in offshore detention have also been further distanced from public scrutiny through the privatization of service provision at these facilities. Papua New Guinea and Nauru, the two

---

2   For a history of Australia's response to refugees and asylum seekers, see Neumann, K. (2004) *Refuge Australia: Australia's Humanitarian Record*, Sydney, UNSW Press.

sites of detention centres under 'Operation Sovereign Borders', are poor, developing countries that receive significant foreign aid from Australia. The Australian government has attempted to cover up abuses faced by asylum seekers in offshore detention through federal legislation that restricts press freedom and discourages whistleblowing by employees of detention centres. Infringements on press freedom have been introduced via amendments made in 2014 to the *Australian Security Intelligence Organisation Act 1979 (Cth)*. This legislation prohibits media reporting of 'special intelligence operations'. Freedom of the press has been further curtailed by the enactment of the *Telecommunications (Interception and Access) Amendment (Data Retention) Act 2015 (Cth)*, which provides the executive branch with new powers to apply for 'journalist information warrants' that can compel telecommunications companies to surrender journalists' metadata, which may reveal a confidential source. Concerns that this would stifle investigative journalism were confirmed after documents obtained under the *Freedom of Information Act* revealed that 'eight stories on Australia's immigration policy [in 2014] were referred to the Australian Federal Police for the purpose of "identification, and if appropriate, prosecution" of the persons responsible for leaking the information' (Williams, 2015). Federal legislation has also criminalized whistleblowing, such as provisions under the *Border Force Act 2015 (Cth)* that allow a prison sentence of up to two years to be imposed on detention centre workers who publicly leak information on conditions at the centres. Medical professionals providing services to asylum seekers on Manus Island and Nauru are subject to a range of sanctions for disclosing any details of the detention environment to third parties. In October 2018, Chief Medical Officer Nicole Montana was dismissed for 'breaching rules' in defying the Nauru government on medical transfers. Only a month earlier her predecessor, Christopher Jones, had been removed from Nauru and had his visa cancelled for similar reasons (Koziol, 2018). Another senior medical officer on Nauru, Dr Nick Martin, was also dismissed for publicizing the deliberate medical neglect of refugees and asylum seekers on the island. In January 2019 he was awarded the *Bluprint for Free Speech Whistleblowing Prize* in London (Doherty, 2019). In accepting the prize, Martin said he was appalled to discover an offshore regime willing to risk the death of a refugee to uphold the Australian government's policy of keeping asylum seekers from entering Australia, concerned only with the public relations fallout of someone's death:

> A child setting themselves on fire was unacceptable, but a young man hanging himself was acceptable, that was OK. You were trying to have a conversation with the Australian Border Force saying 'this person is going to die', and they were essentially saying 'well, let's see if you're right'. (Doherty, 2019)

Despite the veil of secrecy that surrounds offshore detention, human rights activists, filmmakers, and detainees themselves have documented the life of asylum seekers on Nauru and Manus Island (Orner, 2016; Gleeson, 2016). In the years since 2012, the sexual and physical abuse of detainees has been documented by the UN, human rights groups, and detainees. In one case, guards murdered an asylum seeker; medical neglect has been documented, leading in several cases to the deaths of asylum seekers. Self-harm, suicide, and high rates of mental illness are widespread. On 13 February 2017 a group of international legal scholars lodged a Communiqué with the Office of the Prosecutor of the International Criminal Court on the circumstances in Nauru and Manus Island, charging that the detention of refugees and asylum seekers amounts to a crime against humanity (Stanford Law School, 2017). The submission details the range of human rights violations, including systematic and directed attacks. The Papua New Guinea High Court ruled in 2016 that the detention of asylum seekers on Manus Island was unconstitutional.

The conditions and day-to-day circumstances of life for asylum seekers on Nauru and Manus Island have only become visible to Australians through the work of human rights activists, filmmakers, and lawyers who make unofficial visits and, notably, through the efforts of detained asylum seekers themselves. Mobile, digital technologies are vital in producing, tracking, and distributing the artistic interventions explored in the examples detailed below. While some asylum seekers have been resettled in third states, many remain on Nauru and Manus Island, still waiting for their cases to be resolved after five years of incarceration (Grewcock, 2017; Cave, 2017).

Asylum seekers and refugees subject to offshore processing since 2012 on Nauru and Manus Island are largely invisible to the Australian public: they are effectively 'disappeared' through media and information blackouts that also include visa restrictions for lawyers and human rights organizations. These developments do not occur in a vacuum. They are closely related to social attitudes to immigration and outsiders, to dominant tropes in the nation's self-imagination, and the collective memories that are prioritized in these social and political processes. Visual and story-telling media have been utilized by activists and artists opposed to Australia's policies on refugees and asylum seekers to tell different stories.

Creating new visual and narrative cultures of resistance

The advocacy by and creations of Behrouz Boochani, a Kurdish journalist from Iran who has been detained for over six years on Manus Island, are especially convincing evidence of the potency of visual culture. In 2017 Behrouz, along with collaborator and co-director Arash Kamali Sarvestani, released the film *Chauka, Please Tell Us the Time*, which documents life in the detention centre over a period of time and is pieced together from hundreds of mobile phone clips and written texts. This film, along with other forms of visual and material culture and communication, have provided the Australian public access to counter-narratives to the dominant government narratives that generate fear, mistrust, and hatred towards refugees and asylum seekers. Mainstream media outlets have largely been unable to obtain permission for their journalists to travel to Nauru and Manus Island or gain entry to the detention centres. Eva Orner's 2016 film *Chasing Asylum* is the result of an exception to this general rule. It documents asylum seekers' journeys through Indonesia, Cambodia, Lebanon, Afghanistan, and Iran, and ultimately Manus and Nauru and shows the conditions detainees face on Nauru through footage shot by asylum seekers using mobile phones (Orner, 2016). Other evidence has been gathered by official visits to Manus and Nauru by the UNHCR and by international and Australian human rights organizations.

The story of the men and boys who live in the prison-like immigration detention facility emerges through the narrative form of *Chauka, Please Tell Us the Time*. The film is a meditation on the way everyday life proceeds in detention on a remote island such as Manus, giving Australians an account of the physical and psychological strain and trauma of those who are detained. The film is particularly powerful in the context of the Australian policies that have rendered asylum seekers and refugees invisible to the Australian public through these media and information blackouts and visa restrictions on lawyers and human rights organizations. *Chauka* is the name of a solitary confinement cell within the detention centre and is also the name of a bird found only on this island, a bird that is the symbol of the island, decorating its flag.

With the release of the film *Chauka*, Boochani received numerous invitations to appear in person at his film's premiere at international film festivals. The Australian government denied him a visa to travel to any of these. Nevertheless, Boochani has made appearances for interviews at numerous public events and screenings of his film via social media with the assistance of his translator, friend, and collaborator, Omid Tofighian. In this way, the Australian public and an international public have come to know the work, the face, and voice of Boochani and his fellow detainees.

Behrouz Boochani is the subject of numerous feature articles published in the international press during his detention on Manus Island. In 2018 he published a book of poetry, reflection, and criticism called *No Friend but the Mountains* with translator and collaborator Omid Tofighian (Boochani, 2018). Able to be virtually present thanks to technology, Boochani also collaborates with other writers and artists – even while in detention.

The Australian photographer Hoda Afshar has created a portrait of Boochani as well as a video installation that engages with the situation refugees face on Manus Island and Nauru. In describing his creative collaboration with artists and photographers, Boochani says:

> In my book *No Friend But the Mountains*, I describe the experience of refugees being exiled to Manus Island and our experience with the professional photographers

assigned to photograph us at the airport as we arrived. I explain this situation from the perspective of a defenceless subject – a completely passive agent lacking any semblance of power. By contrast, the photographers have the capacity to totally dominate our bodies – targeting us with their cameras, claiming ownership by taking photos of us. A kind of relationship exists between photographer and subject; in fact, a one-sided power dynamic between them.

On Manus, during the years that followed, I have had the opportunity to work closely with some of the most successful and well-known photographers and journalists in the world. However, in some cases, the oppressive power dynamic still conditions our interactions and has given me a strong sense of grievance. Within these relationships, the camera is weaponised and aimed at the subject in an attempt to capture an image of a refugee that evokes the most heightened sense of compassion possible.

In these cases, the refugee is a kind of subject that represents passivity: a being without agency, a being without personhood, a being without the nuances and complexities that constitute the human condition, a being without power, a being without a free and independent identity. In this relationship, the gaze of the camera or the journalist is a weapon that eliminates the personhood of subjects – they 'de-identify' the refugees.

However, the portrait of me by Hoda Afshar stands in opposition to a fixed and static image. It is a critique of the hackneyed impression of a refugee that has become idealised around the world. In this work, the subject is not passive; rather, he is fully aware of the image-making process and active in the production. In fact, he is a co-creator. One might say that the subject is also the creative source behind this work. In this portrait, one can see fire, one can see smoke – clearly, the context of the image is not unlike a comprehensive *mise en scène* produced by an artist. (Boochani, 2018b) (Fig. 11.1)

Behrouz Boochani and more than 547 other men and boys continue to be held on Manus Island without a resettlement option in spite of many having been granted formal refugee status several years ago. More than 359 men, women, and children were still being held on Nauru as of 26 March 2019, according to the Australian Refugee Council.[3] As outlined above, a key issue for lawyers, doctors, human rights activists, and concerned Australians with respect to the detention regimes on Manus Island and Nauru is the veil of secrecy that hangs over all aspects of detention and daily life for the 3,127 asylum seekers that have been sent to Manus Island and Nauru since the second wave of offshore detention arrangements that began in September 2012.

---

3   https://www.refugeecouncil.org.au/operation-sovereign-borders-offshore-detention-statistics/6/

Figure 11.1. Portrait of Behrouz Boochani, Manus Island, 2018.

Source: Hoda Afshar.

In August 2016, *The Guardian* newspaper published the so-called *Nauru Files*. These files detailed 2,116 separate incident reports written by staff in the Nauru detention centre between 2013 and 2015. The incident reports include cases of assault, sexual abuse, self-harm, child abuse, and sub-standard living conditions. The reports were leaked to journalists at *The Guardian* and published in toto. In the absence of regular media access to Nauru, a group of artists, designers, and advocates, together with human rights groups, commissioned an art exhibition featuring works responding to the *Nauru Files*.[4]

This intervention resulted in the exhibition *All We Can't See*, which opened in early 2018. It included works by prominent Australian artists as well as by refugees detained by the Australian government. Supported by Human Rights Watch, the exhibition was seen in Sydney and Melbourne and had an active virtual presence on social media. Well-known Australian artists such as Ben Quilty, Luke Scibberas, and Aida Tomescu are featured alongside refugee and asylum seeker artists such as Abbas Alaboudi and Ravi. Each work responds to one or more of the incident reports. Many of the works transport the audience into the world of abuse and self-harm regularly experienced by those in the Nauru detention centre – including the slashing of bodies, the sewing together of lips, and attempted suicide.

One of these powerful artworks is the photograph by Pia Johnson depicting a naked young woman with her back to the viewer and her nakedness shielded by a translucent curtain, a shower curtain. The incident report Johnson responded to was a complaint by a female asylum seeker to a teacher:

> I was asked on Friday (26-9-2014) by a fellow teacher [REDACTED 1] if I would sit with an asylum seeker [REDACTED 2] who was sobbing. She is a classroom helper for the children. A secondary teacher assistant [REDACTED 3] was present. She talked about several situations, some from Christmas Island, some from RPC3. She reported that she has been asking for a 4-minute shower as opposed to 2 minutes. Her request has been accepted on condition of sexual favours. It is a male security person. She did not state if this has or hasn't occurred. The security officer wants to view a boy or girl having a shower. (*Nauru Files*)

The artistic representations of the refugee issue by Australian artists resonate in other parts of the world, such as Poland, Hungary, Austria, and also the United States of America, where the politics of new nationalism and assertions of 'migrant crises' are also used to punish and deter refugees seeking safety and protection.

Conclusion

The figure of the migrant is by now a central part of contemporary Australian society, part of the ongoing contestation of belonging and of home, of insiders and outsiders, of visible and less visible peoples. Refugees and asylum seekers are one type of migrant, though special obligations are owed to them as outlined in legal instruments such as the Refugee Convention of 1951 and the Universal Declaration

---

4   https://www.theguardian.com/australia-news/gallery/2018/feb/03/all-we-cant-see-illustrating-the-nauru-files

of Human Rights of 1948. Although Australia may be geographically distant from the major refugee-producing regions and also from the many protracted 'crises' in the reception of refugees and irregular migrants, it is nevertheless an important case in the context of the global politics of refugees and migrants. Many Western countries have pointed to the Australian approach to asylum seeker arrivals and its tough border control regime as exemplary and worthy of emulation.

This essay has examined artistic interventions and visual culture as a particular politics – a way of framing, interpreting, and understanding social life and change. These works have been well received among wide audiences in Australia as well as in other parts of the world, notably across Europe and North America. Questions of *representation* and of *recognition* emerge through an elaboration of the specific geographies and the cultures of settlement, cultures of sanctuary, and cultures of home. The artistic and literary interventions detailed above indicate a hierarchy of human life and of the value attached to human life through the practices of immigration detention enforced on refugees and asylum seekers who wish only to reach Australia in order to claim protection. How then do the hierarchies of value attached to human life impact the way humans *see* each other and engage with the visualizations recorded in the context of segregation and exclusion? The discussion of borders that opened this essay suggests that a particular type of border is in operation in the Australian case, a 'border of disappearance'. Through the artistic and narrative interventions examined in this essay, it is made viscerally clear that it is the refugees and asylum seekers on Manus Island and Nauru who live this double disappearance. Australians and the Australian state are implicated in enacting the 'border of disappearance'.

Bibliography

Achiume, T. E. et al. (2017) 'Communiqué to the Office of the Prosecutor of the International Criminal Court: The Situation in Nauru and Manus Island: Liability for crimes against humanity in the detention of refugees and asylum seekers' [Online]. Available at https://www-cdn.law.stanford.edu/wp-content/uploads/2017/02/Communiqué-to-Office-Prosecutor-IntlCrimCt-Art15RomeStat-14Feb2017.pdf (Accessed 10 June 2019).

Augé, M. (1992) *Non-Places: Introduction to an Anthropology of Supermodernity* (trans. J. Howe), London, Verso.

Bauböck, R. (2015) 'Rethinking borders as membranes', in Weber, L. (ed) *Rethinking Border Control for a Globalizing World*, London, Routledge, pp. 169-178.

Boochani, B. (2018a) *No Friend but the Mountains* (trans. Omid Tofighian), Sydney, Pan Macmillan.

———. (2018b) 'This human being', *The Saturday Paper*, 24-30 November, p. 28.

Cave, D. (2017) 'Refugees Trapped Far From Home, Farther From Deliverance', *New York Times Magazine*, 18 November [Online]. Available at https://www.nytimes.com/interactive/2017/11/18/world/australia/manus-island-australia-detainees.html (Accessed 10 June 2019).

Dauvergne, C. (2015) *The End of Settler Societies and the New Politics of Immigration*, New York, Cambridge University Press.

Doherty, B. (2019) 'Nauru doctor wins global free speech award for speaking out on offshore immigration', *The Guardian*, 17 January [Online]. Available at https://www.theguardian.com/australia-news/2019/jan/17/nauru-doctor-wins-global-free-speech-award-for-speaking-out-on-offshore-immigration (Accessed 10 June 2019).

Gleeson, M. (2016) *Offshore: Behind the Wire on Manus and Nauru*, Sydney, Newsouth.

Gordon, A. F. (2008) *Ghostly Matters: Haunting and the Sociological Imagination*, Minneapolis, Minnesota University Press.

Grewcock, M. (2017) '"Our lives is (sic!) in danger": Manus Island and the End of Asylum', *Race & Class*, vol. 59, no. 2, pp. 70-89.

Juss, S. (2017) 'Detention and Delusion in Australia's Kafkaesque Refugee Law', *Refugee Survey Quarterly*, vol. 36, no. 1, pp. 146-167.

Koziol, M. (2018) 'Australia's chief medical officer on Nauru deported amid health policy crisis', *The Sydney Morning Herald*, 17 October [Online]. Available at https://www.smh.com.au/politics/federal/australia-s-chief-medical-officer-on-nauru-deported-amid-health-policy-crisis-20181017-p50a3r.html (Accessed 10 June 2019).

Mezzadara, S. and Neilson, B. (2013) *Border as Method, or, the Multiplication of Labor*, Durham, NC, Duke University Press.

Sontag, S. (2003) *Regarding the Pain of Others*, New York, Farrar, Straus and Giroux.

Orner, E. (2016) *Chasing Asylum: A Filmmaker's Story*, Sydney, HarperCollins Publishers Australia.

Rosenberger, S., Stern, V. and Merhaut, N. (2018) *Protest Movements in Asylum and Deportation*, Cham, Springer. [Online]. Available at https://doi.org/10.1007/978-3-319-74696-8_1 (Accessed 11 June 2019).

Tazreiter, C. (2004) *Asylum Seekers and the State: The Politics of Protection in a Security-Conscious World*, Aldershot, Ashgate.

———. (2010) 'Local to Global Activism: The Movement to Protect the Rights of Refugees and Asylum Seekers', *Social Movement Studies*, vol. 9, no. 2, pp. 201-214.

———. (2015) 'Lifeboat politics in the Pacific: Affect and the ripples and shimmers of a migrant saturated future', *Emotion, Space and Society*, vol. 16, pp. 99-107.

———. (2017) 'The unlucky in the "lucky country": Asylum seekers, irregular migrants and refugees and Australia's politics of disappearance', *Australian Journal of Human Rights*, vol. 23, no. 2, pp. 242-260.

———. (2018) 'Crisis Politics of Asylum Seekers and Migrant Arrivals in Australia', in Menjivar, C., Ruiz, M. and Ness, I. (eds) *The Oxford Handbook of Migration Crises*, Oxford, Oxford University Press, pp. 619-634. [Online]. Available at https://doi.org/10.1093/oxfordhb/9780190856908.013.71 (Accessed October 2018).

Tazreiter, C., Weber, L., Pickering, S., Segrave, M. and McKernan, H. (2016) *Fluid Security in the Asia Pacific, Transnational Lives, Human Rights and State Control*, London, Palgrave Macmillan.

Williams, G. (2015) *The Legal Assault in Australian Democracy* [Lecture to the ACT Law Society], 12 May [Online]. Available at https://www.actlawsociety.asn.au/documents/item/1304 (Accessed 11 June 2019).

Protesting

In Another's Shoes?
Walking, Talking, and the Ethics of Storytelling in *Refugee Tales* and *Refugee Tales II*

Harriet Hulme

Introduction

In 2015 the Refugee Tales project began with a group walk across the English countryside, which was designed to draw attention to the existence of indefinite detention in the UK. During the walk, writers told tales closely based on the experiences of someone who had suffered under the UK immigration system – a refugee, detainee, or asylum seeker – or someone closely connected with the asylum process – an interpreter, lawyer, or visitor to those detained. Those tales were published in 2016 in a collected volume, *Refugee Tales*. In 2017 a second book, *Refugee Tales II*, was published following another storytelling walk across South East England. This intersection of movement and narrative reflects the overall aims of the Refugee Tales project. As has been highlighted by David Herd, who co-edited both volumes with Anna Pincus, the UK asylum process works by regulating the movement and speech of those seeking asylum. Refugee Tales is an attempt to develop a collective response to these dual infringements by bringing those who have experienced indefinite detention into contact with those attempting to change the system, providing an opportunity to walk together and talk together in ways which can create understanding, empathy, and connection.

In this essay I explore the ways in which the three fundamental elements of the project – 'a culturally charged sense of space, the visible fact of human movement, and an exchange of information through the act of telling stories' (Herd, 2016a, p. 133) – are mobilized into an ethical response to the asylum crisis. I begin by discussing the importance of the two forms of collective encounter at the heart of the project: walking and talking. Drawing on the writings of Arendt and Levinas, I explore the ways in which these encounters – one physical, the other verbal – work to create a space, both literal and symbolic, in which the marginalized bodies and voices of those seeking asylum in the UK can be recognized.

I then turn to the third element of the project: the exchange of stories which culminated in the tales published in the two volumes of *Refugee Tales*. The collaborative nature of this storytelling process is highlighted by the paratext of each story, which states that it is the tale of a detainee, a migrant, a refugee 'as told to' an established author. But that 'as told to' is deceptive, for each of the tales has been modified in its conversion from the voice of the original tale teller into the words of the named author. These modifications draw attention to the ethical questions raised by the process of telling someone else's story. For Levinas, in telling another's tale we risk ignoring their alterity in our attempt to define their essence in our own words. Yet Arendt has suggested that it is through storytelling that we can truly reveal another person, simultaneously inscribing the private into the public in ways which allow for forms of collective recognition.

Do the stories told in *Refugee Tales* provide an opportunity to walk in another's shoes, to gain insight into indefinite detention and create a collective challenge to its existence? Or does the fact that these stories have been rewritten in the words of an established author diminish the ethical potential of this narrative impulse? In the second part of the essay, I bring Levinas and Arendt into conversation to explore the relationship between ethics and storytelling. While Levinas and Arendt offer very different approaches to this relationship, this difference, I argue, does not diminish the ethical potential of narrative. Rather, it highlights an ethical imperative at the heart of the narrative impulse, staging the ways in which telling someone else's story always requires us to consider our own ethics of relation. In *Refugee Tales*, this ethical imperative emerges through the narrative strategies deployed by several stories in the text, which foreground their own mediating practices to explore the responsibility involved in telling someone else's story. In so doing, *Refugee Tales* not only gives value and density to the lives of the individuals whose stories are told in its pages but also demands that we, as readers, recognize our own responsibility to approach those stories in the spirit of solidarity and hospitality.

Collective Encounters – Walking

Since 2015 there have been four Refugee Tales walks, each moving across parts of South East England which are 'culturally charged', in that they both resonate with current events concerning the asylum crisis and embody some of the most significant moments of British political and cultural history. Each of these walks has an ethical impetus: through the visible act of movement, the collective nature of that act, and the space in which that act takes place, each walk seeks to challenge the hostility of the political discourse surrounding the asylum process.

The first walk took place in the shadow of three of the UK's Immigration Removal Centres and drew attention to the key purpose of the Refugee Tales project:

to demand an end to 'temporary indefinite detention' in the UK. Unlike other European countries, the UK sets no limit on the length of time an individual can be held in one of these facilities. The government cannot legally detain someone for longer than is 'reasonable', but the ambiguity of this designation means that individuals have been detained for periods ranging from a couple of days to over four years (*Lumba (WL) v Secretary of State for the Home Department* [2011]; Home Office Immigration Statistics, 2017).

The inhumanity of this policy is dramatized by several of the stories in the *Refugee Tales* volumes. 'The Detainee's Tale', as told to Ali Smith, focuses on the dehumanizing nature of the detainment system, which forces detainees to live in rooms with barred windows, behind multiple locked doors, and under constant lighting and to suffer constant invasions of privacy from security officers, who check on them every fifteen minutes. As Rachel Holmes explores in 'The Barrister's Tale', this physical distress is accompanied by the mental trauma of never knowing when this experience will end, as the oxymoronic term 'temporary indefinite detention' renders time elastic:

> How do you measure time that's both temporary and indefinite? [...] [O]ur detainees face unlimited days that can only be counted upwards without the end in sight. [...] Waiting indefinitely to be removed imminently. It's like Beckett and Orwell met for a bender on Bloomsday in The Kafka's Head. (Holmes, 2017, p. 55)

While this linguistic manipulation and labyrinthine bureaucracy would not be out of place in *1984* or *The Trial*, temporary indefinite detention is not a fiction. Nor are the violations of human dignity and freedom at an end when those detained are finally released. Depending on the decision of the Home Office, a detainee can be forcibly 'returned', either to their home country – where they may face arrest, torture, or death – or to the country where they originally entered the EU, where the whole process of application, questioning, and possible arrest and detainment begins all over again. Alternatively, a detainee can be released back into the community to continue their application for asylum. As Amnesty International (2017) notes, this is the case for more than 50% of the detainees who were released in 2017, a figure which only serves to highlight the arbitrary nature of the detainment process. Even if released, ex-detainees are still constrained: they cannot work, must rely on a government-issued Azure card to buy groceries, and must regularly present themselves to be registered by the Home Office, a process which often involves walking long distances, as public transport is not covered by the Azure card (Herd, 2017a, p. 114).

In an essay in the *Times Literary Supplement*, Herd (2016b) explores this abuse of basic human rights by turning to Arendt's discussion of statelessness. Shut out of the 'common world' (Arendt, 1958, p. 53) – a public space which recognizes and supports them – the refugee is prey to a unique type of suffering, a violence 'without bloodshed' in which statelessness becomes a reason to deny them the consideration and respect due to every individual (Arendt, 1943, 76). The detainment centres in the UK are an example of the dispossession of which Arendt speaks: as spaces created within a nation to contain and hide those perceived as unwelcome within that nation, detainment centres remove individuals from the 'common world' in order to deny them the most basic human rights.

In making the 'visible fact of human movement' one of its key elements, the Refugee Tales project seeks to highlight and challenge the erasure of those rights. Herd refers to Arendt's 'space of appearance': as an individual emerges into public sight, they simultaneously demand recognition as a human being, a 'who' rather than a 'what' (Herd, 2017, p. 122; Arendt, 1958, pp. 198, 186). The Refugee Tales walks are one way to create such a space, to allow bodies that have been hidden to appear in the very places designed to hide them from view. Arendt's 'space of appearance' is, crucially, always collective: individuals come together, acting independently but with a shared purpose, creating a plural moment of 'power' which Arendt suggests can begin to effect political change (1958, p. 201). In Refugee Tales, too, it is through the collective, Herd suggests, that a challenge to the erasure of individual rights can best be mounted. The walks bring together people with very different life experiences – the refugee alongside the resident, those denied their basic human rights alongside those who have never had those rights queried – to create a space of appearance in which difference can begin to be mobilized into solidarity (Herd, 2017a, p. 114).

If the visible act of movement is a critical element in generating such a space, the geographical spaces through which the walks pass are no less important to the ethics of the Refugee Tales project. As Herd (2016a) notes, asylum seekers have a 'deeply compromised relation' to the geographical space of the UK: crossing the UK border initiates the possibility of refuge within that national space, yet it is also the act of border crossing which enables a denial of refuge, a denial often presented as essential to the preservation of the integrity of that national space. For Herd, this compromised relation is a product of the ways in which we, as communities and as individuals, understand our national identity as formed in relation to national space: in seeking to preserve that connection, he suggests, we have chosen to respond with hostility rather than hospitality to the refugee crisis (2016b, p. 138).

For Levinas, an ethics of hospitality takes shape precisely in relation to our concept of 'home' – those elements that are fundamentally embedded in our sense of who we are, as nations and individuals. In *The Time of Nations* he writes, 'To shelter the other in one's own land or home, to tolerate the presence of the landless and homeless on the ancestral soil so jealously, so meanly loved – is that the criterion of humanity? Unquestionably so' (1994, p. 9). To be hospitable, according to Levinas, we must encounter the other in those spaces which we guard so jealously as 'ours'. Only through such an encounter can we apprehend that our responsibility towards the other arises precisely in the moment we recognize that other as fundamentally, irreducibly *not us*. To recognize the fundamental separation of the other from the self is to acknowledge that we can choose to close our doors, turning hospitality into the hostility which is both its complement and its converse. But that recognition is also the moment when we can choose to share what is ours with another, the moment when ethics, understood *as* hospitality, takes shape (Smith, p. 249; Levinas, 1991, pp. 172-3).

The locations chosen for the Refugee Tales walks draw attention to the ways in which 'ancestral soil' can be mobilized in the name of both hostility and hospitality. The walks cross spaces which reflect the hostility of contemporary immigration policy. Kent, a county often described as the Garden of England, is now the site of several Immigration Removal Centres, and Westminster is where the hostile 2016 UK Immigration Act was passed by Parliament. But these walks also traverse landscapes which have historically resonated in more hospitable ways. The 2017 walk, for example, began in Runnymede, where in 1215 King John signed the Magna Carta, beginning the process of enshrining the rights of the individual into law. And the 2015 walk followed the Old Pilgrim's Way towards Canterbury, thus mirroring the fictional walk taken by Chaucer's pilgrims in *The Canterbury Tales*. For Herd, *The Canterbury Tales* introduces a connection between hospitality, movement, and narrative into the English language, creating 'a whole new language/Of travel and assembly and curiosity/And welcome' (Herd, 2016c, p. viii). Following in Chaucer's footsteps, Refugee Tales highlights this expression of welcome and curiosity at the heart of our cultural history; in so doing, Herd suggests, we may find ways to recapture these qualities now, to turn a hostile language and landscape into a manifestation of hospitality (Herd, 2016a, p. 139).

The Refugee Tales walks, by juxtaposing the past and present, challenge us to reflect upon our contemporary responses to immigration, to think through our relation to our 'ancestral soil' and how we might mobilize this relation hospitably. To walk from Crawley to Dover via Canterbury is to ruminate on the hospitality at the heart of one of the foundational texts of English language and culture while moving between Immigration Removal Centres that reveal our contemporary hostility to those from 'straunge strondes' (Chaucer, 1974, l.13). To walk from Runnymede to Westminster is to travel from the time and the place where the right to due process was enshrined in law to a time and place where those rights were removed from some individuals by the current UK parliamentary system. To walk in these places is thus to create a 'constellation' between past and present which brings these disparate moments together in illuminating forms (Benjamin, 1973, p. 265). In illuminating the connections between these different temporalities, these constellations offer us an opportunity to recognize that progress is not linear and to accept that sometimes we need to look to the past to find ways to challenge our contemporary experience. In so doing, Herd suggests, we may begin to find ways to act with recognition, responsibility, and hospitality towards those who seek shelter on our 'ancestral soil', to walk in solidarity with those who are *not us* as part of a collective movement for recognition and change.

Collective Encounters – Talking

A similar desire to turn hostility into hospitality motivates the other element of the Refugee Tales project: 'an exchange of information through the act of telling stories' (Herd, 2016b, p. 133). In his 'Prologue' to *Refugee Tales II*, Herd insists that telling stories is a fundamental human right:

> Think of it as
> A basic entitlement
> Like walking
> Telling stories
> [...]
> Not stigmatised
> For seeking asylum
> In this straunge stronde
> But listened to
> As they tell their tales. (Herd, 2017b, pp. 1-2)

Herd's emphasis on the importance of giving individuals the right to speak and, crucially, to be heard echoes Arendt's argument that our freedom to speak is a vital constituent of our human agency, another way to reveal 'who' we are beyond the 'what' of the labels which are used to define us (Arendt, 1958, p. 186).

And yet, for those caught up in the asylum process, the right to speak is indelibly bound up in 'what' that individual is considered to be – an illegal immigrant, an asylum seeker, an appellant – and 'what' they might become – a refugee, a detainee, an individual voluntarily or forcibly returned. In this sense, the decision to use storytelling to challenge the hostility of current immigration policy reflects the fact that the right to speech, like the right to movement, is compromised by the UK asylum process. On the one hand, the asylum process demands that those seeking asylum tell their story in a way that is sufficiently credible to warrant asylum. Yet that credibility is constantly called into question by a system that operates through a guilty-until-proven-innocent approach designed to meet arbitrary net migration targets with limited recognition of the human lives at stake (Grierson, 2018).

The limitations of this approach to storytelling are made explicit in 'The Soldier's Tale', as told to Neel Mukherjee. The tale is narrated by a Home Office employee who is reading the application submitted by Salim, a soldier from Eritrea. Salim's story begins when he escapes from an army prison. From this moment on, Salim suffers horror after horror: forced labour in Sudan; a journey across the Mediterranean in a leaky dinghy; abuse on his arrival in Italy; detainment when he reaches the UK. But for the official reading his tale, the truth of these experiences is called into question by elisions or gaps they perceive in the narrative:

> my suspicions, honed by years of Home Office training, cannot help but be aroused. These are the things that we've been trained to winkle out of applications and use to demolish the arguments for refugee status. [...] sometimes the arithmetic is not quite accurate: the date of birth changes, the number of years on the run [...] can be variable, the accounts contradictory or inconsistent [...] things not adding up properly. (Mukherjee, 2017, p. 86)

The language of this excerpt – to 'demolish', to 'winkle' – combines aggression with a subtle slyness. The onus here is on the individual to ensure that the necessary figures and facts have been provided to create a coherent and verifiable sense of the life they have lived. Storytelling, in this context, operates as a dehumanizing mechanism, one which demands an individual summarize the complexity of a human life in a series of facts which are then judged on their (in)consistency.

Herd refers to this dehumanizing approach as a 'hollowness within', a form of linguistic and narratorial violence which exceeds the obvious (if hidden) existence of indefinite detention or forced detainments or returns (2017a, p. 120). People seeking asylum repeatedly suffer this form of linguistic disenfranchisement: they are 'locked out of' or 'outside the skin of' the language (Herd, 2017a, p. 119; Herd, 2016a, p. 140). For Herd, creating a welcoming environment in which those who have been marginalized can share their stories with other people is one way to begin to combat this exclusion: through such conversations the space between those inside and those outside the language can be, if not eliminated, at least reduced (2016b, p. 142).

Each of the tales in the *Refugee Tales* volumes began as just such a conversation, one between someone with a personal experience of the asylum process and a professional writer. Jackie Kay explores the ways in which such a conversation might operate as an 'act of welcome' (Herd, 2016c, p. v) in 'The Smuggled Person's Tale'. In this tale, the conversation between Kay and 'The Smuggled Person' is described as the access point into a literal moment of hospitality: 'She opened the front door. It was a simple enough thing for her [...]. But to him it was quite something. Over the years travelling, he'd not often been invited into many homes' (Kay, 2017, p. 105). In this narrative, welcoming 'The Smuggled Person' into her house is only the beginning of a more symbolic act of hospitality that emerges, Kay suggests, via conversation. Having shared his story and, crucially, been heard, 'The Smuggled Person' leaves feeling 'beautifully light': '[W]elcome was all that was in his head now, and the rest of the terror for the moment had lifted' (Kay, 2017, p. 112).

Kay's imagined understanding of the thoughts in her interlocutor's head is an example of the ways in which narratives appropriate as well as illuminate the lives they recount, a point I will return to below. Nonetheless, her story highlights the link between conversation and hospitality which, in *Totality and Infinity*, Levinas identifies as central: '[T]he essence of language is hospitality and friendship' (1991, p. 305). Levinas's comment suggests that there is an intimate connection between linguistic exchange and the possibility of hospitality, a connection which he elucidates by suggesting that language enables an opening out of the world to the Other: every conversation 'offers things which are mine to the Other. To speak is to make the world common, to create commonplaces' (1991, p. 76). Levinas's words here intersect powerfully with Arendt's contention that it is the loss of a place in the 'common world' that leads to loss of rights for the refugee. If conversation is an opportunity to 'make the world common', it is also an opportunity to bring another into that world, to share an experience in ways that might begin to challenge the dispossession which Arendt suggests statelessness always entails.

In his 'Afterword', Herd suggests that sharing a story with another is always an opportunity to connect and, in so doing, to begin to challenge the hostility which characterizes the asylum process (2017a, 123). These conversational encounters are not only connective; for Herd, they can also be transformative:

> [T]o tell another person's tale one has to listen at length and very closely; at such length, in fact, that the experience being relayed grafts onto and alters the listener's language. This is what the writers reported; that having collaborated in the ways they did their relation to the language was significantly changed. (2016b, pp. 141-2)

While Levinas proposes that language offers an opportunity to share the world, Herd suggests that the experience of sharing that world can alter language itself. In Herd's reading, conversation becomes collaboration: one person's 'world' is shared with another and in the process, the language of that other is transformed. Crucially, for Herd, that transformed language can then be used to share that world elsewhere in a narrative circulation which, he suggests, is essential to the 'Real/Comprehending welcome' (2017b, p. 2) which the project attempts to create.

Herd's contention that circulating stories can operate as an act of hospitality gives an ethical value to the collaborative storytelling in *Refugee Tales*; in this collaboration, two individuals come together in a conversational encounter which aims to transform the hostility currently faced by (certain) immigrants. But the ethics of this collaborative process are not straightforward. While bringing the story of one person into the language of another can help to share that story, there is also the risk that that re-telling might come to erase the voice it seeks to allow to speak. In the next section, I engage with this risk and this possibility by turning again to the work of Levinas and Arendt to explore how their discussions of the ethics of storytelling intersect with the narrative strategies employed in Refugee Tales.

An Ethics of Storytelling

The collaborative process at the heart of the stories in *Refugee Tales* involved two elements. Firstly, the stories which emerged from those encounters 'had to be grounded in the reality of the experience that the person's original telling presented'. Secondly, 'the writer was invited to take the necessary formal decisions' to shape that tale to be shared with an audience both verbally and, later, via publication (Herd, 2016a, p. 141). These 'necessary' formal decisions emerge in different forms in each tale. Some employ a chronological, first-person structure: 'The Arriver's Tale', as told to Abdulrazak Gurnah, narrates the Arriver's experiences: the 'crime' he committed – describing female circumcision as genital mutilation; his escape to the UK and hopes of asylum; and the moment he is finally granted permission to stay and realizes that the right to remain does not grant him the right to work. Others are more formally experimental, merging prose and poetry, drawing on multiple languages or combining first- and third-person perspectives. Ian Duhig's 'The Walker's Tale', for example, mingles references to Kafka and Yeats and intertextual excerpts from Galeano and Szymborska into a poem which explores the Walker's experience of seeking asylum.

Herd states that the collaborative process was necessary to protect the anonymity of those still caught up in the asylum system who fear reprisal, living as they do under the constant threat of re-detainment. The decision to create these collaborative tales is, then, a reflection of a hostile political climate in which asking an asylum seeker to tell their own tale publicly remains a risk. To change this climate so that 'anonymity is not a shaping conceit' (Herd, 2016a, p. 142) is one of the central aims of the project. Paradoxically, this enforced anonymity is also what gives the act of collaborative storytelling its ethical resonance in the Refugee Tales project, for in requiring someone else to step in and tell another's tale, the project echoes Arendt's suggestion that storytelling is the best way to give value to an individual life. Arendt argues that while an individual can reveal 'who' rather than 'what' they are through speech and action, only when another person tells the story of that individual's life can what is truly unique about that individual emerge. In telling someone else's story, the complexity of that individual life is illuminated, shaped, and revealed as worthy of recognition (Arendt, 1958, p. 184).

In *Refugee Tales*, this illumination is presented as the ethical impetus for the project: as Chakrabarti notes on the book jacket, the tales attempt to rehumanize 'some of the most vulnerable and demonised people on the planet' (Chakrabarti, 2016). Nonetheless, the changes made to the tales in *Refugee Tales* also raise questions about the ethics of telling someone else's story, particularly in contexts where the right of that 'someone else' to tell their own story is already significantly diminished. It would be possible to provide anonymity without involving established writers, for example, simply by removing identifying features from the tales told. And anonymity does not necessarily require that formal changes be made to a story. Herd argues that this collaborative process is essential if the voices of those currently marginalized by the asylum process are to be heard. And yet in deciding to alter those stories, Refugee Tales also risks erasing those voices in the very ways it attempts to enable them to speak.

In *Reality and Its Shadow*, Levinas suggests that this erasure is the risk of all representative art, including storytelling. As discussed above, for Levinas (1991), it is in the face-to-face encounter that the other interpolates us – through expression as much as word – and it is in this encounter that our responsibility to that other emerges. This responsibility develops at that moment in which we recognize the other as fundamentally irreducible to and incomprehensible within our sense-making frameworks: only through acknowledging this absolute difference can we confront the limitations inherent within our ways of knowing the world. To convert that encounter into a narrative is, Levinas argues, a failure to recognize those limitations. If we believe that we can reveal the essence of someone else in a narrative, we suggest that it is possible to understand another sufficiently to reproduce that essence in our own words. In telling a story about someone else we turn those whom we narrate into 'beings that are shut up, prisoners' (Levinas, 1989, p. 139), their alterity constrained for eternity by the framework of the story we have selected for them (Davis, 2017, p. 26).

Levinas's conception of storytelling poses problems for a project like Refugee Tales, which seeks to use narrative practices to reveal the individual lives of those dehumanized by the asylum process. Can storytelling be conceived as an act of illumination, as Arendt suggests, if, as Levinas insists, narrative practices always risk imprisoning the narrated subject? For Hannah Meretoja, storytelling is always caught up in this tension between responsibility and appropriation, elucidation and reductionism, as embodied by the difference in the perspectives taken by Arendt and Levinas (Meretoja, 2016, p. 112). But, Meretoja argues, it is precisely the tension between these two conceptions of the task of the storyteller that allows us to begin to establish what *is* ethical about the act of narrating someone else's tale. Meretoja acknowledges that some modes of storytelling do function as Levinas suggests, 'subsuming singular experiences under culturally dominant narrative scripts'. These 'subsumptive' modes reduce the individual to an abstract conception, perpetuating 'the tendency to see individuals as representative of the groups to which they belong according to gender, sexual orientation, ethnicity, age, class, and so on' (2016, p. 112). But the narrative impulse does not have to function in this way, Meretoja asserts, and not all narratives do. Some storytelling modes 'problematize simplistic categorization of experiences, persons, and relationships'. These 'non-subsumptive' modes 'function as counter-narratives that consciously challenge stereotype-reinforcing hegemonic narrative practice' (Meretoja, 2016, p. 112). For Meretoja, it is this conception of storytelling that underpins Arendt's discussion of the subject in *The Human Condition*.

The distinction Meretoja draws between subsumptive and non-subsumptive modes is a valuable one in discussions of the ethics of storytelling in relation to *Refugee Tales*. In Meretoja's reading, storytelling is neither innately ethical or non-ethical; rather, it is in the ways that we narrate, our narrative strategies and frameworks, that we choose to respond ethically or otherwise to the individual life which we recount. For a narrative such as *Refugee Tales*, which is concerned precisely with giving dignity to the individuals whose tales it tells, these strategies are particularly critical. As will be illustrated below, several of the stories draw attention to their own narrative strategies and mediating practices, highlighting in the process the ethical risks and possibilities of the narrative impulse.

'The Student's Tale' and 'The Refugee's Tale'

As Helen Macdonald explores in 'The Student's Tale', narratives told about refugees often operate in 'subsumptive' ways by reducing the complexity of the lives they narrate to simplistic generalizations:

> I think about all the stories we tell of refugees and how they are always one story or another, never both at once. Tragic stories or threatening stories. Victims or aggressors. Never complicated, always simple, always with clean edges. Easy pigeonholes to fit people who have been forced to take wing. But a hole is not just a pigeonhole. It's the space between two things. [...] It's the space between past and future, between old lives and new. (2017, p. 8)

To recognize a refugee as a victim is a valid response to the experiences we might understand as implicit when the term 'refugee' is used. Yet to conceive of a refugee as *only* a victim is to focus on one end of a continuum that also allows, at its other end, for the conception of a refugee as *only* a threat: it is a simplistic response to a complex situation. Such simplistic responses subsume the individual beneath whichever culturally dominant narrative of the refugee experience we, as readers and writers, seek to reproduce.

Macdonald's play on the word 'pigeonhole' highlights one way in which narratives of the refugee experience might move beyond simply replicating such reductive conceptions. To challenge political and cultural narratives that simplify complex histories requires a narrative approach that focuses on the holes, spaces, and gaps within these pigeonholes: those elements of a lived experience which are surprising, incomprehensible, or challenging to our assumptions. In *Refugee Tales*, this narrative approach takes shape through a contrast between the simplistic labels deployed as the paratextual framework of the text and the complexity of the stories told within that framework. While the title of the text suggests these are 'refugee tales', very few of the tales told actually belong to those who have been granted refugee status in the UK. Instead, as the titles of the individual stories – 'The Migrant's Tale', 'The Voluntary Returner's Tale', 'The Detainee's Tale' – suggest, most are told by those whose claim to be a refugee has not been considered sufficiently valid for the status to be granted. And the stories that follow these labels demonstrate precisely how dehumanizing, limiting, and inconsistent the use of such terms can be. Why is the story of Aziz, 'The Migrant', who was arrested and imprisoned in Syria for criticizing the regime, less of a justification for refugee status than that of Farida, 'The Refugee', who is fleeing religious persecution in Sudan? Why is 'The Detainee' detained for several years despite being a victim of human trafficking? Why is 'The Appellant' forced to prove his immigration status despite living legally in the UK for nearly 30 years?

In highlighting the limitations of such labels, the tales told in *Refugee Tales* attempt to bring to life the complex individual who exists beneath the immigration status. While issues such as labels and stereotypes are not themselves narrative concerns, how narrative strategies respond to, challenge, or affirm these labels and stereotypes reflects the distinction between subsumptive and non-subsumptive practices which Meretoja discusses in *The Ethics of Narrative*. In 'The Refugee's Tale', as told to Patience Agbabi, this distinction is the focus of the text, which explores how stereotypes can be generated or undermined by the narrative approach of the storyteller. The story is narrated by Farida, 'The Refugee'. As was the case in Kay's 'The Smuggled Person', the author imagines the thoughts of the person whose tale is being told. This narrative approach highlights the ways in which a storyteller can attempt to dramatize the internal world of another person in ways which, for Levinas, are fundamentally appropriative. In 'The Refugee's Tale', however, this imagined thought process becomes a way to turn the focus around in order to explore the assumptions of the author herself:

> first time meeting; maybe you say the word
> 'Refugee' in your head when you call me Farida,
> Refugee what is that burn mark on your hand?
> You already have a story of the torture
> I suffered in my war-torn homeland.
> But these marks are from cooking bread for my family,
> this is the first time I'm cooking in my life!
> I never even made a cup of tea
> back home. (Agbabi, 2016, p. 125)

The disjunction between the imagined story of the burn mark and its real origin is the disjunction between the abstract and the concrete, between a general conception of a refugee and the individuality of Farida's experience. For Farida, this disjunction not only reflects but also sustains the experience of becoming a refugee, which is, by definition, an experience of separation from those elements which once constituted her identity: '"[I]t pains me more/than everything to cut myself from my home,/my country, with every section of my claim/" she says. "Now I'm underclass, my head covered with shame. How am I begging when I can't remember my name?"' (2016, p. 131). The term 'refugee' both describes and circumscribes those to whom it is applied: designating an individual as a refugee recognizes that this individual needs to leave behind a previous life to be safe; it also, Farida suggests, results in this individual being subsumed by this new identity in ways which limit how that new life can be lived.

If 'The Refugee's Tale' begins with the failure of the storyteller to recognize the individual behind the label 'refugee', it ends by emphasizing the ethical imperative that they find ways to achieve this recognition. 'The story ends where you put the frame', says Farida, 'but however it begins, remember my name' (2016, p. 132). As Levinas suggests, the storyteller has the power to shape, delimit, and define the life that emerges in the text. There is always the risk that the framing of a story will work to create or regenerate reductive narratives. But Farida's words also suggest that these challenges do not need to present an ethical impasse. Precisely because they have the power to shape the life narrated, the storyteller also has the power to enable that life to emerge in its density and complexity, to ensure that it is not the label 'refugee', but the name of Farida herself that is recognized and remembered. For Arendt, 'no one has a life worthy of consideration about which a story cannot be told' (Arendt, cited in Cavavero, 2000, p. 129). We might, in the context of *Refugee Tales*, reverse this formulation: it is in telling a story about someone's life that we insist that it be recognized as worthy of consideration. In taking a metatextual approach to the narrative she tells, Agbabi confronts and draws attention to the frameworks she, as storyteller, has imposed on the experiences, the thoughts, and the voice of Farida. But she also insists on the importance of making space for that voice and for some of the complexity of Farida's life to emerge from within the anonymity which is the precondition of the text.

'The Lover's Tale'

The ways in which narrative frameworks can operate to illuminate rather than reduce the complexity of a human life is the subject of 'The Lover's Tale', as told to Kamila Shamsie. This is the story of John, a soldier who flees his home after being forced to witness and participate in a series of appalling atrocities. Shamsie records her perceptions of John as he tells his story, noting that his words seem ordered and coherent: she later discovers that he learnt to shape his experiences into narrative as part of cognitive behavioural therapy. For Shamsie, narrative can be a powerful tool in the mediation of traumatic memories:

> Stories allow us to structure our experiences into beginning, middle, end [...]; stories allow us to put forward our own points of view and interpretations; stories, in short, allow us a measure of control over our memories. In lives such as John's, when control is so often in other people's hands, the value of that must be enormous. (2017, p. 12)

In 'Recapturing the Past', Cathy Caruth suggests that, through storytelling, survivors of traumatic events can begin to integrate those events into narrative memory and gain some control over the flashbacks which characterize traumatic recall. But it is precisely because of the force of that traumatic recall that this narrative framework may prove insufficient (Caruth, 1995, p. 153). As John continues to tell his story, his memories overwhelm the artificial coherence of the narrative structure he has imposed upon them: '[T]he ordered re-telling began to fracture, gaps appeared, the story doubled back on itself' (Shamsie, 2017, p. 12). The difficulty of converting the overwhelming and fragmentary nature of traumatic recall into a coherent story highlights the inhumanity of an asylum process which uses consistency as a gauge for truth. It also highlights another reason for the collaborative approach taken by *Refugee Tales*. As Herd notes, in several cases the people whose stories were to be told were so traumatized by the events that had led them to seek asylum in the UK that it would have been inappropriate, if not impossible, to ask them to tell those stories in front of an audience (2016a, p. 141). Mediation through the voice and words of a storyteller is a way to share those stories which might otherwise not be heard.

But how does one narrate an experience which, precisely because it cannot be told in a coherent manner by those who have experienced it, exceeds conventional representational frameworks? In 'The Lover's Story', Shamsie approaches this task by marking not only the descriptions and the details which constitute John's story, but also the gaps. These gaps are highlighted in the content of the story: Shamsie notes when John skims over parts of his story or when specific details are absent. But she also integrates breaks into the narrative framework, cutting John's story into short paragraphs with gaps between each one. At certain points, these gaps are marked by an asterisk; at others, they are simply a white line on the page:

> '[the Captain] put his life at risk for me. He let me go.'
> For the third time, John returned to his country of exile.
>
> *
>
> How could this possibly be the end of the story?

*

Because he allowed John to escape, the Captain's hands were placed in wet cement, which was left to dry, and he was dropped into the sea. His dead body washed up on a beach. John received news of this when he was in exile.

*

(2017, p. 19)

The blank spaces incorporated into and surrounding the narrative of this atrocity fracture the supposed logic which traces the Captain's death back to the fact that 'he allowed John to escape': the cause and effect suggested by the word 'Because' is undermined by the fragmentary narrative which precedes it. As Caruth discusses, many survivors are reluctant to create a coherent narrative from their traumatic experiences because such coherence robs that experience of 'the force of its *affront to understanding*' (1995, p. 154). Finding a way to render such experiences true without suggesting they are coherent is a dilemma inherent in the attempt to narrate a trauma, whether one's own or another's. But in the lacunae which punctuate John's story, Shamsie makes space for this incoherence, allowing that the traumas which have marked John's life may be revealed as much by these gaps and breaches as by the events told.

As Levinas suggests, narrative form can risk overpowering the alterity of another's life, creating an illusion of understanding where none exists. But in 'The Lover's Story', formal strategies also work to highlight the limitations of understanding, to insist upon what cannot be narrated as much as what can be. In this sense, Shamsie's approach reflects Arendt's conception of storytelling in 'Isak Dinesen', in which she writes that 'the story reveals the meaning of what would otherwise remain an intolerable sequence of events [...] without committing the error of defining it' (2001, p. 106). While Arendt highlights here the link between narrative and meaning, she does not position storytelling as a way to *give* meaning to what is intolerable or incomprehensible. Rather, by separating meaning from sequence, Arendt's words suggest that the power of storytelling lies not in its ability to create a linear coherence between disparate parts but in the value it can give to what may be fragmentary or unclear: storytelling illuminates the impenetrability of another life. In 'The Lover's Story' Shamsie uses her narrative frame to highlight those elements of John's life which remain disparate, fragmented, and ultimately incomprehensible, but which, nonetheless, need to be told.

In Another's Shoes? Recognition and Responsibility

The three tales which I have discussed here highlight ways in which responsibility can emerge through narrative strategies that foreground the ethical risk of mediating another's story. As Arendt suggests, however, this responsibility is not only the job of the storyteller: the potential for narrative to reveal the individual life as worthy of recognition requires not only that a story be told but also that it be heard and recognized by an audience that can collectively engage with, witness, and retransmit the story told (1965, p. 198). At the end of *Refugee Tales*, Herd offers a similar assessment of the value of the collaborative storytelling process at the heart of the text: 'What perhaps it means is that a story that belongs to one person now belongs, also, to other people; that other people acknowledge the experience that constitutes the story, but also that in making that acknowledgement they register responsibility' (2016a, p. 142). To register responsibility requires that we collectively recognize what is often kept from view: the stories of those who have been repeatedly marginalized, dehumanized, and villainized by the asylum process.

But to register responsibility also means that we hold ourselves accountable for our own responses to the stories we read. Martha Nussbaum suggests that reading a story about someone else 'means the ability to think what it might be like to be in the shoes of someone different from oneself, to be an intelligent reader of that person's story, and to understand the emotions and wishes and desires that someone so placed might have' (2010, pp. 95-96). Nussbaum's comment positions ethics as understanding: if we can place ourselves imaginatively in another's shoes, we can understand and empathize with them and, therefore, respond with compassion to their situation. But to attempt to stand in someone else's shoes requires us to eliminate the gap and the difference between us and them, to occupy their unique place in the world.

For Arendt, it is in this distance between us and the person whose story we encounter, in the ways that we are *not* them, that we can make space for their unique identity to emerge. Similarly, Levinas argues that it is in accepting that we cannot understand another fully and completely that we can recognize the limits of our sovereignty and, through this recognition, begin to develop an ethics of responsibility towards the other. As Colin Davis notes, Levinas's critique of representative art poses problems for any critic who wishes to suggest that reading might offer an encounter in a Levinasian sense (2017, pp. 25-6). Yet, in one regard at least, the responsibility which can emerge via reading is not so fundamentally estranged from Levinas's ethics of the encounter or from his critique of narrative. If we imagine that we can truly step into someone else's shoes by reading a narrative of their experiences, erasing the distance between us and them, we fail to acknowledge their difference and the limits of our own perspective. It is this limit, this difference and this distance which, for both Arendt and Levinas, allows us to acknowledge the unique, irreducible individuality of another.

In her essay 'Fiction as Restriction', Dorothy Hale refers to Spivak's comment that reading always requires us to 'take a step with' another person (Spivak, 2002, p. 23). For Hale, '"Taking a step with" is to take a leap into the dark: both are predicated on the will to believe in alterity, in the possibility of a law outside and different than the self' (2007, p. 201). To see reading as taking a step *with* someone else as opposed to stepping *into* someone's shoes is, in the context of *Refugee Tales*, to acknowledge the distance that remains between the lived experience and the read experience, between self and other. But it is also to suggest that the experience of reading might hinge upon the question of solidarity rather than similarity. We do not need to stand in someone else's shoes to be able to stand up for their rights. It is, perhaps, in the very ways that we are not able to adequately identify with or understand their experience that the importance of standing up for that individual might manifest itself.

Conclusion

The Refugee Tales project is concerned with establishing an ethical and hospitable response to the asylum crisis by enabling different forms of encounter. The collective walks, which are a key element of the Refugee Tales project, are one way in which such an encounter can occur. Those who walk and talk together, '[n]etworks of visitors and friends' (Herd, 2016b, p. viii), come together to recognize and articulate a responsibility to those who, precisely because they are not us, are marginalized and alienated by our language and our politics. And yet, as Herd insists repeatedly, such encounters are a rarity for those caught in an asylum system which sustains itself by preventing dialogue and keeping people from view. In a political context which deliberately limits the opportunities for us to meet face-to-face with those detained, we need to find other ways for such encounters to occur.

As I have discussed, mediating an encounter through narrative always involves forms of appropriation as well as illumination. Yet this disjunction does not nullify the ethical potential of storytelling. If we define ethics as the attempt to understand the difference between good and bad responses, an ethics of narrative lies precisely in the region between appropriation and illumination, hostility and hospitality. There is no ethics without responsibility and no responsibility without accepting that there is no preconditioned response to any encounter: whether enacted face-to-face, through speech or action, or mediated via a textual narrative, every encounter is a task, an interpolation by another which demands that we choose whether to respond with hospitality or hostility. In the Refugee Tales project, we come face-to-face with this ethical task: through the challenging encounters of walking, talking, and storytelling, the project asks us to reflect on our responses to those seeking asylum and to try to shape these in the spirit of solidarity, hospitality, and responsibility.

Bibliography

Agbabi, P. (2016) 'The Refugee's Tale', in Herd, D. and Pincus, A. (eds) *Refugee Tales*, Manchester, Comma Press, pp. 125-32.

Amnesty International (2017) 'A Matter of Routine: The use of immigration detention in the UK' [Online]. Available at www.amnesty.org.uk/files/2017-12/A %20Matter %20Of %20Routine %20ADVANCE %20COPY.PDF?ya06n1Z2u H6JobP8HmO7R2Pn7nabDymO (Accessed 4 September 2018).

Arendt, H. (1958) *The Human Condition*, Chicago, The University of Chicago Press.

———. (2001) 'Isak Dinesen 1885-1963', in *Men in Dark Times*, New York, Penguin Books.

———. (1943) 'We, Refugees', *Menorah Journal*, vol. 31, no. 1, pp. 69-77.

Benjamin, W. (1973) 'Theses on the Philosophy of History', in *Illuminations* (trans. H. Zohn), London, Jonathan Cape, pp. 255-66.

Caruth, C. (1995) 'Recapturing the Past: Introduction', in Caruth, C. (ed) *Trauma: Explorations in Memory*, Baltimore, The Johns Hopkins University Press, pp. 151-7.

Cavavero, A. (2000) *Relating Narratives: Storytelling and Selfhood* (trans. P. A. Kottman), London, Routledge.

Chaucer, G. (1974) *The Tales of Canterbury*, Boston, Houghton Mifflin Company.

Chakrabarti, S. (2016) Quotation on the front cover of *Refugee Tales*, Herd, D. and Pincus, A. (eds), Manchester, Comma Press.

Davis, C. (2017) 'Truth, Ethics, Fiction: Responding to Plato's Challenge', in Davis, C. and Meretoja, H. (eds) *Storytelling and Ethics: Literature, Visual Arts and the Power of Narrative*, London, Routledge, pp. 23-36.

Grierson, J. (2018) 'Hostile environment: anatomy of a policy disaster', *The Guardian*, 27 August [Online]. Available at www.theguardian.com/uk-news/2018/aug/27/hostile-environment-anatomy-of-a-policy-disaster (Accessed 4 September 2018).

Hale, D. J. (2007) 'Fiction as Restriction: Self-Binding in New Ethical Theories of the Novel', *Narrative*, vol. 15, no. 2, pp. 187-206.

Holmes, R. (2017) 'The Barrister's Tale', in Herd, D. and Pincus, A. (eds) *Refugee Tales II*, Manchester, Comma Press, pp. 53-61.

Home Office Immigration Statistics, April–June 2017 [Online]. Available at www.gov.uk/government/publications/immigration-statistics-april-to-june-2017/how-many-people-are-detained-or-returned (Accessed 31 August 2018).

Herd, D. (2016a) 'Afterword', in Herd, D. and Pincus, A. (eds) *Refugee Tales*, Manchester, Comma Press, pp. 133-43.

———. (2016b) 'Outside the skin of language', *The Times Literary Supplement*, 22 June [Online]. Available at www.the-tls.co.uk/articles/public/outside-the-skin-of-language/. (Accessed 09 November 2018).

———. (2016c) 'Prologue', in Herd, D. and Pincus, A. (eds) *Refugee Tales*, Manchester, Comma Press, pp. v–x.

———. (2017a) 'Afterword', in Herd, D. and Pincus, A. (eds) *Refugee Tales II*, Manchester, Comma Press, pp. 113-23.

———. (2017b) 'Prologue', in Herd, D. and Pincus, A. (eds) *Refugee Tales II*, Manchester, Comma Press, pp. 1-2.

Kay, J. (2017) 'The Smuggled Person's Tale', in Herd, D. and Pincus, A. (eds) *Refugee Tales II*, Manchester, Comma Press, pp. 105-12.

Levinas, E. (1991) *Totality and Infinity* (trans. A. Lingis), Dordrecht, Kluwer Academic.

———. (1989 [1948]) 'Reality and Its Shadow' (trans. A. Lingis), in Hand, S. (ed) *The Levinas Reader*, Oxford, Basil Blackwell Ltd, pp. 130-43.

Lumba (WL) v Secretary of State for the Home Department [2011] UKSC 12, 23 March [Online]. Available at https://www.supremecourt.uk/cases/docs/uksc-2010-0062-judgment.pdf (Accessed 31 August 2018).

Macdonald, H. (2017) 'The Student's Tale', in Herd, D. and Pincus, A. (eds) *Refugee Tales II*, Manchester, Comma Press, pp. 3-9.

Meretoja, H. (2017) *The Ethics of Storytelling: Narrative Hermeneutics, History, and the Possible*, Oxford, Oxford University Press.

Mukherjee, N. (2017) 'The Soldier's Tale', in Herd, D. and Pincus, A. (eds) *Refugee Tales II*, Manchester, Comma Press, pp. 85-91.

Nussbaum, M. (2010) *Not for Profit: Why Democracy Needs the Humanities*, Princeton, Princeton University Press.

Shamsie, K. (2017) 'The Lover's Tale', in Herd, D. and Pincus, A. (eds) *Refugee Tales II*, Manchester, Comma Press, pp. 11-23.

Smith, W. H. (2011) 'Neither Close nor Strange: Levinas, Hospitality and Genocide', in Kearney, R. and Semonovich, K. (eds) *Phenomenologies of the Stranger: Between Hostility and Hospitality*, New York, Fordham University Press.

Spivak, G. (2002) 'Ethics and Politics in Tagore, Coetzee, and Certain Scenes of Teaching', *Diacritics*, vol. 32, no. 3/4, pp. 17-31.

The Civil March for Aleppo
Zero-Level Protest or Networking in Action?

Clara Zimmermann

Introduction

In the late summer of 2015, record numbers of people sought refuge in Europe, eliciting a wide range of public responses. Included among these was an initiative that began a year and a half after the record influx of refugees and asylum seekers: The Civil March for Aleppo proposed participants walk from Berlin to Aleppo 'along the so-called "refugee route", just [in] the opposite direction' (Civil March for Aleppo, 2016b). The March passed through Germany, the Czech Republic, Austria, Slovenia, Croatia, Bosnia-Herzegovina, Serbia, Macedonia, Greece, Bulgaria, and Lebanon (Fig. 13.1). While the main focus of the initiative was the ongoing war in Syria, the March can be understood within the context of the so-called 'long summer of migration' of 2015 (della Porta, 2018). It was this series of events that spawned the initiative, helped to mobilize participants, generated media interest, and elicited broad support for the March from local communities right across East and South-East Europe.

Arising in November 2016 out of a desire to respond to the then five-year-long war in Syria and the ineffective and hypocritical response to it by the international community, the Civil March for Aleppo intended to create a beacon for peace. Many people were spurred to action by their outrage over the siege of Aleppo and the human costs of the war. As the manifesto of the Civil March declared, 'We can't sit in front of our laptops and do nothing. [...] We've had enough of clicking the sad or shocked faces on facebook [sic] and writing "this is terrible" and "we're so powerless". [...] We refuse to take it anymore. We've just withdrawn our consent. We're ready to deny powerlessness' (Civil March for Aleppo, 2016b).

While participants' motivations for and expectations in joining the walk varied considerably, the group was unified by a collective repudiation of the political situation in Syria. The evolving composition of the group was itself dynamically altered by the nature of the March. Attempts to channel the protest's energy – against the war in Syria, the bombing of civilians, and the atrocities that forced people to flee their homes in the first place – into concrete political demands or towards a

Figure 13.1. The Civil March for Aleppo on the route from Rataje nad Sázavou to Zruč nad Sázavou (23km), Czech Republic, in January 2017.

Source: Janusz Ratecki.

specific goal caused controversy within the group. These efforts were ultimately unsuccessful. By highlighting the March's potential to promote and facilitate active engagement among communities and individuals en route, marchers sought to connect people, establish a cross-border network, and create a platform for exchange and dialogue all the way from Berlin to Aleppo. Thus, attempts were made by organizers to re-shape the initial protest into a peacebuilding project. Marchers reached out to activists and experts working in the fields of peacebuilding and community building. One group within the Civil March advocated understanding the protest walk within a larger context of social change. Others wanted to see the March address the precarious situation faced by forced migrants in Europe and challenge Europe's hypocritical migration policy. And, as the author of this essay – herself a participant in the March – learned, many participants had more personal motivations for walking. Overall, the activists were not successful in identifying a unitary aim for the walk, nor were they able to shape and communicate a common vision.

One might well question the meaningfulness of a protest that failed to define its purpose or articulate a vision. This discussion of the Civil March for Aleppo's meaningfulness draws on philosopher Slavoj Žižek's concept of a 'zero-level protest' and on social movement theory. While this essay focuses on the Civil March for Aleppo, the observations it makes also hold true for other protests and civic initiatives.

The concept for the March was first articulated in November 2016 in response to news reports about the siege of Aleppo. And indeed, the initial energy of the protest was directed at the siege and the dire humanitarian situation in that city. When the siege was officially lifted a month later, the main focus of the protest dissipated, necessitating the identification of a new raison d'être for the protest, as Agnew (2017) has pointed out. In an effort to articulate a new aim, organizers justified the long-distance walk in terms of its value as a 'symbol of the biggest humanitarian crisis we are facing' (Civil March for Aleppo, 2016a). This emphasis on the symbolic dimension partly obscured the clarity and focus of the message among the public and even among March participants. Due to organizational shortcomings and the perceived urgency of the undertaking, the activists had elaborated neither a common goal and strategy nor a clear vision prior to departing on the walk in late December 2016. The main rationale behind the effort – whether the March was walking 'to' Aleppo, 'for' Aleppo, or 'to and for' Aleppo – was left unspecified. Most of the activists involved in shaping the idea for the walk considered Aleppo a purely symbolic goal from the outset, yet they presented a quite different image outside of the group in order to attract public attention and foster emotional engagement among people. Notwithstanding impassioned discussions about the purpose of walking thousands of miles in the direction of a war zone from which hundreds of thousands of people were fleeing en masse, no collective position was ever formulated. In the absence of a common vision, activists individually attributed purpose and meaning to the initiative, enriching the narratives about the Civil March with their own personal interpretations.

Aside from the unwillingness to define a common purpose or clearly articulated vision, the organizers of the March took a conscious decision to remain apolitical due to the complexity of the Syrian conflict and a personal reluctance among many of them to take sides in the war. This, too, impeded the ability to articulate explicit political demands. Referring to the responsibility of 'the ones in charge of politics' to formulate political solutions to the conflict, the Civil March rejected positioning itself as anything more concrete than a group that would deliver the 'message' that 'this war has to stop!'. As stated on the homepage of the Civil March, 'We don't want to get into politics – we only want the end of bombing against civilians in Aleppo and other towns in Syria and open humanitarian corridors so that help can get to the people in need' (Civil March for Aleppo, 2016a).

The day-to-day organization of the March varied with time. The walking group itself changed constantly, as most marchers joined the walk for only a limited time. With around 30-40 people usually walking in Germany, the Czech Republic, and Austria, the walking group was larger during the first few weeks of the March, as compared to the 10-20 who walked with the March in the Balkans (Fig. 13.2). The organization of the group has been vividly portrayed by de Rond and Hallett (2019), though their description of 'a typical day' on the March pertains only to the time in Serbia and Macedonia and the initial stages of the walk through Greece.

Figure 13.2. 'Tea break' in Croatia in March 2017.

Source: Janusz Ratecki.

In Greece, whence the March was supposed to cross into Turkey as the next country en route to Syria, major discussions about the purpose and nature of the March arose within the group. Focusing on the geographical goal of reaching Aleppo, many of the activists seemed to accord less importance to the political situation in Turkey. Following the coup attempt in June 2016, the country was in a perpetual state of emergency, which allowed the government to rule by decree. The result has been weakened parliamentary control and judicial oversight, intensified restrictions on the freedom of speech, and a flouting of human rights and the rule of law in the country. These developments, and the fact that peace activism in Turkey is inexorably connected with the Kurdish political movement and, as such, classified by the government as a 'terroristic activity', were pointed out to the group by various parties, including Konuk (2017) (see also Human Rights Watch, 2017; Shaheen, 2017). The Civil March group, faced with the decision of whether to walk through Turkey, was riven with dissent. The group split over disputes regarding its own claim to uphold values of peace and solidarity versus its silence about the Turkish involvement in the war in Syria, the treatment of refugees in Turkey, restrictions on freedom of speech in the country, and the violent conflict between the Turkish government and the Kurdish civilian population. (An alternative and lengthier account of the discussions raised by this dispute is provided by de Rond and Hallett (2019).) As public demonstrations were prohibited under the Turkish state of emergency, the remaining participants in the Civil March decided in May 2017 to apply for a special dispensation from the government to cross the country. Many, however, perceived the Turkish government's stipulations for granting the permit as undermining the integrity of the March. Ultimately, the marching group, which spent almost five weeks on various Greek islands meeting local activists, refugees, and helpers and visiting places symbolic of Europe's political failure to adequately receive refugees, decided it was unwilling to wait any longer for a definitive decision from the Turkish authorities.

The remaining activists flew to Beirut to continue their walk through Lebanon (Fig. 13.3). Not wishing to create the impression that it was cooperating with the Syrian regime, which was in control of territory between the Lebanese border and the city of Aleppo, the Civil March decided not to enter Syria – an action that would have necessitated cooperating with the Syrian regime or employing the services of people smugglers. An official end to the March was announced in August 2017 at the Lebanon-Syria border (Fig. 13.4). What then are we to make of this undertaking, an undertaking that mobilized people against war and human suffering but was consumed by disagreements over its own ways and means? Further, we might ask what lessons are to be drawn for other protest movements.

Figure 13.3. The Civil March for Aleppo in Tyre, Lebanon, in August 2017.

Source: Janusz Ratecki.

Figure 13.4. The official end of the Civil March for Aleppo at the Lebanon-Syria border in August 2017.

Source: Janusz Ratecki.

Zero-Level Protest

The philosopher Slavoj Žižek introduces the term 'zero-level protest' to describe irrational outbursts of violence that carry a vague desire for justice, but which do not articulate any concrete programmatic demands. By way of example, he cites the uprisings in the Paris suburbs in 2005, riots in Ferguson in 2014 and in Baltimore in 2015, and ongoing violent acts committed by Palestinians against Israelis. The *gilet jaune* (yellow vest) protests, which emerged in November 2018 in France in response to President Macron's announcement of a fuel tax, represent another instance of a 'zero-level protest'. Žižek has criticized the yellow vests for making contradictory demands and for 'not know[ing] what they want' (*Slavoj Zizek on Yellow Vests. How to Watch the News, Episode 01*, 2018). In Žižek's view, the violence used by the protestors does not itself further a particular goal; rather, it is simply a manifestation or expression of dissent over a particular situation. Drawing on philosopher Walter Benjamin, Žižek proposes classifying such protests as instances of what he calls 'divine violence'. Benjamin introduces the notion of divine violence in his essay 'Critique of Violence'. His considerations of the existence of a just use of violence afford him the opportunity to describe different categories of violence. Divine violence, according to Benjamin, escapes the means-ends relationship. Thus, discussions over whether violence can be legitimized by just ends does not apply to the category of divine violence (Benjamin, 1974–1989).

Again drawing on Benjamin, Žižek stresses that it is futile to search for a justifying cause for the outbursts of violence in the protests he identifies as examples of 'divine violence'. The use of violence does not betray a hidden or deeper meaning, he argues. The protestors simply do not see any viable alternative in nonviolent resistance or in articulating a meaningful utopian project. The fact that the protestors did not manage to articulate a meaningful project but saw 'blind acting-out' as their only recourse in the face of enforced democratic consensus reveals for Žižek the bankruptcy of the political system. He suggests, moreover, that questions posed by Benjamin about the possibility of a just use of violence cannot be answered on a purely philosophical level. According to Žižek, asking whether the individual's use of violence is justified in terms of a broader notion of 'global justice' articulates a dilemma that cannot be solved, as the discrepancy between individual interest and global justice is too great. Žižek neither justifies nor condemns the use of violence. Instead, he proposes that we accept the fact that divine violence is cruel and unjust, just as the situations in which it occurs are unjust. The only way to exit the 'vicious circle of horror and suffering', he argues, is through concrete social and economic analysis. In other words, if we are to overcome structural injustice, the structures themselves must be critically analysed and the systemic flaws tackled at their origins (Žižek, 2015).

The Civil March for Aleppo as 'Zero-Level Protest'?

While Žižek focuses on violent protest, a zero-level protest in the Žižekian sense can equally be non-violent, since Žižek's criticism is concerned with the fact that zero-level protests, as incidences of 'blind acting-out', lack vision and a set of clearly articulated demands. Thus, Žižek has denounced the non-violent 2011 Occupy protests in the United States, Spain, Greece, and Italy for a lack of imagination and targeted demands, without, however, explicitly identifying them as zero-level protests (Žižek, 2012).

Translated into sociological terms, Žižek's zero-level protest constitutes an 'expressive action' (Klandermans, 2015, p. 222), an action by means of which people express their views. This expression is in itself sufficient a motivation to undertake a particular action. Expressive action is classically understood to stand in opposition to 'instrumental action' (Klandermans, 2015, p. 223), which aims to influence the social and political environment. For Žižek, protest needs to be instrumental. Specifically, meaningful protest needs to serve as a tool for attacking capitalism, since the origins of injustice, he argues, are rooted in the capitalist economic system. Ultimately, protest is assessed by its contribution towards overthrowing that system. Expressive protest, in contrast, stagnates at the zero-level. Thus, for Žižek protest must be more than a manifestation of emotions in order for the undertaking to be meaningful. It remains, then, to assess whether the Civil March was a zero-level protest in the Žižekian sense and whether Žižek's concept allows for a full assessment of the meaningfulness of protest.

From the moment the siege of Aleppo was lifted, prior to the start of the March, the Civil March for Aleppo could no longer articulate programmatical demands or a vision – meeting Žižek's definition of a zero-level protest. The marchers called for an end to the war in Syria, yet this desire to express opposition was stronger than the desire or ability to articulate a means to bring it to an end. All the more pronounced, then, was the desire to demonstrate solidarity with the civilian population. The March intended to show that people cared about those affected by the Syrian war, that they had not forgotten about them and were not indifferent to their fate.

The strong emotional response elicited by the March can be understood against the backdrop of the failure of European politics during the long summer of migration in 2015 and in 2016. The authors of the March's manifesto wrote that the protest walk was intended to help to dispel feelings of powerlessness and helplessness, to 'transform tears and anger into some action' and challenge what people 'have been taught – submission to war, fear of the powerful, a division of people into "good" and "bad"' (Civil March for Aleppo, 2016b). For many, the Civil March was not only an opportunity to oppose the war in Syria, but also a means to challenge European migration policy. Having started in late 2016, the March took place amid the obvious political breakdown of Europe's migration policy. Most states refused to fulfil their humanitarian and legal obligations to receive asylum seekers, leaving civil society to momentarily step in to fill the void. In this context it was relatively easy to use strong emotional appeals to mobilize people to join the March. At the same time, this target of criticism shaped the perception of many participants, who understood the March to be an opportunity to challenge European migration policy.

The organizers of the Civil March did not draw a clear distinction between opposing the war in Syria and tackling European migration policy. As has been pointed out, the March explicitly intended to follow the same route along which people were fleeing to Europe, but in the opposite direction (Alboth, 2016). In many places the March was hosted by communities and organizations set up to help refugees and asylum seekers. The March repeatedly posted on its Facebook page comments critical of European migration policy and shared postings about social initiatives that helped people who had fled their home countries. In January 2017, the Civil March for Aleppo donated money to Fresh Response, an NGO that provides humanitarian support to refugees and migrants on the Serbia-Hungary border. Once it had left its intended route and crossed the Greek mainland, the March visited sites on Lesbos, Chios, and Samos symbolic of the humanitarian tragedies in 2015 and 2016 and of the collapse of a common European asylum system (Fig. 13.5).

Figure 13.5. The Civil March for Aleppo at the 'Cemetery of Refugees' near the village of Kato Tritos on Lesbos, Greece, in June 2017.

Source: Janusz Ratecki.

To the extent that the Civil March was an emotional response to the war in Syria and to European migration policy and lacked programmatic demands and a common vision, it can be accurately characterized as a zero-level protest. Žižek's concept offers a framework for a critical analysis of the protest walk and helps to elucidate its lack of programmatic demands. Yet Žižek's concept does not allow for an assessment of the overall impact of the March. Taking a purely instrumental view, it cannot grasp any potential outcomes, outcomes that are invisible as direct political consequences of the protest. For this reason, we might look to social movement theory as a framework for a broader assessment of the protest's impact.

Social Movement Theory and Social Change

The definitions of social movement vary in the scholarly literature. Amongst other things, social movement has been defined in terms of 'informal networks based on shared beliefs and solidarity, which mobilize about conflictual issues through the frequent use of various forms of protest' (della Porta and Diani, 2006, p. 16). Others define it as a 'collective, organized, sustained, non-institutional challenge to authority, power holders, or cultural beliefs and practices' (Goodwin and Jasper, 2009, p. 4). Another alternative describes it as a 'loosely organized, sustained effort to promote or to resist change in society that relies at least in part in noninstitutionalized forms of collective action' (McAdam and Boudet, 2012, p. 56). Social movements are thus typically comprised of an extra-institutional or non-institutional collective or joint action that promotes change-oriented goals directed at a specific target. Further, social movements contain some degree of organization, temporal continuity, and a sense of shared solidarity and/or collective identity (Flesher Fominaya, 2014).

Whilst Žižek is solely concerned with the instrumental purpose of protests, social movement theory recognizes instrumental social movements that aim to achieve an external goal as well as expressive social movements that focus on the expression of views or emotions. Scholars of social movement theory have developed distinctive or combined models of expressive and instrumental social movements (Klandermans, 2015). In contrast to Žižek's claim, collective action in social movement theory does not necessarily imply the articulation of explicit political demands (della Porta and Diani, 2015).

As a field, social movement studies is broad. In general, however, it could be said that social movement studies offers a framework for the study of 'social change' (della Porta and Diani, 2015). A useful definition of 'social change' is offered by Harper and Leicht, who characterize it as 'the significant alteration of social structure and cultural patterns through time' (2016, p. 5). Social structure refers to 'persistent networks of social relationships where interaction between people or groups has become routine and repetitive'. Culture, in turn, refers to 'shared ways of living and thinking that include symbols and language (verbal and nonverbal), knowledge, beliefs, and values (what is "good" and "bad"), norms (how people are expected to behave), and techniques, ranging from common folk recipes to sophisticated technologies and material objects' (Harper and Leicht, 2016, p. 5). Furthermore, a distinction can be made between non-intentional social changes or trends (e.g. urbanization), and intentional social changes, which are driven by human agency. The latter are either brought about by planned elite decision-making processes or by social movements involving broad segments of the population (Harper and Leicht, 2016, p. 5). The underlying assumption here is that social movements can, with time, significantly influence social structures and cultural patterns.

In a similar way, Flesher Fominaya (2014) uses the term 'prefigurative politics' to highlight the ways in which social movements can transform broader social practices by enacting models of organization, concepts, and conventions that reflect the vision of society to which they aspire. In this sense, social movement theory offers a theoretical framework that allows for an assessment of single instances of civic engagement, such as a demonstration, sit-in, or protest walk, in a broader context and recognizes the non-linear or long-term effects of social actions.

The Civil March for Aleppo as Social Movement?

While not in itself constituting a social movement, the Civil March for Aleppo included a number of elements characteristic of social movements. It was the result of non-institutional collective action undertaken by around 3,000 people who were physically engaged in the undertaking, with many more supporting and following it online. It pursued a change-oriented goal insofar as it aimed to improve the situation in Syria for civilians and to stop the war. The Civil March for Aleppo targeted different groups of people with its insistence on the need for a cessation of hostilities, articulated in the March's manifesto in the simple phrase 'this war has to stop!'. The Civil March addressed official representatives directly by contacting embassies along the route and more extensively by encouraging participants to communicate with their own governmental representatives. From the very beginning, March participants actively sought contact with the media to promote the March's animating idea. People were inspired to join the March or take some action in solidarity with people in Syria, to spread awareness about the humanitarian suffering in Syria and war in general, and to encourage broad media coverage so as to gain credibility in the eyes of political representatives and exert pressure on governments to end the war.

The protest walk itself lasted approximately nine months between December 2016 and August 2017. The organization registered under the name Civil March continues to exist. Since the official end of the March in August 2017, one follow-up event has been organized by the Civilmarch e.V. Activity on the Civil March Facebook page has significantly declined since 2017, and by 2019 it was barely active. In this sense, no active network directly promoting the endeavours of the Civil March for Aleppo has outlasted the protest walk.

The Civil March for Aleppo had different levels of organization. Though open to participation by all (except for a few instances in which people were asked to leave because their behaviour was obstructing the March), the Civil March was characterized by a dynamic, but strict organizational frame, composed of a changing number of activists. In a simplified form, the organizational structure included groups of activists 'on the ground' and online. From a hierarchical point of view, the base of the structure comprised the 'marchers' or 'the March', consisting of a constantly changing group of people who were physically present on the walk. One level higher, there was 'the team', a small group of activists, many of whom intended to support the March during its entire duration and who participated both on the ground and online. Finally, there was the 'leadership', which modified its structure several times. As noted above, the Civil March is a legal entity (Civilmarch e.V.) registered in Germany. As such, it has the right to determine the specific use of its own intellectual and material property, along with the right to articulate 'official' positions or empower certain people to voice them.

Harper and Leicht (2016) draw a distinction between 'social movements' and 'social movement organizations' (SMO). Defining social movements as 'unconventional collectivities with varying degrees of organization that attempt to promote or prevent change' (Harper and Leicht, 2016, p. 134), they understand 'collectivities' as collections of people that are only loosely structured, if at all. The low degree of organization differentiates them from structured SMOs. Unlike SMOs, social movements include all sympathizers, supporters, adherents, and activists.

Applying Harper and Leicht's distinction between social movements and social movement organizations to the Civil March in Aleppo, it becomes clear that it was not in itself a social movement since, with the exception of a few select events, all actions and events around the March were organized either by a central organizing body that was entitled to articulate 'official' positions in the name of the Civil March or by local groups and individuals cooperating with the Civil March.

As Flesher Fominaya (2014) points out, a protest ought to be differentiated from a social movement. Protest, the 'act of challenging, resisting, or making demands upon authorities, power holders, and/or cultural beliefs and practices by some individuals or group' (Goodwin and Jasper, 2009, p. 3), is one possible strategy employed by social movements. Most protests are connected with social movements, but social movements comprise much more than individual protests (Flesher Fominaya, 2014). In this sense, the Civil March for Aleppo was a protest but no social movement. In fairness, the Civil March never claimed to adhere to a larger social movement. Rather, the Civil March can be seen within the context of the mobilizations that occurred during the 'long summer of migration', when many civil initiatives emerged in response to the failure of European migration policy and the war in Syria (see della Porta, 2018). The Refugee Tales Walk in the UK is another example of this type of initiative, and it serves as a useful comparison to the Civil March for Aleppo.

The Refugee Tales: A Walk in Solidarity with Refugees, Asylum Seekers, and Detainees, initiated by the Gatwick Detainees Welfare Group, took place for the first time in June 2015, prior to the arrival of unprecedent numbers of migrants and refugees later that year. Since 2015 the walk has been repeated annually. The Refugee Tales Walk issued a call for an immediate end to the use of indefinite immigration detention in the UK, an instrument covered in that country's Immigration Act. Further, the initiative demands formal recognition of the right of immigrants to work and to education as well as the entitlement to 'a life not (...) held brutally in suspense' (Herd, 2017, p. 143). It aims to raise awareness among a wider audience of the inhuman conditions of detention and post-detention and seeks to exert pressure on officials and change public discourse. The initiative further intends to be an act of welcome in contrast to the hostile environment created by the legal system, and it aspires to give voice to those who are structurally silenced under this system (Herd, 2017; *About Refugee Tales*, n.d.). The walks are framed by cultural events, during which 'tales' – anonymized real stories – of former immigration detainees, refugees, or people working with asylum seekers in the UK, such as lawyers or interpreters, are told and collected. This storytelling is modelled on Chaucer's *Canterbury Tales*. In 2016 the Refugee Tales project compiled a book of *Refugee Tales*, with a second volume appearing in 2017.

A comparison between the Civil March for Aleppo and the Refugee Tales Walk is interesting since both initiatives took place around the same time and against a similar backdrop. While their motivations were different, both projects chose the form of a walk: both groups of activists claimed to walk as an expression of solidarity with displaced people and immigrants more generally, and both walks criticized migration policies in European countries. Whilst the Civil March explicitly rejected the formulation of political demands (other than a vague call for a stop to the war in Syria), the Refugee Tales Walk articulates a precise aim: to end indefinite immigration detention in the UK and, additionally, to improve the situation of immigrants by changing hostile public discourse.

Despite clearly articulating its aims, the Refugee Tales project did not achieve its main political objective. It did not put a stop to indefinite immigration detention in the UK, nor did the use of this practice significantly decline between the start of the project and the time of writing (Amnesty International, 2019). Certainly, the Refugee Tales Walk created awareness about the practice of indefinite immigration detention and the precarious situation of asylum seekers in the UK. Its political impact is nevertheless difficult to assess. Increasingly, the rights of asylum seekers and refugees are being curtailed in many European countries as well as in other parts of the world (Amnesty International, 2018). The Immigration Act of 2016, for example, significantly worsened the legal situation for refugees and immigrants in the UK (Ali Khan, 2016).

However, if we assume that protests – whether as part of a social movement or individually – can contribute to social change, and that they can do so not only by accomplishing immediate political goals, but also by transforming broader social practices and affecting cultural patterns over time, then the meaningfulness of protests ought not solely be determined in terms of their political success or failure. What might be considered instead is the longer-term impact of protests.

Eventful Protest

Taking a non-instrumental view of protest, political scientist and social movement scholar Donatella della Porta (2008) highlights the transformative capacity of what she, with Sewell (1996), calls 'eventful protest': a 'by-product' of the protest is the cognitive, emotional, and relational impact it has on its actors as well as on any associated social movements. First and foremost, protests build networks to increase their impact. These networks, inter alia, produce knowledge, collective identities, and social ties, something della Porta (2008) describes as 'networking in action'. She suggests that protests are particularly 'eventful' and therefore bear an even larger transformative potential when they last for a long time, bring together people from different backgrounds, stress the importance of communication, and engage participants emotionally.

Isin and Nielsen (2008) drawing on the work of della Porta (2008) to highlight the symbolic dimension of collective action as 'collective or individual deeds that rupture socio-historical patterns' (p. 2) insofar as they challenge existing power structures through cultural change. Monforte and Dufour (2013) show how participating in long-term marches of undocumented migrants in Canada, Germany, and France in 2005, 2007, and 2010 has generated a sense of empowerment, pride, and solidarity amongst the participants, and so may be said to have constituted an act of symbolic emancipation of undocumented migrants from their marginal position in society. Della Porta's and Monforte and Dufour's findings are worth considering in relation to the Civil March for Aleppo.

Eventful protests serve as spaces of encounter, spaces in which knowledge and ideas are generated through interaction and exchange. This is all the more true if protests are inclusive and pluralistic (della Porta, 2008). Della Porta (2008) shows that participation in the European Marches, which took place between 1997 and 2002 and targeted EU summits in Amsterdam, Cologne, and Nice, allowed participants to recognize cross-national similarities and so enabled the construction of transnational identities. Monforte and Dufour (2018) argue that the participation of undocumented migrants in the protests had cognitive effects: it raised awareness of their ability to exert claims in the public sphere and act like citizens with legal residency status. In this way, participation in the protests conferred a sense of empowerment. Refusing to be 'invisible', they emancipated themselves from their position in a legal system under which they were not recognized.

The Civil March for Aleppo and the Refugee Tales Walk similarly served as platforms for exchange and dialogue. The daily walk stimulated debates. In the case of the Civil March, the group often started the day with a 'news flash' on the situation in Syria, after which a 'question of the day' could be posed by anyone (Fig. 13.6). The intent was that the question would be discussed in small groups during the day's walk and then addressed by the larger gathering in the evening. Some days participants organized workshops to discuss an issue in depth or to share their knowledge in a specific field with the rest of the group.

Figure 13.6. Morning 'news flash' before the start of the walk from Knežica to Kozarac, Bosnia, in March 2017.

Source: Janusz Ratecki.

As stated in the manifesto, the March intended 'to deny powerlessness' and to challenge what the marchers 'ha[d] been taught': submission to war, fear of the powerful, a division of people into 'good' and 'bad', 'better' and 'worse' (Civil March for Aleppo, 2016b). Individual motivations for joining the March differed greatly, as mentioned above. Yet we can conclude that taking part in a collective action, whatever the motivation for doing so, gave participants a strong sense of empowerment. Maybe this is also what de Rond and Hallett mean when they write that the Civil March 'was also about the participants in the march and their very real existential angst', which the marchers could assuage by walking day in, day out (de Rond and Hallett, 2019).

In her work on protests against the construction of a high-speed train line in Val di Susa, Italy, and the subsequent occupation of the construction sites by protesters in 2006, della Porta (2008) has shown how protests can create communities. The experience of acting together for a protracted time helped generate feelings of solidarity, trust, and belonging amongst the protesters. The occupied site was transformed into a space that allowed for experiments in alternative ways of living, directly affecting the daily lives of the participants. The meaning of the occupation thus transcended opposition to the railway line, turning the occupied sites into common spaces that enabled the growth of a community. We can find other examples of the potential of protests to create community in the airport construction site at Notre-Dame-des-Landes, France, occupied between 2009 and 2018, and in the 2011 occupations of central squares by the so-called Occupy Movements or Movements of the Squares. The latter emerged in Northern Africa, Europe, and the United States and were characterized by a pronounced rejection of neoliberalism, an explicit claim to inclusivity, the absence of leaders and clear programs, the refusal to affiliate with any particular ideology or organization, and the rejection of any form of representation (Fernández-Savater et al., 2017).

The Civil March for Aleppo, too, turned into something that had the quality of a community. Although only a few participants remained with the March for its entire duration, and the rest of the group changed dynamically, the March constituted a space in which people felt welcome and to which many returned. Once on the March many participants, who had planned to join for only a short period of time, postponed their departure. Some quit their jobs or their rental contracts to remain on the March until its end. A number of people re-joined multiple times. The experience of walking together, day in, day out, through the seasons of the year, crossing from one country to the next, created intense engagement amongst the participants and bound them together. As de Rond and Hallett (2019) observe, the March was something that seemed 'deeply meaningful', a space in which 'a set of rare human qualities – of generosity and kindness and physical intimacy' could prosper. The feeling of connectedness with other ex-marchers has remained for many former participants to this day, two years after the protest walk (Fig. 13.7).

Eventful protests carry the potential to create networks. The European Marches and the aforementioned protest walks by undocumented migrants all serve as examples of how protests strengthen connections and foster relationships of solidarity amongst participants and between participants and others. Monforte and Dufour (2013) have shown how the protest marches in Canada, Germany, and France produced social ties not only amongst the migrants, but also between migrants and other social groups.

Throughout the months of walking, around 3,000 people actively participated in the Civil March for Aleppo. Along the route, the marching group engaged with a significant number of individuals, communities, and organizations engaged in social work. The protest forged connections amongst people with different backgrounds, nationalities, and political and religious orientations, and it established a broad trans-national network. Drawing on this network, some former participants set up the initiative Civil Action Network (Civil Action Network, n.d.), which promotes dialogue and solidarity and aims to connect communities in Central Eu-

Figure 13.7. The marching group in Glashütte, in Teupitz, Germany, in December 2016.

Source: Janusz Ratecki.

rope, the Balkans, Turkey, and Syria through realizing common projects, sharing experiences, and exchanging information.

What the Civil March for Aleppo achieved by generating ideas, creating a sense of empowerment, forging community, creating solidarity ties, and fostering connections and friendships was not its principle aim but rather its by-product. These outcomes do not change anything about the lack of a vision and common goal, nor should they obscure organizational shortcomings and the conflicts that existed within the group. Nevertheless, this aspect deserves equal consideration in any assessment of the Civil March.

Conclusion

The Civil March for Aleppo was a nine-month-long protest march dedicated to the civilians in Syria, and Aleppo specifically, which promoted the idea of peace and solidarity. The March took place in the context of the mobilization of large numbers of people during the so-called 'long summer of migration' in 2015-2016. Intending to follow the so-called 'refugee-route' in the opposite direction, participants in the

March walked from Berlin towards Aleppo, ending at the Lebanon-Syria border on 14 August 2017.

The Civil March for Aleppo has been analysed in this essay in light of Žižek's concept of a 'zero-level protest' and social movement theory. With 'zero-level protest' Žižek denotes a type of social protest with no programme or purpose. Zero-level protest can be understood as a manifestation of dissent and anger, a 'violent protest act that demands nothing'. Amounting to nothing but expressing emotions, this type of protest stagnates at a 'zero-level' in contrast to an instrumental protest, which aims to influence society and politics. This essay has extended Žižek's concept of zero-level protest to non-violent protest to engage in a critical analysis of the aims and coherence of the protest walk and to highlight the absence of programmatic demands articulated by the Civil March.

Social movement theory has been posited as an alternative to Žižek's concept. Social movement theory allows individual instances of civic engagement to be assessed within a broader context and takes into consideration the non-linear, long-term effects of social actions. Working from the assumption that protests may have an impact that extends beyond tangible political outcomes, and that protests can contribute to social change by transforming cultural patterns over time, the essay has argued that transformative potential should also be considered when evaluating a protest. This potential is to be found in the ways in which the protest affects its participants on a cognitive, emotional, and interpersonal level. In keeping with della Porta's concepts of 'eventful protest' and 'networking in action', both the Civil March and Refugee Tales Walk might be thought of as powerful potential contributors to long-term change.

Bibliography

McAdam, D. and Boudet, H. (2012) *Putting Social Movements in their Place: Explaining Opposition to Energy Protests in the United States, 2000-2005*, New York, Cambridge University Press.

Agnew, V. (2017) Personal communication with Clara Zimmermann, 19 July.

Alboth, A. (2016) Facebook post, 20 November [Online]. Available at www.facebook.com/anna.alboth/posts/10157904894975515 (Accessed 28 August 2018).

Ali Khan, A. (2016) Analysis: Immigration Act 2016 [Online]. Available at www.asadakhan.wordpress.com/2016/08/02/analysis-immigration-act-2016/ (Accessed 26 May 2019).

Amnesty International (2019) *United Kingdom. Submission to the United Nations Committee Against Torture*, London, Amnesty International Ltd.

Amnesty International (2018) *Amnesty International Report 2017/18. The state of the world's human rights*, London, Amnesty International Ltd.

Benjamin, W. (1974–1989) *Gesammelte Schriften*, 7 volumes, Frankfurt a.M., Suhrkamp.

Bulman, M. and Sims, A. (2016) 'Premature babies in Aleppo removed from incubators after air strikes hit city's only children's hospital', *The Independent*, 19 November [Online]. Available at www.independent.co.uk/news/world/middle-east/premature-babies-in-aleppo-being-kept-under-blankets-on-the-floor-instead-of-incubators-a7427106.html?cmpid=facebook-post (Accessed 28 August 2018).

Civil Action Network (n.d.) *Civil Action Network* [Online]. Available at www.civilaction.net/ (Accessed 27 May 2019).

Civil March for Aleppo (2016) *FAQ* [Online]. Available at www.civilmarch.org/faq/ (Accessed 27 May 2019).

———. (2016) *Manifesto* [Online]. Available at www.civilmarch.org/manifesto/ (Accessed 28 August 2018).

della Porta, D. (2018) *Solidarity Mobilizations in the 'Refugee Crisis': Contentious moves* [Online], Palgrave Macmillan. Available at www.doi.org/10.1007/978-3-319-71752-4 (Accessed 28 May 2019).

———. (2008) 'Eventful protest, global conflicts', *Conference of the Nordic Sociological Association*, Aarhus, 14-17 August.

della Porta, D. and Diani, M. (eds) (2015) *The Oxford Handbook of Social Movements*, Oxford, Oxford University Press.

———. (2006, [1999]) *Social Movements: An Introduction*, 2nd edn, Malden, Blackwell Publishing.

Fernández-Savater, A. and Flesher Fominaya, C. (eds) with contributions by Luhuna C., Elsadda, H., El-Tamami, W., Horrillo, P., Nanclares, S. and Stavrides, S. (2017) 'Life after the squares: reflections on the consequences of the Occupy movements', *Social Movement Studies*, vol. 16, no. 1, pp. 119-151.

Flesher Fominaya, C. (2014) *Social Movements and Globalization: How Protests, Occupations and Uprisings are Changing the World*, Hampshire, Palgrave Macmillan.

Goodwin, J. and Jasper, J. M. (eds) (2015) *The Social Movements Reader: Cases and Concepts*, 3rd edn, Chichester, Wiley-Blackwell. Available at https://usearch.uaccess.univie.ac.at/primo_library/libweb/action/display.do?tabs=detailsTab&ct=display&fn=search&doc=UWI_alma51344759910003332&indx=2&recIds=UWI_alma51344759910003332&recIdxs=1&elementId=1&renderMode=poppedOut&displayMode=full&frbrVersion=4&frbg=&&dscnt=0&scp.scps=scope%3A%28UWI_alma%29%2Cscope%3A%28UWI_R_PHAIDRA%29%2Cscope%3A%28UWI_O_metalib%29%2Cprimo_central_multiple_fe&tb=t&mode=Basic&vid=UWI&srt=rank&tab=default_tab&dum=true&vl(freeText0)=good win%20jeff%20the%20social%20movement%20reader&dstmp=1521704492886.

Harper, C. L. and Leicht, K. T. (2016) *Exploring Social Change: America and the World*, 6th edn, New York, Routledge.

Herd, D. and Pincus, A. (eds) with contributions by Smith, A., Abgabi, P., Abdulrazak, G., Ellams, E., Amoli-Jackson, J., Cleave, C., Collis, S., Herd, D., Lewycka, M., Mohammad, A., Moore, H., Todorovic, D., Watts, C. and Zand, M. (2016) *Refugee Tales*, vol. I, Manchester, Comma Press.

Human Rights Watch (2017) *Turkey: President Bids for One-Man Rule. Parliament Should Reject Constitutional Changes* [Online]. Available at www.hrw.org/news/2017/01/18/turkey-president-bids-one-man-rule (Accessed 28 August 2018).

Klandermans, B. (2015) 'Motivations to Action', in della Porta, D. and Diani, M. (eds) *The Oxford Handbook of Social Movements*, Oxford, Oxford University Press, pp. 219-231.

Konuk, K. (2017) Personal communication with the walking group of the Civil March for Aleppo, 14 April.

Refugee Tales (n.d.) *About Refugee Tales* [Online]. Available at www.refugeetales.org/about-refugee-tales/ (Accessed 19 May 2019).

de Rond, M. and Hallett, T. (2019) 'The long walk to Aleppo: Institutional myths, inhabited institutions, and ideals in the real world', in Reay, T. and Zilbert, T. (eds) *Process and Institutions*, Oxford, Oxford University Press.

Sewell, W. H. (1996) 'Three Temporalities: Toward an Eventful Sociology', in McDonald, T. J. (ed) *The Historic Turn in the Human Sciences*, Ann Arbor, University of Michigan Press, pp. 245-80.

Shaheen, K. (2017) 'Erdoğan clinches victory in Turkish constitutional referendum', *The Guardian*, 16 April [Online]. Available at www.theguardian.com/world/2017/apr/16/erdogan-claims-victory-in-turkish-constitutional-referendum (Accessed 28 August 2018).

Slavoj Zizek on Yellow Vests. How to Watch the News, Episode 01 (29 December 2018) YouTube video, added by RT [Online]. Available at www.youtube.com/watch?v=TrdPchnAR6o (Accessed 29 May 2019).

Žižek, S. (2015) *Refugees, Terror and Other Troubles with the Neighbours: Against the Double Blackmail*, London, Penguin.

———. (2012) *The Year of Dreaming Dangerously*, London, Verso.

Redressing

Academy in Exile
Knowledge at Risk

Kader Konuk

Theodor W. Adorno's *Minima Moralia: Reflections on a Damaged Life* offers a series of short, self-critical aphorisms that reflect on the predicaments of being a German-Jewish émigré in the 1930s and '40s. In his 13th aphorism, 'Protection, help and counsel', for example, Adorno points to the irrevocable breach caused by emigration. He acknowledges that in exile, 'All emphases are wrong, perspectives disrupted' (2005, p. 33). Not only is the émigré's language expropriated, but 'the historical dimension that nourishe[s] his knowledge [is] sapped' (Adorno, 2005, p. 33). Cleft from the historical context upon which knowledge-making is predicated, the émigré's own past is annihilated, Adorno avers (2005, pp. 46-47). The philosopher himself may have been one of the most successful wartime émigrés to preserve, revalidate, and convey the cultural-historical dimensions of his knowledge, yet he stresses the general invalidation of all that the émigré knows: 'it is intellectual experience that is declared non-transferable and un-naturalizable' (2005, pp. 46-47). Notwithstanding its title, Adorno's aphorism 'Protection, help and counsel' does not offer any practical answers to the question of how émigrés are best assisted. Rather, he criticizes the exiled intellectuals' propensity for isolation and highlights one of their coping strategies: the formation of closed political groups that remain suspicious of their own members and hostile towards outsiders.

Other émigrés, among them notably Hannah Arendt, have also reflected on the survival strategies of Jewish refugees. In 'We Refugees' (1943), a rather cynical analysis of the challenges and despair that stateless Jewish refugees faced, Arendt identifies an additional trait of the refugee: 'If we are saved we feel humiliated, and if we are helped we feel degraded' (1994, p. 114). While today's conditions of exile differ from those that characterized the 1930s and '40s, the accounts provided by Adorno and Arendt resonate with the daily struggles of scholars facing exile today – statelessness, homelessness, a loss of resources, uncertain academic status, and a sense of intellectual and social isolation. What, these thinkers seem to ask, is the condition of exile? What might be done to help alleviate exiles' suffering? And, most pressingly, how can their knowledge be preserved for future generations?

Against the backdrop of a global surge in the number of social sciences and humanities scholars seeking refuge from authoritarian governments today, this essay takes Arendt's and Adorno's testimony as a point of departure. To be sure, neither Arendt nor Adorno commented on the specific strategies that facilitated the emigration and employment of German intellectuals abroad. Such initiatives, while essential to discrete individuals, paled against the wholesale devastation of the Holocaust. Yet today's so-called scholar rescue initiatives either have direct roots in or take inspiration from the initiatives that emerged in the 1930s. This essay thus reviews the historical beginnings of some of these initiatives in order to reflect on the challenges facing us today in the field of scholar rescue. It enquires into the ways in which knowledge may be preserved and transferred in exile. It asks what the implications of past experiences are for present-day scholar rescue initiatives in higher education. Which, if any, historical foil is used to justify today's efforts to preserve knowledge from the great forgetting wrought by totalitarian and fascist governments? Finally, this essay enquires into the rationale behind scholar rescue and its justification on humanitarian and utilitarian grounds.

Exile and the Dissemination of Knowledge

Although the present is often referred to as the age of migration or of refuge, neither the exodus of entire communities nor the exile of individuals is new. The practice of exiling individual dissenters who were construed as threats to prevailing social, religious, or state structures can be identified in examples throughout history. Some exceptional individuals have created literature, art, and scholarship that transcends the disruption caused by the experience of exile. The notion that exile may be a fertile ground for the creation of something unique is commonly associated, for example, with the *Divina Commedia*, by the early modern Italian poet Dante; *Les Misérables*, by the French novelist Victor Hugo; *Speak, Memory*, by the Russian expatriate Vladimir Nabokov; *The Origins of Totalitarianism*, by Hannah Arendt; the poetry by the Turkish dissident Nazım Hikmet; *Orientalism*, by the Palestinian scholar Edward Said; and artworks by the Chinese dissident Ai Weiwei.

While these literary, artistic, and scholarly works exemplify the compelling, productive value of individual exile, it is necessary to examine broader historical processes and, specifically, the history of mass expulsion so as to contextualize the experience of individual intellectuals. The collective exile, imprisonment, or killing of dissident intellectuals has been used as a tool by authoritarian and fascist regimes since the early twentieth century. Targeting intellectuals is often one of the first steps towards suppressing criticism and compelling citizens to comply with government policy: disabling the critical elite may prepare the way for perpetrating atrocities. The arrest of Armenian intellectuals in Istanbul in April 1915, for example, enabled the mass deportation of Anatolian Armenians to Ottoman Syria and laid the groundwork for the genocidal killing that ensued. Silencing the Armenian elite facilitated governmental control over once influential minority communities and helped to consolidate Ottoman control of the country.

Similar strategies were employed by the National Socialists in Germany some two decades later. Prominent scholars like Arendt and Adorno were not targeted on an individual basis. Rather, they were affected by the widespread and systematic banishment of certain groups of scholars from German universities and, consequently, the country when the Nazi government passed a law in 1933 concerning the *Wiederherstellung des Berufsbeamtentums*, the so-called 'civil service law'. With this law, the National Socialists established legal grounds for forcing into retirement those professors who were either opponents of Nazism or of 'non-Aryan blood'. As a result, hundreds of Jewish and dissident scholars, deprived of their livelihoods and subject to increasing attack, were forced, where they could, to leave the country without delay.

Many scholars affected by the collective banishment from universities emigrated with the help of organizations that facilitated their being hired at educational institutions and universities abroad.[1] A number of these were founded in response to the flight of scholars from fascism in 1933. For example, the pathologist Philipp Schwartz founded the *Notgemeinschaft deutscher Wissenschaftler im Ausland* (Aid Organization for German Academics Abroad) and coordinated rescue efforts from Switzerland. In the United States, the Institute of International Education initiated the *Emergency Committee in Aid of Displaced Foreign Scholars* that is the precursor of today's IIE-Scholar Rescue Fund. In Britain, the Academic Assistance Council (AAC) was founded, and it continues to operate today as CARA (Council for At-Risk Academics). These organizations were set up to act as advocates for threatened scholars and to assist them in finding host universities in countries that would protect both their personal liberty and their right to conduct their research without interference. Various other organizations, such as the American Guild for German Cultural Freedom or the German PEN-Club in Exile, were able to support writers and intellectuals by arranging visas and disbursing stipends.

Today's initiatives also represent strategies of resistance in the face of the rise of authoritarian regimes globally and the ever-growing number of exiled scholars. These rescue initiatives reflect the commitment to create aid networks in higher

---

1   Engagement on behalf of refugees in higher education did not, as is often assumed, begin with the flight from National Socialism but dates back to the founding of the Institute of International Education (IIE) in New York, which created the Russian Student Fund for refugees after the revolution in 1917 (Duggan, 1943, p. 6; IIE-Scholar Rescue Fund, n.d., online at www.scholarrescuefund.org/about-us/our-history, accessed 18 July 2019).

education but also highlight a tension between humanitarian and utilitarian responses to the growing crisis. The need to respond at a humanitarian level to the persecution of scholars is often confounded by a utilitarianism that seeks to establish the scholar's potential value to the hosting society. In general, it can be said that these initiatives provide invaluable support to individual scholars and perform a vital service in monitoring the infringement of academic freedom worldwide. The US-based Scholars at Risk Network (SAR), for example, keeps tabs on the growing threat to scholars around the world. This international network of higher education institutions and associations works to protect scholars and to promote academic freedom.

Beyond the humanitarian and utilitarian arguments invoked in the discourse of rescue, the question arises as to the political and epistemological dimensions of aid networks for scholars. It is worth considering that the causes and nature of flight in the twenty-first century differ from those in the 1930s. While the *Berufsbeamtengesetz* of 1933 resulted in German scholars being banned from universities mainly on racial grounds, scholars today are often targeted because of their disciplinary affiliations: under attack are entire fields of knowledge rooted in critical traditions like postcolonialism, genocide studies, and gender studies. As the recent examples of Turkey, Hungary, Poland, and Brazil show, these fields are challenging policies and truth claims of right-wing populist governments. It is for this reason that it is important to closely attend to the kinds of knowledge traditions that are represented by exiled scholars but which may also arise out of a condition of exile. Critical thinking might serve as an umbrella term to encapsulate the fields and disciplines that are being systematically undermined today.

Historically we associate the concept and practice of critical thinking with the experience and scholarly output of German and German-Jewish émigrés who disseminated European learning in exile. In the 1930s, film scholar Siegfried Kracauer (1906–1975) sought exile first in Paris and later in New York, literary scholar Erich Auerbach (1892–1957) and physicist/philosopher Hans Reichenbach (1891-1953) first made a home in Turkey, while philosopher Martin Buber (1878–1965) settled in Palestine and philosopher Max Horkheimer (1895–1973) in Switzerland.[2] As a result of this exodus, academic émigré communities sprang up in places like London, Los Angeles, New York, Paris, Jerusalem, and Istanbul. There were two places that at the time claimed to have re-established the form and spirit of the German univer-

---

2 For more on German emigration to the United States, see Berthold et al., 1993; Jay, 1985; Pross, 1955; and Fermi, 1968. Strauss (1991) focuses on emigration within certain disciplines. For more on exile in Turkey, see Cremer and Przytulla, 1991; Widmann, 1973. For a study of German exile in Los Angeles focusing on Thomas Mann, Bertolt Brecht, Theodor W. Adorno, Arnold Schönberg, and others, see Bahr, 2007.

sity abroad: Istanbul University and The New School for Social Research in New York. Both institutions benefited from the German brain drain in profound ways.

At an institutional level, critical thinking has left a lasting mark on The New School for Social Research, which opened its doors in 1919, with educational reformer John Dewey one of the founding members. Alongside other scholars, Dewey had taken a public stance against the United States' entry into the First World War and he was censored by Columbia University's president. As a result, Dewey and his colleagues resigned from Columbia and initiated the process of founding The New School (The New School for Social Research, n.d.).[3] When, in 1933, the director of The New School, Alvin Johnson, became aware of the laws banning socialist and Jewish scholars from German universities, he founded the University in Exile specifically for the benefit of displaced German scholars. In the foreword to the first volume of *Social Research: An International Quarterly of Political and Social Science* published in 1934, Alvin Johnson set the stage for what was framed as a new beginning for higher education. To introduce the establishment of a Graduate Faculty of Political and Social Science that hosted the 'largest organic grouping of continental scholars abroad', he invoked the flight of Byzantine scholars from the Ottomans. In his foreword to the journal he wrote:

> It would be impossible, even if it were practicable, for an organized body of continental scholars to function abroad exactly as they had functioned at home. When the Greek scholars were expelled from Constantinople in the fifteenth century they were not able to set up in the Western world exactly the same scheme of literary education, of training in art, of criticism and philosophy as had been established in the old Byzantine Empire. They were forced to widen their views, to apply Greek methods to Italian and Austrian and French materials. The consequence was a cross-fertilization of cultures, a renaissance that definitely closed the Dark Ages. (1934, pp. 1-2)

Alvin Johnson employed the utilitarian argument to generate support and funding for the continental scholars fleeing to the US. Suggesting that the impact of German scholars in the United States might parallel that of the Byzantine scholars who had fled the conquest of Constantinople by the Ottomans almost five centuries earlier, which represented a substantial contribution to the European Renaissance, Johnson mounted a powerful historical appeal. He was able to raise funding from the Institute of International Education, which set up the *Emergency Committee in Aid of Displaced Foreign Scholars*. The New School received 60 per cent of the grants made by the *Emergency Committee*, which translated into a total of 21 hires (Duggan

---

3   Other sources claim that he either never resigned or returned to Columbia while maintaining close ties with The New School throughout his life: see Foulkes, 2017. For another account of the founding of The New School, see Calhoun, 2009.

and Drury, 1948, p. 69). Johnson saw the flight of German scholars as a potential source of enrichment for the US academy and pointed out that the 'Nazi policy, in destroying academic freedom in Germany, had in effect exiled the German university as the world knew it. Hence the name adopted for the proposed Faculty by the New School: The University in Exile' (Duggan and Drury, 1948, p. 80). While the Emergency Committee supported the assimilation of the individual scholar into the United States, Johnson's vision was the 'assimilation of a Faculty as a whole' (Duggan and Drury, 1948, p. 80). He established the Faculty of the Political and Social Sciences at The New School, which went on to become one of the leading political and social science faculties in the world. As the spread of fascism began to affect other countries, Johnson extended the offer of sanctuary to scholars from countries other than Germany (Duggan and Drury, 1948, p. 78).

At the other end of Europe, in Istanbul, a similar rhetoric was mobilized concerning the renewal of education and culture through a renaissance: The year 1933 was construed as a kind of zero hour for modern tertiary education in Turkey.[4] Turkey's ministry of education decided to close Dar-ül Fünun, the most prominent institute of higher learning in Istanbul, dating back to Ottoman times, and founded Istanbul University in its place. In so doing, the ministry dismissed two thirds of Dar-ül Fünun's faculty and hired European professors and Turkish scholars trained in Europe. As it happened, plans for founding Istanbul University coincided with the National Socialists' rise to power and, hence, with the banishment of German-Jewish and antifascist scholars from German universities. The Turkish government seemed to quickly realize that Nazi Germany's loss through the expulsion of scholars could well be its own gain. The doors of intellectual exchange were opened by exiled scientist Philipp Schwartz, who negotiated with the ministry of education in Turkey and founded the aforementioned organization to assist German academics in emigrating. The *Notgemeinschaft deutscher Wissenschaftler im Ausland* (Aid Organization for German Academics Abroad) put forward the names of more than forty German émigrés, who were immediately hired by Istanbul University; many more were employed by other universities, state-run institutes, museums, and other institutions across Turkey. Among the émigrés to Turkey were well-known composers, architects, and scholars like Ernst Reuter, Fritz Neumark, Bruno Taut, Carl Ebert, and Eduard Zuckmayer.[5]

---

4   In his speech marking the inauguration of Istanbul University, Minister of Education Reşit Galip announced that the new university had no relationship with Dar-ül Fünun. A transcript of the speech can be found in Hatiboğlu, 1998, p. 118.

5   It is estimated that through these channels alone at least eight hundred German professionals and their families could look upon Turkey as their salvation: see Cremer and Przytulla, 1991, p. 27. The Berlin-based organization *Verein Aktives Museum* estimates that 1,040 Germans emigrated to Turkey between 1933 and 1945 (2000).

In 1933, the Turkish minister of education Reşit Galip attached special meaning to the emigration of scholars to Turkey. He construed and welcomed the arrival of European scholars as a form of compensation for the fifteenth-century Byzantine scholars who had fled Constantinople after its surrender to the Ottomans.[6] In the same vein as Alvin Johnson in New York, Galip stressed that the flight of Byzantine scholars had provided an important impetus for the Renaissance. His hope was to instigate a new kind of renaissance that would be achieved through the 'return' of European scholars to Turkey. Galip hoped that by hiring emigrants, Europe's heritage could be reinstated in its birthplace. Classical learning, so the rationale went, would be reborn in the very city it had once deserted.

German scholars – often deeply embedded in humanist education themselves – henceforth contributed to an enormously productive cohort that defined the parameters of secular learning for Istanbul University's new faculties. In the 1930s and '40s, the university hosted the largest concentration of exiled German scholars in the world. Although Istanbul University hired scholars across the disciplines – from philosophy to law and physics – the Faculty for Western Languages and Literatures that philologist Leo Spitzer opened upon arrival in 1933 stands out as a pioneering model for the secularization of education in a predominantly Muslim society.

The rhetoric of renewal was prevalent in both New York and Istanbul. While it would be difficult to measure and compare the respective impact, the historical record suggests that emigration left a lasting mark through the founding and shaping of entire faculties and disciplines. In both Istanbul and New York, new institutional formations were the result of a humanitarian crisis, on the one hand, and the desire to reform higher education, on the other. In Turkey, preserving the foundations of a humanist Europe served the interests of émigrés and Turkish reformers alike. For émigrés, it meant a chance to prevent the loss of their scholarship and, indeed, in many instances, to preserve their very lives; for Turkish reformers, it was a way of reinventing and fashioning themselves as Europeans.[7] The response to the exodus from Germany was comparable in the United States. The American philologist Harry Levin would later say that 'Those losses to European faculties, which have meant such gains for our [faculties], have completed the maturation of American higher learning' (1969, p. 480).

Three points can be taken from this sketch of mid-twentieth-century scholar rescue. The first concerns the perceived value of the exiled or refugee scholar. The hope – expressed so often in the past – that knowledge could be revived through the hosting of European refugee scholars may have been overly optimistic. It was predicated on the assumptions that intellectual life was in a state of stagnation and that

---

6   The Turkish original of this passage can be found in Hatiboğlu, 1998, p. 111.
7   For a study on German-Jewish emigration to Turkey in the 1930s, see Konuk, 2010.

it would be receptive to an injection of new ideas. Such sentiments glossed over the profound difficulties encountered by scholars upon arrival in their respective host countries. Among these difficulties were disciplinary differences, the loss of access to the archives and libraries they left behind, ongoing uncertainties regarding citizenship, the barriers presented by an unfamiliar language, and the pervasive antisemitism faced by many Jewish émigrés. The second point concerns the fact that there was, and still is, an unresolved tension between utilitarian and humanitarian arguments for supporting refugee scholars.[8] At the heart of this dilemma was the question of whether scholars were to be rescued 'merely' because they were in danger or on the grounds that they provided potential benefit to the host country and were thus to be considered particularly 'worthy'. The third point emphasizes the knowledge rather than the scholar as the agent of that knowledge. It relates to the idea that forming exile cohorts facilitated the concentration, absorption, and transformation of knowledge at host institutions. Creating cohorts of refugee scholars is arguably the most effective model for us today – one that foregrounds the conditions and modes of transforming knowledge in exile.

The Value of the Refugee Scholar

In the 1990s, humanities scholars examining the experience of exile in the context of postcolonial cultures highlighted exile as a condition for generating new forms of critical consciousness. Abdul JanMohamed, for example, drew on the trope of exile for his concept of the border intellectual (1992). In his view, border intellectuals – whether exilic or postcolonial – were privileged in the new field of cultural studies for their capacity to contribute to a kind of critical pedagogy (JanMohamed, 1992).[9] Edward Said took up the question of the intellectual in exile in his well-known 1993 Reith Lectures, which explored the concept of displacement and the condition of marginality. Said's interest lay in the masterpieces produced by Adorno, Auerbach, and Naipaul in exile wrought by the displacements caused by the revolutions, fascism, deportations, and the genocides of the first half of the twentieth century. In Said's view, exilic displacement enabled the intellectual to be liberated from his or her usual career or prescribed path. While Said did not deny the challenges and hardship of exile, he emphasized the condition of marginality as a potential asset to the intellectual.[10] He coined the phrase the 'executive value of exile' (1983, p. 8).

---

8   For an article discussing both the refugee crisis in the 1930s and the current challenges for scholar rescue networks, see Lässig, 2017.

9   For the concept of the border intellectual within the framework of critical pedagogy, see Giroux, 1992.

10 To Said, 'the exilic intellectual does not respond to the logic of the conventional but to the audacity of daring, and to representing change, to moving on, not standing still' (1994, p. 64).

Thanks to the work of these and other scholars, exilic detachment came to be seen as a precondition for critical thinking. It has come to be accepted that profound experiences of alienation and detachment sometimes force scholars to shift their thinking in innovative and productive ways. Yet exile is double-sided: while it triggers reflection and recollection and prompts comparisons between the familiar and unfamiliar, it also demands new affiliations with the place of destination. Detachment from one place does not, after all, preclude émigrés from availing themselves of new, if temporary, attachments. Whatever the positive quality born of exile – innovation, improvisation – it is not born from a condition of stasis and lacking. Although some exiles may remain in a state of limbo, they are inevitably drawn into an everyday world that necessitates dealing with invalid passports, temporary visas, statelessness, ongoing trials, inadequate health insurance, and other exigencies before they can ever contemplate translating their knowledge into a new institutional framework. The implication that the loss of home necessarily confers an 'epistemological advantage' over those who remain behind is false and perhaps arrogant. Such an assertion wrongly implies that critical thinking is first made possible by the trauma of deracination and denaturalization and, hence, cannot be learned.

If exile is to remain a useful concept for characterizing scholars' critical distance vis-à-vis (neo)imperialism and authoritarian nation-states, it is necessary to differentiate between different kinds of exile – ranging from exile caused by governments criminalizing scholars (as in present-day Turkey) to that caused by so-called soft forms of repression (as is currently the case in Hungary and Poland). Historicizing the figure of the 'refugee scholar', a figure that has been referred to as exile, émigré, refugee, expatriate, displaced scholar, pariah, or, as is the trend now, simply person 'at risk', is helpful in identifying the intellectual traditions that inform current international aid efforts in higher education.

The current 'brain drain' from Turkey and the Middle East – as well as the persistent signs of 'soft repression' in Eastern Europe – requires that we rethink the paradigms for constructing support networks. As has been demonstrated, intellectual emigration from Europe in the 1930s was legitimized by invoking the Renaissance, a claim that was doubtful even then and would be utterly misplaced today. Notwithstanding the fact that institutes of higher education in the global North thrive on the international exchange of scholars, the integration of refugee scholars remains a challenge. Insufficient research has been done on the refuge sought by Middle Eastern literati, scholars, and journalists in Europe in the 1970s and '80s, for example. Those who found refuge from coups and other forms of political turmoil created diasporic networks that supported political resistance in their respective home countries. In Europe, exiles from the Middle East were, moreover, the driving force behind the recognition of the Armenian genocide, the establishment of the Kurdish Institute in Paris, and the flourishing of a transnational Kurdish literature.

In recent years, hundreds of critical scholars in the humanities and social sciences in Turkey have been banned from practising their professions, criminalized, and prosecuted. In the face of such repression, scholars are now seeking exile in order to continue their critical work abroad (Konuk, 2018). In the past three years, most applications to Scholars at Risk, Scholar Rescue Fund, the French program PAUSE, and the Philipp Schwartz Initiative have originated in Turkey, suggesting that Turkish academics are currently one of the most threatened groups of scholars worldwide.[11] The erosion of academic freedom, however, is not merely symptomatic of the rise of political Islam, and it is far from being a development peculiar to Turkey. Examples from other countries perhaps involve less prominent verbal assaults on academic freedom, but they are nonetheless characteristic of the current conjuncture. In 2015, for instance, the Russian government accused the Centre for Independent Social Research in St. Petersburg of acting as a foreign agent, and in 2016 it endangered the future of the European University at St. Petersburg by revoking its teaching license. This university was founded as a distinguished private graduate school at the time of the Soviet Union's collapse in 1991. Likewise threatened is the Central European University (CEU) in Hungary, an American–Hungarian institution founded by the philanthropist George Soros with the aim of promoting liberal values. Other initiatives funded by Soros in Eastern Europe have become targets, too, with the former North Macedonian prime minister explicitly calling for a 'de-Sorosization' of society.[12] The Open Society Foundations moved staff from Budapest to Berlin in 2018 and closed its office in Istanbul, and CEU is currently in the process of relocating the entire university to Vienna. In Poland in 2018, the government took concrete measures to criminalize suggestions that the Polish state or Polish people were complicit in the Holocaust. As has been reported in the press, LGBT activists, artists, and scholars are increasingly under state-directed attack in multiple countries. To name but one example: For the past year, Brazilian colleagues have reported that there is growing pressure on critics of the government, with gender and LGBTI studies programmes being targeted in particular.

We might ask what difference it makes if the scholars seeking refuge today are not the philosophers and humanists trained in the Weimar Republic, but rather the sociologist from Nigeria threatened because of her work on Boko Haram, the

---

11 The first round of calls for applications by the Philipp Schwartz Initiative in 2019 resulted in the award of 26 out of 38 fellowships to applicants from Turkey and seven to applicants from Syria (Philipp Schwartz Initiative, 2019).
12 In Romania, Soros was named a 'financial evil' (Lyman, 2017). Available online at https://www.nytimes.com/2017/03/01/world/europe/after-trump-win-anti-soros-forces-are-emboldened-in-eastern-europe.html. (Accessed 5 April 2017).

Pakistani political scientist with a PhD from a prestigious US institution, the Kurdish literary critic from a provincial Turkish college, or the scholar from Hungary whose entire field – gender studies – has been defunded in that country? One of the most obvious differences between émigrés of the past and exiles today concerns the status of transnational mobility. Not only is such mobility often a path to career advancement, but as a human rights concept the freedom of movement has also come to be seen as an integral feature of academic freedom. National governments are generally invested in internationalizing their institutions for economic reasons but also with the aim of advancing knowledge and scholarly excellence. In distinction to the émigrés of the 1930s, many scholars today are already participants in a globalized academy in which English is the lingua franca. As members of a global, if highly inequitable, academy, scholars today are less profoundly threatened by the possibility of losing what Adorno referred to as 'the historical dimension that nourished his knowledge'. For the privileged, polyglot few, whose training was undertaken abroad and whose professional networks remain active, exile is a personal horror but one that is mitigated by a tenuous safety net. For the vast number of scholars whose training has been regional, whose sphere of influence local, and whose skills and knowledge are not readily transferable, exile continues to pose an existential threat.

Academy in Exile

It was growing awareness about the acute needs of dissident Turkish scholars that motivated me to call for a brainstorming session with recently exiled scholars in late 2016, which would prepare the way for fundraising initiatives. Our initial idea was to host a cohort of scholars in Germany and develop a model that emulated places like The New School and Istanbul University, where émigrés were able to continue being productive.[13] Mindful of the need to involve threatened scholars themselves in the process of generating safe spaces in higher education, Academy in Exile was founded in Germany in 2017. Academy in Exile started as a joint initiative of the Institute for Turkish Studies at the University of Duisburg-Essen, the Kulturwissenschaftliches Institut (KWI) in Essen, and the Forum Transregionale Studien Berlin. The Wissenschaftskolleg zu Berlin (Institute of Advanced Study) and the Volkswagen Foundation provided start-up funding and personnel support.

---

13 In 2018, Arien Mack at The New School reinvested in the institution's historical legacy and initiated The New University in Exile Consortium, a network that connects universities and colleges which host scholars at risk. https://newuniversityinexileconsortium.org. (Accessed 16 August 2019).

Academy in Exile offers scholars the opportunity to resume their research in Germany. Unlike comparable initiatives that support scholars at risk, we focus on intellectuals who are threatened specifically *because* of their academic or civic engagement for human rights, peace, and democracy. Without wanting to discredit the vital work of seemingly similar initiatives, it is worth pointing out that other tertiary educational aid organizations usually refrain from taking a clear stance with regard to the political leanings of the scholars seeking their support. At an international level we can think of reasons why aiding scholars at risk is potentially contentious. Many tertiary educational institutions are dependent on revenue provided by overseas student tuition. Inevitably, this impinges on the ability of university administrations – and possibly also individual faculty members – to engage in open critique of these countries.[14] Yet even at German institutions, where there is no tuition and where academic freedom is protected under the constitution, the risk of triggering a diplomatic crisis is a factor in deciding whether or not to host a threatened scholar. Similar conflicts of interest are posed by foreign governments offering to fund professorships or support entire departments – in some instances, it is the very funding that acts as a smoke screen for the repression that has driven scholars into exile in the first place.[15] Academy in Exile is mindful of such forms of intervention and tries to navigate these difficult waters in scholar rescue.

Academy in Exile provides a forum for reflecting on the pressing challenges to intellectual life, critical thinking, reason, social justice, and diversity that we face today. Academy in Exile fellowships afford scholars the opportunity to continue their careers in Germany and to work on a research project of their own choosing in a multidisciplinary environment. Fellows contribute to and shape the research agenda and intellectual profile of the Academy generally. AiE is based on a model that creates multidisciplinary cohorts of scholars from the same region or around a unified theme, with the aim of enabling threatened scholars to collaborate with one another.

In October 2017, AiE published the first call for applications addressed to scholars from Turkey. Reflecting the immense need experienced by scholars at risk in Turkey at the time, we received 105 applications for six fellowships. A committee of ten scholars – all experts on Turkey – reviewed and rated the applications according to academic merit and risk. The review process involved explicit discussion of the academic and humanitarian aspects of the process itself. Decisions were made

---

14　Without specifically considering the issue of revenue from overseas students, Craig Calhoun points out that the very structure of universities in the US is transformed in such a way that 'questions of academic freedom are inextricably entangled with the political economy of higher education and research' (2009, p. 581).

15　For the current debate over Chinese influence at Australian universities, see Pearson, 2019.

on the basis of the applicant's academic merit, 'at risk' status, and potential contribution to the research profile and agenda of the Academy. With new funding made available from IIE-Scholar Rescue Fund and the Freudenberg Foundation, the Academy was able to increase the number of the initial six fellowships to nine. In late 2018, Academy in Exile received additional funding from the Andrew W. Mellon Foundation and began to host a new cohort of scholars at the Freie Universität Berlin. Thanks to support from various other German and international foundations, we were able to award long-term fellowships of 12 to 24 months and short-term emergency stipends of three months to additional scholars. Discrete aspects of the Academy's program are being developed and coordinated by Volker Heins, Egemen Özbek, Georges Khalil, and Vanessa Agnew.

In May 2019, we published a second round of calls for applications that was open to scholars at risk from around the globe. AiE received 65 applications predominantly from Turkey, Nigeria, and Eurasia, but also from Hungary and Brazil. We awarded fellowships to scholars from Hungary, Brazil, Afghanistan, Azerbaijan, and Turkey. To date, AiE has awarded a total of 30 fellowships to scholars at risk and funds two large cohorts in Berlin and Essen. We assist fellows with integrating into the European scholarly community and finding long-term positions. The aim is to forge new ways of responding to the threats posed to institutions of higher learning by populism, the curtailment of free speech, religious extremism, the spread of disinformation, and state-sponsored persecution.

AiE fellows are piloting new teaching formats to respond to the threat to critical thinking in crisis regions. Fellows are developing online tandem-taught courses and virtual learning communities across borders. We envision developing what we are calling a *critical thinking toolbox* for use in places where academic freedom is restricted. These courses will promote not only analytical skills among students but also academic autonomy as a defining feature of a healthy democracy. AiE proposes making such courses widely available so that this innovative model might be replicated by other interested programmes and institutions. The pedagogical aim of tandem teaching across borders involves equipping students with essential knowledge and tools for analytical thinking and critique across a range of scholarly contexts.

Conclusion

Critical thinking has long been the collective term for methodologies that foster self-critical awareness and analytical skills in the arts, humanities, and social sciences. Although the term is used loosely and refers to a whole range of methodologies, from critical theory to secular criticism, feminist theory, and postcolonial studies, its role in contributing to democratic processes and an open society seems uncontested. The pressing question arises as to how to preserve, promote, and transform critical thinking – particularly in collaboration with scholars from Turkey, Hungary, Brazil, Palestine, Syria, and Afghanistan, and other countries that are subject to repression. In light of the rise of authoritarian regimes and populist movements worldwide, we need to reinvest in the concept of critical thinking to mobilize it in policies of higher education. In this era of post-truth politics and the aggressive dissemination of misinformation, we are called upon to protect educational institutions that foster enquiry, reflective learning, and the ability to reason. By enquiring into the ways in which we define and engage with critical thinking, there is an opportunity to understand the conditions that have brought us to this juncture – what AiE is calling, with a nod to Bertolt Brecht's 'An die Nachgeborenen', 'these dire times' – and to re-evaluate the very premises on which our profession is based.

The boundary between the postcolonial scholar who seeks an international reputation and the scholar who seeks refuge is blurred in today's globalized academic world. Given these circumstances, we are called to continuously review and adjust the guidelines of international aid efforts in higher education and the autonomy of universities and research institutes. The ultimate aim is to rethink academia and the notion of the freedom of teaching and research (*Lehr- und Forschungsfreiheit*) in light of the challenges that refugee scholars face today.

Bibliography

Adorno, T. W. (2005) *Minima Moralia: Reflections on a Damaged Life* (trans. E. F. N. Jephcott), London and New York, Verso.

Arendt, H. (1994) 'We Refugees', in Robinson, M. (ed) *Altogether Elsewhere: Writers on Exile*, Boston and London, Faber and Faber, pp. 110-119.

Bahr, E. (2007) *Weimar on the Pacific: German Exile Culture in Los Angeles and the Crisis of Modernism*, Berkeley, University of California Press.

Berthold, W., Eckert, B. and Wende F. (1993) *Deutsche Intellektuelle im Exil: Ihre Akademie und die 'American Guild for German Cultural Freedom'*, Munich, Saur.

Calhoun, C. (2009) 'Academic Freedom: Public Knowledge and the Structural Transformation of the University', *Social Research*, vol. 76, no. 2, pp. 561-598 [Online]. Available at www.jstor.org/stable/40972273 (Accessed 19 August 2019).

Cremer, J. and Przytulla, H. (1991) *Exil Türkei: Deutschsprachige Emigranten in der Türkei 1933-1945*, Munich, Verlag Karl M. Lipp.

Duggan, S. and Drury, B. (1948) *The Rescue of Science and Learning: The Story of the Emergency Committee in Aid of Displaced Foreign Scholars*, New York, The MacMillan Company.

Fermi, L. (1968) *Illustrious Immigrants: The Intellectual Migration from Europe, 1930-1941*, Chicago, University of Chicago Press.

Foulkes, J. (2017) 'On James Baldwin and The New School: What It Means to be a Progressive University', *Public Seminar*, 27 December [Online]. Available at https://preview.publicseminar.org/2017/12/on-james-baldwin-and-the-new-school/ (Accessed 17 August 2019).

Giroux, H. A. (1992) 'Paulo Freire and the Politics of Postcolonialism', *Journal of Advanced Composition*, vol. 12, no. 1, pp. 15-26 [Online]. Available at www.jstor.org/stable/20865825 (Accessed 21 July 2019).

Hatiboğlu, M. T. (1998) *Türkiye Üniversite Tarihi: 1845-1997*, Ankara, Selvi Yayınevi.

IIE-Scholar Rescue Fund (n.d.) *Our History* [Online]. Available at www.scholarrescuefund.org/about-us/our-history (Accessed 18 July 2019).

JanMohamed, A. R. (1992) 'Worldliness-without-World, Homelessness-as-Home: Toward a Definition of the Specular Border Intellectual', in Sprinker, M. (ed) *Edward Said: A Critical Reader*, Oxford, Basil Blackwell, pp. 96-120.

Jay, M. (1985) *Permanent Exiles: Essays on the Intellectual Migration from Germany to America*, New York, Columbia University Press.

Johnson, A. (1934) 'Foreword', *Social Research: An International Quarterly of Political and Social Science*, vol. 1, no. 1, February, pp. 1-2.

Konuk, K. (2018) 'What Does Exile Have to Do with Us? Academic Freedom in Turkey', in Bachmann-Medick, D. and Kugele, J. (eds) *Migration: Changing Concepts, Critical Approaches*, Berlin, de Gruyter, pp. 211-225.

Konuk, K. (2010) *East-West Mimesis: Auerbach in Turkey*, Stanford, Stanford University Press.

Lässig, S. (2017) 'Strategies and Mechanisms of Scholar Rescue', *Social Research: An International Quarterly*, vol. 84, no. 4, Winter, pp. 769-807.

Levin, H. (1969) 'Two *Romanisten* in America: Spitzer and Auerbach', in Fleming, D. and Bailyn, B. (eds) *The Intellectual Migration: Europe and America, 1930-1960*, Cambridge, Belknap, pp. 463-484.

Lyman, R. (2017) 'After Trump Win, Anti-Soros Forces Are Emboldened in Eastern Europe', *The New York Times*, 1 March [Online]. Available at https://www.nytimes.com/2017/03/01/world/europe/after-trump-win-anti-soros-forces-are-emboldened-in-eastern-europe.html (Accessed 5 April 2017).

The New School for Social Research (n.d.) *Our History* [Online]. Available at https://www.newschool.edu/nssr/history/ (Accessed 18 July 2019).

The New University in Exile Consortium (n.d.) [Online]. Available at https://newuniversityinexileconsortium.org (Accessed 16 August 2019).

Philipp Schwartz Initiative (2019) 'Threatened researchers find refuge in Germany: Philipp Schwartz Initiative funds another 38 fellows', 24 June [Online]. Available at https://www.humboldt-foundation.de/web/press-release-2019-13.html (Accessed 19 August 2019).

Pross, H. (1955) *Die deutsche akademische Emigration nach den Vereinigten Staaten 1933-1941*, Berlin, Dunckner & Humboldt.

Pearson, E. (2019) 'China's efforts to curb Australia's academic freedom: what universities can do', *The Strategist*, 4 April [Online]. Available at https://www.aspistrategist.org.au/chinas-efforts-to-curb-australias-academic-freedom-what-universities-can-do/ (Accessed 15 August 2019).

Said, E. W. (1983) 'Secular Criticism', *The World, the Text, and the Critic*, Cambridge, MA, Harvard University Press, pp. 1-30.

———. (1994) *Representations of the Intellectual: The 1993 Reith Lectures*, New York, Vintage Books.

Strauss, H. A. (1991) *Die Emigration der Wissenschaften nach 1933: Disziplingeschichtliche Studien*, Munich, Saur.

Verein Aktives Museum (2000) *Mitgliederrundbrief*, vol. 43, May [Online]. Available at www.aktives-museum.de/fileadmin/user_upload/Extern/Dokumente/rundbrief-43.pdf (Accessed 20 March 2009).

Widmann, H. (1973) *Exil und Bildungshilfe: Die deutschsprachige akademische Emigration in die Türkei nach 1933*, Bern, Herbert Lang; Frankfurt a.M., Peter Lang.

Scholar Rescue
The Past of the Future

Jane O. Newman

Like 'exile', the term 'refugee' is a difficult one to gloss.[1] As the German-Jewish philosopher and political theorist Hannah Arendt, herself a refugee, first in France and then in the United States, wrote in her famous essay 'We Refugees' (1943), refugees themselves often do not choose or even like the term; they would prefer to be treated as normal 'immigrants', with all the trials and challenges which that status itself entails. Refugees are, rather, those who seek refuge, protection, and asylum, Arendt writes, because of 'some act committed or some political opinion held' (2007, p. 264). Many of her academic colleagues who sought refuge from Hitler's Germany at the time had been persecuted less for any such positions or deeds, but rather for who they were, namely German Jews.

Arendt's hesitations about using the term 'refugee' may be appropriate in such cases and may also help to explain the origin of an alternative way of describing the work done to save those of her academic colleagues who had to flee the authoritarian Nazi regime, namely 'scholar rescue'. The Institute of International Education (IIE), best known for hosting the Fulbright scholarship program, for example, was founded in 1919 in the wake of the First World War, but it expanded exponentially during the Second World War and was instrumental in creating what was called the Emergency Committee in Aid of Displaced Foreign Scholars at the time. The Emergency Committee facilitated placement for countless German-Jewish scholars at colleges and universities, libraries and research centres in the United States (Samuels, 2019). The Council for At-Risk Academics (CARA) in the UK was founded in 1933, also in response to the dangerous situation faced by scholars in Germany

---

1   This article is based on a lecture given at the National Humanities Center (NHC), Research Triangle, North Carolina, in March 2018. Hence its focus. I am grateful to NHC for inviting me to present on the topic of scholar rescue to their Board of Trustees. I am especially indebted to the President of the NHC, Robert Newman, and the NHC Director of Scholarly Programs, Tania Munz, for their extraordinary efforts in developing a programme to host a scholar at risk at the NHC in collaboration with Duke University. Going forward, the programme can serve as a model for other research centres and colleges and universities, both in the United States and around the world.

during the Second World War. And the name of the Philipp Schwartz Initiative (PSI) in Germany, now housed in the Humboldt Foundation, honours the Hungarian-born neuropathologist Philipp Schwartz who, soon after being dismissed from his position at the university in Frankfurt in 1933 because he was Jewish, founded the Emergency Assistance Association for German Scientists Abroad, which helped place several hundred German-Jewish academics in Turkey during the war.[2] Again, the German-Jewish scholars aided by these organizations sought sanctuary not necessarily for any particular 'acts committed' or politically suspect kinds of research. Rather, they were persecuted simply for who they were, or perhaps more accurately, because of who they no longer were after 1935, namely citizens of Germany entitled to the protection of (rather than persecution by) the state.

The huge number of 'stateless' persons in Europe after 1945 and elsewhere after 1948 has not been rivalled until today, with some 65 million refugees and internally displaced persons (Betts and Collier, 2017), among them many academics, now at risk. As Arendt writes: Having 'lost' their 'occupations', they have also 'lost' the 'confidence' they were 'of some use in this world' (2007, p. 264). Looking to the past, back to Arendt's generation, can help us to orient ourselves today as we move forward and confront the continuing harassment and mistreatment of scholars. 'Lost ... language', the 'loss of the naturalness of reactions, the simplicity of gestures, the unaffected expression of feelings', are all gone, she writes, left behind on the other side of the 'rupturing' of one's private and public-professional life because of displacement.

It is not only these words from the 1943 essay 'We Refugees' that still resonate, however. Arendt's objections in her book *The Origins of Totalitarianism* (1949), published somewhat later, to the so-called 'regime' of 'human rights' that was inaugurated more or less immediately after the end of the Second World War with the founding of the United Nations and the ratification of the Universal Declaration of Human Rights in 1948 also continue to ring true. Such efforts were of course designed to champion the rights of all human beings in the face of the betrayal of so many of them by the authoritarianism of their birth states. But they did little to address the measures imposed on them by the states to which they fled. Already in 1940, for example, the 'Alien Registration Act' in the US led to mass forced registration of immigrants and also to countless arrests and the imprisonment of many; the quieter authoritarianism of a 1942 curfew imposed on the German Jews of Los Angeles, who, as 'enemy aliens', could not leave their homes between eight

---

2   Many of these organizations still exist and continue to support scholar rescue. The IIE in New York now houses the Scholar Rescue Fund (SRF), which offers fellowship opportunities and has, since its founding in 2002, helped some 1,200 scientists, artists, and scholars find safe havens where they can continue their work. The international organization Scholars at Risk (SAR) also assists in the placement of several hundred scholars a year around the world.

in the evening and six in the morning and had to remain within a five-mile radius of their residences during the day, may have seemed eerily familiar to them from their experiences in Germany. In the face of such state-based controls on both sides of the Atlantic, possessing the 'human rights' meant to guarantee the transstate rights of those who had 'formally lost their nationality' during the war and of 'those who could no longer benefit from' any 'citizenship rights' they might still have had (such as refugees and asylum seekers) must have seemed of distant utility indeed. These realities formed just one of the reasons why Arendt objected to the discourse of human rights, for she understood that the guarantee of such rights in the 1940s was, as political scientist Ayten Gündogdu writes, mostly 'aspirational'. 'Universal' human rights can always be 'proclaimed', she writes, but must in the end also be 'politically enacted, recognized and affirmed in ... institutions, orders, and communities [on the ground] if they [were and] are to find stable guarantees' (2015, p. 7). The right to have human rights is thus classically hampered by what sociologist Yasemin Soysal (cited in Gündogdu, 2015, p. 10) refers to as the enforcement or 'implementation deficit' that always was and still is more the rule than the exception, with the 'discrepancy between formal [human] rights and their practice' leaving ample room for the nation-state to dictate who comes and who goes.

Arendt's objections to relying only on a rhetoric, or discourse, of human rights that in the end may be powerless to control the policies and acts of nation-states are still relevant. Repatriation agreements are signed and deportation orders enforced depending on the political needs of the day. This powerlessness is nevertheless itself not universal, as the work of the scholar rescue organizations detailed above shows. Indeed, it was precisely the capacity of non-state-based institutions in the early to mid-twentieth century, such as IIE, CARA, and Schwartz's Emergency Assistance Association for German Scientists Abroad, working together with the colleges and universities and the research centres, institutes, and libraries at which many academics found a place, to guarantee these scholars' survival that must be remembered. Indeed, in times such as the early twenty-first century, when there has been active resistance to authoritarian regimes – concrete 'acts' of resistance, in other words – on the part of students and faculty alike, scholar rescue is more urgent than ever.[3] It is important to underscore that such work is nevertheless not only an act of mercy or just a 'humanitarian issue' (Betts and Collier, 2017, p. 10). Scholar rescue also creates the conditions of possibility for profoundly innovative academic work. Indeed, the institutions hosting scholars and the disciplines in which they work often benefit just as much, if not more, from scholar rescue than the individual scholars themselves. This was certainly the case in the United States in the mid-twentieth century when so many of the German-Jewish scholars

---

3   For up-to-date statistics by location, see the annual reports published by Scholars at Risk (SAR), entitled *Freedom to Think*.

reached US shores. It is to this exemplary moment that I now turn as a way of beginning to assess the promise – but also the challenges – of erecting the 'new institutional architecture' of scholar rescue in the global academy for which Betts and Collier call (2017, p. 5).

***

The academic conditions on the ground in Germany when Hitler came to power have been well studied (see Bialas and Rabinbach, 2007, for example). In 1933, one of the first major acts that he passed was the so-called 'Restoration of the Professional Civil Service', which either dismissed or forcibly retired most 'non-Aryan' civil servants, including many university faculty members as well as teachers, professional judges, and municipal and government workers at all levels. A similar law was soon passed that imposed the same fate on lawyers, doctors, tax consultants, and musicians. It is shocking to realize how quickly it all transpired. While those who had served at the front in the First World War were exempt for a time, this loophole was rapidly closed two years later with the passing of a second law, the 'Law on the Retirement and Transfer of Professors as a Result of the Reorganization of the German System of Higher Education'. These anti-Jewish laws, the first since the so-called emancipation of the Jews in 1871, decimated higher education in Germany. Some 1,200 German-Jewish colleagues were dismissed. The percentages give a better sense than the raw numbers do of what this actually meant at the time: as of approximately 1920, for example, between 25 and 47 per cent of all university faculty in the humanities were Jews. The figure was similar in other disciplines. When the world-renowned mathematician David Hilbert, who taught at the University of Göttingen, was seated next to Bernhard Rust, the Nazi minister of education, at a banquet in 1934, he was asked by Rust: 'How is mathematics at Göttingen, now that it is free from the Jewish influence?' Hilbert allegedly replied: 'There is no mathematics in Göttingen anymore' (Menzler-Trott, 2001, p. 142).

In most cases, the Nazi purges of the professoriate of course meant that the vacated positions were soon filled by party loyalists, usually ignorant of the disciplines for which they were being made responsible. More troubling, however, is that other more or less reputable scholars kept their jobs by toeing the line, enthusiastically embracing the task of supporting the state to which they owed their employment. The immense multi-volume 'scholarly study' published in 1941 entitled *The German Way in Language and Poetry* (*Von deutscher Art in Sprache und Dichtung*), edited by Franz Koch and others, for example, was a project that had been developed the year before in Weimar at the 'Wartime Mobilization Conference of German University Germanists'. It contains essays by prominent scholars that are sometimes still cited today (Newman, 2007). The conference was but one example of the multidisciplinary 'War Effort of the Humanities' known as the 'Aktion Ritterbusch' under the leadership of Professor Paul Ritterbusch, rector of the University of Kiel between 1940 and 1945. Such programmes meant that the 'Gleichschaltung' – or enforced political conformity – of the universities under the Nazis was thorough and quick (see Hausmann, 1998).

In the face of conditions such as these, it is no surprise that the German-Jewish scholars were eager to take advantage of any way out they could find. Many got help from Philipp Schwartz, the Jewish neuropathologist mentioned above, who, having escaped from Germany in 1933, founded the Emergency Assistance Association for German Scientists Abroad in Zurich. Schwartz, together with the Swiss educator Albert Malche, who had been advising the newly established Turkish Republic about the reform of their higher education system since 1932, facilitated finding numerous positions in Turkish higher education for persecuted scholars. (They were in competition with Albert Einstein in this project; Einstein also tried to get the Turks to hire forty German-Jewish academics, but he was turned down, as the Turks wanted to choose their own invitees.[4]) Contracts for up to five years were signed and several hundred academics were ultimately placed. It is important to note that as 'humanitarian' as such hiring initiatives might sound (and the Turkish government still insists they were), these initiatives were also extremely strategic, part of the plans by the founder of the modern Turkish state, Mustafa Kemal Atatürk (1881-1938), who served as Turkey's first president from 1923 until his death, to secularize and westernize the country (see Konuk, 2010). Alongside more cosmetic changes, like ordering all men in 1925 to wear a western-style top hat instead of the traditional fez, Atatürk decided in 1933 that the venerable Turkish institution of higher learning, the very traditional Dar-ül Fünun, had to be transformed into a western-style Istanbul University.

The state-initiated creation of a secularized system of Turkish higher education was to be undertaken under the leadership of a carefully selected cadre of refugee scholars, who were thus invited in a more or less instrumental fashion to accept academic positions not as Jews, but rather as 'Europeans' in support of Atatürk's plans; their contracts stipulated clearly what they were and were not allowed to profess. Their number included the famous literary scholars Leo Spitzer and Erich Auerbach, who joined Traugott Fuchs, Heinz Anstock, and Eva Buck, the ancient historian Clemens Bosch, the economist Alexander Rüstow, and the philosophers Ernst von Aster and Hans Reichenbach as well as the architect Bruno Taut and the composer Eduard Zuckmayer. While the manner in which the arrival of the German-Jewish academics in Turkey was celebrated suggests that the situation was an intellectually rich, vibrant, and, above all, welcoming one in which the scholars could thrive, private letters and recently discovered documents reveal just how fearful they continued to be, since they knew that an active Nazi spy network in Istanbul was keeping tabs on their activities, both private and professional, even as Nazi functionaries and their contacts within the Turkish Ministry of Education

---

4   For more on this specifically, see Reismann, 2007.

sought to contain the growing influence on university culture of the refugee scholars by appointing additional non-Jewish German faculty members whose loyalties lay with the Nazis (see Konuk, 2010). The situation was perhaps not so dire as in Shanghai, where the German-Jewish refugees were literally confined in ghetto-like neighbourhoods (Bei, 2013), but it was unsettling all the same. Somewhat later, after German–Turkish relations had soured and Turkey declared war on Germany in 1944, many of the émigrés were perversely interned by the Turks as German nationals.

These details with regard to the conditions faced by German-Jewish scholars in Turkey are instructive, especially if we compare their asylum at Atatürk's state-sponsored universities to what many of them experienced when they came to the United States. Again, it was the non-governmental Emergency Committee in Aid of Displaced Foreign Scholars, working together with the Institute of International Education (IIE), that served as a clearinghouse for scholars whose applications were reviewed and for whom placement was sought (see Samuels, 2019). Files of the Emergency Committee housed at the New York Public Library contain multiple letters from the Committee to college and university presidents requesting their aid. The case of the German-Jewish literary scholar Erich Auerbach (1892-1957) is revealing of the precarity of these scholars' lives. Auerbach applied several times to the Committee while he was still in Germany and also during his years in Istanbul. It is troubling to note that his dossier was in fact declared 'closed' in 1942; as it turns out, he did not leave Turkey until 1947, after the war. At first, Auerbach found a temporary position at Penn State University, but it was not renewed after a year because he did not receive a clean bill of health (Kadir, 2011). He then spent a year at the Institute for Advanced Study at Princeton, a private foundation established with a gift from the department store magnate Louis Bamberger, before he received an offer in 1950 to join the faculty at Yale University in the form of a permanent position. In a case such as Auerbach's, placement was thus only the result of a combination of private philanthropy and efforts on the part of several universities, each with its own policies and needs.

In other cases, institutions of higher education came up with larger-scale infrastructural responses. This was famously what happened at The New School in New York, which under its founder and then director, Alvin Johnson, and with the financial support of philanthropist-businessman Hiram Halle, part-owner of Gulf Oil, and the Rockefeller Foundation, provided a haven in the United States at the so-called University in Exile, which sponsored more than 180 individuals and their families, securing them both visas and jobs (see Friedlander, 2019). On the basis of its excellent faculty, which included economists (Karl Brandt, Gerhard Colm, Arthur Feiler, Eduard Heimann, and Emil Lederer), psychologists (Max Wertheimer and Erich von Hornbostel, who was also a leading musicologist), social policy experts (Frieda Wunderlich), and one sociologist (Hans Speier), as well as the philosopher

Hans Jonas, the University in Exile received authorization from the Board of Regents of the State of New York in 1934 to offer master's and doctoral degrees. The work of many other German-Jewish scholars associated with The New School, such as the philosopher Leo Strauss, who taught for a long time at the University of Chicago and then at St. John's College in Annapolis, Maryland, and the psychologist Erich Fromm, who taught at The New School for more than fifteen years while also a professor at Bennington College, in Vermont, remains influential today. In this case, too, it was non-governmental bodies – research institutes and colleges and universities – that, working together with private donors and organizations like the IIE, mobilized to house the scholars.

As we consider the afterlives of these efforts and the investment in the future of the global academy that the present and ongoing scholar rescue efforts represent, it is important to underscore how profound the impact of the work of this generation of scholars was on the shape of the US academy in the twentieth century. One of the most well-known among them is the art historian Erwin Panofsky (1892-1968), most famous for his studies of iconology and iconography. Panofsky was one of the first art historians to move away from the study of style as an art historical method to use the history of ideas and deep knowledge of visual clues to unpack early modern and especially northern European art (see Holly, 1985). His early essay (1934) on the famous 'Arnolfini Portrait' by Jan van Eyck, which now hangs in the National Gallery in London, explains that it is not just a portrait or even merely a depiction of a wedding ceremony. It is also a visual contract testifying to the event and an account of the rights and responsibilities of the holy sacrament of marriage itself, which are visible in the many details of the image. The essay and approach made his name. Panofsky's methods set the terms of art historical debates until his death in 1968 and still determine how early northern European art is read. But Panofsky was lucky. He was already well known in art historical circles before the war and had had a visiting appointment at New York University (NYU) in 1931. He was thus able to relocate permanently to the US after 1933 with relative ease. He taught at both NYU and Princeton before moving to the Institute for Advanced Study in Princeton in 1935.

Panofsky was nevertheless well aware of the desperate plight of many other German-Jewish scholars and was himself influential in assisting colleagues well beyond his discipline of art history. He was instrumental, for example, in eventually arranging for the medieval and early modern historian Ernst Kantorowicz (1895-1963) to join him at Princeton (see Lerner). The German-Jewish Kantorowicz has long been considered a controversial figure. His early book on the twelfth-century Hohenstaufen emperor, Frederick II, published in 1927, was full of praise for the charismatic figure of Frederick and depicted him as a tragic hero and the idealized embodiment of the German nation. The Nazi general Hermann Goering allegedly presented a copy of the book with a personal inscription to Mussolini, and

Hitler is said to have read it twice. It may have been the reputation of this book that helped the Jewish Kantorowicz, who, like so many others, was forced into retirement by the Nazis in 1935, to survive until 1938, at which point he fled, arriving in the United States after a short stay in Oxford. He landed first at the University of California, Berkeley, where in 1950 he would refuse, along with many other faculty members, to sign the McCarthy-era 'loyalty oath' pledging not to become a member of the Communist Party. He was all too familiar, he said, with the way universities could be instrumentalized by the state; he would rather resign. And he did. Panofsky then prevailed upon Robert Oppenheimer, then the head of the Institute for Advanced Study in Princeton, to create a position for Kantorowicz there, which Oppenheimer did, thus providing Kantorowicz with the time and space he needed to complete his monumental *The King's Two Bodies* (1957), which recasts his argument about leadership. The book is a study of what Kantorowicz calls 'medieval political theology'; it traces the ways in which theologians, historians, and canon lawyers in the Middle Ages and early modern period used the figure of Christ as both man and God to define 'the king' as both a mortal individual – with his 'body natural' – and an institution identified with the 'body politic' of the office, which transcends time. Kantorowicz's examples may derive from pre- and early modern Europe, but his analysis is still compelling today. Historians, literary scholars, and political scientists still use *The King's Two Bodies* to understand how authority and charisma can come to be vested in a single individual rather than in the clunky, but sometimes less authoritarian apparatus of the office he or she occupies.

The case of Paul Oskar Kristeller, who lived from 1905 to 1999, is one of the most fascinating stories of this generation. His refugee route and intellectual and physical journeys were as complicated as they get (see Rubini, 2014, pp. 293-343). Like so many of the German-Jewish scholars referenced here, Kristeller had a promising early career in Germany. He studied with all of the major scholars in classics, history, and philosophy during the inter-war years and imbibed both their vast learnedness and their methods. An interesting though little-known fact is that Kristeller was also a student of the phenomenologist Edmund Husserl and the existential psychologist Karl Jaspers; perhaps most shocking is that he even worked with the existential philosopher and soon-to-be Nazi supporter Martin Heidegger from 1931 to 1933 (see Boutcher, 2006). After 1933, Kristeller fled Germany, first to Italy, where the famous Italian historian of Renaissance philosophy Giovanni Gentile, who happened to be Mussolini's culture minister at the time, found his learned colleague employment. But in 1938, after the imposition of Italy's racial laws, Kristeller left Europe entirely. He initially found a temporary teaching job at Yale before being hired by Columbia University, where he worked from 1939 until his death. Kristeller did not reveal to his colleagues that he was Jewish until the very end of his life. As in the case of Panofsky, it would be difficult to overstate Kristeller's importance in the multiple fields in which he worked, primarily the history of philosophy and of Renaissance Humanist philosophy in particular, but also for medieval and Renaissance studies in the United States and around the world. He was one of the founders of the main professional organization for Renaissance studies, the Renaissance Society of America, for example, and was also the president of the Medieval Academy of America. Without his *Iter Italicum*, which describes numerous un-catalogued manuscripts of Renaissance philosophy in detail, we would have a very skewed idea of the real nature of fifteenth- and sixteenth-century European philosophy. He was also the founding editor and editor-in-chief of what is known as the *Catalogus Translationum et Commentariorum*, an ongoing project that aims to catalogue all extant classical works as they were published during the Middle Ages and Renaissance. These field-defining learned tomes aside, his *The Renaissance Philosophy of Man*, which Kristeller edited with Ernst Cassirer and John Herman Randall, and which was first published in paperback in 1948 and is still in print, helped to shape and continues to shape the conception of the European Renaissance among undergraduate students across the country, as did his several other introductory books, also issued in paperback and priced to sell to a growing collegiate audience after the war. That we even know that there was something like a rebirth of ancient philosophy during the Renaissance is largely due to Kristeller's work. As it turns out, despite concealing his own origins, Kristeller too helped other German-Jewish scholars to find safety in the US, as I discuss below.

The men all landed at some of the most prestigious and established universities and research centres in the country. This was one of the reasons why their work had the immense impact that it did. Their successes were nevertheless hard won, since anti-Semitism was rampant in the American academy at the time and especially in the Ivy League. Indeed, it may have been for this reason that the German-Jewish academic refugees marketed their great learnedness in the US, since it was, in addition to their 'Europeanness' – rather than their Jewishness – what set them apart. There were also other campuses, however, many of them in the still heavily segregated South of the United States, that welcomed the refugees with open arms and to which the New York-based Emergency Committee turned over and over again (see Landsberger and Schweitzer, 1996). A mass appeal to college and university presidents on 2 November 1933, for example, sought placement for the scholars. Duke University President William P. Few appears to have responded the very next day asking for a list, and by the end of November he had sent requests for materials on seven scholars (King, 1996). It is important to remember, however, that as ready as Few was to provide assistance, the offer was – as in the case of Atatürk's plans for higher education in Turkey – also extremely fortuitous. Duke was a relatively young institution at the time and during the 1930s undergraduate enrolment increased 50 per cent and graduate enrolment 87 per cent, even as faculty growth lagged behind at only 34 per cent. While the institution had profited enormously from James B.

Duke's largesse at a time of economic depression, the rapid expansion of the campus meant that there were multiple unmet needs, and the opportunity presented by the Emergency Committee offered decided advantages. Distinguished scholars would be available to help in staffing new or expanded academic programmes and to bring Duke much desired prestige. And they were available at no expense, since the Emergency Committee and the Rockefeller Foundation were paying most of the scholars' wages. At the time, no long-term financial commitment was required of the university; this changed as the ranks of the displaced academics swelled.

There were still other institutions in North Carolina where the German-Jewish refugees – both scholars and artists – found a home, including the University of North Carolina at Chapel Hill, which hosted the German-Jewish philosopher Werner David Falk (Falk, 1996). Falk had fled Germany in 1933 and, via Oxford and Melbourne, arrived in North Carolina in the 1960s, which is where he would spend the remainder of his career. Black Mountain College, a famed institution near Asheville, North Carolina, also hosted refugees (see Levine, 2106). Less well known, but just as – if not more – important, are the numerous Historically Black Colleges and Universities (HBCUs), including Durham's North Carolina Central University (formerly known as the North Carolina College for Negroes), that welcomed the eminent scholar of classical philosophy Ernst Manasse (see Schweitzer, 1996). Manasse had been a colleague of Kristeller, both in Germany and in Italy. These connections turned out to be crucial, for when the Emergency Committee could find only a minimally paid, one-year position for Manasse at the Museum for Classical Art in Urbana, Illinois, which would not have allowed him to support his family, another German-Jewish classicist, Ernst Abrahamson, who was teaching at Howard University in Washington, D.C., at the time, arranged, together with Kristeller and Panofsky, for Manasse to receive the job offer in Durham. The paradox that Manasse had been an oppressed minority in Germany and was now teaching, as the only white instructor on the campus, members of an equally unjustly oppressed minority at North Carolina Central was something about which he wrote and spoke often in his 34 years as a faculty member there. Finally, like Manasse, though not a humanist strictly speaking, the German-Jewish sociologist Ernst Borinski, who arrived in the United States in 1938, began teaching at Tougaloo College in Mississippi in 1947. Maria Lowe has written that Borinski 'embodied the characteristics of both a bridge leader and a transformative intellectual, and worked behind the scenes and utilized the academy's resources and his status as an "outsider" to contribute to undermining Mississippi's racial status quo'. Throughout the 1940s, '50s, and '60s, Borinski worked both in and outside the classroom as a civil rights activist; his so-called Sociology Science Forums were designed to bridge the gap between the races by bringing together Tougaloo students with members of the surrounding white communities. Countless other academic refugees from a racist regime in Europe were able to continue their work at HBCUs.

These are only a few of the German-Jewish refugee scholars who arrived on the shores of the United States during and after the war. In addition to helping to shape many of the core disciplines within American academe, they had a profound impact on generations of students of colour in a still pre–Civil Rights era in the US. There were countless others, including a number of learned women academics, including the German-Jewish classicist, Eva Fiesel, today virtually unknown, who played similar roles in the education of women in the US at a time when this was not the norm. Fiesel was the author of a still important book on Etruscan grammar based on her dissertation (see Hallett, 2018). She received her PhD in classics from the University of Rostock in 1920 and some years later secured a position at the University of Munich, where she taught until she was dismissed in 1933. She managed to escape with her thirteen-year-old daughter (she was a single mother, having divorced her husband in 1926 when he aligned himself with Hitler in Munich) and arrived in the United States via Florence. Fiesel's initial appointment was as the only woman faculty instructor at Yale for a year. She then received an offer to join the faculty of Bryn Mawr College, a prestigious women's college. Tragically, Fiesel died soon thereafter, very young, of cancer, leaving her daughter Ruth alone. Ruth later attended Bryn Mawr College as a scholarship student. Ruth Fiesel, Miss Fiesel, as we called her, was this author's Latin and Greek teacher in elementary and middle school at the Friends' Central School, a Quaker private school in Philadelphia, where Latin, Greek, and German were taught to girls and boys alike beginning in the seventh grade. Fiesel wrote a Latin language instruction book entitled *Living Latin*, in which she taught Latin not as a dead language, but as one school children could speak and use to converse with one another about the issues that concerned them most. Such lessons are part of the living legacy that the work of the German-Jewish scholars represents. The organizations, schools, colleges, and universities that housed them testify to the work of countless individuals and institutions committed to scholar rescue. Looking to the structures and impact, but also the challenges, of their work in the past reveals the importance of remaining committed to building an international academy today via our own efforts.

Bibliography

Arendt, H. (2007) 'We Refugees', in Kohn, J. and Feldman, R. H. (eds) *Arendt, The Jewish Writings*, New York, Schocken Books, pp. 264-74.

Bei, G. (2013) *Shanghai Sanctuary: Chinese and Japanese Policy toward European Jewish Refugees during World War II*, Oxford, Oxford University Press.

Betts, A. and Collier, P. (2017) *Refuge: Rethinking Refugee Policy in a Changing World*, Oxford, Oxford University Press.

Bialas, W. and Rabinbach, A. (eds) (2007) *Nazi Germany and the Humanities*, Oxford, Oneworld Press.

Boutcher, W. V. (2006) 'From Germany to Italy to America: The migratory significance of Kristeller's Ficino in the 1930s', in Hartung, G. and Schiller, K. (eds) *Weltoffener Humanismus: Philosophie, Philologie und Geschichte in der Deutsch-Jüdischen Emigration*, Berlin, transcript Verlag, pp. 133-154.

Edgcomb, G. S. (1993) *From Swastika to Jim Crow: Refugee Scholars at Black Colleges*, Malabar, FL, Krieger Press.

Falk, J. (1996) '"Carolina Vignettes": W. David Falk', in Landsberger, H. A. and Schweitzer, C. E. (eds) *They Fled Hitler's Germany and Found Refuge in North Carolina*, Raleigh, Center for the Study of the American South/Academic Affairs Library, pp. 69-74.

Friedlander, J. (2019) *A Light in Dark Times: The New School for Social Research and its University in Exile*, New York, Columbia University Press.

Gündogdu, A. (2015) *Rightlessness in the Age of Human Rights: Hannah Arendt and the Contemporary Struggle of Migrants*, Oxford, Oxford University Press.

Hallett, J. (2018) 'The Endeavours and Exempla of the German Refugee Classicists Eva Lehmann Fiesel and Ruth Fiesel: Zwischen Exemplarität und Transformation', in Finkmann, S., Behrendt, A. and Walter, A. (eds) *Antike Erzähl- und Deutungsmuster zwischen Exemplarität und Transformation*, Berlin, de Gruyter, pp. 655-689.

Hausmann, F.-R. (1998) *Deutsche Geisteswissenschaft im Zweiten Weltkrieg: Die Aktion Ritterbusch (1940-1945)*, Heidelberg, Synchron.

Holly, M. A. (1985) *Panofsky and the Foundations of Art History*, Ithaca, Cornell University Press.

Kadir, D. (2011) 'Auerbach's Scar', in Kadir D., *Memos from the Besieged City: Lifelines for Cultural Sustainability*, Stanford, Stanford University Press, pp. 19-40.

King, W. E. (1996) 'Duke University Opens its Doors', in Landsberger, H. A. and Schweitzer, C. E. (eds) *They Fled Hitler's Germany and Found Refuge in North Carolina*, Raleigh, Center for the Study of the American South/Academic Affairs Library, pp. 25-39.

Koch, F., Fricke, G. and Lugowski, K. (eds) (1941) *Von deutsche Art in Sprache und Dichtung*, 5 vols., Stuttgart, Kohlhammer.

Konuk, K. (2010) *East West Mimesis*, Palo Alto, Stanford University Press.

Landsberger, H. A. and Schweitzer, C. E. (eds) (1996) *They Fled Hitler's Germany and Found Refuge in North Carolina*, Raleigh, Center for the Study of the American South/Academic Affairs Library.

Lerner, R. E. (2017) *Ernst Kantorowicz: A Life*, Princeton, Princeton University Press.

Levine, E. (2016). 'From Bauhaus to Black Mountain: German Émigrés and the Birth of American Modernism', *The Los Angeles Review of Books*, 16 May [Online]. Available at https://lareviewofbooks.org/article/bauhaus-black-mountain-german-emigres-birth-american-modernism/.

Lowe, M. (2008). 'An Unseen Hand: The Role of Sociology Professor Ernst Borinski in Mississippi's Struggle for Racial Integration in the 1950s and 1960s', *Leadership*, vol. 4, no. 1, pp. 27-47.

Menzler-Trott, E. (2001) *Gentzens Problem: Mathematische Logik im nationalsozialistischen Deutschland*, Basel, Birkhäuser.

Newman, J. O. (2007) 'Baroque Legacies: National Socialism's Benjamin', in Bialas, W. and Rabinbach, A. (eds) *Nazi Germany and the Humanities*, Oxford, Oxford University Press, pp. 238-266.

Panofsky, E. (1934) 'Jan van Eyck's Arnolfini Portrait', *The Burlington Magazine for Connoisseurs*, vol. 64, no. 372, pp. 117-119 and 122-127.

Reisman, A. (2007) 'Jewish Refugees from Nazism, Albert Einstein, and the Modernization of Higher Education in Turkey (1933-1945)', *Aleph*, no. 7, pp. 253-281.

Rubini, R. (2014) *The Other Renaisssance: Italian Humanism between Hegel and Heidegger*, Chicago, University of Chicago Press.

Samuels, S. (2019) '"An Outstanding and Unusual Contribution": The Emergency Committee in Aid of Displaced Foreign Scholars', *Penn History Review*, vol. 24, no. 2, pp. 71-99.

Scholars at Risk (2018) *Free to Think* [Online]. Available at https://www.scholarsatrisk.org/resources/free-to-think-2018/(Accessed 1 August 2019).

Schweitzer, C. E. (1996) 'Ernst Moritz Manasse: A Black College Welcomes a Refugee', in Landsberger, H. A. and Schweitzer, C. E. (eds) *They Fled Hitler's Germany and Found Refuge in North Carolina*, Raleigh, Center for the Study of the American South/Academic Affairs Library, pp. 41-50.

List of Contributors

Vanessa Agnew (University of Duisburg-Essen and Australian National University): Vanessa Agnew is professor of Anglophone Studies at the University of Duisburg-Essen and senior researcher in the Humanities Research Centre at The Australian National University. She was educated at the University of Queensland (BMus), New York University (MA), University of Wales (PhD), and Open University (BSc), and was tenured in German studies at the University of Michigan in 2008, where she worked until 2013. Her *Enlightenment Orpheus: The Power of Music in Other Worlds* (Oxford University Press, 2008) won the Oscar Kenshur Prize for Eighteenth-Century Studies and the American Musicological Society's Lewis Lockwood Award. She has co-edited *Settler and Creole Reenactment* (Palgrave, 2010), special issues of *Rethinking History* 11 (2007) and *Criticism* 46 (2004), and book series *Historical Reenactment* (Palgrave) and *Music in Society and Culture* (Boydell and Brewer). Other co-edited books include *The Routledge Handbook of Reenactment Studies* and *Reenactment Case Studies: Global Perspectives on Experiential History* (Routledge, 2020). Her children's book on refugee flight, *It's Not That Bad*, is appearing with Sefa-Verlag.

Meltem Gürle (University of Cologne): With advanced degrees in both philosophy and literature, Meltem Gürle is a comparative literature scholar from Istanbul working on the modernist novel. Her research interests are modernity and modernism, the theory of the novel, and the Bildungsroman. Presently she is working at the University of Cologne as a researcher and writing a book on the Turkish Bildungsroman. Apart from her academic work, she is the author of *The Red Sweater* (2017), a collection of essays on literature and everyday life, and *Talking to Roko* (2018), a philosophy book for children.

Hande Gürses (Simon Fraser University): Hande Gürses holds a PhD in literary studies from the University College London. Her work on Orhan Pamuk has appeared in *Fear and Fantasy in a Global World* (Brill/Rodopi, 2015), *Global Perspectives on Orhan Pamuk* (Palgrave, 2012), and other academic and non-academic journals. Her primary research interests include contemporary world literature, cosmopolitanism, ecocriticism, and critical animal studies. She is also interested in inclusive pedagogies and contemplative practices in higher education. She was previously a visiting lecturer in the comparative literature program at the University of Massachusetts, Amherst, where she taught courses on the international short story, dystopian literatures, and ecocriticism. At the University of Massachusetts Amherst she was the recipient of the Teaching for Inclusiveness, Diversity, and Equity Fellowship and an active member of the Contemplative Pedagogy Working Group. Most recently, she co-edited a volume on ecocritical approaches to contemporary Turkish literature, entitled *Animals, Plants, and Landscapes: An Ecology of Turkish Literature and Film* (Routledge Press, 2019). Currently, she is affiliated with the World Literature Program at Simon Fraser University.

Harriet Hulme (The University of Hong Kong): Harriet Hulme is a post-doctoral fellow in the Society of Fellows in the Humanities at The University of Hong Kong, where she is working on a project entitled *On the Threshold: Locating an Ethics of Hospitality Between Home and Homelessness*. The project draws both on her 16,500 km bicycle journey across Europe and Asia and on examples from contemporary literature to explore how the tension between the domestic and the nomadic shapes our understanding of hospitality. She holds a PhD in comparative literature (2016) from University College London. Her first monograph, *Ethics and Aesthetics of Translation: Exploring the Work of Atxaga, Kundera and Semprún* (UCL Press, 2018) explores the ethical theories of translation offered by Benjamin, Deleuze, Derrida, and Ricœur as part of an interrogation of ethical as well as political thought within the work of three bilingual European authors.

Aslı Iğsız (New York University): Aslı Iğsız is associate professor of Middle Eastern and Islamic studies at New York University. Her work examines cultural politics in relation to and within the Middle East, with a special focus on Turkey. Her research interests are situated at the intersections of political violence, cultural policy, and the politics of representation, with a critical eye on the implications of the past for the present. Her first book, *Humanism in Ruins: Entangled Legacies of the Greek-Turkish Population Exchange* (Stanford University Press), was published in 2018. Currently, she is working on a new book project on transregional cultural politics informed by the notion of civilization, with Turkey as a particular focus. Iğsız is also co-editor of the Middle East e-zine *Jadaliyya*'s Turkey page.

Kader Konuk (University of Duisburg-Essen): Kader Konuk is professor and chair of Turkish studies at the University of Duisburg-Essen in Germany. In 2017, she founded the Academy in Exile, which offers over 30 scholars at risk fellowships to continue their research in Berlin and Essen. Konuk completed her PhD in comparative literature at the University of Paderborn in 1999. Between 2001 and 2013 she was assistant and then associate professor of comparative literature and German studies at the University of Michigan, Ann Arbor. Trained as a comparatist in German, Turkish, and English literature, Konuk focuses on the disciplinary nexus between literary criticism, cultural studies, and intellectual history. Her research is situated at the intersections between religious and ethnic communities, beginning with the Ottoman modernization reforms and continuing on to Turkish-German relations in the twenty-first century. Her work examines cultural practices that evolve in the context of East-West relations (travel, migration, and exile). In her monograph *East West Mimesis: Auerbach in Turkey* (Stanford University Press 2010), she investigates the relationship between German-Jewish exile and the modernization of the humanities in Turkey. *East West Mimesis* won the prizes for the best book in both of her disciplines. It received the René Wellek Prize from the American Comparative Literature Association and the DAAD award from the German Studies Association.

Nazan Maksudyan (Freie Universität Berlin and Centre Marc Bloch): Nazan Maksudyan is Einstein guest professor at the Friedrich-Meinecke-Institut at the Freie Universität Berlin and a research associate at the Centre Marc Bloch (Berlin). She was a 'Europe in the Middle East' (EUME) Fellow in 2009-10 at the Wissenschaftskolleg zu Berlin and an Alexander von Humboldt Stiftung Postdoctoral Fellow at the Leibniz-Zentrum Moderner Orient (Berlin) in 2010-11 and 2016-18. From 2013 to 2016, she worked as a professor of history in Istanbul and received her habilitation in 2015. Her research focuses on the history of children and youth in the late Ottoman Empire, with special interest in gender, sexuality, education, humanitarianism, and non-Muslims. Among her publications, *Orphans and Destitute Children in the Late Ottoman Empire* (Syracuse University Press, 2014) is one of the pioneering contributions to the social history of children and youth in the Ottoman Empire. Her edited volume, *Women and the City, Women in the City* (Berghahn, 2014), provided a gendered lens on Ottoman urban history. Her book, *Ottoman Children and Youth during World War I* (Syracuse UP, 2019) adds a new dimension to the historiography of the war by exploring the varied experiences and involvement of Ottoman children and youth. Maksudyan is among the founders of the Association of Middle East Children's and Youth Studies (AMECYS). She is also one of the managing editors of '1914-1918-online: International Encyclopedia of the First World War'.

Jane O. Newman (University of California, Irvine): Jane O. Newman is professor of comparative literature at University of California, Irvine. Her first two books, *Pastoral Conventions* (Hopkins, 1990) and *The Intervention of Philology* (North Carolina, 2000), discuss the German seventeenth century; she has also published essays on sixteenth- and seventeenth-century English, German, and neo-Latin political theory, literature, and culture and the disciplinary history of Renaissance and Baroque studies. Newman's third book, *Benjamin's Library: Modernity, Nation, and the Baroque*

(Cornell, 2011), received an honourable mention for the 2012 Modern Language Association (MLA) Scaglione Prize in Germanic Languages and Literatures. Her translation of a collection of Erich Auerbach's essays, *Time, History, and Literature. Selected Essays of Erich Auerbach* (Princeton, 2014, paperback 2016) won the 2015 MLA Scaglione Prize for Best Translation of a Scholarly Work. Newman has held Fulbright, Guggenheim, and Humboldt fellowships, was the M.H. Abrams Fellow at the National Humanities Center (Research Triangle, North Carolina) (2015-16), and held a Berlin Prize at the American Academy in Berlin (Spring 2017). She is chair of the University of California Systemwide Coordinating Committee for Scholars at Risk. Newman is currently completing *Auerbach's Worlds: Early/Modern Mimesis between Theology and History*.

Egemen Özbek (Academy in Exile): Egemen Özbek is the academic coordinator of Academy in Exile, a joint initiative of the Department of Turkish Studies at the University of Duisburg-Essen, the Berlin-based Forum Transregionale Studien, FU Berlin, and the Kulturwissenschaftliches Institut Essen. Before taking this position, he taught modern Middle Eastern history at Carleton University in Canada. He received a PhD (2017) in cultural studies from Carleton University, with a doctoral dissertation that focused on the post-2010 commemoration of the Armenian genocide in Turkey. *Commemorating the Armenian Genocide: A Transnational Politics of Memory*, the ensuing book, is being prepared for publication with Routledge. He has recently published an article, 'The Destruction of the *Monument to Humanity*: Historical Conflict and Monumentalization', in *International Public History*. He has an MA in modern Turkish history and a BA in cultural studies. Previously he taught courses on modern Turkish history and collective memory in Turkey. His current research focuses on digital mapping of Armenian refugee routes and narratives.

Debarati Sanyal (University of California, Berkeley): Debarati Sanyal is professor of French at the University of California, Berkeley. She is the author of *Memory and Complicity: Migrations of Holocaust Remembrance* (Fordham University Press, 2015), translated into French as *Mémoire et complicité: Au Prisme de la Shoah*, with an introduction by Eric Fassin (Presses universitaires de Vincennes, 2019), and *The Violence of Modernity: Baudelaire, Irony and the Politics of Form* (Hopkins, 2006). Her research interests include nineteenth-century French literature, memory studies, Holocaust studies, and critical refugee studies. She is the editor of an issue of *Critical Times*, entitled *Time and Politics in Contemporary Critique: Entanglements and Aftermaths*, and co-editor of a double issue of Yale French Studies entitled *Noeuds de Mémoire: Multidirectional Memory in French and Francophone Culture*. She is currently completing a book on aesthetic expressions and political imaginaries of the refugee 'crisis' in Europe.

Christiane Steckenbiller (Colorado College): Christiane Steckenbiller is assistant professor of German studies and a faculty member in race, ethnicity, and migration studies at Colorado College in Colorado Springs, USA. Previously she taught at the College of Charleston and received her PhD in comparative literature in 2013 from the University of South Carolina. Her research focuses on twentieth- and twenty-first-century German and postcolonial Anglophone literature, with an emphasis on migration and minority discourses, colonialism and postcolonialism, cultural geography, and urban studies. Her articles have appeared in *Die Unterrichtspraxis/Teaching German*, *Monatshefte*, and *The German Quarterly*. She is currently working on a book project on migration narratives, in which she explores representations of the contemporary migrant and refugee experiences and the myriad ways in which individuals attach meaning and symbolism to their everyday lived spaces.

Claudia Tazreiter (University of New South Wales): Claudia Tazreiter is associate professor of sociology at the University of New South Wales, Australia. Her research is in the fields of political sociology, social theory, visual cultures, race, ethnicity, and migration with a focus on the social and affective impacts of forced and irregular migration, on human rights culture, the role of civil society in social change and visual cultures of dissent. She is the author of numerous articles, chapters, and books including *Asylum Seekers and the State: The Politics of Protection in a Security-Conscious World* (Ashgate 2004, 2006), *Fluid Security in the Asia Pacific: Transnational Lives, Human Rights and State Control* (Palgrave, 2016), and the *Handbook on Migration and Global Justice*, edited with Leanne Weber (forthcoming, Edward Elgar). Claudia convenes the *Forced Migration Research Network* at the University of New South Wales. She has held visiting appointments at the Institute for Political Science, University of Vienna (2018), Center for Place, Culture and Politics, City University of New York (CUNY) (2014), and the Centre for International Studies (CERI) Sciences Po (2011), and is a fellow at the Institute for Migration and Intercultural Studies (IMIS), University of Osnabrück.

Ngũgĩ wa Thiong'o (University of California, Irvine): Ngũgĩ wa Thiong'o is distinguished professor of comparative literature and English at the University of California, Irvine. He is author of *Mũrogi wa Kagogo* (English: Wizard of the Crow) (2004); the critical volumes *Something Torn and New* (2009), *Globalectics* (2012), *In the Name of the Mother* (2013), and *Secure the Base* (2016); three volumes of memoirs, *Dreams in a Time of War* (2010), *In the House of the Interpreter* (2012), and *Birth of a Dream Weaver* (2016), as well as a major reworking of his prison memoir *Detained* (1981) as *Wrestling with the Devil* (2018). He is currently translating his recent Gĩkũyũ epic, *Kenda Mũiyũru: Rũgano Rwa Gĩkũyũ na Mũmbi* (2019) into English as *The Perfect Nine: The Story of Gĩkũyũ and Mũmbi*. He received the 2001 Nonino International Prize for

Literature, the 2014 Nicolás Guillén Lifetime Achievement Award for Philosophical Literature, the 2016 Pak Kyong-ni Literature Award (South Korea), the 2018 Grand Prix des mécènes of the GPLA (Cameroon), and the 2019 Erich-Maria-Remarque Peace Prize, as well as thirteen honorary doctorates and the University of California, Irvine Medal. He is a member of the American Academy of Arts and Sciences and the American Academy of Arts and Letters.

Zeynep Türkyılmaz (Academy in Exile/Forum Transregionale Studien and Freie Universität Berlin): Zeynep Türkyılmaz received her PhD from the Department of History at the University of California, Los Angeles (UCLA) in 2009. Her dissertation, 'Anxieties of Conversion: Missionaries, State and Heterodox Communities in the Late Ottoman Empire', is based on research conducted in Ottoman, British, and American missionary archives and focuses on the Kizilbash Alevis, Nusayri-Alawites, and Crypto-Christians of Pontus. She was an Andrew W. Mellon Foundation Sawyer Seminar postdoctoral fellow at the University of North Carolina at Chapel Hill in 2009-2010 and a Europe in the Middle East/The Middle East in Europe Seminar (EUME) postdoctoral fellow at the Wissenschaftskolleg zu Berlin in 2010-2011. She worked at Dartmouth College as an assistant professor of history between 2011 and 2016. She is a research fellow of Academy in Exile at Forum Transregionale Studien in Berlin. Currently, she is working on two projects, one on Ezidis in the period spanning the Ottoman empire to the nation-state; the second project deals with the so-called Pontus Question from 1916 onwards. Her research and teaching interests include state formation, gender, nationalism, colonialism, and religious communities, with a focus on heterodoxy and missionary work in the Middle East from 1800 to the present.

Clara Zimmermann (University of Vienna): Clara Zimmermann has been studying law (MA) and philosophy (BA) at the University of Vienna since October 2014. In 2017-18, she spent a year in the law faculty of the University Assas in Paris under the auspices of the Erasmus+ Programme. Clara Zimmermann has volunteered for Caritas Austria, assisting with child care in a home for refugees and asylum seekers. She also volunteered for six months in a home for elderly and handicapped women in Qubeibah, Palestine (West Bank), and has worked on a voluntary basis for Amnesty International. In 2016-17, she helped co-organize the European peace initiative Civil March for Aleppo. As a result of her engagement with this project, she has broadened her research interests to include social movement studies. Since 2018, she has been part of the NGO Vienna Asylum Law Clinic, within the context of which she will run workshops on asylum law, conduct research, and cooperate with NGOs working in asylum law.

Index

Page numbers in *italic* denote figures.

A

abandon(ed) 130, 151–152, 182, 204; belongings 23, 57; bodies 74; child 73; creature 131; family 151; properties 59n1
abduction 34–35, 37, 43n14, 46–47
Abdulhamid II 46; massacres (1985–96) 101; Hamidian regime 46; Hamidian Tribal Troops 46
Abrahamian, Antaram 99, 102–103
abuse 200, 215, 221, 229, 233; child 220; physical 22, 44, 104, 217; sexual 22, 104, 217, 220
Academic Assistance Council (AAC) 271
Academy in Exile 24, 279–281
activism 20, 165; migrant 189n30; peace 250
Afghanistan 51, 54, 159, 218, 281–282
Africa 52, 91, 95–96, 119–120, 124, 178, 180; African-American 91; asylum seekers 119; assumed backwardness 124; East 91; languages 90, 92; men 121; North 17, 165, 213, 262; safety 126; South 94; women 123
Afrin 43
Agamben, Giorgio 162, 172, 187n28
Agbabi, Patience 238–239
Aid Organization for German Academics Abroad *or* Emergency Assistance Association for German Scientists Abroad (*Notgemeinschaft deutscher Wissenschaftler im Ausland*) 271, 274, 286–287, 289
Aleppo 51, 65, 68, 78, 103, 248–251, 263–264; Civil March for 20, 247, 248, 249, 252, 253–254, 255, 257–264, 304; orphanage 65; siege of 247, 249, 254
Alevi 44, 304
Algeria 139–140, 142, 145, 151; Algerian Civil War 142; asylum seeker 23, 139; origins 142
Alice 139, 142, 144, 151
alterity 228, 236, 241, 243
American Guild for German Cultural Freedom 271
Amnesty International 229, 259, 304
Anatolia(n) 21–22, 60; Armenians 271; eastern 104; peninsula 52; plateau 64; Railway 63, 68, 78; western 99
antisemitism 276
Anzaldúa, Gloria 89
Arabization 43
Arendt, Hannah 20, 162, 172, 180, 227–228, 230, 232, 234–236, 241–242, 269–271, 285–287; common world 229, 234; *The Human Condition* 237; 'Isak Dinesen' 241; plural moment of 'power' 230; *The Origins of Totalitarianism* 270, 286; 'space of appearance' 230; statelessness 229; story-

telling, 21, 228, 234–235, 239, 241; 'We Refugees' 269, 285–286
Armenia 33, 42, 67; Friends of 61; Russian 42; Soviet 43, 60
Armenian 42–43, 51, 60, 63–64, 66, 68, 71–72, 99, 102; adult males 60; annihilation of 63; cause 66; clergy 105; community 63, 71, 101; deportation 62–65, 67, 75, 79; deprived of state protection 59; elite 271; extermination of 64, 66; flight 21; General Benevolent Union 61; genocide 21–22, 35, 59–60, 64–65, 67, 104, 277; intellectuals 270; majority 99; massacres 63–64; neighbourhood 105; of Istanbul 105; Ottoman 52, 59–60, 62, 68, 69, 71; persecution of 66; 'question' 63, 67; refugees 22, 60–61; Relief Fund 61; religious organizations 61; settlement plan 60; state 59; stateless 60; survivors 61, 104; ancient urban centres 104; violence against 63; women and children 60–61, 70, 77; *see also* Anatolia
arrival 45, 51, 55, 110, 117, 128, 211, 233, 275, 289; boat 213; irregular 194; migrant 213, 258; of asylum seekers 214–215, 222; of European scholars 275–276; of family 151–152; of grandchildren 105; of non-European Others 117; of refugees 53, 211; of 'undesirables' 194; place of 129; refugee 214; scenes of 21; spontaneous 215; 'unauthorized' 214
assault 34–37, 44, 220
assimilation 43–44, 202, 274; forced 60
asylum: acceptance 159; applicant 22, 126; applying for 62, 123, 128, 229; arrivals 214; awaiting 140; barriers to 59; case 151, 152; claims 53, 173; crisis 227–228, 243; detention 172n13; granting of 151, 169, 203; hopes of 235; interview 22–23; path to 24; policies 118, 121; process 23, 227–228, 232–233, 236, 240, 242; protection 162, 203; qualifying for 205; right to 205; seekers 17–19, 22–24, 46, 52–53, 119n3, 121, 123–124, 140–141, 144, 150, 162–163, 172–173, 203, 211–219, 221–222, 227, 230, 232–233, 235, 240, 243, 247, 254, 259, 285, 287; system 235, 243, 254; visual 164; *see also* Africa, Algerian, Syria
Atatürk, Mustafa Kemal 37n7, 289–290, 293
Auerbach, Erich 272, 276, 289–290
Auschwitz 162–163, 172
Australia 17, 21, 53, 60–61, 110, 211–213, 215, 217–218, 222; approach to asylum seekers and refugees 213, 214, 216, 222; Border Force 216; Department of Immigration and Border Protection 215; Federal Police 216; government 218, 221; history of settling refugees 214–215; human rights organizations 218; immigration policy 216; immigration system 214; offshore detention 212; offshore processing 215; protection obligations 213; refugee policies 19, 214, 217; state 213; territory 213
Australian Refugee Council 219
autonomy of migration 182
Aykan, Yavuz 40
Azoulay, Ariella 186–188
Azure card 229

B

Baba Sheikh 47–48
Balkans 20, 42, 60, 249, 263
'bare life' 19, 162–164, 172–173, 177, 180, 183, 187, 189

Barthes, Roland 144–145, 147
Batman 37, 43, 45
Bauman, Zygmunt 19, 162
Beckett, Samuel 229
belonging 45, 150, 163n7, 180, 185, 189, 261; contestation of 221; ecologies of 165, 168; ephemeral 185; legitimacy of 19; sense of 19, 123, 140
Benjamin, Walter 165, 169, 175, 180, 231, 252–253
Berlin 20, 54, 62, 64, 66, 68, 111, 118–121, 124–125, 128, 133, 247–248, 264, 278, 281; -Baghdad Railway 62–64; book bonfires 90; GDR 121–122, 125; Senate 121, 126; Treaty (1878) 67
biopolitics 159, 162, 172, 206–207; affirmative 177; contemporary 207
body 19, 52, 150, 163, 168, 170–171, 176, 180, 182, 185, 187, 212; collective 189; contamination of 175; human 176; illegitimate 161; natural 292; of knowledge 63; politic 292
Boochani, Behrouz 19, 213, 217–219, 220
book burning 90, 95; *see also* Berlin
border: administrative 37n7; British 162, 230; changing 131; citizenry without 186; contemporary 163–164; control 41, 177, 222; creation of 43; crisis 161; crossing 18, 45, 52, 118, 130, 167, 173, 182, 188, 211, 230, 248; demarcated 41; digital 173n14; dislocation of 162; dispositif 180, 185; encampments 175; expansion 162; externalization 17, 25, 193; French 162; gates 53; guards 212; hybridized 213; immunity 176–177, 181; internal 193; international 60, 62; Lebanon-Syria 20, 251, 252, 264; management 130; medicalization of 175; migration across 42; militarization 118; national 128, 213; nation-state 212; outer 127; policing 118, 120, 130, 163; porous 41; practices 162, 164, 214; preemptive filtering 183; regime 118, 163, 172, 181, 185; resistance to 182; securitarian logic 164; security 161; Serbia-Hungary 254; -scapes 163–164, 168, 173, 183; solidarities 184; Spanish 165; surveillance 18, 163, 173; technological 182; thematization of 121; tightening of 18, 52; Turkish 194; zone 18, 119–120, 131–132, 162
Borinski, Ernst 294
brain drain 273, 277
Brecht, Bertolt 53, 90, 282
Bruno, Giordano 89, 91
Bryn Mawr College (USA) 295
Buchenwald 164

C

Cadava, Eduardo 144, 150
Calais 53, 160, 163–168, 170–173, 176, 180, 182–185, 187–188; camp 177, 188; encampments 164, 183; fence 170; Great Wall of 162; informal camps 159; 'Jungle' 19, 159–161, 172–173, 183–185, 186; prefecture 161
camp 18, 23, 35, 65, 68, 69, 78–79, 103, 105, 162, 164, 169–170, 172, 177, 182, 184–185, 187–189; concentration 62, 65, 67, 162, 164, 170; container 160; contemporary 163; death 170; deportation 65, 75; destruction of 169; extermination 162, 172n13; French 19; humanitarian 163; informal 159; internment 162; jungle 159; makeshift 159; Nazi 162, 164, 170–172; paradigm 162; protest 121, 125–126; refugee 36–37, 103–105, 117, 159, 162–163; self-organized 163; state-funded 159–160

Canada 35, 140–141, 151–152, 260, 262
Caruth, Cathy 240–241
Catania, Sicily 118–120, 129–130
Catholic 42, 89–90
Cazeneuve, Bernard 161, 169
census 21, 34, 36, 40–41
Central European University (CEU) 278
Chakrabarti, Shami 235
Chaucer, Geoffrey 231; *The Canterbury Tales* 20, 231, 259
Chauka, Please Tell Us the Time 217–218
cinema 147–148, 164–167, 168, 169–170, 175, 177
citizenship 182, 185, 189, 212, 276; equal 163; full 42; national 36; rights 33, 43, 287; Russian 41; thematization of 121; universal 36, 42
Civil March for Aleppo; *see* Aleppo
Clifford, James 19
climate change 17, 23, 25
climate migrants 17
'Coalition of the Willing' 34
Cold War 61, 199
collective 37, 230, 242, 256; actions 184, 256–257, 260–261; banishment 271; being 185; body 189; catharsis 140; challenge 228; encounter 227–228, 232; exile 270; expulsions 161; good 91; historical consciousness 18; identity 256, 260; institutional 256; memory 22, 40, 217; mobilization 189; movement 232; nature 228; oeuvre 184; position 249; power; recognition 228; repudiation 247; response 227; self-designation 185; sites 18; towns 43; walks 243
colonialism 119–120, 122, 171–173, 180; consequences of 121; German 118, 125; post- 272; temporality of 177
Columbia University 273, 293

commemoration 24
Committee for the Release of Political Prisoners in Kenya (UK) 93
Committee of Union and Progress 46, 63, 67, 101
compassion 48, 134, 160–162, 189, 219, 242; hygienic 184
concentrationary 164, 169; aesthetic 169; space 187; universe 164, 169, 177
conflict 17, 23, 51–53, 60, 131, 134, 194, 249, 263; armed 119n3; colonial interests 131; issues 255; of ideas 92; of interests 280; sectarian 53; Syrian 249; violent 251
Conrad, Joseph 96
conscription 21, 36, 40–42
control 121, 126–127, 132–133, 145, 151, 163–164, 173, 181–183, 196–197, 240, 287; access 119; biometric 177, 180; birth 199; border 41, 173n14, 177, 222; community 40, 47; governmental 271; immigration 215; mechanisms 127, 131; Muslim 130; number 197; Ottoman 39, 42, 60, 271; parliamentary 250; population 199; relinquishing 132; societies of 175; spatial 118–119, 123, 126–128; state 18, 40, 287; technologies of 163n7
Cortes-Rocca, Paola 144, 150
Council for At-Risk Academics (CARA) (UK) 271, 285, 287
crisis 117, 130–131, 154, 194, 272; agent of 19; asylum 227–228, 243; border 161; diplomatic 280; global displacement 52, 62, 194; humanitarian 248, 275; male identity 130; migrant 117, 121, 214; of numbers 194; of human mobility 18; of solidarity 194; refugee 24, 52–53, 128, 172, 198, 230; regions 281

D

Dabiq 33–34
Dar-ül Fünun 274, 289
Davis, Colin 236, 242
de Genova, Nicholas 117–119, 130, 132
de la Chenelière, Évelyne 140, 142
Demnig, Gunter: Stolperstein ('stumbling stone') Project 54
democracy 24, 171, 280–281
demographic production of knowledge 195–196, 206–207
demography 25, 195–199, 201, 204, 206–207
deportation 43, 59, 62–65, 71, 73, 76, 101, 104–105, 160, 169, 195, 203, 276, 287; camp(s) 65, 75; forced 22, 36, 102; mass 194, 271; Nazi 169; orders 63; route 65; *see also* camps; *see also* forced migration
Der Zor 22, 103–104
Dersim genocide 35
detention 160, 218–220; arrangements 220; centres 19, 159, 161, 212, 216–218, 221; environment 216; facility 218; historical forms of 163; histories of 170; immigration 222, 258–259; indefinite 214, 227–229, 233; mandatory 53; of asylum seekers 217; of refugees 21, 217; offshore 212, 215–216; open-air sites of 163; post-258; regimes 219; sites of 164, 215; spaces of 162
disappearance 165, 182, 212–213, 222; data 182; mass 169; spaces of 212; strategies of 182; tactics 185; themes of 213; *see also* border of disappearance
displacement 19, 23, 59, 146, 176, 195, 202, 206–207, 276, 286; concept of 276; enforced 43; exilic 276; experience of 140–141, 146, 151, 154; focus on 194; forced 23; global 52; human 62, 193; internal 23; mass 119–120, 128, 132–133, 194, 198; multi-layered routes of 21; of refugees 160; onward 62; palimpsest of 20–21; postwar 195; state of 144; *see also* crisis
Diyarbakır, Amid, Diyarbekir 35n5, 37–38, 40, 45
Dublin Regulation 120, 126, 173
Duhig, Ian 235
Duke University 285n1, 293

E

Einstein, Albert 289
Elie, Jérôme 17
El-Tayeb, Fatima 125, 133
Emergency Committee in Aid of Displaced Foreign Scholars 271, 273, 285, 290
emplaced 24–25
encounters 127, 131, 227, 235, 243; conversational 234; failed 53; first 22, 122; Levinasian 242; talking/verbal 232, 243; walking/physical 228, 243; with hostile groups 39; with political authorities 36
Erpenbeck, Jenny 22, 117–118, 120–128, 133
ethics 234, 242–243; of hospitality 230–231; of narrative 243; of relation 228; of responsibility 242; of storytelling 228, 234–235, 237
ethnicity 122, 132, 201, 236
eugenics 25, 195–197, 199–202
Europe 35, 43–44, 52, 54, 59, 262; border crisis 161; Council of 204; crisis for 117; de facto colonies of 119; democratic processes in 53; divisions within 134; Eastern 197, 277–278; exclusion of racialized Others 125; Fortress 18, 175, 181; histories of

21; humanist 275; migration to 44, 52, 121, 248; Northern 197, 291; periphery 128; political failure 251; postwar 197; 'sick man of' 42; South-East 247; Southern 128, 197; Western 21, 51, 60, 125, 196, 198

European: asylum system 255; border zone 132; colonial past 134; Commission 193; confrontation 119–120; economy of recognition 180; historiography 17; literatures 91; Marches 260, 262; migrant crisis 117; migration 17, 178, 254–255, 258; non- 117, 127, 130–133; overseas possessions 199; public 117; refugee association 195, 199; Renaissance 273, 293; repressed colonial heritage 129; Union 18, 118, 121, 131, 161, 173, 177, 193–194

EU–Turkey Statement (2016) 194

Evliya Çelebi 37–39

exile 18, 20, 22, 24, 33, 35, 45, 66–67, 90–91, 93–95, 105, 121, 162, 167, 172, 183, 218, 240–241, 269–272, 274–280, 285; enforced 24; Ezidi 36; forced 93, 96; German 22, 275; hardship of 276

experience: Armenian 68; autochthonous 22; common 22; contemporary 120–121; intellectual 269–270; of alienation 277; of asylum seekers 24, 233, 235; of displacement 140–141, 146, 151, 154; of exile 35, 91, 270, 276; of fleeing 33; of indefinite detention 227; of life 148, 151; of liminality 153; of migration 168, 214; of persecution 23; of separation 238; of sharing 234; of space 128; of temporality 153; of violence 121; refugee 17–18, 20–23, 36, 45, 53, 127, 132, 140, 164, 218, 237–238; shared 105, 140, 151, 263; traumatic 45, 153, 241

Ezidi: agency 36; armed and confrontational 39; as infidels 34; citizenship 42; communal identity 40, 45; communities 21, 33, 38, 41–43; conversion of 43, 46; culture 21; destruction of villages 43; disempowerment 36; enforced displacement 43; exile 36; extermination of 34, 39; groups 33; homelands 48; knowledge of landscape 39; Kurds 38, 43; lifeworld 37; massacre of 35; migrants 44; persecution of 35–36; population 34; refugee experience 36; refugee routes 37, 49; religious structure 40–41; resistance 21, 36; seclusion 39; secrecy 37; settlements 42; Spiritual Council 48; spiritual leader 47; suppression 38; traditions 48; tribes 39–40; Turkish 45; veiled in invisibility 33; *see also* genocide

F

Falardeau, Philippe 23, 139–140, 146–147, 149

Falk, Werner David 294

fascism 24, 122, 195, 197, 199, 202, 271, 274, 276

Felman, Shoshana 153–154

ferman (pogrom) 21, 35–36, 38, 40, 43, 46

Fiesel, Eva 295

forced migration 17, 24, 36, 118, 120, 128–129, 132, 193; *see also* deportation

Foucault, Michel 176n17, 181, 187n28, 206

France 96, 125, 159, 161–162, 164–165, 169, 183–184, 187, 189, 198, 252, 260, 262, 285
freedom 229; academic 24, 91, 272, 274, 278–281; fighter 94; of enquiry 24; of movement 118, 132, 279; of research 282; of speech 232, 250–252; of teaching 282; press 215–216
French camp 19; demographic research 199, 202; international jurists 203; mandate 60; Republic 185; spheres of interest 131; state 159, 165, 185; territory 187
fugitives 41, 89, 188

G

Galeano, Eduardo 235
Galton, Francis 196–197
gender 33, 49, 60, 122, 128, 130, 132, 187, 236, 272, 279
Geneva Convention 22
genocide 21, 34, 36–37, 45, 48, 59, 63–69, 71, 105, 272, 276; Armenian 21–22, 35, 51, 59–60, 64–65, 67, 104, 278; Assyrian 35; Ezidis 43, 46–48; Shengal 37; victims of 65; *see also* Dersim
George, Sylvain 47, 165–170, 173, 175, 177, 180, 187
German PEN-Club in Exile 271
Germany 18, 20, 22–24, 44–46, 62–65, 67–68, 96, 117, 123–125, 128, 132, 195, 205–206, 247, 249, 258, 260, 262, 271, 274–275, 279–280, 285–290, 292, 294; colonial legacy 133; East 126; Federal Republic of 126; Democratic Republic (GDR) 20, 123, 125; integration in 126; Nazi 90, 274; reunification 125; West 123; xenophobia in 19
Gĩkũyũ language 92, 94–95
Gilroy, Paul 119–120, 128, 131, 133–134

Greece 20, 52, 60, 131, 165, 173, 193, 247, 250, 253–255
Greek Orthodox 42, 193
Greek-Turkish population exchange 193, 195, 204–205
Gurnah, Abdulrazak 235

H

Hale, Dorothy 242
Harvey, David 126, 128
Heller, Charles 18, 161n5, 196n7
Herd, David 227, 229–236, 240, 242–243, 258–259
heritage 20, 129, 275
Historically Black Colleges and Universities (HBCUs) (USA) 294–295
historiography, historicization 17–18
Holmes, Rachel 229
Holocaust 23, 61, 67, 122, 203, 270, 278
hospitality 21, 23, 51, 53, 55, 117, 121, 133, 164, 228, 230–234, 243; discourse 23; ethics of 230; recipients of 24
host(ing) 20–22, 24, 51–53, 96, 164, 194, 204, 273, 275, 279–281, 285, 287, 294; communities 19, 22, 254; country 17, 52–53, 142, 202, 276; history of 20; institutions 24, 276; potential 18; refugee 21; societies 23, 272; universities 271, 275
hostility 37, 39, 45, 59, 66, 117, 120, 132, 206, 228, 230–232, 234–235, 243, 257, 259, 269
human rights 24, 182, 280, 286–287; activists 214, 216–217, 219; advocates 19; basic 229–230; conceptions of 205, 279; defender 62; discourse of 287; flouting of 250; formal 287; fundamental 184; groups 217, 221; international 195, 203; internationally ratified 17; organizations 217–218; 'regime' 24; rhetoric

of 185; sacrificing 49; standards 215; universal 287; violations 19, 217
humanitarian 19, 160, 165, 194, 196, 206–207, 215, 249, 257, 270, 272, 276, 281, 287, 289; aid 25, 196; approach 163; assistance 203; camps 163; care 162; corridors 249; crisis 249, 275; governmentality 162; intake of refugees 215; international law 51; intervention 164; management 165; modern 61; obligations 254; protection 163; reason 162–163, 175; reduction of refugees 182; tragedies 254
Hussein, Saddam 43
Huxley, Julian 200–202

I

identity 37, 40, 42–43, 51, 139, 141–143, 153, 176, 239, 242; card 44; categories of 143; collective 256; communal 40; European 130; fake 142; fractured 57; group 149; imperial 130; Muslim 40; national 169, 230
immigration 204, 214–216, 231; checkpoints 162; control 215; detainees 259; detention 218, 222, 258–259; irregular 175; nation 214; officials 162; policy 231–232; regulations 23; restriction movement 197; social attitudes to 217; status 238; system 214, 227
Immigration Act (UK) (2016) 231, 258–259
Immigration Removal Centres 228, 231
incarceration 17, 23, 89, 92, 160, 217
Index Librorum Prohibitorum 90
Institute for Advanced Study (Princeton University) 290–292

Institute of International Education-Scholar Rescue Fund (IIE-SRF) 271, 273, 281, 285, 287, 290–291
internally displaced person (IDP) 35, 37, 286
interview 37, 45–46, 163, 218; asylum 23; protocol 22
invisibility 18–19, 33, 53, 164; selective 18; strategic 183; /surveillance nexus 18
Iraqi Kurdistan 21
irregular migrants 18, 24, 52, 161, 175, 211, 213–214, 222
Islamic State (IS) 21, 33–35, 37, 43–45, 47–48
Istanbul (Turkey) 22, 37, 62, 65, 103, 105–107, 111, 199, 202, 270, 272, 274–275, 278, 289; University of 197, 198, 273–275, 279, 289
Italy 52, 67, 127–129, 132–133, 173, 195–197, 204, 233, 253, 261, 292, 294

J

Jensen, Anna 65
Jewish 24, 286, 289–290, 292–293; anti- 288; communities 42; émigrés 276; German- 269, 272, 285–286, 288–289, 292–295; influence 288; population 175; refugees 269; scholars 271, 273–274, 286, 288, 290–291
Johnson, Alvin 273–275, 290
justice 48, 66–67, 94; desire for 252; global 253; redistributive 19; social 280

K

Kafka, Franz 235; *The Trial* 229
Kanco, Hüseyin 46–47
Kant, Immanuel 23, 51–53, 67
Kantorowicz, Ernst 291–292
Kay, Jackie 233, 238

Kenya (Nairobi) 24, 90, 92–95
Kirchhoff, Bodo 22, 117–120, 127–128, 130–131, 133
Kristeller, Paul Oskar 292–294
Kurdish Regional Government (KRG) 35, 45–46

L

Lachance, Martine (movie character) 139–140, 144–145, *145*, 151,153
Lalish 47–48
Las Meninas 148–150
Laub, Dori 153–154
Lazarean project 169
Lazarus 169
Lazhar, Bashir (movie character) 23, 139–142, 149–150, 153–154
League of Nations 60–61
Lebanon 52–53, 60–61, 117, 218, 247, 251, 252; -Syria border 20, 251, 252, 264
Lepsius, Johannes 63, 66
Levinas, Emanuel 20, 227–228, 231, 234, 236, 238, 241–242; 'ancestral soil' 230–232; conversation 228; encounters 230, 236, 242; hospitality 230; *Reality and Its Shadow* 236; representative art 236, 242; storytelling 228, 234, 236, 239; *The Time of Nations* 230; *Totality and Infinity* 234
Lieu de mémoire 18
'long summer of migration' 18, 118, 247, 254, 258, 263

M

Macdonald, Helen 237
Magna Carta 231
Magnin, Marie 186–187
Malche, Albert 289
Manasse, Ernst 294
Manus Island 19, 212–213, 215–219, 220, 222

Mardin 38, 43
Marx, Karl 96
Massey, Doreen 122, 124, 128
Mediterranean 18, 51–53, 117–120, 122, 131, 161, 171, 182, 213, 233
memorialization 19, 53
memory 18, 21–22, 54, 112, 122, 165–166, 169–170, 177, 185; collective 22, 40; communal 45; culture 19, 24; 'land of' 18; making 20; narrative 240; social 102; state structuring of 23
mental: breakdown 101n5; illness 19, 217; instability 201; trauma 229
Meretoja, Hanna 236–238; ethics of storytelling 237–238; 'non-subsumptive' 236–238; 'subsumptive' 236–238
Meskeneh 65
Middle East 17, 21, 33, 49, 51–52, 119, 277–278
Midyat 43, 45
migrant 44, 52, 117–118, 127, 129–130, 133, 159n1, 165, 169, 173–175, 180, 182, 184–185, 202, 205–206, 213, 221–222, 228, 254, 258, 262; agency 182; assimilation of 202; climate 17; crisis 117, 221; deaths of 122; distribution of 118; economic 162; experiences 214; itineraries 182; mobilities 118–119, 177, 183; movement 183; nameless 128; permanent 18; right of 118; travellers 127; undocumented 260, 262; workers 215; *see also* activism, forced migration, irregular migrants
mobility 123, 128, 177, 183, 189, 194, 207, 279; appropriating 118; forced 21; greater 41; human 18; imperceptible 183; mass 25; pattern of 21; physical 204; priority of 182; right of 177;

struggle for 181; transnational 279; unfettered 185
Montréal 139
Mujama'at 43
Mukherjee, Neel 232–233
Murad, Nadia 48; Nadia's Initiative 35
Muslim 34, 39, 41, 45–46, 54, 60–61, 130, 193; communities 41–42; empire 39; families 104; identity 40; neighbours 44–46; society 275; Sunni tribe 42; superiority 42; Turkish- 60

N

Nansen International Office for Refugees of the League of Nations 60
narrative 22, 124, 127, 152–153, 163, 218, 227, 231, 233, 236–243, 249; approach 237–238; appropriation, 233; circulation 234; counter- 38, 217, 236; creative 152; critique of 242; cultures 217, 237; documentary 166; dominant 237; fragmentation 241; framework 239–240; gaps 233; government 217; healing 153; impulse 228, 236–237; interventions 212, 222; national 24, 128; of survival 60; of victimhood 36; pattern 22; potential of 228; powerful 66; practices 236; reductive 239; restraint 127; scripts 236; strategies 228, 234, 237–238, 241; structure 240; textual 243; trauma 241
National Humanities Center (Research Triangle, North Carolina, USA) 285n1
national identity 169, 230
National Institute of Demographic Studies (INED) 198
National Public Radio (NPR) 48
National Socialism 54, 67, 126, 133, 271n1

Nauru 212–213, 215–222
Nazi 121–122, 125, 271, 288–290, 292; deportation 169; government 271; ideology 126; past 54, 164; policies 197, 274; regime 285; scientific racism 202; spy network 289; *see also* camp
Niepage, Martin 66
No Friend but the Mountains 218
Nora, Pierre 18
Nussbaum, Martha 242

O

occupation 34, 126, 261–262; British 104–105
Office of the High Commissioner for Human Rights 34, 61
offshore: detention 215–216, 220; processing 17, 19, 53, 215, 217; regime 216; sites 163
Old Pilgrim's Way 231
Operation Sovereign Borders 216
Oranienplatz 121, 125–126
orphanages 48, 61
Orwell, George 229; *1984* 229
Ottoman Empire 21, 42, 46, 59, 61–63, 68, 69; Archives 37, 39; reforms 40

P

Pacific Solution 17–18, 215
Panofsky, Erwin 291–294
Papua New Guinea (PNG) 19, 212–213, 215, 217
PAUSE (*Le Programme national d'Accueil en Urgence des Scientifiques en Exil*) 278
Penn State University (USA) 290
perpetual world peace (*Ewiger Frieden*) 52

Index 315

persecution 17, 21–23, 35–36, 38, 40, 45–46, 51, 61, 66–67, 82, 119n3, 159n1, 205, 238, 272, 281, 286
Persian Empire 33, 40
Pezzani, Lorenzo 18, 196n7
Philipp Schwartz Initiative (Humboldt Foundation, Germany) 278, 286
photograph 35, 57, 65, 67–68, 144–150, 153, 164–165, 185–189, 218–219, 221; documentation 21; forms 212; historical 68; image 186; inventory 67; prohibition 64, 67; record 68; still 147
pilgrimage 30, 38
Pincus, Anna 227
postcolonial 96, 117, 119–120, 125, 180, 272, 276, 282
post-war: demographic concerns 198, 207; demographic engineering 196; demographic epistemes 207; demographic production of knowledge 206–207; demographic research 206; displacement 195; environment 203; Europe 197; international conceptions 205; mass population transfers 205; national reconstruction efforts 198; public attitudes 66; refugee crisis 198; unemployment 204; Western Europe 196
poverty 17, 53, 57
power: authorial 149–150; axes of 122; colonial 126; dynamics 42, 47, 140, 142, 218–219; governmental 186; hierarchies 127; imbalance of 127; occupying 131; of death 172; of language 150; over life 177; over space 126; position of 143; relationship 92, 94, 120, 130, 142; ruling 131; social framework of 206; sovereign 148, 152, 162, 180, 182; state 188; structures 140, 260; vantage point of 129; world-making 182

R
race 122, 128, 132, 187, 197, 201–205, 294; human 202; Nordic superior 199; notion of 201; Turkish 59
racialized: bodies 177; histories of terror and dehumanization 172; others 125, 175; paradigms 204; reconfigurations of hierarchies 206; refugees 161n2; terms 129; terror 171; violence 164, 170, 187
racism 117, 194, 197, 201–202
Rancière, Jacques 165, 177n18, 189
reading 39, 94, 118, 121, 127, 133, 139, 152, 164, 173, 188, 232–234, 237, 242–243; critical 120, 134; semiotic 151; spatial 118, 120; symbolic 119
reception centre 23
recognition 42, 164, 176, 222, 230–232, 235, 239, 242, 278; collective 228; economy of 180; formal 258; international 67; limited 232; logic of 180
reenactment 20, 24
refuge 17, 61, 95–96, 104, 122, 270; denial of 230; place of 24; possibility of 230; right to 53; seeking 40, 52, 91, 96, 247, 270, 277–279, 282, 285
refugee: accounts 22; activists 122; association 195, 197, 199; camps 36–37, 103–105, 117, 159; centres 126; concerns 19; encampments 163; exile 22; experiences 20–23, 36, 45, 53, 140, 162, 237; flight 18, 21–22, 59; host 17, 21; issues 21, 221; law 62; management 25; memories 18; policies 19, 118–119, 126, 214; problem 193, 204; quotas 57; reenactment 20; regime 59; remembrance 18; rights 18, 61–62; route 18–19, 21, 25, 33, 35–37, 43–

45, 47–49, 57, 247, 263, 292; scholars 275–277, 282, 289–290, 295; situations 53, 61; status 59, 212, 215, 219, 233, 238; suffering 127; testimonies 172; trajectories 195; trek 20; violence 19; *see also* crisis
Refugee Convention (1951) 213, 215, 222
Refugee Tales project 227–228, 230, 232, 235–236, 243, 259
Refugee Tales walk 228, 230–231, 258–260, 264
refugeehood 19, 59, 61, 203
refugeeism 17–18, 23–24, 120, 128, 194
Renaissance 273–275, 277, 292–293
repression 23, 160–161, 277–278, 280, 282; military 43; soft 277
rescue 24, 47–48, 61, 96–97, 271–272, 276; *see also* scholar
resettlement 17, 33, 205, 214–215, 219
resistance 36, 103–104, 133, 141, 163–165, 172–173, 176–177, 180, 182–183, 212, 253, 271, 278, 287; Ezidi 21
right to disappear 176, 180–183
rights 41, 165, 180, 182–183, 205, 230–231, 243, 287, 291; access to 214; articulation of 185; citizenship 33, 43, 287; civil 294–295; discourses of 180, 183; equal 162; individual 62, 230; loss of 234; of asylum seekers 259; of the stranger 51; trans-state 287; universal 185; violation of 160; *see also* human rights, refugee
Rohner, Beatrice 65
Rohrbach, Paul 63, 66, 68
route 64, 193, 254; Balkan 57; clandestine 159; deportation 65; escape 19; finding 20–21; intended 254; major 52; migration 36, 46; of displacement 21; of terrorist infiltration 183; physical 195; survival 45; trade 52; walking 20; *see also* refugee

Russian Empire 33, 41
Russo–Turkish War 42

S

Sappho 97
Sarvestani, Arash Kamali 217
Sauvy, Alfred 199, 202–205
scholar rescue 24, 270–271, 275, 280, 285, 287–288, 291, 295; Fund 278, 281
Scholars at Risk (SAR) 97, 272, 278
scholars at risk 97, 280–281
Schwartz, Philipp 271, 274, 278, 286–287, 289
secular 24, 61, 275, 282, 289
Shamsie, Kamila 239–241
Shengal/Sinjar 21, 33–34, 43, 45–46; district 35; liberation of 35; Mountains 33, 37, 38; *see also* genocide
Sicily 118, 127, 129–131
slavery 171–173, 177, 180–181
Smith, Ali 229
social movement 165, 249, 255–260, 264
solidarity 94, 166, 169, 194, 203–204, 228, 230, 232, 243, 250, 254–257, 259–263; international 92, 203
Sommer, J. W. Ernst 66
space: abject 172, 183–184; approach to 124; appropriation of 118, 130; civil 186; claims to 118, 129, 132; common 183, 261; competition over 118; contaminated 181; control of 119, 123, 126; European 133; experience of 128; fortified 160; legal acquisition of 126; liminal 62, 150, 153; national 230; of detention 162; of extremity 171; partition of 166, 173; political 162, 184; power over 126; public 90, 180, 229; sovereign 212; transitory 131

'Space of appearance' 180, 187, 230
spatial 120–121; appropriation 132; claims 118; control 118, 128; dislocation 36; disobedience 129; fabric 121; fixed 214; layout 151; locations 132; management 119; practices 118–119; reading of migration 118; relocation 60
Spitzer, Leo 149–150, 164, 275, 289
Spivak, Gayatri 242
statelessness 24, 57, 180, 185, 188, 229, 234, 269, 277
Stoler, Ann 122, 128
Stone, Brangwen 121
storytelling 19–20, 127, 151, 153, 227–228, 232, 235–238, 240–241, 243, 259; appropriation 236; collaborative 234–235, 242; dehumanizing 233; ethics of 227, 234–237, 243; hospitality 231–232, 234, 243; power of 241; responsibility 228, 236, 241–242
suicide 19, 129, 140–141, 144, 150, 153, 165, 217, 221
surveillance 18, 24–25, 132, 160, 163, 166, 173, 175, 177, 181–182
survival 20, 22, 39, 60, 91, 105, 144, 176, 182, 287; community 39; means of 21; mode of 21; right to 189; route 45; strategies 36, 39, 43–44, 269; struggle for 58
Syria 20, 22, 33, 43, 51–52, 60–61, 63, 65, 102–104, 159, 238, 249–251, 257, 260, 263, 282; asylum seeker 161; borders 33; conflict 249; desert 21, 60; Lebanon- 20, 251, 263; Ottoman 271; political situation 247; refugees 194, 205; regime 251; war-torn 21, 247, 251, 254–255, 258–259
Szymborska, Wisława 235

T

technology (technologies) 181; disciplinary 173; of biometrics 183; of capture 167; of control 163n7; of information management 175; of management and governance 176
The New School for Social Research 273, 279, 290–291; Faculty of the Political and Social Sciences 274; University in Exile (New York City, USA) 274
Third World 199, 206
third-country resettlement 17
Timmermans, Frans 193–194
topography 21, 51–52, 118
Tougaloo College (Mississippi, USA) 294–295
trauma 37, 47–48, 131, 140, 150–151, 153, 163, 218, 241, 277; and narrative 240; mental 229; multilayered 131; trans-generational 35; victimology of 165
Treaty of Sèvres 59
Turkey 21, 24, 33, 43–46, 51–53, 64, 66–67, 69, 72, 102, 117, 161, 170, 193–194, 196–197, 205, 250–251, 263, 272, 274–275, 277–278, 280–282, 286, 289–290, 293

U

United Kingdom 20–21, 53, 94, 159–160, 162, 183, 227–229, 230, 233, 235, 238, 240, 258–259, 285; asylum process 227, 232; Home Office 229, 232–233; Immigration Act (20 16) 231; immigration system 227; Immigration Removal Centres 228; parliamentary system 231
United Nations 188, 194, 198, 286; Educational, Scientific and Cultural Organization (UNESCO) 200–201;

Genocide Convention (UNGC) (Convention on the Prevention and Punishment of the Crime of Genocide) 34n4; High Commissioner for Refugees (UNHCR) 17, 52, 159n1, 211, 214, 218; Security Council (UNSC) Resolution (2379) 34

United States 21, 24, 60, 175, 196–199, 203, 205–206, 221, 253, 271, 273–275, 285, 290, 292–295

University of California: Berkeley 292; Irvine 89n1

University of North Carolina at Chapel Hill 294

V

Velázquez, Diego 148

violence 39, 42, 63, 121, 131, 139, 151, 163, 165, 180, 188, 194, 212, 251–253; anti-refugee 19; dehumanizing 164; history of 131; linguistic 233; mass 23; narratorial 233; of migration management 131; of sovereign power 180; outbursts of 251, 253; racialized 164, 170, 180, 187; securitarian 161; sexual 48, 59; sporadic 39; state 176; without bloodshed 229; *see also* divine

Viranşehir 43, 45

visual: allusions 173; archive 169; asylum 164; culture 211–212, 217, 222; documentation 67; interventions 211, 213–214; media 217; memories 170; poetics 164, 166; productions 189; representations 164; technologies 181n22; work 212

W

Walk in Solidarity with Refugees 20, 258

walking 20, 105, 109, 118, 227–228, 232, 243, 248–249, 261–262; long distance 229; routes 20

'Wanderlust Life Jacket' 57, 58

Wegner, Armin T. 21, 62–68, 69–79

welcome culture 18, 23

World War I 56, 59–60, 62, 66, 273, 285, 288

World War II 17, 20, 24, 55, 121, 162, 175, 194–195, 197–199, 202, 211, 285–286

X

xenophobia 19, 117

Y

Yale University 93, 290

Yazidi, Yezidi; *see* Ezidi

Yeats, W.B. 235

Z

zero-level protest 247, 252, 243–255, 264

Žižek, Slavoj 20, 248, 252–256, 264

Social Sciences

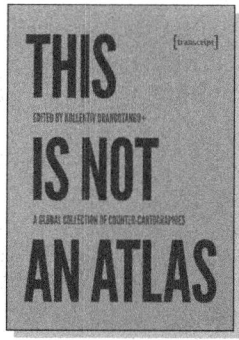

kollektiv orangotango+ (ed.)
This Is Not an Atlas
A Global Collection of Counter-Cartographies

2018, 352 p., hardcover, col. ill.
34,99 € (DE), 978-3-8376-4519-4
E-Book: free available, ISBN 978-3-8394-4519-8

Gabriele Dietze, Julia Roth (eds.)
Right-Wing Populism and Gender
European Perspectives and Beyond

April 2020, 286 p., pb., ill.
35,00 € (DE), 978-3-8376-4980-2
E-Book: 34,99 € (DE), ISBN 978-3-8394-4980-6

Mozilla Foundation
Internet Health Report 2019
2019, 118 p., pb., ill.
19,99 € (DE), 978-3-8376-4946-8
E-Book: free available, ISBN 978-3-8394-4946-2

**All print, e-book and open access versions of the titles in our list
are available in our online shop www.transcript-verlag.de/en!**

Social Sciences

James Martin
Psychopolitics of Speech
Uncivil Discourse and the Excess of Desire

2019, 186 p., hardcover
79,99 € (DE), 978-3-8376-3919-3
E-Book: 79,99 € (DE), ISBN 978-3-8394-3919-7

Michael Bray
Powers of the Mind
Mental and Manual Labor
in the Contemporary Political Crisis

2019, 208 p., hardcover
99,99 € (DE), 978-3-8376-4147-9
E-Book: 99,99 € (DE), ISBN 978-3-8394-4147-3

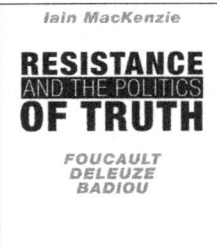

Iain MacKenzie
Resistance and the Politics of Truth
Foucault, Deleuze, Badiou

2018, 148 p., pb.
29,99 € (DE), 978-3-8376-3907-0
E-Book: 26,99 € (DE), ISBN 978-3-8394-3907-4
EPUB: 26,99 € (DE), ISBN 978-3-7328-3907-0

**All print, e-book and open access versions of the titles in our list
are available in our online shop www.transcript-verlag.de/en!**